A must read for all – regardless of race or religion

Prophet Muhammad (ﷺ): 1001 Universal Appreciations & Interfaith Understanding & Peace

Dr Mohammed A. Lais

Prophet Muhammad (ﷺ):
1001 Universal Appreciations & Interfaith
Understanding & Peace

2nd Edition August, 2016

ISBN - 978-0-9930375-4-2 Paperback

Published & Distributed by
1001 Appreciations
152-160 City Road
London EC1V 2NX

I am grateful to
Almighty Allah (SWT)
for inspiring me to write this book
on His Apostle Muhammad (ﷺ),
with the appreciations of those
who do not follow Islam
as their faith.

The Author

My choice of Muhammad…world's most influential person…he was the only man in history who was supremely successful on both the religious and secular levels.

Michael H. Hart

The sayings of Muhammad are a treasure of wisdom not only for Muslims but for all mankind.

M.K. Gandhi

Dedication

This Book is dedicated to
My Late Son-in-Law
Salim Islam
& also to
My Grandchildren
Nousheen, Raiyan,
Suraiya, Najah & Zakariya

Acknowledgements

At the very outset I would like to express my most sincere thanks to many religious authorities and personalities including the Archbishop of Westminster, Diocese of Europe, Hindu Temple of East London; Jalaram Mandir; Gurdawa Southall; Central London Sikh Temple; Britannia Hindu Temple Trust, Wimbledon Buddhist Temple, Tony Blair Faith Foundation and Chaplaincies of University College London, Cambridge University, Harvard University and Edinburgh University for being involved in this research project. My gratitude also goes to many interfaith organisations.

I am enormously indebted to Professor Jagdish Gundara, Institute of Education, London for his significant support. Whatever his circumstances, he always provided guidance on many aspects of the research including designing and developing questionnaires, selecting participants, etc., until the book was ready for publication. I am grateful to Mr Farid Panjwani, Lecturer, Institute of Education, London for his tremendous input into this book. I would also like to express my sincere thanks to Professor John Eade, Roehampton University, for providing wonderful support during the research.

My heartfelt thanks go to several Right Honourable MPs and Lords including Frank Dobson MP, David Amess MP, David Blunkett MP, Tony Benn MP, Michael Meacher MP, Debbie Abrahams MP, Jeremy Corbyn MP, Stephen Timms MP, Lord Neil Kinnock and Lord Norman Lamont.

I would like to express my sincere gratitude to Principal Moulana Abdur Rahman Madani, Jamiatul Ummah Madrasha for being a huge inspiration behind my research work.

I am grateful to Moulana Imam Abdul Qayyum, Imam, Moulana Dr. Abul Kalam Azad, Moulana Mahmudul Hasan, Moulana Abu Sayeed Ansarey and Moulana Dr A.S. Azadi for their kind contributions in my research work.

The historian Mr Mojlum Khan also offered valuable information and suggestions regarding the book's completion. For this all of them deserve my sincere thanks.

I am greatly indebted to Reverend Dr Damian Howard SJ, Heythrop College, University of London, for kindly writing the Foreword of this book. This amply depicts the relevance and the context of my effort.

I am hugely appreciative for the efforts of Mr Jon Dal Din, Director, Westminster Interfaith Group, London, for his kind support in taking part in the research as well as recruiting the research participants.

Special thanks go to the Councillor Mushtaq Ahmed, who suggested preparing sermons ahead of Friday prayers to aid in the dissemination of the book's primary message.

I also gratefully acknowledge the support from Dr Ahmad Al Dubayan, Director, Regents Park Mosque, his secretary Mrs Siddika Mannan and Dr Ahmed Makhdoom, Director of Goodge Street Mosque for helping me in contacting HRH Prince Charles.

I am indebted to HRH Prince Charles for providing me with the copies of his lectures that he delivered at Oxford University.

I have received enormous inspiration and information from the lectures and the website of Dr Zakir Naik, the dynamic Indian public religious speaker and the founder and President of the Islamic Research Foundation. I am immensely grateful to him and his Research Foundation.

My heart-felt gratitude goes to Allison McKechnie, my copy editor for her great help, effective comments, appropriate corrections, special care and professional services towards editing the manuscript which have improved the work significantly.

Credit must also go to Dr Abdullah Al-Maruf, Islamic Foundation, Bangladesh and also to the library staff at Aligarh University, India for their kind help in offering relevant materials for the research.

My thanks go to my youngest son Hasnet Lais, who supported my work in many different aspects, despite his own commitments of work and other pressures. Furthermore, my eldest son Kalam Lais, daughters Samira and Shahana as well as son-in-law Yousuf have contributed to the research, for which I am very grateful. And a very special feeling is reserved in my heart for my beloved and late son-in-law, Salim Islam, who showed a lot of interest and enthusiasm in my work.

I express my sincere thanks to Dr A.T.M. Jamil and Mr K.M. Abu Taher Choudhury for their amicable support and encouragement in completing the book. I extend sincere thanks to my brothers and sisters, many of my friends, relatives and well-wishers from different parts of the world, as well, who have motivated me in my work.

Also thanks are due to Stephen Baker from 'Ebooks by Design' who helped repair and sort out the layout.

And last but not the least, my heartfelt thanks go to my wife Momtaz Lais who kept me far from all sorts of family distractions and tribulations, thus helping me complete the work within the scheduled time.

Table of Contents

The Author

Dr Mohammed Abul Lais, son of the late Hajee Abdus Satter, was born in 1949 in the village of Dullab Pur in the district of Moulvi Bazar, Bangladesh. Education wise, he did his primary from Kanak Pur Primary School and secondary from Ajamoni High School before moving to Moulvibazar Govt High School in 1964 to complete SSCE in science group in 1966. The guidance of his older cousin Col (Rtd.) M.A. Matin was very significant in his education. He studied at Govt. College Sylhet to earn a combined BSc degree in Mathematics, Physics and Statistics in 1970. He spent the next few years first as a teacher of Mathematics, then as a Senior Operator at Fenchugonj Fertiliser Factory.

Another of Dr Lais's role models, his father's maternal uncle Rafiqur Rahman Khan (Supt. of Police) was always on hand to encourage him in his further education. In 1974, he left for the UK to advance his education. However, his education was interrupted as he went to Saudi Arabia where he worked for about a decade. After returning to the UK, he was engaged in formal and informal teaching and joined the Camden Career Service in 1992 as a Career Assistant based at the Surma Community Centre, under Camden Education Department. He became a qualified Careers Officer by gaining the Postgraduate Diploma in Careers Guidance (PG Dip CG) from East London University in 1995.

Dr Lais noticed that many Bangladeshi children cannot reach their fullest potential in education because of inadequate support from the National Curriculum. As a result they were failing in examinations and were being labelled as underachievers in education. To address this reality and support Bangladeshi children in education he embarked on a PhD study, joining Imperial College as a Research Officer. He gained his PhD from Middlesex University in 2004. The doctoral research was a breakthrough for a great majority of Bangladeshi children in the UK which earned him two awards from the Bangladeshi Community in Camden, where he lived with his family for some 40 years. He moved to

University College London in 2005 and received a FRSA Award in the same year and a National Research Award in 2006. He was involved in many research projects for universities including Oxford, City, Queen Mary, Roehampton and Edinburgh.

The recent tension between the Muslims and non-Muslims became an issue of great concern for Dr Lais, which led him to a self-funded research project for about 3 years on social cohesion based on the teachings of Prophet Muhammad (ﷺ). From this research he published this book titled as follows:

Muhammad (ﷺ): 1001 Universal Appreciations and Interfaith Understanding and Peace.

Such a large compilation of appreciations of the Prophet (ﷺ) of Islam is something which has been attempted for the first time in history. Dr Lais received another award at the House of Lords for outstanding performance through this book from the Right Honourable Lord Nazir Ahmed on behalf of International Imam Hussain Council, in May 2014. He received another Crest Award from School of Oriental and African Studies (SOAS), University of London (in partnership with Community Leadership Foundation) for the advancement in 'Interfaith Dialogue' in 2015.

Foreword

Seriously and thoughtfully entertaining the religious claims of those who follow another spiritual path is not something the majority of Christians of past centuries have been particularly inclined to do. For most of recorded human history, religious affiliation has been bound tightly to political belonging; belief in the official religion was tantamount to a civic duty and conversion away from it an act of treason. Why would one take an interest in what could only be construed as erroneous beliefs, especially if, as was frequently the case between Muslims and Christians, they were those of the enemy camp? By the standards of the modern era, in which religious freedom is a much cherished good and increasingly acknowledged as a human right, and diversity something to be celebrated and explored, this paradigm seems narrow-minded and parochial, not to say ungenerous. It is worth recalling that the opprobrium heaped by Christians and Muslims upon one another dates, by and large, from this epoch, now so strange and distant for most westerners.

This is the context in which it is best to appreciate this book. It is clearly a labour of love: love of the truth, love of Islam and love of the man who brought the Qur'an to the Arab nation, Islam's prophet, Muhammad. It is a response to the vilification, slander and abuse which has been heaped upon this remarkable man over the course of history and sets out to make accessible to the reader another picture of him, a portrait of a great hero and spiritual leader who galvanized a new spiritual and imperial project and transformed for good the world we share. Dr. Mohammed Lais has worked tirelessly to gather the testimony of an impressive array of witnesses, Muslim and non-Muslim, who have registered their admiration and esteem for Muhammad and for his extraordinary achievements. The book presents ample evidence that Christians have learned that their beliefs do not oblige them to think of Muhammad as an impostor, a false prophet, that there is no inevitable incompatibility between committed, orthodox Christian faith and admiration for the person and qualities of Muhammad. And so it is that, in these pages, Orientalists, men of letters, Christian ministers, politicians, Jews, atheists, scholars and great figures from history, all rub shoulders, their words fondly recorded for posterity. The pages of this volume testify to a generosity of spirit which is truly a sign of hope in these tumultuous times.

Rev. Dr Damian
Howard SJ Heythrop College,
University of London
October 2013

Note on the second edition

The re-issue of this book could not come at a better time because it seems there is heightened tension in many parts of the world, much of it due to religious misunderstanding and fear of different cultures. Many people get their knowledge of other religions and cultures from the media, from half-forgotten things learned at school and other sources. Misconceptions and misinformation spread and obscure the realities of the situation, giving rise to unnecessary fear and even hatred.

The way to combat this is to go beyond the superficially accepted 'facts' and find out first-hand what the real story is. When it comes to the Prophet Muhammad, Islam and the Qu'ran there are so many misconceptions among people of other religions and of no religion, that it is difficult to know where to start dealing with the misunderstandings.

This book helps enormously with this, particularly as it is written from the perspective of interfaith relations and the opinions of non-Muslims over centuries. It places the great religion of Islam in the historical context and discusses its relationship with other religions in a way that is very helpful to those outside the faith who want to understand more.

The book remains largely the same, with some sections tightened up and moved for greater clarity, and some corrections made to assist in readability. Dr Lais's desire to share this vital knowledge with others shines through. For those who are interested in learning more, there is a select bibliography listing many key texts on Islam, the Qur'an and the Prophet Muhammad.

The Publisher
June, 2016

Notes to the Reader

1. This book is written out of research conducted on peace and understanding amongst Muslim and non-Muslim communities based on the teachings of Prophet Muhammad (ﷺ). The research aimed to study the perceptions of politicians, priests from multi-faith communities, celebrities, etc., about his teachings on social issues including the issues of dealing with neighbours, the poor, orphans, women and the helpless, and the issue of equality, such as women's rights, etc. Although the literature review / history suggested that a great many works have been produced by Muslim scholars in appreciation of the Prophet Muhammad (ﷺ), his teachings, Islam and the Qur'an, no similar work has yet been done to collate the appreciations by the non-Muslim scholars on the subject and offer guidance for interfaith understanding and peace.
2. Therefore, an extensive investigation was conducted into the appreciation, judgements, opinions, gratitude and thoughts of non-Muslims about the characteristics of Prophet Muhammad (ﷺ), the influence and impact of Islam, and the teachings and guidance of the Qur'an across history. This could possibly inform the Muslim as well as the non-Muslim communities on how the differences between them can be bridged so that they can coexist harmoniously.
3. The literature on the Qur'an, Islam or the life of Prophet Muhammad (ﷺ) dates back to two centuries after the death of the Prophet (ﷺ). It was then the Muslim scholars started their scholarly work about the Qur'an, Islam and the Prophet (ﷺ). These works were consulted by other Muslim and non-Muslim scholars in history and have been passed on from generation to generation. At the present time, there are a significant number of non- Muslim scholars all over the world who have produced works on these subjects and the information they provide is mainly based on the original works compiled by Muslim scholars of that period.
4. Similarly, the appreciations by non-Muslims in this book are based on the materials written by Muslims. In some other cases, some non-Muslims have recorded their praise for Islam, based on their direct

knowledge gained from studying the Qur'an and its translation and or their Muslim friends' circle.

5. The spelling of the name of the Prophet Muhammad (ﷺ) has appeared differently across history, e.g. Muhammed, Muhammad, Mohamed, Mohammed and Mohammad. In the medieval West he was known as Mehond and Mehomet. Earlier his followers were referred to as 'Muhammadans'.
6. R- This sign is used after the names of Companion's of the prophet.
   Radhiallahu '**anhu** is an Arabic phrase **meaning**, "May God Be Pleased With Him."
7. (ﷺ) This sign is an Arabic abbreviation of 'Sallallahu Alayhi Was Sallam' meaning "Peace be upn him." This is uttered by Muslims after mentioning the name of Prophet Muhammad.
8. Limitations: One of the limitations of the present study, owing to financial constraints, is that it does not cover 'Jihad' and its theology. Both of these are specialist areas. The author of this book feels that separate studies could be conducted to explore these two areas.
9. Declaration: Wherever appropriate, the authors were contacted to get their copyright permission to use their quotations. The participants of interviews have provided their written consent to use their quotes. The identification of authors being non-Muslim were made through several steps, including asking the person, consulting personal profiles, findings, networking with other possible sources and by the names themselves. However, the methodology used has the limitation of identifying by name and in some cases of conversion to Islam only the original non-Muslim names are retained.

CHAPTER ONE

Introduction

Rationale

The failure of many writers and thinkers from the Western world to explore the truth about Prophet Muhammad (ﷺ), the religion of Islam and the Qur'an – the revelation to the Prophet (ﷺ), has contributed to the building of a misleading and inaccurate perception of Islam. This misrepresentation originates from the writings of a number of Orientalists such as the Venerable Bede (673–735), John of Damascus (675–749), Paul Alvarus, William Langland (1332–1386), William Dunbar (1470), Ranulf Higden (or Higdon) (1280–1364, John Mandeville (14th century), Durante degli Alighieri (known as Dante, 1265–1321), William Muir (1819–1905) and George, Lord Byron (known as Byron, 1788–1824) and has been adopted, as a matter of tradition, by large sections of the Western world. As a result, the perceptions of many about the Muslims have been skewed and stereotyping of their religion abounds. This has led to the stigmatisation of Muslim communities and the Islamic faith worldwide. Muslims have been generally treated with hostility, resentment and bias. Often they were left feeling marginalised from the host society they lived amongst. This created huge distrust amongst interfaith communities and contributed to the view that Muslims are obstacles to social harmony and that non-Muslims are not welcome in an Islamic society. In other words, it is quite wrongly perceived that Muslims cannot live cohesively with others and fail to establish common ties in an interfaith community.

There are also studies by Muslim and non-Muslim scholars such as

Anita Rai's *Muhammad: Uncovering the Truth* (2006) suggesting that not adhering to the teachings of the Prophet Muhammad (ﷺ) or adopting distorted interpretations of Islam have contributed to the current stance between Muslims and non-Muslims.

However, there have been a great number of non-Muslim biographers, authors, poets, writers, novelists, historians, philosophers, politicians, academics, educationists, professionals, emperors, priests, atheists, etc., throughout history who have recorded positive perceptions of Prophet Muhammad (ﷺ), many of whom have committed themselves to a truthful study of the Prophet's life, the Qur'an and Islam. British novelist William Makepeace Thackeray[1] observed: *Next to excellence is the appreciation of it. Appreciation is made about a positive effect.* With regard to Prophet Muhammad's appreciation, it is related to his character, qualities, manners, spirituality and relations with others. His personality is not only commendable but also exemplary because it emphasises his humbleness and accessibility as a person, in spite of his top position as the last Messenger of God, and as the unquestionable Muslim leader.

Among those who have expressed admiration for the Prophet of Islam are Thomas Carlyle, Dr Henry Stubbe, George Bernard Shaw, Napoleon Bonaparte, Mahatma Gandhi, Karen Armstrong, the Duke of Edinburgh, Prince Charles, politicians including former President Nelson Mandela, former US Secretary of State and presidential hopeful Hilary Clinton, and the university chaplaincies of Harvard, Cambridge, University College London and many others. They recognised his matchless qualities; the value and significance of his teachings, the influence and impact the Prophet, the Qur'an and Islam have on civilisation, and expressed favourable opinions and thoughts on all these aspects. Unfortunately, however, their views have not received extensive coverage, compared to those who have historically tended to malign the Prophet, Islam and its followers.

Originality

As far as we know, this is the first extensive compilation of appreciations, opinions, thoughts and attributes of non-Muslim dignitaries across human history:

- Exploring what is little known about Prophet Muhammad (ﷺ), Islam and the Qur'an
- Revealing the truth about the life and teachings of Prophet Muhammad (ﷺ) which encourage interfaith understanding.
- Involving key figures in qualitative interviews to gain their views about the Prophet (ﷺ).
- Exploring the social impact of burning the Qur'an, the revelation to the Prophet (ﷺ) and mankind.

Target group

This book is for all - Muslims and non-Muslims. It will be of interest to many Muslims, who will develop a strong appreciation for the extent of knowledge and respect held by non-Muslims towards Prophet Muhammad (ﷺ), Islam and the Qur'an. It will also provide them with helpful insight to the expectations which non-Muslims have of them.

Furthermore, many non-Muslims will learn from the opinions of non-Muslim scholars about the degree of respect and reverence they share for Prophet Muhammad (ﷺ), Islam and the Qur'an. This will raise their awareness regarding the wilful distortion and misrepresentation of Prophet Muhammad's character and how, in general, a false portrait has been painted about Prophet Muhammad (ﷺ), Islam and the Qur'an that generates a negative image of the Muslims in Western minds.

Both Muslims and non-Muslims will become more sensitive and aware about the dangers which extremism and fanaticism pose to faith, society and the state. They will be enlightened on how the teachings of Prophet Muhammad (ﷺ), Islam and the Qur'an encourage mankind to live in a cohesive society, irrespective of faith, colour, creed, gender, nationality or status of an individual.

Pre-Islamic Arabia

To understand the tremendous achievements of Prophet Muhammad (ﷺ), it is very important to gain an understanding of the religious, social and political situation of the time in which he lived. The development which had taken place in the Arabian Peninsula during the time of Prophet Jesus over 500 years previously was on the brink of collapse. The 7th century witnessed one of the worst periods in the history of the Arabs. Idolatry, adultery, robbery, gambling, killings, infanticide, slavery, etc., were the norm among them. The people were divided into clans and engaged in tribal conflicts. Women were denied any legal rights. Taking of revenge, committing of murder, shedding of blood were done for pride. Although polygamy was acceptable, marriage and divorce were frequent without any social limits or restrictions. The Arabs had no concept of or respect for law and order in any sector the society. Poverty was widespread and the gap between the rich and the poor was huge. The oppression of the poor by the rich and the elite was unprecedented. All types of crimes were committed easily. Orphans, women and widows were treated badly; might was right; human rights and dignity were unknown and burying girl children alive was the norm. People could hardly discern good from evil. In brief, the darkness of ignorance and injustice prevailed across the Arabian Desert.

At such times Prophets and Messengers are sent by God to rescue humanity from the shackles of bondage to others than Him and bring back His law and order to the regions. Being born at such a time Prophet Muhammad (ﷺ) was able to unite this degraded people and many a nation with them, by spreading the message of the revelation he received from God. The author J.H. Denison makes the point that the period was infested with catastrophes when Prophet Muhammad (ﷺ) was born to lead the world:

> *It was among these people that the man was born who was to unite the whole known world of the east and south.*[2]

British historian and Member of Parliament Edward Gibbon, said in his most important work, *The History of the Decline and Fall of the Roman Empire*:

> *In this primitive and abject state, which ill deserves the name of society, the human brute, without arts and laws, almost without sense or language, is poorly distinguished from the rest of the animal creation.*[3]

Thus, the worst of times are usually when a Prophet or a messenger of God is sent to bring humankind from out of darkness into light.

A full biography of Prophet Muhammad (ﷺ) is beyond the scope of this book. Yet a few words on him as an introduction to the theme of the book are nonetheless relevant. Prophet Muhammad (ﷺ), having been born as an orphan in 570 AD in Makkah, and raised by Abu Talib, his uncle and a very powerful and prominent person in the tribe, worked as a shepherd as a young boy and at about 15 years of age joined his uncle in business, taking caravans with him between Makkah and Syria. Soon, word of his wisdom, intelligence and most of all his impeccable trustworthiness, spread amongst the Arabs and he earned the title of "Al-Ameen", the "trustworthy". On a sojourn to Syria young Muhammad (ﷺ) drew the attention of an experienced monk, Bahira,[4] who had the knowledge that another Prophet was coming to mankind and was aware of the signs and symptoms he would possess. The monk spotted such miraculous signs in Muhammad (ﷺ) and asked his uncle Abu Talib to arrange protection for the future Prophet. Shortly afterwards, Prophet Muhammad (ﷺ) earned renown as a very successful trader who served with great integrity. He was, thus, employed by a rich, intelligent and able businesswoman, Khadijah, who later proposed marriage to him. It was 595 AD, he was at that time 25 years old and she was 40, twice married before[5] she had married the Prophet (ﷺ). Khadijah (RA), more advanced in years than the Prophet (ﷺ), was a source of comfort and reassurance during the time of test and trial when he was opposed and shunned by all.

The deplorable situation of his countrymen was painful to him and made him pensive. He lost his interest in the caravan trade. With a view to finding a way out of the appalling conditions of his people, he started to meditate in solitude in a cave of Hera, a mountain, 2080 feet high at the north west corner of Makkah, about 5 km away. In 610 AD when he was about 40, the Angel Gabriel came to him with the revelations that came to be known as the Qur'an, from God (Allah). He commanded him to preach that

> *There is only one God, without partner, God the Eternal, the Uncaused Cause of all beings, He begets not, and neither is He begotten, and there is nothing that could be compared with Him and that God would hold people accountable for their actions in this world on the Day of Judgment, and that he, Prophet Muhammad (ﷺ), was the final Messenger of God.*[6]

The British author Karen Armstrong says that having heard the narration of the Prophet regarding God's message being received by him, his wife Khadijah (RA) who knew him all the while to be such a tender and kind-hearted person, readily believed him to be the Messenger of God[7] and the message sent to him to be His revelations. She was, thus, the first Muslimah (Muslim woman). His uncle Abu Talib never accepted Islam, but continued to extend his staunch support and protection to Prophet Muhammad (ﷺ) in the face of relentless opposition and enmity from the Quraish, his own clansmen. Verses of the Qur'an were regularly revealed to the Prophet (ﷺ) and he preached to people, urging them to abandon worshipping idols, to worship the One and Only God, and to testify that there is no other god but God, and to accept Prophet Muhammad (ﷺ) as the Prophet and the Messenger of God.

At the start of his mission, the Prophet faced a lot of opposition. Although the likes of Ali ®, Abu Bakar ®, Uthman ®, and Omar ®, who came to be known as the Caliphs of the Prophet, and a number of his other companions accepted Islam, it was rather difficult to preach outside of his close family in Makkah, which was a safe haven for idolaters. The Ka'aba, in Makkah, had been the centre of worship since ancient times, but held as many as 360 deities.

Despite the opposition and enmity of the Quraish, his clansmen, he continued to preach the message of God – that He is the One and only God – the God of Abraham and Moses; that He neither begot a son nor is He begotten; that He neither has a partner nor has the need for any; that the true domain is His; that all men are equal in His eyes but accountable to Him on the Day of Judgement in the Hereafter, for all their deeds in this world. And slowly but surely people, particularly from the lower echelons of society, came to accept Islam. This drew the attention of the tribal leaders and the elite in society. They feared they would lose control and power if Prophet Muhammad's message became popular with the Makkans. So, they did their best to ensure that Prophet Muhammad (ﷺ) never threatened the status quo in Makkan society. They imposed a ban on him and his followers, excluding them from all social events and business dealings – which made their survival excruciatingly difficult.

During this period, Prophet Muhammad (ﷺ) endured two personal losses. The first was the death of his beloved uncle Abu Talib, his ardent supporter, and the second the demise of his loving wife Khadijah (RA), leaving him nearly shelter-less but for the protection of Allah, his Lord. Despite Abu Talib not accepting Islam, he was affectionate towards Prophet Muhammad (ﷺ) and the two had a very loving relationship. He did not criticise or present any obstacle in the way of Prophet Muhammad(ﷺ)'s preaching the message novel to the Arabs. Whatever Prophet Muhammad (ﷺ) had achieved in his mission so far was greatly aided by the honest support of his beloved uncle. Khadijah (RA) was not just his wife but also Prophet Muhammad's dearest friend and soulmate. Losing her meant losing a part of him.

Faced with the torture and subjugation he and his followers were subjected to by the Makkans, and the dangers they faced, at the invitation of a group of recent converts to Islam of Madinah, an oasis city some 460 km north of Makkah, Prophet Muhammad (ﷺ) left Makkah one night with his close friend Abu Bakr. For about 10 years he had toiled in Makkah preaching the way of life God had revealed to him for humanity. However, it was time to seek a new beginning in Madinah. 622 AD, the year of migration of the Prophet (ﷺ) to Madinah, marked the beginning of the new Islamic Hijri calendar.

Madinah at that time witnessed a lot of disputes, conflicts, bitterness and unhappiness amongst the various clans, the predominant reasons being ethnic and socio-economic issues. There was not, at that moment, in Madinah any credible and capable leader who could lead them all in negotiating and resolving their conflicts, disputes and differences, impartially and equitably. This provided an excellent opportunity to the Prophet (ﷺ) to step into the void as their leader.

Soon, the Prophet (ﷺ) succeeded in establishing a coalition between the residents of Madinah, who welcomed him and those who had migrated from Makkah with him.

The Jews of Madinah were expecting a new Prophet to emerge from their own ethnicity and community. They knew that the Prophet (ﷺ) had been rejected by the Makkans. Yet, they accepted him as a leader in the hope of having peace and law and order in society. The Makkans would not let him have peace, however. The battles of Badr and Uhud were forced on him by the Quraish and the idolaters of Makkah. These were battles for survival for him and his followers.

As the Prophet (ﷺ) withstood these onslaughts of a social order in Madinah. He proceeded by setting down laws, as he was guided through the Qur'anic revelations, protecting the rights of slaves, orphans, women, the poor and the weak in society. The traditional tribal loyalties that fuelled rivalry, feuds and vengeance were to be substituted with the loyalty to Allah, i.e. "submission to the will of one and only God" – a way of life that the Qur'an advocated and he professed and which has come to be known as Islam. However, it was easier said than done.

As the followers of Islam grew in numbers, attracted by the teachings and example of the Prophet (ﷺ), his enemies became uncomfortable and suspicious that the ever-increasing strength of the newly established social order was usurping their authority. These enemies of the Prophet (ﷺ) were joined by a few members of Jewish clans of Madinah and the area around, even though they had a treaty with him. This resulted in many more wars, battles and assaults initiated by the enemies which the Prophet (ﷺ) and his followers had to fight in the following years, to survive and to continue to spread the message he was entrusted to convey to mankind. Meanwhile, he continued to be a generous leader, not initiating any war, always sparing women, the children, the weak and the old and non-combatants, always kind and considerate, forgiving his enemies. Thus slowly but surely people came to the field of Islam and the era of Islamic expansion from Madinah[8] started to unfold.

These developments were nervously watched by the enemies of Islam: the Quraish and the Makkans. In a final attempt to eliminate the Prophet (ﷺ) and his followers, whose numbers were growing steadily, they combined their forces, raised a huge army of about 10,000 and proceeded to Madinah. The Prophet (ﷺ), advised by one of the Sahabies (followers), Salman Farsi, ordered a trench to be dug around the city to prevent the enemies from entering it and lay in wait for the confederates. This battle, for the very remarkable defence strategy through the trench adopted by the Prophet (ﷺ), became known as the 'battle of the trench'.

The Quraish and their allies laid siege to the city and waited for days but, as providence would have it, no war needed to be fought – one night a terrible storm ravaged the camps. Weak from cold and hunger and the prolonged siege, the enemy was demoralised and dispirited and in the darkness of night decamped and fled. The hand of God played its role to aid the Prophet (ﷺ) and his followers.

It was about 6/7 years since the Prophet (ﷺ) had emigrated from his city of birth. In March 628 AD, as the month of pilgrimage started, he announced one morning to the Muslims that he found himself in a dream to be standing in the Harram of Makkah holding the key of Kaabah, the sacred house of worship. This was a clear sign of the imminent victory of the Prophet (ﷺ) and Islam. Prophet Muhammad (ﷺ) announced his intention to go on pilgrimage and asked his followers to join him. They were not to carry any weapons and were to undertake the journey in ihram, the state of consecration. It was a grave and highly risky expedition, as if lambs were venturing into a den of wolves. Many advised against it but the Prophet (ﷺ) was determined.

When the caravan reached a place called Hudaybiyyah near Makkah, the Prophet(ﷺ)'s camel knelt to the ground and refused to budge. The Makkans, however, would not let them into the city, either. The Muslims camped at Hudaybiyyah. Tensions rose, over the confrontation and the heated discussions between the Makkans and Muslims as to whether the pilgrims would be allowed to enter and perform the pilgrimage or not. The stalemate ended through the signing of a truce, with the Quraish and the Makkans agreeing to allow the Prophet (ﷺ) and the Muslims to perform pilgrimage only the next year. This displeased many of the companions of the Prophet (ﷺ). But God, the All-Knowing and the Wise, termed the "Truce of Hudaybiyyah" as the ultimate victory for the Muslims through a revelation of the Surah (Chapter) "Al-Fatah" in the Qur'an.

The "Truce of Hudaybiyyah" characterised the Prophet (ﷺ) and Muslims not as men of war, aggression and arrogance like the Quraish of Makkah, but to be of the spirit of peace, tolerance and forbearance, being allied with the "People of the Book", the true followers of Allah and His Apostle Muhammad (ﷺ), who prostrate themselves before God praying, who were described in the Qur'an as follows: "Thou seest them bowing, prostrating, seeking bounty from God and good pleasure. Their mark is on their faces, the trace of prostration. That is their likeness in the Torah and their likeness in the Gospel.(48:29)" Following this truce, between 628 AD and 630 AD more people converted to Islam than all those who had converted up to that point.

During March 629 AD, in the month of Dhul-Hijjah, it was time for the Prophet (ﷺ) and his followers to undertake the pilgrimage promised. More than 2600 of his companions joined him this time. The Quraish evacuated the city, their elders from the nearby mountain top watching as Prophet Mohammad (ﷺ) along with the Muslims entered the city in great humility chanting the slogans of surrender to the Almighty: "O Allah, here I am. You have no partners. O Allah, here I am. All the praises are yours and the dominion is yours. You have no partners. Here I am."

Later, during 629 AD, the Quraish broke the Treaty of Hudaybiyyah. The Prophet (ﷺ), at the head of an army of about 10,000 volunteers, marched out of Madinah and arrived at Taif, a city close to Makkah. To assess the intent and the preparations of the Muslim contingent, a few notable leaders of the likes of Abu Sufian, Abbas, Budail and the Chief of Khuzzah, went stealthily out of Makkah and met the Prophet (ﷺ). It was evident to them that Muhammad (ﷺ) was not be stopped this time and it was inevitable that the Quraish would have to surrender. Yet, a few wanted to put up a fight. The Muslims soon beat them. Then, it was almost without any resistance that the army of the believers entered Makkah.

Mounted on his camel "Qaswa", the Prophet (ﷺ) rode to the precincts of Kaabah. As he recited the Qur'anic verse, "The Truth has come and the falsehood has perished away. Surely, the falsehood is certain to perish", he smashed the stone effigies of false gods decked around the holy shrine of Kaabah, the Quraish watching from the rooftops of their houses or from their places of hiding. Generous protection was granted to them by the generous head of the Muslim Army, the Prophet, the Mercy to the Worlds, Muhammad (pbuh), who sought no revenge, reprisal or retaliation on these tormenters of the early Muslims, who were keen to banish him from the face of the earth for the faith he preached and who eventually caused him to flee his birthplace, the beloved city Makkah. His message, then, to humanity was the revelation he received from his Lord, "Behold, We have created you all out of a male or a female, and have made you into nations and tribes, so that you may come to know one another. Verily, the noblest of you in the sight of God is the one who is most deeply conscious of Him. Behold, God is All-Knowing, All-Aware." [Qur'an 53:5-9]. True to the calling of his Lord, in victory, today, the Prophet (ﷺ) was God-conscious, was humble and compassionate, forgiving and self-effacing, kind and considerate. This demonstration of the mercy and magnanimity of Muhammad (ﷺ) led many, including the staunchest of foes, to embrace Islam. [9] [10] [11] [12].

Conquering Makkah thus, Prophet Muhammad (ﷺ) returned home to his adopted home city of Madinah, much to the surprise and pleasure of his companions known as the "Helpers", who were so named because of the help they gave him. They believed that he was the Prophet, and when his fellow countrymen of Makkah rejected him, they sheltered him, and they fought for him when he was attacked by the enemies. It was with them that he established the very first "Islamic state" ever in the society of Madinah with the Qur'an as its constitution, the revelation of

God to Muhammad (ﷺ) and humanity.

Not long afterwards, in 630 AD, Prophet Muhammad (ﷺ) passed away – about 80 days after he performed his first pilgrimage (which also happened to be his last) to Makkah and addressed the Ummah delivering his final sermons. He declared, "Muslims are to deal justly with one another, to treat women kindly, to abandon the blood feuds and vendettas inspired by the spirit of jahiliyyah. Muslim must never fight against Muslim. Know that every Muslim is a Muslim's brother and that the Muslims are brethren. It is only lawful to take from a brother what he gives you willingly. So, wrong not yourselves."

Reactions from Christians and the reasons behind them

The view that Islam's primary goal was to eradicate non-Muslims from the face of earth has no foundation in the history of the Muslims. Despite the swift expansion of Islam and the large number of territories conquered by Muslims, there is no record of the non-Muslim natives of those areas and countries being compelled to embrace Islam. Rather, Jews and Christians were granted religious freedom to practise their faith. The expansion of Islam, however, raised fear and suspicion in Christian circles and the wider non-Islamic world, as the threat of an impending Muslim conquest of their territories plagued people's minds. Islam was becoming a major player on the global scene and was competing with the other faiths practised there. The rate at which the Muslim frontiers were spreading sent alarm bells ringing across Christendom, which felt it necessary to subdue the momentum of advancing Muslim armies before they reached their doorstep.

The Christian fear and loathing of Muslims reached such levels that lies were concocted and spread by the clergy to demonise Muslims. Thus, the seeds of suspicion were sown in the hearts and minds of many Europeans, that Muslims posed a great threat to their survival and that Islam was about to replace Christianity. The consequence of Christian stigmatisation of Islam was that the study of the Islamic faith became a discipline much distorted by prejudice.

The Christian scholars recognised the potential of Islam to become a major force in Europe. Having recognised the devotion among the followers of Prophet Muhammad (ﷺ) to their faith, they felt it was pointless attacking the theological tenets of Islam, as these seemed to be etched on the hearts of the Muslims. Instead, they resorted to a demonisation campaign against Prophet Muhammad (ﷺ), spreading falsehood and lies about his character, in order to tarnish the reputation of Islam and the Muslims. Among the unfounded claims that they made about the Prophet were that he was an impostor, a fake, a womaniser, one who claimed to receive revelation during fits of epilepsy and who preached his religion at the point of the sword (God forbid). These lies spread about Prophet Muhammad (ﷺ) drove a wedge between Muslims and Christians and this has survived to this day.

As far back as 622 the Byzantine emperor Heraclius hurled insults at Prophet Muhammad (ﷺ) by calling him a work of the devil and an antichrist. The English historian Roger Wendover (d. 635/1237) also promoted the view that Prophet Muhammad (ﷺ) was an impostor. He called him a "false prophet of the Saracens" and also someone who suffered from "epileptic fits". In the 19th century, it was a commonly held view that Prophet Muhammad (ﷺ) was an impostor. A few examples of literature dating back to that period which supports this idea include *The Life of Mahomet, the Famous Oriental Impostor* published by J. Lee (1815) and "Imposture, Deception, and Credulity (1838) (Family Library, No.lxiii). The Scotsman Alexander Ross had many insulting titles for Prophet Muhammad (ﷺ) including: "The Great Arabian Impostor", "Great Hypocrite", "Great thief" *(*"A needful Caveat", appended to the translation of the Alcoran of Mahomet, by Ross, 1649*)*.

In the late 15th century the Scottish poet Walter Kennedy spoke satirically about Prophet Muhammad (ﷺ) to William Dunbar, also Scottish poet. He referred to Prophet Muhammad (ﷺ) pejoratively, calling him a devil and dog, with the intention of showing that he was a false Prophet.

The Qur'an categorically states that the monotheistic faiths of Judaism and Christianity were inspired by God and, as a result, the Muslims were commanded never to view the followers of those faiths, "the people of the book", in a hostile manner. Yet Christendom began to show hostility towards Islam and the Muslim world, resorting to demonisation of the Prophet (ﷺ) and Islam. The Crusades were launched by Christians against Muslims and this was accompanied by a propaganda war against Muslims, cunningly crafted by Christian scholars. In the book *De Haeresibus*, John of Damascus (675–749) branded the Islamic faith as heresy. Guibert de Nogent (d. 518/1124), saw no sense in Islam's prohibition of alcohol and pork. Other examples of vitriolic slander against Islam and Muslims came from Guillaume de Tripoli, as well as Ramon Lull (d. 716/1316), who was beating the drum of war against the Muslim world. Muslims were also accused of idolatry by Marco Polo and Prophet Muhammad (ﷺ) was accused of forgery by French Scholar Ernest Renan. Roger Wendover (d. 635/1237) and John Maundeville (d.757/1356) had spread malicious and baseless reports about the Prophet of Islam.

As the hostility between Christians and Muslims reached boiling point, the Islamic faith was further denigrated and misrepresented by non-Muslims who were deeply suspicious and fearful of Muslims. The Qur'an was translated into Latin by Peter the Venerable (1094–1156), not to serve any academic purpose, but to slander Muslims. This was followed by Robert of Ketton (1143). Many other translations followed, by Mark of Toledo (1190–1200), Francis of Assisi (1181–1226) and Ramon Lull, all of whom continued with skewed interpretations of Islam. The likes of Ranulf Higden (d. 1364) and John Mandeville (1300–1372) continued to distort the true message of Islam, a tradition which predated them. The era of the Crusades was perhaps the most effective and instrumental period of history where Islam was hugely maligned.

Many unfounded and baseless assertions about Prophet Muhammad (ﷺ) were circulated for centuries and an endless list of pejoratives were used to describe Islam and Muslims. Saint Eulogius (d. 859) used very foul language about Islam. In the most extreme allegation, Diceto followed Sigebert (1030–1112) in stating that the Muslims worshipped Prophet Muhammad (ﷺ) as God. Edward Herbert (1583–1648) wrote that Prophet Muhammad (ﷺ) preached against Pope Boniface's usurpation of the title of universal Bishop.

According to Pedro de Alfonso, Prophet Muhammad (ﷺ) used religion as the means to achieve his personal ambition of power and rulership. Du Pont said that Prophet Muhammad (ﷺ) allowed Muslim men to have up to ten wives, and Muslim women to have ten husbands. This falsehood continued for centuries and could be found in much European literature. The ignorance about Prophet Muhammad (ﷺ)'s life was so profound that some had mistaken Ali for Prophet Muhammad's uncle, like the Latin author Joinville (1224–1317). The ignorance and hostility did not stop there. According to Pedro, the name of Prophet Muhammad's father, 'Abdullah', meant the slave of an idol. Hottinger said that the very mention of Prophet Muhammad's names caused him to shiver. From these remarks, it becomes clear that Islam has been the most maligned religion in the West. H. Reland claimed Islam as the most malicious religion. Peter Heylyn (1599–1662) wrote in a geographical treatise, *Mikrokosmos,* that the orphan Prophet Muhammad (ﷺ) was sold to a wealthy merchant called Abdulmutalife.

The representation of Muslims in Christendom in the Middle Ages was remorseless, to say the least. Christian legends dating back to this period are unrelenting in their demonic depiction of Muslims and their Prophet Muhammad (ﷺ). Henry Stubbe, a British writer and scholar, said that the influence which these portrayals exercised in the archives of European literature is an unmistakable phenomenon. Muslims were referred to by a catalogue of pejoratives that included Infidel, Miscreants, Paynims, Pagans, Heathens, Heathen hounds, Enemies of God, Turks, Allophili, Hagerenes, Ishmaelities, Canes, Moabites, Aliens and Gentiles; and occasionally Goths and Vandals. The most disparaging reference which gained popular currency was 'Saracens'. Contrary to the belief – promulgated by Muslim-hating Christians – that the term 'Saracens' was adopted by Muslims who "claimed to be descending from Sarah, with the object of concealing their low birth", subsequent Orientalist scholarship on the etymology of the word 'Saracens' concluded it to be a derivative of the Arabic word 'Serq', meaning to 'steal', hence the Saracens, according to Christian scholarship, were equated with thieves. The 'Turks' – another in the list of sneering descriptors for Muslims – were invariably identified with 'Magog', which in Christian and Muslim doctrine refers to one half of the promethean, godless force which will be unleashed to wreak havoc as a prelude to the final day of judgement. With the Arabs frequently equated with the other sacrilegious half, known as 'Gog', early Christian notions spared no Muslim in their aim to brand the Islamic faith and its adherents as a bulwark against the forces of good. The falsehoods propagated about Muslims became popular currency and ultimately led to a much-skewed understanding of Prophet Muhammad (ﷺ).

These perceptions were thoroughly ingrained in scholarly circles, which also demonised prominent Muslim intellectuals and thinkers. The myths surrounding Muslims went unchallenged and a consensus emerged in the Christian clerical class that Muslims harboured polytheistic tendencies, culminating in the veneration of Prophet Muhammad (ﷺ). These opinions were touted by historians who would note the Muslim adulation of Prophet Muhammad (ﷺ) reflected in the content of the hymns they would recite. To compound the Muslim incredulity, Christian notions of the Saracens attached to them the associations of incantation, with prominent sages such as Al-Kindi and Ibn Sina represented as the custodians of witchcraft and magic.

Christians had the tendency to always blame the Muslims and discovered a new way to create enmity with them. Stubbe highlights that the Christians lost no opportunityto display enmity with the Turks. Thus, the characterisation of Muslims in medieval Christian reports is replete with fabricated and unsubstantiated generalisations and abuse. Among the charges levelled against Prophet Muhammad (ﷺ) was that he was an impostor who faked his prophethood (God forbid). When interviewed by the Sultan of Babylon regarding faith, the King of France, Louis IX, labelled Prophet Muhammad (ﷺ) an impostor and an ignoble human (It is mentioned in the pages of history that the Christians treated Mahomet as an impostor (*Complete history of Turks, vol 2, ch 3, 1701* (God forbid). In the work 'Tribus Impostribus' Jurist Johannes Joachim Müller (1633–1733) deemed Prophet Muhammad (ﷺ) an impostor (God forbid). *(The Berlin Journal, No. 19. Fall 2010.p.10.* Some entertained wild tales about Islam, and foolishly predicted that Muslims will leave their faith and flock to Christianity. This was noted in *Flowers of History* (Bonn, 1849, 2:515). Many others also prophesied the demise of Islam, speaking of impending doom and catastrophes awaiting the Muslims.

A piece titled "A Spiritual Conference, between two doctors", involving Sheikh Sinan and Doctor Ahmed, promoted the idea that Prophet Muhammad (ﷺ) was an impostor and that he falsely claimed to have eradicated idolatry (God forbid). A poem called "The Temple of Imposture" (1708) presents Prophet Muhammad (ﷺ) in the most devilish of forms: "Thus modern Arts on Ancient Plans improve, a bedlam-serpent swallows Makkah's Dove".

A true measure of the hatred against Islam and Muslims can be seen from the reluctance of many medieval Europeans to credit Islam for the intellectual and scientific achievements of the Renaissance period, despite there being a clear link between the two. Even when there was a desire to develop a more sober understanding of the Islamic faith, perceptions were marred by the centuries of lies and misrepresentation about Islam. The 15th and 16th centuries were replete with the spreading of falsehood about Muslims and, once again, prophecies which predicted the end of the Muslim world flourished. Examples include the writings of John Bale (1495-1563) and Henry Smith (1560-1591). Towards the end of the 16th century (1572 and 1575), much was written in the European countries against Islam. One of the predictions included the destruction of Makah and Madinah.

A very popular view in Christian churches was that Muslims were infidels as well as idol worshippers who worshipped none other than Prophet Muhammad (ﷺ). A common prayer read in the churches during the reign of Elizabeth I placed the Turks, Muslims and Prophet Muhammad (ﷺ) in the same category as enemies: "Almighty and everlasting God...we thy rebellious children, in great danger to be oppressed, by thine and our sworn and most deadly enemies the Turks, Infidels...The Turk goeth about to set up, to extol, and to magnify that wicked monster and damned soul Mahumet...", etc. (Liturgical Services of the Reign of Queen Elizabeth, pp. 532-533. Parker Society, 1847). According to the historian Matthew Paris, Prophet Muhammad (ﷺ) was an object of worship among the Saracens. Written in 1270, the "Golden

Legend" described Prophet Muhammad (ﷺ) as an "Enchanter" and "False Prophet" (This can be traced back to the period of the "Speculum Historiale", the "Roman de Mahomet" and "Hildobert of Tours").

British army officer, author and journalist R.V.C. Bodley notes that it was a commonly held belief that Prophet Muhammad (ﷺ) was an epileptic, but he also mentions that these epileptic episodes may have been caused by Prophet Muhammad's realisation that something of a higher provenance was calling him. The fact that Prophet Muhammad (ﷺ) showed a high level of military insight and endurance is, according to Bodley, proof that the charge of epilepsy against him may have been blown out of proportion.

The celebrated British author John Davenport has summarised the overwhelming number of accusations against Prophet Muhammad (ﷺ) into the following four categories:

1. The promulgating of a new and false religion as a revelation from God, it being, on the contrary, but a mere invention of his own, for the purpose of gratifying his ambition and lust.
2. That Mohammed propagated his religion by the sword, thereby causing enormous waste of human blood, vast human misery.
3. The sensual character of his paradise as described in the Koran.
4. The encouragement he has given to licentiousness by legalizing polygamy.

The charges against Prophet Muhammad (ﷺ) were many, and reflected the enmity which many non-Muslim Europeans in particular harboured towards Prophet Muhammad (ﷺ) and Muslims. In addition to these commonplace charges is another which states that Islam is inherently hostile to non-Muslims and other religions in general and that it cannot accommodate others into its realm.

From what has been discussed above, it may be seen that some Christians always had enmity towards Prophet Muhammad (ﷺ) and his followers. Prophet Muhammad's characteristics, e.g. greatness, humbleness, truthfulness, integrity, etc., turned some Christians away from him and his religion. His personality was hardly recognised by his staunch enemies, who feared his popular appeal. Instead of giving recognition to him, they tried to attach a bad name to him. They would belittle the religion of Islam and its followers at every opportunity. Some of the things they would say regarding Muslims in general were that they were violent, oppressive towards women, etc. They generated propaganda against the Qur'an, saying that its teachings were promoting violence and it promotes a dangerous way of life. They also created the impression that Prophet Muhammad (ﷺ) was overwhelmed with lust for women and treated them with utter disrespect.

Research questions:
The main research questions are as follows:

a. How valid are the historically disparaging views about Muhammad, Islam and the Qur'an?
b. What causes the misunderstanding between Muslims and non-Muslims?
c. Are Muslims capable of co-existing with other communities?

Aims
To answer these questions there are three aims of this book:

1. To investigate the truth about Prophet Muhammad (ﷺ), Islam and the Qur'an
2. To investigate the reasons for the misunderstanding between the Islamic world and the West and
3. To investigate if Muslims can live cohesively in an interfaith community based on the teachings of Islam

Objectives
In order to meet the aims, an extensive investigation was conducted into the appreciation, judgements, opinions, observations and thoughts recorded by non-Muslims about the characteristics of Prophet Muhammad (ﷺ), the influence and impact of Islam and the teachings and guidance the Qur'an made by non-Muslims across history and also to find out if the Islamic guidance encourages Muslims to live cohesively in

a society.

Data collection

The data for the research were collected as follows:

1. Though semi-structured interviews with, among others, politicians (MPs, peers), multi-faith priests, leading university chaplaincies, professionals and institutes of interfaith organisations. Semi-structured interviews were mainly conducted face to face in London and on the phone abroad.
2. By collecting comments by non-Muslims on Islam from its early stages until the present.

The qualitative questions related to the 7th century Arab situation, the revelation of the Qur'an, the characteristics and teachings of Prophet Muhammad (ﷺ), links between terrorism and Islam, perceptions of Prophet Muhammad (ﷺ) in the West, Muslims' civic responsibilities and cohesive living with interfaith communities which has been a great challenge in the West. The questions also included a current pressing issue, the burning of the Qur'an – a new issue in the world which has not been investigated so far.

Recommendations for this research/book:

This book is written out of research which has been endorsed by the following organisations, politicians, priests and leaders. Having considered the significance of the study at such a delicate period of Muslim/non-Muslim relations, they feel that such a study is essential.

- Right Honourable MP (British) Frank Dobson
- Right Honourable MP (British) David Amess
- Archbishop's House, Westminster
- Dioceses in Europe
- Tony Blair Faith Foundation
- Britannia Hindu Temple, Highgate, London
- Jalaram Mandir, London
- Buddhist Temple, South London

- Synagogue, East London
- Sikh Temple, Southall

Summary of chapters

In order to refute the charges made and uncover the truth, I have gathered extensive appreciation of Prophet Muhammad (ﷺ), Islam and the Qur'an made by non-Muslims. I have gathered this information by reviewing books and by conducting interviews with prominent personalities. The appreciations are conceptualised, categorised and thematically analysed and divided into eight chapters, based on the above themes.

Chapter two refutes the charges made in chapter one, such as Prophet Muhammad (ﷺ) being an imposter, infidel, fake (God forbid), etc., and focuses on the enormous appreciation of his characteristics. Tremendous admiration is showered on him and, according to some, he was one of the bravest, most generous, simplest, honest, trustworthy, just, noble and influential men in history. The themes which emerged are divided in three parts. Part one considers the 'greatness' of the Prophet, part two his 'simplicity' and part three his 'honesty'.

Chapter three provides evidence that the Prophet Muhammad (ﷺ) was a real protector of women, slaves, the poor and orphans, etc. This chapter also clarifies the reasons for his multiple marriages and discusses how Islam does not discriminate against anyone.

Chapter four considers the influence, impact and teachings of the religion of Islam and how Islam educated the Europeans. Islam guides humanity in life's affairs and it means peace; there is no place for violence in it. It is essentially a rational religion and a blessing for mankind which enlightened Europe when it was in deep darkness.

Chapter five deals with the influence, impact and teachings of the Qur'an and its scientific contributions to mankind.

Chapter six provides evidence that Islam was not preached at the point of the sword. Rather, it was the simplicity of the Prophet which attracted others to Islam. This chapter also demonstrates that there is no link between Islam and terrorism.

Chapter seven deals with the false and vilified images of Islam, and is divided into two parts. Part one indicates how lack of knowledge about Prophet Muhammad (ﷺ) has created a wrong image of his in the West and beyond. Part two deals with the new issue of burning the Qur'an and how it contributes to social tension and violence and presents an obstacle to peace and unity. Also, it explores how politics and the media are also responsible in suppressing the truth about Islam and its Prophet.

Chapter eight has two parts. Part one deals with diversity in Islam and focuses on how Zakat (Islamic tax) can help establish a healthy society which cares for neighbours, and the poor, etc. Part two deals with social cohesion and reveals that the teachings and the guidance of Prophet Muhammad (ﷺ), the Holy Book 'the Qur'an' and the religion 'Islam' do encourage Muslims and others to live peacefully like brothers in a family, irrespective of differences in faith, nationalities, cultures, colour or any other factors. Every individual belongs to one and the same class, which is 'humankind'.

CHAPTER TWO

Prophet Muhammad (ﷺ): Characteristics

Prophet Muhammad (ﷺ) possessed impeccable qualities. He was very gentle in manners, kindhearted to everyone, amicable to all, magnanimous in nature, tolerant of the faults of others, polite in dealings and firm in action. He was always trustworthy, pious and devoted to God and uncompromising in the face of injustice and oppression.

The Prophet's personality was of someone who was courteous, good natured and understanding of the shortcomings of others. All of the positive characteristics and qualities that can be found in human beings, which help forge better relations with others, could be found in Prophet Muhammad(ﷺ)'s character. When it came to establishing and standing up for any person's rights and justice, the Prophet (ﷺ) would be fair but firm. When dispensing justice, he had a very balanced outlook. His engaging manner attracted people towards him. Despite the high position he reached, he always kept his feet on the ground.

Prophet Muhammad (ﷺ) combined exemplary personal ethics with a great command of wisdom, knowledge and erudition – a rare combination hardly found in any person. These qualities led his followers to refer to him as an authoritative and advisory voice on many issues, ranging from social and economic organisation, to human relations and the worship of God, etc. What is most amazing is that Prophet Muhammad (ﷺ) possessed wisdom of the highest level without any formal education and without his learning from the books of previous religions or of any subjects as he was unlettered. His kindhearted manner extended to all, including children.

There were many moments in his life when his loving and caring nature towards the young was noticeably demonstrated.

Based on his qualities, this chapter is divided into three parts: The greatness of Prophet Muhammad, his simplicity, and his honesty.

Part One:

The Greatness of Prophet Muhammad (ﷺ)

Most Influential

Prophet Muhammad (ﷺ) is considered as the most influential person in history by Michael Hart, an American author who heaps much praise on Prophet Muhammad (ﷺ) for his impact on two levels. Prophet Muhammad (ﷺ) successfully penetrated the realm of both the secular and the religious and contributed to political development during his time. Hart has ranked him as number one amongst the 100 most influential people in history. He says:

> *My choice of Muhammad to lead the list of the world's most influential persons may surprise some readers and may be questioned by others, but he was the only man in history who was supremely successful on both the religious and secular levels.*
>
> *Of humble origins, Muhammad founded and promulgated one of the world's great religions, and became an immensely effective political leader. Today, thirteen centuries after his death, his influence is still powerful and pervasive.*[13]

Hart's decision to rate Prophet Muhammad (ﷺ) even above Jesus (pbuh) as the world's most influential personality must be put into perspective. He compares the attributes and influences of both these individuals in terms of the growth and progress of their faiths and declares Prophet Muhammad (ﷺ) to have been more successful in that regard. Hart reminds us of the role played by St Paul in the development of Christianity, which possibly explains why Jesus is not considered to be of the same level as Prophet Muhammad (ﷺ) in his estimation. As far as Prophet Muhammad (ﷺ) is concerned, the doctrines of Islam and the codes of conduct it imparts can be credited to him, as he exemplified himself as the best model of the faith he professed. Unlike Jesus (pbuh), Prophet Muhammad's message had a considerable political element, which affords him a unique distinction.

It may initially seem strange that Muhammad has been ranked higher than Jesus. There are two principal reasons for that decision. First, Muhammad played a far more important role in the development of Islam than Jesus did in the development of Christianity. Although Jesus was responsible for the main ethical and moral precepts of Christianity (insofar as these differed from Judaism), St. Paul was the main developerof Christian theology, its principal proselytizer, and the author of a large portion of the New Testament.

Muhammad, however, was responsible for both the theology of Islam and its main ethical and moral principles. In addition, he played the key role in proselytizing the new faith, and in establishing the religious practices of Islam...It is probable that the relative influence of Muhammad on Islam has been larger than the combined influence of Jesus Christ and St. Paul on Christianity.... Furthermore, Muhammad (unlike Jesus) was a secular as well as religious leader. In fact, as the driving force behind the Arab conquests, he may well rank as the most influential political leader of all time.[14]

Hart reveals that within a short time the Arabians were influenced by Prophet Muhammad (ﷺ) and were able to establish a state from the boundary of India to the Atlantic Ocean – which was the largest territory under single control in history.[15]

Hart points out that Islam's spread must be attributed to the precedent set by Prophet Muhammad (ﷺ), in particular his combined emphasis on religious and worldly matters, and perceiving them as a harmonious whole. For such incomparable blending he should be judged as the most important person in history. He continues by saying:

We see, then, that the Arab conquests of the seventh century have continued to play an important role in human history, down to the present day. It is this unparalleled blend of secular and religious influence which I feel entitles Muhammad to be considered the most influential single figure in human history.[16]

The prolific Chinese author Liu Chai-Lien admired the Prophet of Islam and claimed that God would not have created the universe or any creatures if he had not created According to Lin:

> *The Prophet was the most cherished person of the whole creation, wherefore the Lord God said to Jesus: "Had it not been for Mohammed, I would not have created heaven, earth, men and spirits." So there can be no doubt that his was a special life.*[17]

Liu maintains that the Prophet was the most praiseworthy amongst all of God's creatures. His characteristics, action and sayings, etc., were of the highest quality:

> *In creation, the Prophet was the most honourable; his natural endowments and gifts, and his aspirations, were of the highest; his family and his dwelling-places were most noble and distinguished. There was not a single thing connected with him which was not most honourable, hence he is called the Most Holy Prophet.*[18]

Authors Kerry Brown and Martin Palmer wrote in their book *The Essential Teachings of Islam* that Prophet Muhammad (ﷺ), a central person of Islam, is a human being and not divine who is given the highest tribute:

> *The key figure of Islam is of course Muhammad. While Muhammad is considered to be only a human being and in no way divine, he is accorded great respect.*[19]

The French scholar Ernest Renan wrote in 1851 that Prophet Muhammad (ﷺ) was alive through the whole of history, "in the full light of history".[20]

The Prime Minister of Fiji, Commodore Josaia Voreqe Bainimarama, paid tribute the Prophet Muhammad (ﷺ) in a speech on the occasion of the Prophet's birthday, declaring him as one of the most influential spiritual leaders of the world. The Prime Minister said in his speech:

My Fellow Fijians, Today we join hundreds of millions around the world in celebrating the birth and life of one of the world's most influential spiritual leaders – the Prophet Muhammad, peace be upon him. For Muslims everywhere, the Prophet Muhammad's life and message are the very core of Islam, and guide their faith....[21]

The celebrated author Isaac Mason, a British missionary with the Friends Foreign Mission Association in China narrated an interesting story about how Islam was first spread in China. The story goes that the emperor of China sent his astronomer to the West to find out about a new star which had appeared in the sky. After a year-long journey, the astronomer reached the Prophet and asked him to travel to China. The Prophet, instead, sent his messenger Saad ibn Waqqas. Having heard the astonishing tales of the Prophet, the emperor ordered a mosque to be built in Canton, China. Mason states:

The account given of the first entry of Moslems into China says that in the sixth year of K'ai Huang of the Sui dynasty, (A.D. 586) there was seen in the sky a strange star; the Emperor commanded the Chief Astronomer to divine its meaning, and he said that an extraordinary person was appearing in the West. The Emperor sent an envoy to investigate, and he arrived in Mecca after about a year's travelling. The envoy desired Mohammed to proceed to the East, but he declined; he sent, however, his maternal uncle Saad Wakkas, and three others, to accompany the envoy to China. The envoy secretly had a portrait of the Prophet made to take back with him; this was given to the Emperor who proceeded to worship it, and when he arose, the scroll was there but the picture had vanished. Saad Wakkas explained that this was due to the influence of the Prophet who had forbidden to men the worship of images and the "kowtow." The Emperor was so impressed that he gave directions for the building of the "Prophet Remembrance", a mosque at Canton.[22]

Another Chinese Emperor, Hong-Wu (also known as Zhū Yuánzhāng, 1368–1398) had high regard for Prophet Muhammad (ﷺ).

He expressed his admiration in a poem of 100 words which was displayed in many mosques in China. The poem, translated into English is as follows:

> *Since Creation of Universe Heaven has already appointed, Faith Preaching Giant Saint,... To guide all creations, King of all Kings, Leader of Holy Ones...*
> *Away from all wrongdoings, Mercy to the World, Walking ancient Crowned Path, Evil vanquished to One, Religion Pure and True, Muhammad, The Noble High One*[23]

Greatest Personality

The Orientalists' myths regarding Prophet Muhammad (ﷺ) must be set aside in view of their falsity. The fabrication surrounding Prophet Muhammad's personality has been a huge disservice to those generally interested in the truth. The hundreds of millions of people claiming adherence to Islam can be seen as a product of Prophet Muhammad's efforts and the examples that he set. Given the huge number of people who have adopted Islam as a faith and chosen to live by its guidelines, we cannot dismiss Islam and its messenger Prophet Muhammad (ﷺ), summarily. Thomas Carlyle, the Scottish writer, essayist, historian and teacher, said that the myths regarding Prophet Muhammad (ﷺ) must be cast aside due to their implausibility. In his words:

> *Our current hypothesis about Muhammad, that he was a scheming impostor, A falsehood incarnate, that his religion is a mere mass of quackery and fatuity, begins really to be now untenable to any one. The lies, which well meaning zeal has heaped round this man, are disgraceful to ourselves only. When Pococke inquired of Grotius, where the proof was of the story of the Pigeon trained to pick peas from Mahomet's ear and pass for an angel dictating to him? Grotius answered that there was no proof! It is really time to dismiss all that. The words this man spoke has been the life guidance now*

> *of a hundred and eighty millions of men these twelve hundred years.*[24]

The attribute of sincerity is essential when determining a person's heroism. However, a person insisting he is sincere defeats the object. One who is sincere need not tell others that he is sincere. For those claiming sincerity are full of insincerity and pretence. Rather, sincerity should be reflected in their actions. The sign of a genuinely sincere person is one who keeps his noble deeds to himself and never makes a public act drawing attention to himself. In fact, one may argue that a sincere person is someone who does not consciously acknowledge his acts of sincerity, but rather someone who fears that he may succumb to insincere intentions, given his awareness that, as a fallible individual, he like anyone else is prone to inconsistency and error. Being unconscious of one's sincerity, then, is a prerequisite of a sincere person. Vanity, pomp, and smug self-congratulation are not in a sincere person's vernacular and a sincere person is never afflicted with these malaises. Carlyle says:

> *But of a Great Man especially, of him I will venture to assert that it is incredible he should have been other than true. It seems to me the primary foundation of him, and of all that can lie in him, this. No Mirabeau, Napoleon, Burns, Cromwell, no man adequate to do anything, but is first of all in right earnest about it; what I call a sincere man. I should say sincerity, a deep, great, genuine sincerity, is the first characteristic of all men in any way heroic. Not the sincerity that calls itself sincere; ah no, that is a very poor matter indeed; a shallow braggart conscious sincerity; oftenest self-conceit mainly. The great man's sincerity is of the kind he cannot speak of, is not conscious of; nay, I suppose, he is conscious rather of insincerity; for what man can walk accurately by the law of truth for one day? No, the great man does not boast himself sincere, far from that; perhaps does not ask himself if he is so; I would say rather, his sincerity does not depend upon himself; he cannot help being sincere! The great fact of existence is great to him.*[25]

Sir John Glubb, a British soldier, scholar and author, claimed that he was not doubtful about Prophet Muhammad's success, which was due to his great personality and certainly not to military actions. In the present time we think of him as a strong man who was a leader, but the truth is that Prophet Muhammad (ﷺ) was naturally a soft person. We have no example of him giving tyrannical commands or punishing those who did not comply with his instructions.[26]

The British author Anita Rai praises the Prophet Muhammad (ﷺ) for the great personality he showed by marrying Khadijah (RA), who was 15 years older than him and twice married before. Rai felt that such a marriage is not disgraceful, offensive or abhorrent; rather she admires the Prophet for his great personality.[27]

The American author Amit Pal reveals in his book *Islam Means Peace* that the idea that Islam is a violent religion is dispelled once we reflect on the teachings and practice of Prophet Muhammad (ﷺ). In particular, the early stages of his Prophethood provide compelling proof of his and his followers' pacifying nature and their aversion to violence and chaos. Amit Pal says:

> *My journey of exploration starts with the founder of the religion, the Prophet Muhammad, and Islam's holy book, the Qur'an. The prophet is a role model for devout Muslims. In support of the fact that Islam places an emphasis on nonviolence, scholars point to the conduct of the Prophet Muhammad in Makkah. For 12 long years, he endured persecution in that city without fighting back, emphasizing instead the virtues of forbearance (sabr) and patience.*[28]

Major Arthur Glyn Leonard, an American author, reported that on one occasion Martin Luther sat at a table with a few friends, and when describing to them his view of the world, he used the analogy of kings, princes, aces, etc., in a pack of cards. According to Luther, the Pope reigned supreme over these lofty men until an "ace" was revealed by God, who overcame the temporal powers. In Luther's opinion, Prophet Muhammad (ﷺ) was this ace, since from him alone emanated a social, political and cultural revolution of unprecedented proportions.

In a conversation that Luther had one day with some friends at table, he spoke of the world as a vast and magnificent pack of cards composed of emperors, kings, princes and so forth. For several ages these had been vanquished by the Pope. Then God had come upon the scene, and chosen the "ace," the very smallest card in the pack - himself, in a word - and overthrown this conqueror of worldly powers and principalities. Mohammed, as much as Luther, was one of "God's Aces." Seldom, indeed, in the history of the world, has so great a human river flowed from a source so puny. Never did the divine manifest itself in a single pip, so seemingly small and insignificant as a cause, yet so pre-eminently and consistently great as an effect![29]

Prophet Muhammad(ﷺ)'s activities were for all and forever. He explained that God's creation was for worldly and religious purposes. An in-depth study of the Qur'an reveals that Prophet Muhammad (ﷺ) exerted all of his energy and thoughts on the completion of his great mission. Leonard adds:

Mohammed was a thinker and a worker not only for his own, but for all time. He recognized that man was equally a political and religious product of God's creation. He understood that as a counterpoise to man's materialism and to the destructive in his nature, is that indefinable essence which we call the spiritual and the constructive. The more one looks into and understands the Koran, the more obvious is it that Mohammed concentrated all the active and vigorous energies of his vivid and powerful imagination, also his virile mentality, on the accomplishment of his great design.[30]

Edward Sell, an Orientalist and historian, admired Prophet Muhammad (ﷺ) for his strength of personality in influencing the local people in Madinah at a time when there was no law and order in society. Quarrels and fights were the order of the day and it was difficult for the local politicians to resolve these situations. However, after the advent of Prophet Muhammad (ﷺ), the situation started to change. The great personality of the Prophet influenced not only the ordinary people but also the leaders. Edward Sell asserts:

> *There were plenty of quarrels in Madinah. Muhammad by his claims, and also by the force of his own personality, soon acquired even a greater influence than the ancient kahins (local politicians) ever possessed, for his authority was becoming political as well as religious.*[31]

Deepak Chopra, an Indian author, wrote in the 'author's Note' of his book *Prophet Muhammad: A Story of the Last Prophet* about the spiritual side of the Prophet. He admits that Prophet Muhammad (ﷺ) appealed to him most because the Prophet reformed humankind by reaching into the inner level of the divine. Such an achievement was only possible with divine guidance. Chopra further says that the Prophet's achievements through this divine guidance guided him to become a leader in daily life.[32]

The celebrated author Barnaby Rogerson states that according to Islam, what merits all mankind could have, Prophet Muhammad (ﷺ) possessed alone himself. Rogerson also quotes the mystic poet Rumi who described the Prophet as proof of the existence of God. But the Prophet himself said that he was an ordinary human being.[33]

In the view of John William Draper, the American scientist, philosopher and historian, the influence which Prophet Muhammad (ﷺ) exercised over mankind is not surpassed by anybody. His leadership over vast peoples and his role as spiritual mentor for over a billion people could explain and do justice to his prophethood. His influence can be felt all across the earth. Draper highlights:

> *Four years after the death of Justinian, A.D. 569, was born in Makkah, in Arabia, the man Muhammad, who of all men, has exercised the greatest influence upon the human race. To be the religious head of many empires, to guide the daily life of one-third of the human race, may perhaps justify the title of a Messenger of God… The towering personality of Muhammad has left bright and indelible imprints on all mankind.*[34]

Carlyle observed that Prophet Muhammad (SAW earned the title of *Al-Ameen* (the trustworthy). He was a very faithful, caring, and generous person; whatever he spoke was meaningful and he used to remain silent when there was nothing to say. He had beautiful physical attributes, personal qualities, and an excellent approach which pleased people. Carlyle added:

> *But, from an early age, he had been remarked as a thoughtful man. His companions named him "Al Amin, the Faithful." A man of truth and fidelity; true in what he did, in what he spoke and thought. They noted that he always meant something. A man rather taciturn in speech; silent when there was nothing to be said; but pertinent, wise, sincere, when he did speak; always throwing light on the matter. This is the only sort of speech worth speaking! Through life we find him to have been regarded as an altogether solid, brotherly, genuine man. A serious, sincere character; yet amiable, cordial, companionable, jocose even; - a good laugh in him withal: there are men whose laugh is as untrue as anything about them; who cannot laugh.*[35]

Professor Tor Julius Efraim Andrae (Tor Andrae), a Swedish scholar, stated that the scholars in history compared Prophet Muhammad (ﷺ) with Numa, the second king of Rome and Theseus, the founder-king of Athens. The scholars admired Prophet Muhammad (ﷺ) as a wise and informed lawgiver.[36] Andrae also mentioned that scholars considered Prophet Muhammad (ﷺ) to be a genuinely sincere, unusual personality, a great man, an original man, etc.[37]

A recent scholar of Islam, Karen Armstrong, expressed admiration for Prophet Muhammad (ﷺ) in her book *Muhammad: Prophet for our time.* She wrote that if the Prophet was viewed like any other significant person in history, she had no doubt that, in comparison with others, he is the greatest genius of the world.[38]

The prolific author Arthur Naylor Wollaston agrees with the above statement. According to him:

> *[T]the Prophet of Islam – a genius who, whatever may be the*

verdict of posterity in regard to his "mission", has had a more potent influence on the destinies of mankind than has been vouchsafed to any son of Adam who has left footprints on the sands of time.[39]

Karen Armstrong claims that Prophet Muhammad's life was a reflection of how the divine permeates society and how the faithful and God-fearing live their lives. He revealed God's action on the earth and showed how to surrender to God.[40]

Armstrong continues saying that Prophet Muhammad (ﷺ) even before the prophethood was commissioned, was known as Al-Ameen, 'the trustworthy', among the people of Makkah. He had the skill to inspire confidence in others, and had an influential and whole-hearted personality. He never looked over his shoulder and if he needed to speak to someone, he turned completely to face them. When shaking another person's hand, he did not take out his hand first.[41]

Dr Henry Stubbe, a British writer and scholar, wrote in his book *An Account of the Rise and Progress of Mahometanism* that Prophet Muhammad (ﷺ) is perhaps the only figure in the history of mankind of whom opinions are split right down the middle, be they positive or negative. With much of the world revering him and many others condemning him, there is hardly anyone who has left a similar legacy. What cannot be denied is how instrumental Prophet Muhammad (ﷺ) was and still is for a huge part of the earth's population. The irony, however, is that Prophet Muhammad (ﷺ), despite his adulation of Jesus (pbuh) and his command to his followers to respect Jesus, is nonetheless scolded and described in the most irreverent and derisory terms by many Christians in the world. He wrote:

There is no man under heaven who has been the object of so much discussion, due either to extreme hatred or great love, as the Prophet Mohammed. Exalted in the East and discarded in the West, the Prophet has acquired a position which is difficult to define and for which it is impossible to find a parallel. He has been a central figure, to a large part of mankind, during the last thirteen centuries. His great enemies were the infidels of Makkah, but their

> *hostility is as nothing compared to that shown by the Christian nations, which casts the story of the Jews and their detestation of Jesus entirely into the shade. It is a strange irony of fate that Mohammed, who so manifestly honoured Isa [Jesus] and respected his teachings, has been made the object of the grossest abuse and the vilest calumny by the followers of Isa.*[42]

A famous Hindu poet, Rana Bahgwan Das, paid high compliments to Prophet Muhammad (ﷺ) for giving direction to the misguided and providing care to the needy. He paid tribute to the Prophet who would be a leader here and in the hereafter. He expressed this in a poem:

(Urdu)
"As-Salam ay Hadi-e- gumgashtagan
As-Salam ay shafa-e-Bechargan
As-Salam ay Malik-e-har do Man
As-Salam ay Wajha-e-Takhliq-e- Zaman"

(English)
(I salute the guide of the misguided
I salute the helper of the helpless
I salute the master of the two worlds
I salute him who is responsible for the creation of the universe).[43]

Major Arthur Leonard highlights the remarkable characteristics of Prophet Muhammad (ﷺ) in acquiring knowledge and achieving something gradually while avoiding hastiness. The odd failure here and there did not stop him from carrying on. Calmness and patience were among the great qualities he developed. Leonard brands the Prophet as a truly remarkable man:

> *What appears to me as so remarkable and so significant, so truly characteristic of the man, is the way in which he never lets go his grip of the central idea and purpose, but follows it up step by step. And as he follows, he makes every point that he can, seizes every*

opportunity, takes every advantage of every ordinary event and occurrence that is going on around him, makes the best of every reverse, turns even his set-backs and reverses into moral victories; and accepts it all as inevitable with the calmness of a philosophy that emanated from his own wondrous egoism and that inexhaustible fund of patience and reserve of courage which so distinguishes his character. In this respect alone Mohammed truly was a remarkable man.[44]

Leonard uses a farming analogy to explain that Prophet Muhammad (ﷺ) worked as an instrument of God to establish the religion despite facing huge difficulties, and suffering at the hands of his enemies. His good manners helped him endure misfortunes and led him to eventual victory.

His hand was to the plough—the plough God. God was the goal, the end, the summit of human existence and ambition. Humanity was the soil, and to get there he must furrow his way through its enmities and affections. Firm and exceptional natures are thus moulded out of miseries, misfortunes and afflictions. As a result of his work history shows us more and more that Mohammed was firm and exceptional to the very highest degree.[45]

In a similar manner, Diwan Chand Sharma, a Member of Parliament, Indian Congress Party, admires the Prophet Muhammad (ﷺ) for his compassion and control over the situation of his time. If Prophet Muhammad (ﷺ) was renowned for anything, it was his natural kindness. He had a very amicable nature that left a positive impression upon many:

Muhammad was the soul of kindness and his influence was felt and never forgotten by those around him.[46]

Edward Gibbon affirms that Prophet Muhammad (ﷺ) was a highly talented person whose tremendous achievements entitle him to the high regard of all:

The talents of Mahomet are entitled to our applause.[47]

The quickness with which Prophet Muhammad (ﷺ) assumed the seat of power and the reverence with which he was regarded in his community was extraordinary. This was to have a tremendous impact on the rest of the world. John Austin, a British philosopher and writer, echoes the same idea:

> *In little more than a year he was actually the spiritual, nominal and temporal rule of Madinah, with his hands on the lever that was to shake the world.*[48]

William Draper maintains that Prophet Muhammad (ﷺ) had numerous attributes which helped him excel as a leader and guide of others. He had qualities which were advantageous in many disciplines and aspects of life. As a soldier, he led from the front and as a spiritual instructor his words spoke volumes and touched the hearts of many people. His religious ethos was not abstract but simple – simple enough for those of other backgrounds to digest and practise. Unlike so many religious personalities and sages throughout history, Prophet Muhammad (ﷺ) never bogged his followers down in dry dogma and polemics.

Rather, he was devoted to bettering the prevailing social and economic climate of his time, by commanding his followers to pay Zakat – "the due from the income of the rich and affluent to the poor". Draper says:

> *Mohammed possessed that combination of qualities which more than once has decided the fate of empires. A preaching soldier, he was eloquent in the pulpit, valiant in the field. His theology was simple: "There is but one God." The effeminate Syrian, lost in Monothelite and Monophysite mysteries; the Athanasian and Arian, destined to disappear before his breath, might readily anticipate what he meant. Asserting that ever-lasting truth, he did not engage in vain metaphysics, but applied himself to improving the social condition of his people by regulations respecting personal cleanliness, sobriety, fasting, prayer. Above all other works he esteemed almsgiving and charity.*[49]

Draper notes that religious pluralism was something which Prophet Muhammad (ﷺ) endorsed. His teachings would often state how there was much to be shared among the virtuous people on this earth, irrespective of faith. In this sense, Prophet Muhammad (ﷺ) transcended the often rigid and narrow frameworks of salvation of his time. In Draper's words,

> *With a liberality to which the world had of late become a stranger, he admitted the salvation of men of any form of faith provided they were virtuous. To the declaration that there is but one God, he added, "and Mohammed is his Prophet." Whoever desires to know whether the event of things answered to the boldness of such an announcement, will do well to examine a map of the world in our own times. He will find the marks of something more than an imposture. To be the religious head of many empires, to guide the daily life of one-third of the human race, may perhaps justify the title of a messenger of God... Too often, in this world, success is the criterion of right.*[50]

Christian Snouck Hurgronje, a Dutch scholar of Oriental cultures and languages, mentionsed that the great personality of Prophet Muhammad (ﷺ) is well known widely. His creation of the *'League of Nations'* to establish a unique system of brotherhood is commended everywhere.[51]

W. Montgomery Watt, Professor of Arabic and Islamic Studies at the University of Edinburgh, acknowledges that Prophet Muhammad's conviction in his message and fortitude to suffer and bear the brunt of whatever came his way for the sake that his message prevails, is testimony to his resilience. The good character and integrity of his followers and those who were attracted by his character are further evidence of his uprightness, and the fact that he never deliberately compromised or jeopardised the security and well-being of his people. The suggestion that Prophet Muhammad (ﷺ) was a false prophet does not fit in with Prophet Muhammad's profile and the descriptions of his character which many have provided. Given his stature, it is a travesty that misinformation about Prophet Muhammad (ﷺ) runs rife in the Western world.[52]

Professor Watt maintains that a historical appreciation of Prophet Muhammad's mission magnifies his achievements. That his predicament was unbearable by many standards, and he faced insurmountable odds, is undeniable, yet Prophet Muhammad (ﷺ) met the expectations that were placed on him. His administrative competence, leadership qualities and indefatigable conviction in a higher being and power were all essential ingredients for him to usher in an epic chapter in the history of mankind.[53]

Stanley Lane-Poole, a British Orientalist and archaeologist, points out that the drastic overhaul which could be seen in the character and nature of the Arab population is owing to the genius of Prophet Muhammad (ﷺ). His propagation of Islam and promises of victory resonated strongly with the Arabs, who were desperate to escape from their shackles and self-inflicted wounds.

Prophet Muhammad's message helped inculcate revolutionary zeal among the Arabs, and the swiftness with which this occurred is difficult for the modern man to digest. More often than not, revolutions and mass social upheavals are spearheaded by personalities oozing intellect and charisma, and Prophet Muhammad (ﷺ) certainly possessed those traits. His unflinching support for the Islamic cause caused both him and his followers to be undaunted and undeterred by any of the practical obstacles and possible harm that may ensue, when delivering the message. Prior to Prophet Muhammad (ﷺ), the Arabs were sad spectacles of savagery, yet Prophet Muhammad (ﷺ) managed to successfully instil in them a unity of purpose for the greater good. He was known to have granted security to those requesting it and would always come across as the most amicable of persons in discussions. Often, people would be in awe of him. He had a tremendous drawing power and charisma. British Orientalist Stanley Lane-Poole says:

> *The change had been caused by one man. Muhammad the Arabian prophet began to teach the religion of Islam in the beginning of the seventh century, and his doctrine, falling upon a people prone to quick impulses susceptible of strong impressions, worked a revolution. What he taught was simple enough. He took the old*

faith of the Hebrews, which had its disciples in Arabia, and, making such additions and alterations as he thought needful, he preached the worship of one God as a new revelation to a nation of idolaters. It is difficult for us in the present time to understand the irresistible impulse which the simple and unemotional creed of Mohammed gave to the whole people of Arabia; but we know that such religious revolutions have been, and that there is always a mysterious and potent fascination in the personal influence of a true prophet.[54]

Lane-Poole observes that Prophet Muhammad (ﷺ) taught the people whatever he received through the revelation. The Arabs were involved in barbaric activities which he brought to an end. The Prophet was their most faithful protector. According to Lane-Poole,

Mohammed was so far true, that he taught honestly and strenuously what he believed to be the only right faith, and there was enough of sublimity in the creed and of enthusiasm in the Prophet and his hearers to produce that wave of overmastering popular feeling which people call fanaticism. The Arabs before the time of Mohammed had been a collection of rival tribes or clans, excelling in the savage virtues of bravery, hospitality, and even chivalry, and devoted to the pursuit of booty. The Prophet turned the Arab tribes, for the nonce, into the Moslem people, filled them with the fervour of martyrs, and added to the greed of plunder the nobler ambition of bringing all mankind to the knowledge of the truth...He was the most faithful protector of those he protected, the sweetest and most agreeable in conversation. Those who saw him were suddenly filled with reverence; those who came near him loved him; they who described him would say, "I have never seen his like either before or after." He was of great taciturnity, but when he spoke it was with emphasis and deliberation, and no one could forget what he said...[55]

Lane-Poole remarks that despite suffering untold oppression and torture at the hands of the Quraish and those who were hostile to his message, Prophet Muhammad (ﷺ) forgave all their transgressions, granting them clemency. This is nowhere better illustrated than in his conquest of Makkah, which occurred with no report or record of blood being spilled. Those under Prophet Muhammad's command followed suit and would not harass any member of the community and engage in any crime. Lane-Poole explains:

> *He freely forgave the Koraysh all the years of sorrow and cruel scorn in which they had afflicted him and gave an amnesty to the whole population of Mekka. Four criminals whom justice condemned made up Mohammad's proscription list when he entered as a conqueror to the city of his bitterest enemies. The army followed his example, and entered quietly and peacefully no house was robbed, no women insulted. One thing alone suffered destruction. Going to the Kaaba, Mohammad stood before each of the three hundred and sixty idols, and pointed to it with his staff, saying, 'Truth has come and falsehood has fled away" and at these words his attendants hewed them down, and all the idols and household gods of Mekka and roundabout were destroyed.*[56]

Lane-Poole maintains that one thing which really reinforces Prophet Muhammad's humble nature is the fact that the power he assumed did not prompt him to revel in the material excesses of the world. Furthermore, Prophet Muhammad (ﷺ) was never an extrovert. He was not one for boisterous play and could never be remotely seen as behaving and talking like a braggart. His compassion extended to those of any age. Prophet Muhammad (ﷺ) would always take time to show how much he loved and valued children. Also, he was not the type to condemn and invoke bad wishes and omens on others.

Maintaining healthy social relations with any peer group was of great importance to Prophet Muhammad (ﷺ). This meant not discriminating when it came to race, gender or status. This was all part of Prophet Muhammad's public presentation and principles which he internalised as a human being. Lane-Poole adds:

> *His eating and drinking, his dress and his furniture retained, even*

when he reached the fullness of power, their almost primitive nature. The only luxuries he indulged in were arms, which he highly prized, a pair of yellow boots, a present from the Negus of Abyssinia. Perfumes, however, he loved passionately, being most sensitive to smells. Strong drink he abhorred... 'He is more modest than a virgin behind her curtain', it was said of him. He was most indulgent to his inferiors, and would never allow his little page to be scolded whatever he did. 'Ten years', said Anas, his servant, 'I was about the Prophet, and he never said as much as 'uff' to me'. He was very affectionate towards his family. One of his boys died on his breast in the smoky house of the nurse, a blacksmith's wife. He was very fond of children; he would stop them in the streets and pat their little heads. He was the most faithful protector of those he protected, the sweetest and most agreeable in his conversation.[57]

Lane-Poole points out that the victory of Makkah was a bloodless triumph! The Prophet did not take any vengeance on those who once wanted to kill him and caused all sorts of pains and sufferings for him and finally compelled him to be ousted from the city. But instead of taking any revenge he gave a general amnesty to all. As a result, everybody was safe at their homes and outside. It was a unique example in history. In Lane-Poole's words:

But what is this? Is there no blood in the streets? Where are the bodies of the thousands that have been butchered? Facts are hard things; and it is a fact that the day of Prophet Muhammad's greatest triumph over his enemies was also the day of his grandest victory over himself. He freely forgave the Qureysh all the years of sorrow and cruel scorn they had inflicted on him; he gave an amnesty to the whole population of Makkah. Four criminals whom justice condemned, made up Prophet Muhammad's proscription list; no house was robbed, no woman insulted. It was thus that Prophet Muhammad (ﷺ) entered again his native city. Through all the annals of conquest, there is no triumphant entry like unto this one.[58]

John Eade, a Professor of Sociology and Anthropology and former Executive Director of CRONEM (Centre for Research on Nationalism, Ethnicity and Multiculturalism which links Roehampton and the University of Surrey), considers that there is something more 'normal' Prophet Muhammad's character compared to other historical figures. This aspect of his personality may lead others easily to follow him on a practical level.

According to Professor Eade,

> *Unlike Jesus, Muhammad was in many respects an everyday person. He was a merchant. What's interesting about him is that he had an everyday life but was chosen to be the spokesperson for Allah. Unlike Jesus who never married and never had children, Muhammad is clearly different. He appears to be a kind of normal person.*[59]

A noted British author, Geoffrey Parrinder, says that one would be hard pushed to identify a single person in the history of mankind who is subject to the level of vilification and misconception as Prophet Muhammad (ﷺ). The pejoratives that have been assigned specifically for him cannot compare to any others, whether historically or in current times. It is unfair that Prophet Muhammad (ﷺ) has been dubbed a womaniser (God forbid), especially when his life merited no such slander. The fact that he lived happily and faithfully with Khadijah (RA), 15 years his senior and married again only after she passed away is a testimony to his uprightness. The wives he took after Khadijah (RA)'s death were at an old age and he married them for various reasons apart from the ones conventionally passed to us by biased and Islamophobic commentators. Prophet Muhammad's relationship with his wives and women in general compares far more favourably than that of many Christian figures in history.[60]

Geoffrey Parrinder goes on to say that Prophet Muhammad (ﷺ) was required to work in many environments at various times, but it this not affect him much. From his beginnings as a shepherd through the caravan trade to solitary meditation on the mount he moved on to preaching a religion, exile to Madinah and then achieving victory! American author

R.B. Smith was very doubtful if any other person could retain the humbleness all throughout his life as Prophet Muhammad (ﷺ) had. Parrinder echoed this opinion:

> *On the whole, the wonder is not how much but how little, under different circumstances, Muhammad differed from himself. In the shepherd of the desert, in the Syrian trader, in the solitary of Mount Hira, in the reformer in the minority of one, in the exile of Madinah, in the acknowledged conqueror, in the equal of the Persian Chosroes* [a famous and powerful king of ancient Persia] *and the Greek Heraclius, we can still trace a substantial unity. I doubt whether any other man, whose external conditions changed so much, ever himself changed less to meet them. The accidents are changed; the essence seems to me to be the same in all.*[61]

Prophet Muhammad's cerebral nature and logical attributes were central to his character. He possessed the ability to recollect information and think creatively at a very high level. Everything from his mental capacity to his diet was afforded the greatest degree of care, and his dress never suggested he was someone full of pomp and pride. Washington Irving, the American author, biographer and historian admired Prophet Muhammad (ﷺ) for his amazing qualities, bright thoughtful mind and creative nature. He commented:

> *His intellectual qualities were undoubtedly of an extraordinary kind. He had a quick apprehension, a retentive memory, a vivid imagination and an inventive genius...He was sober and abstemious in his diet, and a rigorous observer of fasts. He indulged in no magnificence of apparel, the ostentation of a petty mind; neither was his simplicity in dress affected but a result of real disregard for distinction from so trivial a source.*[62]

James Michener, another American author, describes the characteristics of Prophet Muhammad (ﷺ). He thinks that no one can doubt the fact that Prophet Muhammad (ﷺ) was kind and compassionate to all people, irrespective of their wealth, status etc. His wife Khadijah

(RA) was attracted to his ethical trading policies and warm nature. During their married years, Prophet Muhammad (ﷺ) was always faithful to Khadijah (RA) and always remained humbled by the fact that Allah had chosen him as a Prophet for mankind. Though he was initially afraid of his limitations of literacy, the angel encouraged him to read and preach, which later brought Islamic revolution on the earth. He believed and taught others that death is natural and should not be linked to any supernatural event. Michener adds:

> *Orphaned at birth, he was always particularly solicitous of the poor and needy, the widow and the orphan, the slave and the downtrodden. At twenty he was already a successful businessman, and soon became director of camel caravans for a wealthy widow. When he reached twenty-five, his employer, by recognizing his merit, proposed marriage. Even though she was fifteen years older, he married her, and as long as she lived, remained a devoted husband. Like almost every major prophet before him, Muhammad fought shy of serving as the transmitter of God's word, sensing his own inadequacy. But the angel commanded 'Read.' So far as we know, Muhammad was unable to read or write, but he began to dictate those inspired words which would soon revolutionize a large segment of the earth: 'There is one God.' In all things Muhammad was profoundly practical.*[63]

Roche Forlong, a Major General of the Indian Army who was trained as an engineer in Scotland and England, paid tribute to Prophet Muhammad (ﷺ). Having done thorough research for over forty years on the character, virtues, behaviour and dealings of the Prophet Muhammad (ﷺ) Forlong came to the conclusion that Prophet Muhammad (ﷺ) is among the greatest of persons who have ever lived on earth and he justly received deep respect from all – whether in public or in private. In Forlong's words:

> *After long, very full and candid study of the great Arabian and his faith, his public and private character, virtues and defects; his times and circumstances a study extending over forty years and in close*

connection with Muhammadans of all sets and nations, we must confess that the Prophet stands high in the list of the greatest of the earth's rulers and the makers of history. Alike, in camp and council, as a governor of men, administrator and organiser of brave and turbulent tribes or settled nations, Muhammad commanded the respect of statesmen, friends and foes; and was loved, honoured and esteemed by all privileged to know him privately or publicly[64].

The celebrated historian Edward Montet studied the lives of the prophets of different times. He compares other prophets with Prophet Muhammad (ﷺ) and claims that there had been no Prophet who was as credible as he was. Montet declares that: "*No Prophet has ever been as completely vindicated as he was.*"[65]

The writer G. Lindsay Johnson highlights that throughout history, there has been a lot of misinformation about Prophet Muhammad (ﷺ) and little appreciation of the fact that he led a very noble and honourable life. His time on this earth was spent in devotion to God and encouraging others towards righteousness and piety. Extremism was something he spoke out against, and a reading of his life would vindicate this. The calumnies uttered against him and his message are unfounded. Lindsay Johnson wrote in his book *The Two Worlds*:

The ignorance displayed by most Christians regarding the Muslim religion is appalling... Mohammad alone, among the nations at that time, believed in one God to the exclusion of all others. He insisted on righteousness as the source of conduct, of filial duty, and on frequent prayers to, the Ever-living God, and of respect to all other peoples, and of justice and mercy to and moderation in all things, and to hold in great respect learning of every kind... Most of the absurdities which Christians would have us believe to exist in the Qur'an were never uttered by Mohammad himself, nor are they to be found in a correct translation of the work.[66]

It is unfortunate that Prophet Muhammad (ﷺ) rarely gets the credit for the good he imparted to mankind. An impartial assessment of his life and times is always refreshing amidst the prejudiced, contemptible scholarship which regrettably flourishes. According to the German author Dr Emanuel Deutsch:

> *It has been the fashion, to ascribe whatever is good in Mohammadanism to Christianity. We fear this theory is not compatible with the results of honest investigation. For, of Arabian Christianity at the time of Muhammad, the less said perhaps the better...By the side of it...even modern Amharic Christianity, of which we possess such astounding accounts, appears pure and exalted.*[67]

Like so many other celebrated world scholars, Gustave Le Bon, a French historian and sociologist, asserts Prophet Muhammad (ﷺ) to be the greatest man that history ever knew.[68]

Le Bon further claimed that, if it were not for prejudice, Western writers would acknowledge his great works. In Le Bon's words:

> *If the value of men was to be measured by the great acts they did, Muhammad (peace be upon him) was one of the greatest figures throughout history. Western scholars started to be fair with Prophet Muhammad (peace be upon him), though religious bigotry made several other historians blind to acknowledge his virtue.*[69]

Owing to his lofty status, there has hardly been a person in history whose time on this earth has been recounted in such comprehensive detail as Prophet Muhammad (ﷺ). The eminent scholar John Davenport said:

> *It may be truly affirmed that of all known legislators and conquerors, not one can be named, the history of whose life has been written with greater authenticity and fuller detail, than that of Mohammed.*[70]

Carlyle challenged the hostile Orientalists, insisting that Prophet Muhammad (ﷺ) was a true man, who was adequate in doing anything in comparison with many rulers in history.[71]

Richard Bell, a British author, wrote in his book *Introduction to the Qur'an* that Prophet Muhammad (ﷺ), a human being, worked as God's spokesman for the divine will delivered to him by the angel Gabriel. The Prophet, standing on the border between the divine and the earthly, passed the message to all including himself. Sometimes God sent messages to him to pass on to the people, sometimes he sent commands for the people; at other times he sent directions and guidance for all including the Prophet himself, and all the while he was working as the honest and true representative of God on the earth.[72]

Annie Besant was a prominent British Theosophist, women's rights activist, writer and orator and supporter of Irish and Indian self-rule. She regarded Prophet Muhammad (ﷺ) as the great messenger of the Supreme. According to her, anyone who studied about the Prophet, how he preached and the simple lifestyle he maintained would certainly develop respect for the great Prophet. Besant seems overwhelmed with admiration for Prophet Muhammad (ﷺ). She concedes that repeated reading about the Prophet makes her more humble and respectful to him, the powerful teacher of the Arabian Peninsula. In her words:

> *It is impossible for anyone who studies the life and character of the great Prophet of Arabia, who knows how he taught and how he lived, to feel anything but reverence for that mighty Prophet, one of the great messengers of the Supreme. And although in what I put to you I shall say many things which may be familiar to many, yet I myself feel whenever I re-read them, a new way of admiration, a new sense of reverence for that mighty Arabian teacher.*[73]

Besant was concerned about the unjustifiable claims of some people who raised questions about Prophet Muhammad's multiple marriages, which some argue were motivated by sheer lust. She points to the fact that he married a woman who was forty and older than him when he himself was only twenty-five years of age. He continued to lead a loving married life with her until he was 50, when she died. By no means and standards can it be assumed that lust and sexual passion had been behind his marrying. The other marriages he contracted were for social or political reasons, either to protect a widow from an evil society or to resolve the conflict between tribes. This is not a way to judge the life of a man of his calibre. Besant highlights that:

> *But do you mean to tell me that the man who in the full flush of youthful vigour, a young man of four and twenty, married a woman much his senior, and remained faithful to her for six and twenty years, at fifty years of age when the passions are dying, married for lust and sexual passion? Not thus are men's lives to be judged. And you look at the women whom he married, you will find that by every one of them an alliance was made for his people, or something was gained for his followers, or the woman was in sore need of protection* [74]

The Russian philosopher and author Leo Tolstoy was one of the greatest writers of the world. He reckons that Prophet Muhammad (ﷺ) was unique in many aspects. Among these included achieving the respect of his enemies, which resulted in many of them accepting Islam. Even though the enemies knew him as Al-Ameen – trustworthy – they did not express their respect. Tolstoy explains:

> *There has been no prophet who gained the respect of his enemies save the prophet Muhammad. This is why a lot of them embraced Islam later on. It seems surprising that those who declared themselves enemies of him certainly knew that he was trustworthy and was calling them to the truth; they even respected him in the depth of their hearts, but they concealed this respect for they did not want to be accused of leaving their faiths.*[75]

Tolstoy noted how Prophet Muhammad (ﷺ) tolerated the persecution from the pagans while he invited them towards the One God and him, the apostle of God. Prophet Muhammad (ﷺ) did not claim to be the only Prophet; rather, he accepted Moses and Jesus as prophets of God. In Tolstoy's words:

He endured in his first years of inviting people to Islam tremendous tyranny and persecution from the pagans and others, just like every Prophet before him. He invited people to the truth, without these massive adversities undermining him and his cause, but instead strengthened his determination to carry on with his propagation. He did not claim to be the only prophet, but he believed in Moses and Jesus as prophets, and called people to this belief. He also said that the Jews and Christians must not be coerced to leave their religions, but he said that they should fulfill the commandments of their prophets.[76]

The British poet Edwin Arnold had a very high regard for Prophet Muhammad (ﷺ), a talented teacher who had established a huge kingdom with a new faith and civilisation. The spread of Islam should not be rejected, but rather accepted. Arnold wrote:

That marvellous and gifted teacher created a vast empire of new belief and new civilisation, and prepared a sixth part of humanity for the developments and reconciliations which later times will bring. For Islam must be conciliated; it cannot be thrust scornfully inside or rooted out. It shares the task of the education of the world with its sister religions.[77]

Washington Irving noted that Prophet Muhammad's facial appearance was ruddy and when a divine revelation descended on him, his face became very bright; his followers took it as mystical light of prophecy. Irving claims that the Prophet was a man of tremendous wisdom and talent. In his words:

His complexion was ruddier than is usual with Arabs, and in his excited and enthusiastic moments there was a glow and radiance in his countenance, which his disciples magnified into the supernatural light of prophecy. His intellectual qualities were undoubtedly of an extraordinary kind. He had a quick apprehension, a retentive memory, a vivid imagination, and an inventive genius.[78]

William James Durant, a prolific American writer, historian and philosopher, admired Prophet Muhammad (ﷺ) saying that he was a great Prophet who established monotheism. He was selected by God to serve mankind:

Muhammad was a great Prophet and a unique supreme monotheist who was chosen to reclaim the [sic] humankind.[79]

In another account, Durant claimed Prophet Muhammad (ﷺ) to be the greatest figure in history in terms of exerting effective influence on the people.

If we rated the greatness by the influence of the great on people we will say –Muhammad is the greatest of the great in history.[80]

George Bernard Shaw, an Irish playwright and a co-founder of the London School of Economics (LSE), argued that the present world needs leaders like Prophet Muhammad (ﷺ) for the general peace and happiness. Shaw observed:

I believe that if a man like him were to assume the dictatorship of the modern world he would succeed in solving its problems in a way that would bring it the much needed peace and happiness: I have prophesied about the faith of Muhammad that it would be acceptable to the Europe of tomorrow as it is beginning to be acceptable to the Europe of today.[81]

Bosworth Smith notes the achievements of Prophet Muhammad's early life. The Prophet established trust in the society that led him to be known as Al-Amin. The wise monk prophesised him as a Prophet and he became well-known as honest to the employer, Khadijah (RA), with whom he had a happy marriage. In his opinion:

He was a man of few words, and he had few friends: notable chiefly for his truthfulness and good faith, they called him Al Amyn, the Trusty. His tending his employer's flocks; his journeys to Syria; possibly his short-lived friendship there with Sergius or Bahira, a

> *Nestorian monk; his famous vow to succour the oppressed; his employment by Kadijah in a trade venture, and his subsequent happy marriage with her, are about the only note-worthy external incidents in his early life.*[82]

Martin Lings, an English writer and scholar, had made similar observations about Bahira, the Nestorian monk. Bahira noticed something very strange when a caravan from Makkah arrived. He noticed that a small piece of low-hanging cloud moved above the group of Makkan travellers which included the boy Prophet Muhammad (ﷺ) and formed shade from the sun. When they stopped walking, the cloud also stopped. To add to his amazement, he saw a tree stretching its shade on them too. The wise monk thought this could be due to the presence of a Prophet who was expected at that time. He invited the Makkan caravan to his cell, and after having observed the boy closely, the Monk found the signs of prophethood in him. The monk explained this to Muhammad's uncle and advised him to take good care of the future Prophet. Lings writes:

> *One glance at the boy's face was enough to explain the miracles to Bahira; and looking at him attentively throughput the meal he noticed many features of both face and body which corresponded to what was in his book.*[83]

The story of the monk Bahira is also narrated by the American author Elsa Marston. The monk noticed that the cloud created a shadow on the head of Prophet Muhammad (ﷺ) as he walked in the sun. According to the monk, that was a sign of greatness and a future Prophet.[84]

With reference to the great personality of Prophet Muhammad (ﷺ), Elsa Marston also points out that his articulate speaking and strong personality and character drew the attention of his people.[85]

Marston further claims that Prophet Muhammad (ﷺ), due to his great personality and having no lust for any worldly benefits, rejected offers from the Makkan rich and the merchants who tried to deviate him from preaching the new religion:

> *At first the rich merchants ignored the Prophet. As his criticisms grew sharper, merchants assumed he was seeking wealth and power. They tried to buy him off with promises of riches, power, and prestige. He rejected every offer, saying his mission had nothing to do with these things.*[86]

The Reverend Stephens pays high tribute to Prophet Muhammad (ﷺ), saying that he was a great patron of his people, who did not have a rational religion, organised political structure or good morals. However, the Prophet (ﷺ) established all of those essential elements of the society. Revd Stephens highlights:

> *First of all, it must be freely granted that to his own people Muhammad was a great benefactor. He was born in a country where political organizations, and rational faith, and pure morals were unknown. He introduced all three. By a single stroke of masterly genius he simultaneously reformed the political condition, the religious creed, and the moral practice of his countrymen. In the place of many independent tribes he left a nation: for a superstitious belief in gods many and lords many he established a reasonable belief in one Almighty yet Beneficent Being; taught men to live under an abiding sense of this Being's superintending care, to look to Him as the Rewarder, and to fear him as the Punisher of evil-doers.*[87]

Thomas Carlyle says that Prophet Muhammad (ﷺ) was a very reflective and contemplative individual. He would pay great attention to his heart and the nature of mankind in general. As a deep thinker, he would always keep himself tuned in with the current state and condition of his people. An essential trait and characteristic of his prophethood was sincerity. Some have suggested that Prophet Muhammad's purity as a human being was symbolic of a divine involvement, or at least a divine element in his life. His message was in accordance with the natural disposition of man and could not be compared with the teachings of others. Prophet Muhammad (ﷺ) questioned the very purpose of life and existence and was very eager to unearth the nature of man, and probe into matters like death.[88]

Carlyle notes that it was when Prophet Muhammad (ﷺ) retreated to lonely locations for meditation that he encountered the divine realm. It was at those places and occasions where Prophet Muhammad (ﷺ) connected with an eternal spirit, something which reminded him of the limitation of man but the reality of an everlasting divinity and the afterlife. He could not find any solace and any satisfying answer regarding man's purpose in life in the prevailing belief systems and traditions of his people. What really distinguished Prophet Muhammad (ﷺ) from other prominent people during his time was that he had the intuitive ability to explore matters and reality beyond the apparent, beneath the face value and the superficial meaning. This was a rare foresight, and one which could see the pretentiousness and artificiality of things. An example would be Prophet Muhammad's rational objection to polytheism and the idolatrous practices of the time. What is certain is that Prophet Muhammad (ﷺ) was not seeking the acceptance and following of his people for the sake of his personal fame and fortune only.[89]

Alphonse Marie Louis de Prat de Lamartine, a French writer, poet and politician, states that the objectives which Prophet Muhammad (ﷺ) set for himself would be considered by many to be beyond human capability. The crux of his message and his teaching was to bring human beings into an affinity with their creator. When we consider the deeply entrenched polytheism that prevailed during his time, his active promotion of monotheism would have been considered daring by anyone's standards. The limitations of his environment and insufficient resources would have prompted many to pack in their mission, yet Prophet Muhammad (ﷺ) did not even consider the possibility that his message would not be successful. It can be argued that Prophet Muhammad (ﷺ) bequeathed perhaps the most radical and enduring legacy of anyone in history, judging by the phenomenal spread of Islam. De Lamartine notes:

> *Never has a man set for himself, voluntarily or involuntarily, a more sublime aim, since this aim was superhuman; to subvert*

> *superstitions which had been imposed between man and his Creator, to render God unto man and man unto God; to restore the rational and sacred idea of divinity amidst the chaos of the material and disfigured gods of idolatry, then existing. Never has a man undertaken a work so far beyond human power with so feeble means, for he (Muhammad) had in the conception as well as in the execution of such a great design, no other instrument than himself and no other aid except a handful of men living in a corner of the desert.*[90]

He went on to say that when we reflect on how Prophet Muhammad (ﷺ) had to overcome numerous obstacles and limitations, and then ponder how he achieved what he did despite these weaknesses, it makes him as a person even more remarkable. History is a testimony to the creation of empires and armies which after periods of existence met its demise. Prophet Muhammad (ﷺ) was not only successful in these fields, but his real success lay in the ability to penetrate the hearts of men. According to him:

> *If greatness of purpose, smallness of means, and astonishing results are the three criteria of a human genius, who could dare compare any great man in history with Muhammad? The most famous men created arms, laws, and empires only. They founded, if anything at all, no more than material powers which often crumbled away before their eyes. This man moved not only armies, legislations, empires, peoples, dynasties, but millions of men in one-third of the then inhabited world; and more than that, he moved the altars, the gods, the religions, the ideas, the beliefs and the souls.*[91]

One of Prophet Muhammad's most remarkable achievements was his unifying potential which he exploited to its fullest. His declaration of monotheism was so risky and dangerous when the normative traditions and *status quo* were all firm believers in polytheism. His message sent shock waves across the elite and ruling factions as it definitely signaled the presence of an unadulterated monotheism in the Arabian scene. The struggles and victimhood he had to endure for the sake of preaching the worship of one God speaks volumes for his forbearance and determination. There is no doubting Prophet Muhammad's courage for going against time-honoured beliefs and traditions and not being apologetic for his preaching. Seeing as he combined the functions of Prophet, statesman and moral educator all in one, the discussion about his greatness needs no invitation. De Lamartine adds:

> *On the basis of a Book, every letter which has become law, he created spiritual nationalities which blend together peoples of every tongue and race. He has left the indelible characteristic of this Muslim nationality the hatred of false gods and the passion for the One and Immaterial God. This avenging patriotism against the profanation of Heaven formed the virtue of the followers of Muhammad; the conquest of one-third the earth to the dogma was his miracle; or rather it was not the miracle of man but that of reason.*[92]

Ronald Victor Courtenay Bodley was a British army officer, author and journalist who noted that that Prophet Muhammad's achievements were many. From facilitating Islam's swift expansion beyond its borders, to propagating a faith which today claims over a billion followers, what we often lose sight of is that despite the greatness of these achievements, the real victories of Prophet Muhammad (ﷺ) which ought to be celebrated are the more subtle points of his life. Because he wanted to desperately overturn the abject status of his people, and despite the hostilities faced by his clan, family and wider society, he established credibility and honourable reputation for himself and the faith he preached. On a social and personal level, the strides Prophet Muhammad (ﷺ) made to convince his society and his followers that Islam was the God-given vehicle for change and progress is more of a monumental achievement than the spread of Islam during his time, especially when considering the plight of many Arabs. He maintains:

> *I seldom think of Mohammed as God's Messenger whose followers make up one seventh of the world's population. I seldom think of him as the inspirer of the soldiers whose conquests were exceeded*

> *only by those of Britain's imperial armies. I seldom think of him as the author of that amazing book of laws and theology and verse, the Koran. I think of him rather as the boy who made good among his own people. I think of him as the scoffed at, persecuted young man with an ideal who forced his family to acknowledge him to have been right. For what Mohammed did with the sword and from the pulpit was far less of an achievement than confounding the saying about prophets being without honor in their own countries and changing the minds of his relatives. And that must be borne in mind, if one is to appreciate this "success story" of the desert. For that is what it is. Not quite, perhaps, the log-cabin-to-White House formula, but something akin.*[93]

The adjustments Prophet Muhammad (ﷺ) had to make so that his message was relevant to the changing circumstances obtaining in his period are nothing short of remarkable:

> *I doubt whether any man whose external conditions changed so much ever changed less to meet them...*[94]

George Sale, a British Orientalist and solicitor, best known for his translation of the Qur'an into English (1734) reported that, having heard the incident in Mount Hera from Prophet Muhammad (ﷺ), his wife Khadijah (RA) ® realised that he would be the next Prophet and she consulted her Christian cousin, Waraqa, a learned man of the time. Waraqa assured her that the same angel appeared before Moses and now came to Prophet Muhammad (ﷺ). Sale notes that

> *Khadijah (RA) received the news with great joy, swearing by him in whose hands her soul was, that she trusted he would be the prophet of his nation, and immediately communicated what she had heard to her cousin, Waraqa Ibn Nawfal, who, being a Christian, could write in the Hebrew character, and was tolerably well versed in the scriptures; and he as readily came into her opinion, assuring her that the same angel who had formerly appeared unto Moses was now sent to Mohammed. This first*

overture the prophet made in the month of Ramadan, in the fortieth year of his age, which is, therefore, usually called the year of his mission.[95]

British writer H.G. Wells wrote that Prophet Muhammad (ﷺ) made a sermon during the last pilgrimage. It is treated as a great sermon by Muslims through which the Prophet commanded several key roles for mankind to follow in their lives on the earth. These commandments are still followed in the daily lives of a huge number of the world's population.[96]

Sadhu T.L. Vaswani, an Indian philosopher and educationist who set up Sadhu Vaswani Mission in Hyderabad, Sindh, India had deep respect for Prophet Muhammad (ﷺ) and regarded him as the mighty hero of the world. Leading a life always threatened by his foes, he preached the religion and brought the Arabs out of darkness:

A Hero Prophet. I salute Muhammad as one of the world's mighty heroes; Muhammad has been a world force, a mighty power for the uplift of many peoples. Read the old records, and you will glimpse the grace and beauty of his life. A king and a spiritual leader, he yet mends his clothes. He hearkens to the call of the Unseen. "O thou enwrapped in thy mantle! Arise and preach" They persecute him; his very life is in danger; but he is loyal to the Call; he moves about preaching the way of peace. Muhammad was a he is and a prophet; and I have often meditated on the last word whispered by him before he passed away: "Lord; grant me pardon, and join me to the fellowship on high!" Who will not say that such a man was 'beautiful' in Me (please check the word "Me" in the original quotation), beautiful in death '? And consider for a moment what the faith he preached has achieved. Islam has given the world a religion without priests. Warn abolished infanticide in Arabia; lslam enjoined on the faithful total abstinence from drink, Islam emphasised the great qualities of faith, courage, endurance and self-sacrifice.[97]

Major Arthur Glyn Leonard highly appreciated Prophet Muhammad

(ﷺ) for his extreme devotion and submission to God. He claimed that the Prophet was the greatest and the most truthful person on the earth:

> *If ever a man on this earth found Allah, if ever a man devoted his life to Allah's service with a good and great motive, it is certain that the Prophet of Arabia (Muhammad) is the man. Muhammad was not only the greatest but truest man that humanity has ever produced.*[98]

Edward Gibbon firmly says about the authenticity of the Qur'an which is from God and there is no confusion or doubt at all on what Prophet Muhammad (ﷺ) had preached. He discarded polytheism and installed monotheism. He taught that everything on the earth is perishable and the Creator is the Sustainer. The truths proclaimed by him were firmly believed and adopted by his followers. Gibbon adds:

> *The creed of Mahomet is free from suspicion or ambiguity; and the Koran is a glorious testimony to the unity of God. The prophet of Makkah rejected the worship of idols and men, of stars and planets, on the rational principle that whatever rises must set, that whatever is born must die, that whatever is corruptible must decay and perish. In the Author of the universe, his rational enthusiasm confessed and adored an infinite and eternal being, without form or place, without issue or similitude, present to our most secret thoughts, existing by the necessity of his own nature, and deriving from himself all moral and intellectual perfection. These sublime truths, thus announced in the language of the prophet, are firmly held by his disciples, and defined with metaphysical precision by the interpreters of the Koran.*[99]

Major Leonard further lists some of the important contributions of Prophet Muhammad (ﷺ). Through the magnetic teachings of Islam, the Prophet Muhammad (ﷺ) had brought the people from their tribal lives to an ordered society. His honest desire had worked very favorably.

> *It was the genius of Muhammad, the spirit that he breathed into*

the Arabs through the soul of Islam that exalted them. That raised them out of the lethargy and low level of tribal stagnation up to the high watermark of national unity and empire. It was in the sublimity of Muhammad's deism, the simplicity, the sobriety and purity it inculcated the fidelity of its founder to his own tenets that acted on their moral and intellectual fiber with all the magnetism of true inspiration.[100]

Lala Lajpat Rai, an Indian author, politician and leader also known as 'The Lion of Punjab' paid tribute to Prophet Muhammad (ﷺ) by ranking the Prophet in the highest position amongst religious preachers:

I have not the least hesitation in declaring that I entertain highest respect for the Prophet of Islam. In my opinion he holds the highest rank amongst Religious Teachers and Reformers.[101]

The celebrated British author John Davenport praises Prophet Muhammad (ﷺ) for his keenness for education, although he was unlettered. He placed knowledge before wealth and encouraged people to travel far to acquire education:

Through its brightest periods, nay, even from its origin, Mohammedanism was, comparatively, favourable to literature. Mohammed himself said that "a mind without erudition was like a body without a soul; that glory consists not in wealth, but in knowledge;" and he charged his followers to seek for learning in the remotest parts of the globe.[102]

Tor Andrae felt that the Prophet spoke in a way that was not like the way other people spoke. The words he spoke had in-depth meaning and reality. This was because he lived in regular fellowship with reality.[103]

Prophet Muhammad's outstanding wisdom, personality and virtue have been studied over the centuries by a wide range of philosophers, historians, authors, etc., and they have praised him. George Sale, in 1734, compared the greatness of Prophet Muhammad (ﷺ) to that of Numa and Theseus.[104]

George Sale holds that Prophet Muhammad (ﷺ) was a man of great intelligence. Many historians had praised him for his balanced methods of ruling and keen memory, which developed significantly over his years of experience. His amicable characteristics and personal attributes made him popular with all:

> *He had indisputably a very piercing and sagacious wit, and was thoroughly versed in all the arts of insinuation. The eastern historians describe him to have been a man of an excellent judgment, and a happy memory; and these natural parts were improved by a great experience and knowledge of men, and the observations he had made in his travels. They say he was a person of few words, of an equal cheerful temper, pleasant and familiar in conversation, of inoffensive behaviour towards his friends, and of great condescension towards his inferiors.*[105]

One of the most remarkable things about Prophet Muhammad (ﷺ) was that his attributes related to virtually every important human function and need. Whether in the aspect of trade, governance or law, he straddled all aspects of human and social organisation. K. S. Ramkrishna Rao, an Indian Professor of Philosophy, applauds him in his work "*Muhammad The Prophet of Islam*". Rao regards the Prophet as the perfect model for human life:

> *The personality of Muhammad, it is most difficult to get into the whole truth of it. Only a glimpse of it I can catch. What a dramatic succession of picturesque scenes! There is Muhammad, the Prophet. There is Muhammad, the Warrior; Muhammad, the Businessman; Muhammad, the Statesman; Muhammad, the Orator; Muhammad, the Reformer; Muhammad, the Refuge of Orphans; Muhammad, the Protector of Slaves; Muhammad, the Emancipator of Women; Muhammad, the Judge; Muhammad, the Saint. All in all these magnificent roles, in all these departments of human activities, he is alike a hero.*[106]

Prophet Muhammad (ﷺ) grew up an orphan and in this sense did not have the tender love and care from parents, which is so important for a person's emotional well-being. The fact that his fortunes changed and he assumed power and status did not change the fact that he knew that as humans, all were equally accountable before God. He had gone through much during his prophethood, and endured the highs and lows with his companions. None of this deterred him from his ultimate mission, which was to spread the word of God. K.S. Ramkrishna Rao adds:

> *Orphan hood is an extreme form of helplessness and his life upon this earth began with it; Kingship is the height of material power and it ended with it! From an orphan boy to a persecuted refugee and then to an overlord, spiritual as well as temporal, of a whole nation and arbiter of its destinies, with all its trials and temptations, with all its vicissitudes and changes, its lights and shades, its ups and downs, its terror and splendour, he has withstood the fire of the world and came out unscathed to serve as a model in every phase of life. His achievements are not limited to one aspect of life, but cover the whole field of human conditions.*[107]

Something which has been acknowledged by non-Muslims, and for which Prophet Muhammad (ﷺ) always gets praise, is that he was a unique amalgam of a Prophet, a lawgiver and a chief of his people. Professor Rao further points out:

> *In the person of the prophet of Islam we see the rarest phenomenon on earth walking in flesh and blood i.e. the union of the theorist, the organizer and the leader in one man.*[108]

A British politician (requested to be anonymous) has paid high tribute to Prophet Muhammad (ﷺ):

> *Muhammad's had a very edifying and educating effect on humanity. After describing Islam as 'beautiful', he said Muhammad was 'an enormously civilizing force.*[109]

It was Prophet Muhammad's conviction in the most High which saw him exercise a tremendous influence over his people. John Medows Rodwell (1808–1900), a friend of Charles Darwin and an English clergyman of the Church of England, writes in the preface of the translation of the Qur'an:

> *Muhammad's career is a wonderful instance of the force and life that resides in him who possesses an intense faith in God and in the unseen world. He will always be regarded as one of those who have had that influence over the faith, morals and whole earthly life of their fellow men, which none but a really great man ever did, or can exercise; and whose efforts to propagate a great verity will prosper.*[110]

Maharaja Peshkar Sir Kishen Pershad Bahadur, *Yamin us-Sultanat*, GCIE was twice the Prime Minister of Hyderabad State. He paid rich tribute to Prophet Muhammad (ﷺ) who was selected as Prophet of God and was very keen to follow him as the leader. He has expressed his feelings in his poem:

> *My life I offer for Ahmad, the Chosen one*
> *Behold, he is undoubtedly my Guide.*
> *My humble person,*
> *He did uplift to eminence.*
> *Behold, the glory of the Glorious God.*[111]

Reverend Stephens compares Prophet Muhammad (ﷺ) with Moses; both of whom revived a pure religion from their common father, Abraham. However, Prophet Muhammad's achievements were extensive by installing monotheism in place of polytheism and abolishing many vicious crimes of the human society he was born in. Stephens notes that:

> *The aim of Muhammad was revived among his countrymen the Arabs, as Moses revived among his countrymen, the Jews, the pure faith their common forefather Abraham. In this he succeeded to a very great extent. For a confused heap of idolatrous superstitions he substituted a pure monotheistic faith; he abolished some of the most*

vicious practices of his countrymen, modified others: he generally raised the moral standard, improved the social condition of the people, and introduced a sober and rational ceremonial in worship … The vices most prevalent in Arabia in the time of Muhammad which are most sternly denounced and absolutely forbidden in the Qur'an were drunkenness, unlimited concubinage and polygamy; the destruction of female infants, reckless gambling, superstitious arts of divination and magic. The abolition of some of these evil customs and the mitigation of others, was a great advance in the morality of the Arabs, and is a wonderful and honourable testimony to the zeal and influence of the Reformer. The total suppression of female infanticide and of drunkenness is the most signal triumph of his work.[112]

It is a privilege for Muslims that they are the followers of Prophet Muhammad (ﷺ), as his teachings have enlightened people. Pandit Sunder Lal Sharma was so enamoured by Prophet Muhammad's personality that he claimed that hardly anyone of his stature had ever been seen in human history. The Pandit says that the Muslims are very lucky as they have a Prophet like Prophet Muhammad (ﷺ). However, they would be unlucky if they do not obey his teachings; his teachings are like a light in the darkness. He studied Islam in university and was very influenced by the Prophet (ﷺ), as he remarks:

Muslims are fortunate in having Muhammad as their prophet; they are more than unfortunate if they violate his teachings – so nice and so illuminating indeed. These teachings, in my opinion, have proved to be beacon light to mankind. As a student of the history of Islam which has been my subject since my university days I have been deeply impressed by the personality of the Prophet of Islam, the like of whom is seldom born in history.[113]

Mawde Royden was a British preacher and suffragist. She claimed that Prophet Muhammad (ﷺ) established the idea of one Glorious God. The equality of mankind in Islam is no fiction. Nobody on earth has ever established freedom as was accomplished by Prophet Muhammad (ﷺ)[114]

Dr John Clark Archer, Professor of Comparative Religion at Yale University, New Haven, USA, in an article entitled "Our Debt to the Muslim World", observes:

> *This tremendous movement came out of Arabia borne by Arabs. The Caliphate and its sole dominion was established by the Arabs, ruled by them and regulated on Arabic principles. The Arabic book of Religion, the Qur'an and its tongue provided articulation for all Muslim lands. The very spirit which infused the Muslim world was Arabic and it was the basis, the driving force of culture.*[115]

As far as history's greatest and most prominent figures are concerned, Prophet Muhammad (ﷺ) is right up there in many people's estimation, mainly owing to his ability to elevate the deadened spirits of men. Sadhu T.L. Vaswani, an Indian educationist, remarks:

> *I salute Muhammad as one of the world's mighty heroes. Muhammad has been a world force, a mighty power for the uplift of many peoples.*[116]

Samuel Marinus Zwemer was Professor of mission and religions at Princeton Theological Seminary. He says:

> *Muhammad was an able reformer, eloquent and well spoken, courageous and daring, a great thinker. We cannot attribute to him anything that contradicts these qualities. The Qur'an that he brought and his history bear witness to the truth of these claims.*[117]

Guru Nanak, the great founder of the Sikh religion, a world-renowned saint and sage, had profound respect for Prophet Muhammad (ﷺ). Accordingly, he performed pilgrimage to Makkah twice and visited the tomb of the Prophet Muhammad (ﷺ) in Madinah. He used to study the Qur'an in search of the divine message. His love for the Prophet and Islam was reflected in his lifestyle. The great Guru Nanak's teachings included many Islamic aspects, recorded in the Granth Sahib. Some of them are mentioned below:

God is one. He is the Truth and the Truthful. He has created heavens and earth out of nothing. He is infinite, fearless and harmless. He is immortal. He is not born, nor is any one born of him. He is above resemblance to any one, nor is He capable of incarnation into any human form. He is Rahman (Beneficent) Rahim (Merciful) and Everlasting."... "The age for the Vedas and Puranas is gone: now the Qur'an is the only book to guide the world." "The saints, reformers, martyrs, Firs, Sheikhs and Qutubs will reap untold benefit if they will send Daruds (God's blessings) on the Holy Prophet."... "The only reason as to why man is constantly restless and goes to hell is that he has no regard for the Prophet.[118]

The editor of Sat Updaish (Newspaper) claimed that Islam was not preached by the sword. Rather it was the Prophet's demeanour which attracted people to Islam:

Some people say that Islam was preached by the sword, but we cannot agree with this view. What is forced on people is soon rejected. Had Islam been imposed on people through oppression, there would have been no Islam today. Why? Because the Prophet of Islam had spiritual power, he loved humanity and he was guided by the ideal of ultimate good.[119]

U.S Army General James Gavin considers Prophet Muhammad (ﷺ) to have exercised the greatest impact on history of any leader. He claims that Prophet Muhammad (ﷺ) has the greatest contributions amongst all world leaders.[120]

Although Prophet Muhammad (ﷺ) did not have any formal education, he was a genius with God-given potentials, possessing the talents of occupation and vocations enabling him to face obstacles, dilemmas of situations, the perils of life and helping him take decisions in the many difficult situations of life and in the fields of war, wisely and successfully. Major General Forlong observes:

Without culture or training, Mahamad bravely and with strong self-reliance entered upon many of the most difficult questions of state craft - economic and international laws - slavery and relations of the sexes in all their complications, as well as on many grievous burdens which no other rulers of Arabia or Western Asia had ventured to tackle. Where he found laws and customs too formidable to arrest, he mitigated them and made it difficult and dangerous for the oppressor to oppress.[121]

Gandhi, one of the greatest politicians of modern times, asserts that Prophet Muhammad (ﷺ) is not only for the Muslims but for all humanity. Gandhi proclaimed:

The sayings of Muhammad are a treasure of wisdom not only for Muslims but for all mankind.[122]

Dr Gokalchand, PhD, Barrister-at-Law, maintains that the Arabians, having been taught by Prophet Muhammad (ﷺ), in turn had taught the whole world:

When the teachings of the Arabian Prophet infused a new life into the uncivilized Arabs, they became the Teachers of the whole Western world and the banner of learning, conquest and divine help began to fly over Bengal on one side and Spain on the other side.[123]

Alphonse de Lamartine showers Prophet Muhammad (ﷺ) with a number of praiseworthy titles. He believes that Prophet Muhammad (ﷺ) certainly enriched many aspects of human life and none could be compared with him. Lamartine highlights:

Philosopher, Orator, Apostle, Legislator, Conqueror of Ideas, Restorer of Rational beliefs ... The founder of twenty terrestrial empires and of one spiritual empire that is Muhammad. As regards all standards by which human greatness may be measured, we may well ask, is there any man greater than he?[124]

Alfred Martin, a Unitarian minister and writer on religion, states that there is considerable ignorance regarding Prophet Muhammad (ﷺ) and his message:

> *Chronologically the latest of the great moral leaders whose life and work we are studying is Mohammed. Like Moses, the Prophets, Jesus and Paul, Mohammed belonged to the Semitic branch of the human family. He was the founder of the least appreciated and most misunderstood of the world's great religions.*[125]

A noted Indian leader, Lala Hardayal, testifies to the greatness of the Prophet of Islam:

> *Hazrat Muhammad, the Prophet of Islam was a very great man. His honesty and probity as a poor young man earned him the social title of the Just: Al-Amin. His immense contribution to civilization remains an outstanding and astounding fact of history.*[126]

The famous author Reynold A. Nicholson paid tribute to Prophet Muhammad (ﷺ) in his *A literary History of the Arabs:*

> *Possessed and inspired by the highest idea of which man is capable, fearlessly preaching the truth revealed to him, leading almost alone what long seemed to be a forlorn hope against impregnable stronghold of superstition, yet facing these tremendous odds with a calm resolution which yielded nothing to ridicule or danger, but defied his enemies to do their worst, Muhammad in the early part of his career presents a spectacle of grandeur which cannot fail to win our sympathy and admiration.*[127]

The famous historian William Muir, in-spite of his markedly hostile attitude towards Prophet Muhammad (ﷺ), admitted the greatness of the Prophet in his book *Life of Mahomet*:

> *I have thus, as proposed, endeavoured to sketch the original sources for the biography of Mahomet. I have examined the Coran, and have admitted its authority as an authentic and contemporary*

record. I have enquired into the origin and history of Mahometan tradition, and shown that it contains the elements of truth; and I have endeavoured to indicate some canons, by which fact may be distinguished from the legend and fiction so closely commingled with it. I have enumerated those early biographical compilations which can alone be regarded as worthy of attention, and have shown that no later authors are possessed of an original and independent authority. The principles thus laid down, if followed with sagacity, perseverance, and impartiality, will enable the enquirer to arrive at a fair approximation to historical fact. Many Gordian knots regarding the Prophet of Arabia will remain unsolved, many paradoxes still vainly excite curiosity and baffle explanation; but the groundwork of his life will be laid down with confidence; the details will be substantially filled in with all reasonable amplitude; and the student will be able to determine with certainty the leading features of his character.[128]

Muir further lauds Prophet Muhammad (ﷺ) for his greatness and for forgiving those people who once vowed to banish him from the face of the earth and made his life in Makkah impossible, which compelled him to leave his city of birth for Madinah. After about 10 years of forced exile in Madinah, when Makkah was conquered by Prophet Muhammad (ﷺ) and he entered the city a victor with his companions, the generous Prophet Muhammad (ﷺ) was prompt to forgive all of his declared enemies and adversaries:

The conduct of Mahomet on the conquest of Makkah, was marked by singular magnanimity and moderation. It was indeed for his own interest to forgive the past, and to cast all its slights and injuries into oblivion. But it did not the less require a large and generous heart to do this.[129]

Dr Samuel Johnson pays high tribute to Prophet Muhammad (ﷺ). Highlighting his wonderful character, Dr Johnson says:

His purely historical character, his simple humanity claiming to be a man among men, his intense realism avoiding all mystical remoteness, the thoroughly democratic and universal form under which his idea of divine monarchy led him to conceive the relations of man the force of ethical appeal all affiliate Muhammad with the modern world.[130]

A Great Leader

Sir John Glubb notes that the Messenger of God, Prophet Muhammad (ﷺ), had inborn skills in political affairs and international relations besides whatever divine assignment he was entrusted with. There were many examples of how he had avoided fights and engaged the enemies in discussion which at a later stage led to conversion. That was how he won over the Arabs.[131]

The celebrated French conqueror Napoleon Bonaparte paid high ribute to Prophet Muhammad, saying that the Prophet was a great leader for humankind. Having united the conflicting Arabs, he reached out with his message of Islam to the wider world:

Mohammad, in reality, was a great leader of mankind. He preached UNITY among Arabs who were, till then, torn asunder due to internecine quarrels, sometime resulting in bloody warfare. He brought them out of the depth of degradation and taught them the way in which they should live as human beings. His followers conquered half of the world in a short time and the discipline which they maintained under his leadership was simply marvellous, and so was their bravery, courage and devotion to the cause which they loved and cherished. This, coupled with the contempt for death as taught by their leader, made them great soldiers and fighters like of whom history rarely produces. I simply marvel at the achievements of this Son of the Desert within a period of 15 years only - a thing which Moses and Christ could not do in fifteen hundred years. I salute this great-man; I salute his qualities of head and heart.[132]

Jules Masserman, an American psychoanalyst and Professor at Chicago University compares the leadership qualities of some great leaders of the world and claims that Prophet Muhammad (ﷺ) was the greatest of all time. Many of the world's statesmen, rulers and thinkers can be grouped as leaders in a particular category. What distinguished Prophet Muhammad (ﷺ) from all these other personalities was that his leadership incorporated characteristics which cut across many dimensions:

> *People like Pasteur and Salk are leaders in the first sense. People like Gandhi and Confucius, on one hand, and Alexander, Caesar and Hitler on the other, are leaders in the second and perhaps the third sense. Jesus and Buddha belong in the third category alone. Perhaps the greatest leader of all times was Mohammed, who combined all three functions. To a lesser degree, Moses did the same.*[133]

Dr Daniel C. Peterson, a Professor from Brigham Young University, USA, claims that, even after 1400 years Muhammed (ﷺ) remains a leader, as he was once with his immediate followers.[134]

Phillip K. Hitti, a scholar of Islam, narrates that there is evidence in history of many people who have founded a religion, some a nation and others a state. But there is no evidence of a single person doing all three, except in the case of Prophet Muhammad (ﷺ).[135]

British author James William Hampson Stobart extols Prophet Muhammad (ﷺ), saying that his activities were unparalleled:

> *Judged by the smallness of the means at his disposal, and the extent and permanence of the work that he accomplished, no name in the world's story shines with a more spacious lustre than that of the Prophet of Mecca.*[136]

Stobart adds that his teachings were followed in life by many generations throughout history:

> *To the impulse which he gave, numberless dynasties have owed*

their existence, fair cities and stately palaces and temples have arisen, and wide provinces became obedient to the faith. And beyond all this, his words have governed the belief of generations, been accepted as their rule in life and their certain guide to the world to come.[137]

The prolific British author Pierce De Lacy Johnstone says that the noble character of Prophet Muhammad (ﷺ) made him popular among people from all walks of life. As Johnstone explains:

Gradually his genius, earnestness, and high moral character gathered around him a little band of followers, men and women of all ranks, and all alike absolutely devoted to their leader.[138]

John Adair, in his book *The Leadership of Prophet Muhammad* (ﷺ), notes that the Prophet (ﷺ) always advised against taking the extreme path in any walk of life and favoured a middle path in all activities:

This avoidance of extreme – an essentially moderate approach - was characteristic of Muhammad. The Qur'an reflects his own practical wisdom in religious practice as in living life generally.[139]

A Great Statesman

The American Professor Jules Masserman states that Prophet Muhammad's combination of religious and political functions puts him on a unique platform among the great rulers in history. By contrast with the pomp that surrounded the Pope, Prophet Muhammad's personality did not reflect self-importance. Even when we compare him with the likes of Caesar, Prophet Muhammad (ﷺ) could not boast of a huge entourage, army and security apparatus. If there was ever a rightful claim to rule by divine mandate, then Prophet Muhammad (ﷺ) is surely the most deserving of this accolade. His austerity and simplicity simply magnified his great standing in history:

Head of State as well as Church, he was Caesar and Pope in One;

but he was a Pope without the Pope's pretensions, and Caesar without the legions of Caesar, without a standing army, without a bodyguard, without police force, without a fixed revenue. If ever a man ruled by right Divine, it was Muhammad, for he had all the powers without their supports. He cared not for the dressings of power. The simplicity of his private life was in keeping with his public life.[140]

Prophet Muhammad's statesmanship and eye for governance was a hallmark of his prophethood. Taking care of the affairs of his people was important for him as a religious leader and also as a political leader.[141]

The distinguished scholar W. Montgomery Watt admires Prophet Muhammad's wisdom as a statesman. The Qur'an is a guideline to follow that also incorporates policies relating to the social context, which, however, required the talent and wisdom of Prophet Muhammad (ﷺ) to interpret. His political and social far-sightedness helped in the rapid spread of Islam.[142]

Watt adds that Prophet Muhammad (ﷺ) was a skilful and good administrator. His selection of people for office was precise and politically sound. The policies he established helped Islam tremendously to spread far and wide even after his death.[143]

American author Elsa Marston observes that Prophet Muhammad (ﷺ) was gradually developing diverse skills encompassing religious, social, economic and political matters, and proved himself as a statesman:

Meanwhile, the Prophet's role expanded from spiritual guide to leader in all aspects of life. He became the head of a community that relied on his authority in economic, social, and political affairs, as well as religious matters. He proved his statesmanship through his personal qualities of wisdom, good judgment, and patience. Before long, this role began to take on even larger dimensions.[144]

Marston notes that Prophet Muhammad (ﷺ) not only became a statesman but was successful in many other roles as well:

Muhammad filled many roles in his vigorous life of sixty two years

> *– trader, merchant, visionary, prophet, leader, administrator, warrior, strategist, and statesman*[145]

Marston concludes that a great many of the world's people are guided by the Islamic spirit which was initiated and infused, 14 centuries ago, by the praiseworthy Prophet Muhammad (ﷺ):

> *The Islamic belief in God has brought spiritual guidance to countless millions of people the world over and may be the fastest-growing of all religious faiths today. Although sometimes sadly misunderstood, and affected by the anxieties and discord of our times, Islam holds a high ideal for human beings' relationship with God and with other human beings.*
> *And it started with the vision and faith of one extraordinary man in an Arabian town, nearly 1,400 years ago - Muhammad, the Praised One.*[146]

Lord Kinnock sheds some light on Prophet Muhammad(ﷺ)'s political sensibilities by stating he had a preference for a more consensual form of government as opposed to one-way rule:

> *From what I know, he was an advocate of shared decision making, which is slightly similar. But in terms of the society at that time, it would have been extraordinary for anyone to have been a confident advocate of representative democracy. Teachers like Muhammad favoured democratic practice more than autocratic practice.*[147]

A Great Lawgiver

The celebrated author George Rivorie praises the Prophet very highly, saying:

> *He laid the foundation of a universal government. His law was one for all. Equal justice and love for everyone.*[148]

Prophet Muhammad (ﷺ) was honoured by the US Supreme Court as one of the greatest lawgivers of the world in 1935. A frieze of Prophet Muhammad ( ) was erected in the court, with an inscription reading:

> *Muhammad (c. 570–632) The Prophet of Islam. He is depicted holding the Qur'an. The Qur'an provides the primary source of Islamic Law. Prophet Muhammad's teachings explain and implement Qur'anic principles.*[149]

Henri de Boulainvilliers, a French writer and historian, insisted that Islam was a superior religion to Christianity. He demonstrates that Prophet Muhammad (ﷺ) was a wise lawgiver who set up a reasonable religion whilst Judaism and Christianity were submerged in dubious dogmas.[150]

As far as prisoners of war are concerned, the practice of Prophet Muhammad (ﷺ) provides a clear example of mercy and compassion that should be extended to them. A prisoner's basic needs of food, clothing and shelter must be met by the Muslims and it is forbidden to inflict any physical harm or torture upon such a prisoner. In this regard, an Indian author Dr N.K. Singh says:

> *The Prophet Muhammad (ﷺ) had noble attitude toward the prisoners. Out of the seventy two captives, only two were executed, viz., al- Nadr b. al-Harith and Uqbah b. Abi Miaqit who were notorious for their unrelenting hostility towards the Muslims. The rest of the captives were treated with utmost kindness and consideration. Said one of these in later days:*
> *"Blessing on the men of Madinah, they gave us wheaten bread to eat when there was little of it, contenting themselves with dates".*[151]

The celebrated author John Alden Williams points out that the Muslims scholars addressed Prophet Muhammad (ﷺ) as the Lawgiver:

> *Muhammad is often referred to by the Muslim philosophers as "The Lawgiver," since from his governing of the early community and the example of his life the Islamic Law has been systematized. The Law is usually seen as of Divine origin, but mediated by the Prophet.*[152]

Edward Sell also acclaimed Prophet Muhammad (ﷺ) as a lawgiver who introduced law, order, policies and religious reforms which played a great role in establishing the commonwealth. According to Sell,

> *His work at this time was beneficial. In the place of lawlessness and disorder he introduced law and order. Religion played an important part in the creation of the common-wealth.*[153]

Prophet Muhammad (ﷺ) was the pioneer of providing impartial family law – equally for husband and wife. A woman, like her husband, has the right to divorce. He was very strict about the laws he implemented. Major General Forlong says:

> *The great lawgiver saw in marriage only a civil contract which the testimony of two witnesses made complete, but which the woman, like her husband, could annul on grounds of immorality and general bad conduct; as by leaving each other without suitable subsistence, habitual cruelty, or if the husband threaten his wife with bodily injury, or force her to degrading labor. "If ye husbands have rights, so have your wives," said Mahamad, "therefore shall the wife plead her own cause against the unjust and rapacious husband. … He shall maintain her and hers in a manner suitable to their condition*[154]…

It was common during Prophet Muhammad's time for people to treat others favourably if they were rich and noble, and to discriminate against those of low rank and status. All of the Prophet Muhammad's personal characteristics and morals pointed to a kind-hearted person who gave everyone their due. His interpersonal skills and social relations were of the highest standard. He had a very personable and amicable manner with others and always showed compassion towards children:

> *A remarkable feature was the urbanity and consideration with which Mahomet treated even the most insignificant of his followers. Modesty and kindness, patience, self-denial, and generosity, pervaded his conduct, and rivetted the affections of all around him.*

> *He disliked to say No; if unable to reply to a petitioner in the affirmative, he preferred to remain silent... He possessed the rare faculty of making each individual in a company think that he was the most favoured guest. When he met any one rejoicing, he would seize him eagerly and cordially by the hand. With the bereaved and afflicted he sympathized tenderly. Gentle and unbending towards little children, he would not disdain to accost a group of them at play with the salutation of peace. He shared his food, even in times of scarcity, with others; and was sedulously solicitous for the personal comfort of every one about him. A kindly and benevolent disposition pervades all these illustrations of his character.*[155]

Pandit Gopal Krishna, editor of the daily *Bharat Samachar* has paid the highest tributes to the Prophet. Gifted with a high moral character he had been sent to transform the world. He showed light to the Arabs who were sunk in darkness. The benevolent Prophet never had taken revenge against anyone. He was a carer of the poor, the helpless and women:

> *God had sent him to reform the world. He had been endowed with the strength of character and moral qualities of a great reformer and of a great man. He transformed the downtrodden evil society of Arabia into a very refined, virile and virtuous society. The Prophet of Islam was very kind-hearted and never took revenge on personal grounds, nor turned away any supplicant from his door. He was responsible for the emancipation of women and he made no distinction between a rich and a poor person.*[156]

Forlong reports that Prophet Muhammad (ﷺ) established relations with other countries who sent their ambassadors to Arabia. These foreign diplomats had opportunities to observe very closely the lifestyle, dealings and the preaching of Islam by Prophet Muhammad (ﷺ). One of them claimed that he did not find any comparison to Prophet Muhammad (ﷺ) who could rule someone with the same status as Prophet Muhammad (ﷺ) did. Although he was the head of state, he lived the life of the simplest of persons who required no bodyguards as the leader. He was the real hero in true sense:

"I have seen," said one of his royal ambassadors, "Khosru, Emperor of Persia, and the Christian Monarch Heraklius, but I have never seen a man ruling his equals as does Mahamad. … Though head of Church and State, he was a Pope without his pretensions, and a Caesar without his legions, bodyguards, palaces and great revenues. If ever a man had a right to say he ruled by Divine right, it was Mahamad; for he had all the power without the instruments and supports." He was indeed "one of the greatest heroes the world has ever seen—alike as a warrior, legislator, poet and man of genius." Though scarcely able to read and write, he is the author of a book, at once a code of laws, of prayers, and a Bible all in one, which is revered to-day by probably one-sixth of the whole human race, and which is a miracle in purity of style, wisdom and truth.[157]

The long-term effects of Prophet Muhammad(ﷺ)'s message can be seen by how dominating his monotheism was. His preaching had the effect of uprooting the age-old beliefs and religious practices associated with polytheism. The monotheism of Prophet Muhammad (ﷺ) had taken over the idolatry of the Arabs. His message was also an encouragement to cooperate with one another in good deeds. Sir William Muir says in this context:

And what have been the effects of the system which, established by such instrumentality, Mahomet has left behind him? We may freely concede that it banished for ever many of the darker elements of superstition which had for ages shrouded the Peninsula. Idolatry vanished before the battle-cry of Islam; the doctrine of the unity and infinite perfections of God, and of a special all-pervading Providence, became a living principle in the hearts and lives of the followers of Mahomet, even as it had in his own. An absolute surrender and submission to the divine will (the very name of Islam) was demanded as the first requirement of the religion. Nor are social virtues wanting. Brotherly love is inculcated within the circle of the faith; orphans are to be protected, and slaves treated with consideration; intoxicating drinks are prohibited, and Mahometanism may boast of a degree of temperance unknown to any other creed.[158]

Unlettered but Talented

R.V.C. Bodley states that, having started a career as a shepherd and although with no opportunity for schooling, Prophet Muhammad (ﷺ) was more advanced in clear thinking and expressing ideas than any average child of his time.[159]

Bodley adds that after switching his career from shepherd to the caravan trade, the unlettered Prophet Muhammad (ﷺ) gradually developed substantial skills and experience as a substantial businessman over the time. This made him popular amongst many merchants, including his uncle. Even before reaching the age of twenty-five, his reputation and honesty spread to different parts of the Arabian world.[160]

Bodley further notes that Prophet Muhammad's dealing with people from other countries provided him with opportunities to widen his thoughts. He never confined himself only to the divine world like his predecessors; rather he learnt about the world and its problems in a practical way and worked on what he was ordered by God to complete.[161]

Bodley narrates an interesting story about the wisdom of Prophet Muhammad (ﷺ) in connection with the black stone, placed at one corner of the Kaabah, which the Muslims believe to have been sent down from the heavens by God to Prophet Adam (pbuh) and Eve (pbuh) as a token indicating the place where an altar should be built for prayer. The original Kaabah was built where this stone was dropped. While rebuilding the Kabaah, which was destroyed in the great deluge at the time of the Prophet Noah (pbuh), Prophets Abraham (pbuh) and his son Prophet Ismail (pbuh) placed this sacred stone at the south eastern corner of Kaabah. Owing to another flooding of Makkah, five years before Prophet (ﷺ) received his first revelation from God, the Kaabah was required to be rebuilt. Although the removal of the sacred stone was unchallenged, its replacement, after the rebuilding of the Kaabah, caused huge disagreement amongst the senior personalities as to who would receive the great honour of replacing the stone back in its niche. While no solution was reached and chaos ensued, someone suggested seeking advice from the person who would first enter the courtyard of Kaabah in the morning. And all agreed on that. Next morning, by some coincidence, Prophet Muhammad (ﷺ) arrived there, ahead of all. Being given the task of solving the problem, Prophet Muhammad (ﷺ) took off his wrapper and spread it on the ground and he himself placed the stone on the wrapper. He then asked the chiefs and the leaders of the clans to hold the corners and take it to the Kaabah. As they followed his instructions, the Prophet (ﷺ) lifted the sacred stone and placed it at the designated place at the corner of the Kaabah. The solution was straightforward and it stopped a conflict which could have bloody consequences.[162]

Sir John Glubb[163] and Elsa Marston[164] have narrated similar stories about Prophet Muhammad's wisdom and how a conflict which could have been bloody had been avoided.

Dr Daniel C. Peterson is consistent with the above statements. He opines that the future role of Prophet Muhammad (ﷺ) as a leader was indicative in that incidence.[165]

On this topic, Geoffrey Rowell states that being unlettered does not prevent a person from exerting a great influence on others. Sometimes, other aspects of their personality compensate for this and help leave behind an indelible impression on others. History is replete with examples of unlettered yet enigmatic personalities who have gone on to establish prolific legacies. Prophet Muhammad (ﷺ) was one of them:

> *He was clearly a powerful and charismatic person. There are quite a lot of instances in history where powerful and charismatic leaders have the quality of inspiring people, even when they were illiterate.*[166]

John Henry Haaren was an American educator and historian. He wrote in his *Famous Men of the Middle Ages* that although Prophet Muhammad (ﷺ) was unlettered, he was not ignorant. He was a wise person. Haaren notes:

> *Mohammed had no school education. He could neither read nor*

write. But he was not ignorant. He knew well how to do the work entrusted to him, and was a first-rate man of business... He spent much of his time in thinking about religion. He learned all that he could about Judaism and Christianity; but he was not satisfied with either of them[167]*...*

He further maintains:

Mohammed was very earnest and serious. In a cave in Mount Hira, near Makkah, he spent several weeks every year in prayers and religious meditations. He declared that, while praying in his cave, he often had visions of God and heaven. He said that many times the Angel Gabriel appeared to him and revealed to him the religion which he taught to his followers. As he himself could not write, he committed to memory all that the angel told him, and had it written in a book. This book is called the 'Koran' which means like our own word Bible the 'Book'. The Koran is the bible of Mohammedans.[168]

Author Pierce De Lacy Johnstone argues that being unlettered is not a bar to acquiring knowledge. Prophet Muhammad (ﷺ) was unlettered but his wisdom was of great importance. According to Johnstone,

The question whether he could or could not read is not of great importance, and is at this date insoluble. He always called himself the "Unlettered Prophet," and appealed to the perfect harmony and eloquence of his Qur'an as being therefore a miracle, sufficient to prove his prophetic mission. Inability to read would not have been a bar to acquisition of knowledge, and a retentive memory (such as was common in Arabia) would secure it.[169]

The Reverend Bosworth Smith stresses that the Christian philosophy and principle will accept that the Qur'an is God's word and Prophet Muhammad (ﷺ) is His messenger. Prophet Muhammad (ﷺ), although unlettered, had been selected by God to reveal the Qur'an through him, which inspired countless books, now bedecking the bookshelves of mankind worldwide:

I boldly assert that one day the loftiest of human philosophies and the most veracious principles of Christianity will confess and bear witness that the Qur'an is the Word of God and that Muhammad is the Messenger of God. An unlettered and unlearned prophet was chosen by God to bring the Qur'an to mankind, a book that has in the course of history produced thousands of other books and treatises, brought libraries into being and filled them with books, and placed before mankind laws and philosophies and educational intellectual and ideological systems. He arose in an environment where there was no trace of learning and civilization. In the whole of Madinah there were only eleven people who knew how to read and write, and in all the branches of the Quraysh, in Makkah and its environs, not more than seventeen people were literate.[170]

The American author Washington Irving asserts that although Prophet Muhammad (ﷺ) was not lettered, he was intelligent and brilliant. Lack of formal education did not put him behind in any aspect of his dealings. Irving, points out:

His intellectual qualities were undoubtedly of an extraordinary kind. He had a quick apprehension, a retentive memory, a vivid imagination, and an inventive genius. Owing but little to education, he had quickened and informed his mind by close observation, and stored it with a great variety of knowledge concerning the systems of religion current in his day, or handed down by tradition from antiquity.[171]

A Great Reformer

Samuel Parsons Scott, a lawyer and writer from Hillsboro, Ohio, in his *History of the Moorish Empire in Europe* (Vol I), attributes all the success of Europe to the Prophet Muhammad (ﷺ). He writes that the reform which Prophet Muhammad (ﷺ) had to undertake at social and political levels cannot be appreciated enough. It was truly a formidable task and the achievements of Muslims throughout history in many ways owe their genius to Prophet Muhammad (ﷺ). Being the messenger of One God and propagating His divine message asking people to shun the polytheistic belief system that was then current in Arabia, was a tough proposition that threatened the very social fabric of Makkah and the strongholds of their chieftains. When we take time to contemplate the purpose of religion and what God intended for all human beings, in terms of morality, and the bettering of society, the idea which Prophet Muhammad (ﷺ) promoted truly reflects his prophethood.[172]

R.V.C. Bodley argues that, although many themes of the Qur'an appeared in the earlier divine books, no one can ever undermine the position of Muhammad, the person who reformed religion and brought an energetic force which has been inspiring mankind over the centuries.[173]

Thomas Carlyle highlighted that the Arabs were mired in the lowest levels of barbarism whan Prophet Muhammad (ﷺ) appeared in the land of the desert to reform the nation. He started life as a shepherd, then became a caravan trader and then a Messenger of God, who helped the Arabs come out of the darkness into light. Arabian history became very well known to the entire world through the hero Prophet Muhammad (ﷺ). Carlyle elaborates:

> *To the Arab Nation it was as a birth from darkness into light; Arabia first became alive by means of it. A poor shepherd people, roaming unnoticed in its deserts since the creation of the world: a Hero Prophet was sent down to them with a word they could believe: see, the unnoticed becomes world-notable, the small has grown world-great; within one century afterwards, Arabia is at*

> *Grenada on this hand, at Delhi on that; - glancing in valour and splendour and the light of genius, Arabia shines through long ages over a great section of the world. Belief is great, life-giving. The history of a Nation becomes fruitful, soul-elevating, great, so soon as it believes. These Arabs, the man Mahomet, and that one century, - is it not as if a spark had fallen, one spark, on a world of what seemed black unnoticeable sand; but lo, the sand proves explosive powder, blazes heaven-high from Delhi to Grenada! I said, the Great Man was always as lightning out of Heaven; the rest of men waited for him like fuel, and then they too would flame.*[174]

The famous explorer Mungo Park remarks that Prophet Muhammad (ﷺ) brought significant reforms socially which changed the life style of his people and elevated their status. One of the norms of Arabian society was the rampant consumption of wine, which he outlawed. Park observes:

> *The beverages for the pagan Negroe's are beer and mead, of which they frequently drink in excess. The Muhammadan converts drink nothing but water.*[175]

Prophet Muhammad (ﷺ) was the greatest of reformers who offered tremendous services to the human community: guiding his nation to believing in one true God instead of the many false deities, leading them to piety and peace instead of vengeful killings and war, inspiring them to lead a happy and simple life in place of being submerged in arrogance and hatred. His contributions put them on the road to progress and civilisation. Leo Tolstoy brings home the point:

> *Undoubtedly, the Prophet Muhammad is one of the greatest reformers who rendered extensive service to the human community. As an indication of his greatness, it suffices to mention that he guided an entire nation to the light of truth and made it incline to serenity and peace and opted to live a life of asceticism. He forbade acts of bloodshed or human sacrifice. He opened up for his nation the way to progress and civilization. That was a great feat which nobody – no matter how powerful he may be – is able to achieve.*

Such a man, indeed, is highly respectable and estimable.[176]

The author J.H. Denison wrote in his book *Emotion as the Basis of Civilization* that the centuries before Prophet Muhammad (ﷺ) were marked by a sharp decline in moral standards, social relations and peaceful co-existence. There was virtually no hope that civilisation could restore a sense of normality and balance, as it was plummeting further into darkness and despair. The Christian world was not fostering the ethics of Jesus and could not unite its ranks. Man seemed on the brink of cultural oblivion and progress was a distant dream. It was at this critical juncture in human history that Prophet Muhammad (ﷺ) was born and, subsequently, went on to gift his people and ultimately the world with a religion and social, economic and political system that gave it the much-needed moral restoration and order it craved.[177]

Sir H.A.R. Gibb warned that it would be a gross mistake if Prophet Muhammad (ﷺ) is considered to be interested in politics and war only. He was rather keen to educate and train his people so that they could reform society.[178]

Anita Rai, the author of the book *Prophet Muhammad (ﷺ): Uncovering the Truth,* indicates that the Prophet wanted to teach the people to worship one God, the Almighty, the Creator of all, and establish a relationship with Him directly instead of other intermediaries.[179]

Edward Sell asserts that the character of Muhammad (ﷺ) helped significantly to reform the Arabian tribes. His qualities made him not only a religious leader but also a statesman – a great man, whom history will remember forever:

> *His perseverance against great odds at Makkah, and his patience under persecution there call forth sympathy for the patriot and the religious reformer. His quickness to realize the advantage of the exodus from Makkah to Madinah, his readiness to change his point of view when the Jews failed to help him, and his skill as an opportunist call for admiration, if we view him only as a successful Arab chief, who founded a kingdom on a religious basis, himself*

becoming Caesar and Pope. In these respects he was a great man, who will stand out conspicuous so long as history remains to tell his tale.[180]

Professor T.L. Vaswani paid tribute to Prophet Muhammad for bringing huge reforms to society. The Prophet, through preaching Islam, made significant changes including stopping infanticide and many other evils:

And consider for a moment what the faith he preached has achieved. Islam has given the world a religion without priests; Islam abolished infanticide in Arabia; Islam enjoined on the faithful total abstinence from drink; Islam emphasised the great qualities of faith, courage, endurance and self-sacrifice.[181]

George Sarton, a Belgian historian, admires the Prophet Muhammad (ﷺ) for the sanction against alcohol, which has been a blessing, while strong and harmful alcohol is in use in the daily life of men in the West. The consumption of alcohol and the resulting drunkenness can so badly impair the social fabric of men's lives that it justifies banning the use of it many a time.[182]

Thomas Patrick Hughes, a famous British author, notes that Prophet Muhammad (ﷺ) did not claim to be the founder of a new religion but was the reformer of the one religion prophesied by the Prophets of God before him. He is the last and the greatest amongst all Prophets of God. He deserves respect for having all-round skills, qualities and the experience of all. He is no doubt the greatest hero, Hughes claims:

In forming an estimate of Muhammad's prophetical pretensions, it must be remembered that he did not claim to be the founder of a new religion, but merely of a new covenant. He is the last and greatest of all God's prophets. He is sent to convert the world to the one true religion which God had before revealed to the five great lawgivers – Adam, Noah, Abraham, Moses, and Jesus! We give Muhammad credit as a warrior, as a legislator, as a poet, as a man of uncommon genius, raising himself amidst great opposition to a pinnacle of renown; we admit that he is, without doubt, one of the greatest heroes the world has ever seen.[183]

George Sale wrote that the Arabs united together under the religion of the great Prophet Muhammad (ﷺ) and the religion spread over a large part of the world:

And the Arabs being then united in one faith, and under one prince, found themselves in a condition of making those conquests which extended the Muhammadan faith over so great a part of the world.[184]

Dr Marcus Dods notes that the Arabs advanced beyond the powerful nations at the time:

Mohammad's religion reformed all existing dogmas and brought the Arabs ahead of the super powers of the time.[185]

R.V.C. Bodley says that the fact that Prophet Muhammad (ﷺ) had been elevated to the peak of statesmanship did not detract from the fact that his principal objective, and the one which gave him most comfort and satisfaction, was purging the centre of Islam – Makkah – of its pagan and polytheistic influences. A great accomplishment of Prophet Muhammad (ﷺ) was that for all his achievements, including the conquering of territory and the successful conversion of many to Islam, he never compromised his religious values and remained firm and principled throughout his Prophetic mission. He never lost sight of what was truly important for him and his followers. Even at the height of his power, Prophet Muhammad (ﷺ) led a very frugal existence and never succumbed to the pomp and excessive splendour of many of his contemporaries:

Now he was tired. He needed rest. In a few days he had become one of the most powerful rulers in Arabia. He was pope, he was Caesar. Before the year was over, he would be the only ruler who counted, the founder of a nation, of an empire, of a faith. But this did not

> *elate him as much as the thought that the Kaaba, the center of the world, was now cleaned of its infamous idols. If he died that night, he would consider the most important part of his mission accomplished.*[186]

Claude-Etienne Savary, a French Orientalist, pioneer of Egyptology and translator of the Qur'an, had a similar view to Henri de Boulainvilliers (see below). He believed that Prophet Muhammad (ﷺ) was a genius, second to none. Savary said that having been born amongst the idolaters, Prophet Muhammad (ﷺ), preached and worshipped the religion of one God. Savary declared the Prophet (ﷺ) as one of the greatest men who ever lived.[187]

When Europe was wallowing in misery, Muslims were making the fullest potential of the wisdom which Prophet Muhammad (ﷺ) had imparted to them, by advancing intellectually and materially. Much of this progressive inheritance is owing to Prophet Muhammad's efforts and sacrifice. Bertrand Russell affirms:

> *The supremacy of the East was not only military. Science, philosophy, poetry, and the arts, all flourished in the Muhammadan world at a time when Europe was sunk in barbarism. Europeans, with unpardonable insularity, call this period 'the Dark Ages': but it was only in Europe that it was dark – indeed only in Christian Europe, for Spain, which was Muhammadan, had a brilliant culture.*[188]

The Prophet of God

The famous scholar William Montgomery Watt states that Prophet Muhammad (ﷺ) was prophesised by a Syrian monk, Bahira as a future Prophet of God at the age of 15 years, while he was there on business together with his uncle. The knowledgeable monk, discerning divine signs in Prophet Muhammad (ﷺ), warned his uncle to take precautions to protect him from his enemies.[189]

Johann Wolfgang von Goethe was the greatest writer, poet, novelist, playwright and natural philosopher of the German tradition. Of Prophet Muhammad Goethe asserted:

> *He is a prophet and not a poet and therefore his Koran is to be seen as Divine Law and not as a book of a human being, made for education or entertainment.*[190]

Goethe also claimed:

> *The message of Mohammad is following toward its noble destination like a pure, fresh and transparent rivulet.*[191]

Michael Hart says that when Prophet Muhammad (ﷺ) was forty years old he was convinced that God was speaking to him and selected him to spread the message of God, the true religion.[192]

The British author Michael Cook points out that Prophet Muhammad's role as a Prophet was understood from some signs in his early life. A divine light at his birth helped his mother to see faraway castles, and also the Arabs, the Jews and the Christian scholars became aware of the coming Prophet.[193]

British author Arthur Gilman asserts that Prophet Muhammad (ﷺ) communicated directly with God and had the command to preach as the Prophet of the most High:

> *Now, Mohammad had, he thought, been in direct communication with the messenger Allah (God); he had distinctly been commissioned to preach; and had been told what to say; and had*

been assured that he was the prophet of the most High.[194]

The savagery which many armies unleashed throughout history against innocent non-combatants is something which cannot be said of Prophet Muhammad (ﷺ). One can see this from the transgressions of the Christian crusaders and the British army's plunder of Africans. Prophet Muhammad's mission and triumphs were motivated simply out of religious and the highest moral concerns. He never gave in to the primitive and brutal temptations of those before and after him. Arthur Gilman echoes this idea:

> *In comparison, for example, with the cruelty of the Crusaders, who, in 1099, put seventy thousand Muslims, men, women and helpless children to death when Jerusalem fell into their hands; or with that of the English army, also fighting under the Cross, which in the year of grace 1874 burned an African capital, in its war on the Gold Coast, Muhammad's victory was in very truth one of religion and not of politics; he rejected every token of personal homage, and declined all regal authority; and when the haughty chiefs of the Koreishites appeared before him he asked: "What can you expect at my hands? "Mercy, O generous brother; "Be it so; you are free"! he exclaimed.*[195]

Dr Gottlieb William Leitner, a British Orientalist who studied the Arabic language and learnt a significant part of the Qur'an by heart says that Prophet Muhammad (ﷺ) never declared himself a perfectionist. He, too, could have made mistakes. Once when the Prophet (ﷺ) was busy receiving and preaching to a delegation of the higher ups of Makkan society, a poor and a blind companion of him approached him for advice and consultation. In a momentary show of aversion, the Prophet (ﷺ) turned his face. This is the simple and pure admonishment from the Lord and the Prophet (ﷺ), the truthful, had no hesitation at all in disclosing it to the folk as usual as the rest of the Qur'an was shared instantly with them. Such was the magnitude of truthfulness of him. Dr Leitner appears surprised how the ignorant call this Prophet an imposter! He exclaims:

Muhammad himself did not make any claim to infallibility. On one occasion he had a revelation censuring himself severely for having turned away from a beggar in order to speak to an illustrious man of the commonwealth, and he published this revelation, the very last thing which he would have done had he been an impostor, as ignorant Christians call the great Arab Prophet.[196]

The Swedish Professor Tor Andrae has also mentioned about the divine light during the birth of Prophet Muhammad (ﷺ). It is said that Muhammad's mother did not experience the pangs of pregnancy. Once, while she was in a state between sleep and waking, she heard a voice saying that she was bearing a son who would be the future Prophet; subsequently, she heard another voice telling her to name him 'Ahmad'. Jesus prophesied the coming of another apostle with the name of 'Ahmad'. Similar predictions were popular among the Jewish scholars who, after the birth of Prophet Muhammad (ﷺ), announced that the star 'Ahmad' has arisen.[197]

In addition to the above claim of seeing divine light during the pregnancy, Prophet Muhammad's mother Amina heard a divine voice asking her to make over the child to one God and name him "Muhammad". The Jews, Christians, Zoroastrians, and pagans had prophesised the arrival of Prophet Muhammad (ﷺ).[198]

Samuel Marinus Zwemer pointed out that Muhammad (ﷺ) was a Prophet and his life was the epitome of the principles he preached. The religion of Islam was, thus, reflected in the ways of the life of Prophet Muhammad (ﷺ). According to Zwemer,

The religion which Mohammed founded bears everywhere the imprint of his life and character. Mohammed was not only the prophet, but the prophecy of Islam.[199]

David Kerr maintains that, as the Qur'an accepts Prophet Muhammad (ﷺ) as the last Prophet of God which was also foretold in the earlier scriptures, Jesus son of Mary (pbuh) also said that he was the Prophet of God and it was mentioned in the earlier book, the Torah, and confirmed that another Prophet is coming in the lineage whose name is 'Ahmed' i.e. Prophet Muhammad (ﷺ).[200]

David Kerr also declares that the Qur'an is a set of guidelines which enshrines the principle of unity of God from the inception of mankind until Islam was completed and revealed to Prophet Muhammad (ﷺ) as the last Prophet of God.[201]

A Sikh intellectual, Sardar Diwan Singh Maftoon, admired the Prophet greatly. He had deep respect for the Prophet, his teachings and the mode of daily prayers. He states:

> *Since the time I have learnt the Prophet of Islam's saying that the highest crusade is to speak the truth before a tyrant ruler, I could hardly measure the grandeur of a personality who has considered the expression of truth before a tyrant as the highest crusade. I have also been extremely impressed by the Prophet of Islam's prayer that he may be placed among the poor. I was born in a Sikh family, but I am as much a believer of the Prophet of Islam as any Muslim.*[202]

Elsa Marston states that having heard about the claim of Prophet Muhammad (ﷺ) to be the Prophet of God, people wanted him to perform miracles, if he was a real messenger. However, Prophet Muhammad (ﷺ) repeatedly denied having any divine powers, saying that the Qur'an was the only miracle that was given to him:

> *Muhammad steadfastly repeated that he claimed no supernatural powers. His role was to preach the truth and warn his people of the results of wrongdoing. The Koran, he said, was the only miracle involved in his mission.*[203]

The claim that Prophet Muhammad (ﷺ) was a false Prophet cannot be historically supported. If he were a mere pretender as so many people claim, then it would have made sense for him to have compromised his message and principles for material gain and security. But there are many occasions in his life when Prophet Muhammad (ﷺ) did not think twice about jeopardising his physical and economic security and well-being, in order for his message to survive and prevail. He was given every financial and material incentive to relinquish his teachings and put an end to his preaching of monotheism, but he resisted the temptation and the pressure. There were periods when the notable men of Quraish, the elite of Makkan society, approached him with the intention of swaying Prophet Muhammad (ﷺ) from his mission but all of this was to no avail. Besides claiming messenger-ship, Prophet Muhammad (ﷺ) was open to the fact that like other human beings, he was also susceptible to weakness and errors, but this admission only reinforced his honesty and distanced him even more from the hateful scholarship over centuries which has stigmatised him to the core. The prolific British author Alfred Martin says:

> *That Mohammed was not an impostor can be proved by reference to several significant incidents in his career. As a young man Mohammed had received a handsome salary for serving as custodian of the "Kaaba" that enshrined the sacred stone worshipped by resident believers and by visiting pilgrims. But in time there came to be associated with this object of veneration certain superstitious practices which Mohammed could not conscientiously endorse. To criticise them meant loss of his position and salary, yet he did not hesitate to denounce them and promptly sacrificed his profitable custodianship. Surely such conduct was not that of an impostor. Again, when implored by his wealthy uncle to desist from his preaching of "radical" views, Mohammed to name his own price for the silence his uncle desired, he repudiated the tempting offer, preferring the luxury of free thought and free speech with poverty, if need be, to the luxury of ease and wealth with a tarnished soul. Read his own brave and uncompromising utterance: "Were I to be offered the sun in my right hand and the moon in my left hand to induce me to abandon my undertaking, the offer would be futile, for I will not rest until the Lord carry his cause to victory, or till I die for it." Could such be the part of an impostor?... And nothing but blind prejudice and lazy indifference to truth can account for the perpetuation of the charge.*[204]

Reverend Bosworth Smith emphasises the authenticity of the religion as preached by Prophet Muhammad (ﷺ) and he did not know any reason to support the claim that Prophet Muhammad (ﷺ) was an imposter. All he found proved to be the truth. In Smith's words:

> *Nor could anyone have done what Mohammed did without the most profound faith in the reality and goodness of his cause. Fairly considered, there is no single trait in his character up to the time of the Hegira which calumny itself could couple with imposture: on the contrary, there is every thing to prove the real enthusiast arriving slowly and painfully at what he believed to be the truth.*[205]

John Kaltner, an Associate Professor of Religion, asserts that Prophet Muhammad (ﷺ) is the Prophet as well as the Messenger of God. He conveyed the will of God faithfully to mankind and left no need for any further Prophet to be sent to the earth. That is why Prophet Muhammad (ﷺ) is known as the last Prophet of God.[206]

Washington Irving, who wrote a biography of Prophet Muhammad (ﷺ), came to the conclusion that many charges made by hostile Orientalists about him are not genuine. He pointed out that numerous false reports had been associated with his name:

> *The question now occurs, was he the unprincipled impostor that he has been represented? Were all his visions and revelations deliberate falsehoods, and was his whole system a tissue of deceit? In considering this question we must bear in mind that he is not chargeable with many extravagances which exist in his name. Many of the visions and revelations handed down as having been given by him are spurious.*[207]

Armstrong, wrote in his book *Lord of Arabia* that Prophet Muhammad (ﷺ) appeared, all of a sudden, in the dark age of Arabia and unified different people over a great many parts of the world by preaching Islam, the call for submission to the will of God:

> *Suddenly out of this monstrous chaos was born a Great Man, preaching a Great Religion – the Prophet Mohamed preaching*

Islam. Islam united the Arabs, purified them, bound them into one people. Mohamed filled them with a great Faith. His power increased rapidly. Within ten years he controlled all Arabia. His successors and followers advanced across the Euphrates into Persia and beyond. Northwards they went through Syria into Asia Minor and stormed at the walls of Constantinople. Westwards they swept along the African coast across the Sahara to the Atlantic and up into Spain and threatened France. Within a hundred years they had expanded their rule until the Arab Empire stretched from the Straits of Gibraltar to the Indus River and from Central Africa to the Persian frontier.[208]

The great philosopher Karl Marx said that any sensible person should accept the Prophet Muhammad (ﷺ) as the messenger of the Almighty. In his words:

Every man who has a mind – should really confess that Muhammad is messenger from God.[209]

Maximilian Karl Emil "Max" Weber, the German sociologist, philosopher, and political economist offers a definition of a prophet. According to his definition, it means an individual who possesses certain qualities and characteristics by dint of which he is distinguished from ordinary people. He is known as having supernatural or exceptional powers or qualities which ordinary people do not possess. This definition fits Muhammad (ﷺ) very well.[210]

The views of David Noel Freedman, an American biblical scholar, author, editor, archaeologist and ordained Presbyterian minister are consistent with the above definition of prophet and he says these characteristics match with those of Muhammad (ﷺ).[211]

The uniqueness of Prophet Muhammad's Prophethood is that unlike the previous Prophets before him, he did not resort to physical miracles as a way of legitimising his Prophethood in the eyes of the masses. If anything can be considered miraculous about Islam and Prophet Muhammad (ﷺ), it is the tremendous spread of Islam, beyond its frontiers. An Indian historian, M.N. Roy, has observed:

Every prophet establishes his pretension by the performance of miracles. On that token, Mohammad must be recognized as by far the greatest of all prophets, before or after him. The expansion of Islam is the most miraculous of all miracles.[212]

An Indian author, Venkata Ratnam, in his book *An Essay on Islam,* highlights that Prophet Muhammad (ﷺ) never said that he was equal to God, rather he claimed to be a messenger of the Almighty:

Muhammad never made himself equal with God. He always professed himself as the messenger of God, teaching His will to men. The Islam of Muhammad with its stern discipline and stern morality proved itself the only practical religion. Muhammad the Prophet of God has done more good than any other man.[213]

Carlyle said in his speech, "Prophet Muhammad (ﷺ): The Hero as Prophet" that he brought about a great change from idolatry to monotheism – guiding people from darkness into light. However, the great hero did not claim himself to be God, but a messenger of God:

From the first rude times of paganism among the Scandinavians in the North, we advance to a very different epoch of religion, among a very different people: Muhammadanism among the Arabs. A great change; what a change and progress is indicated here, in the universal condition and thought of men! The Hero is not regarded as a God among his fellow men; but as one God-inspired, as a Prophet;...[214]

He Served the Whole World

Prophet Muhammad (ﷺ) had succeeded where Judaism and Christianity had failed – in the domain of raising the civility of his people. Alfred Martin says:

> *To his everlasting credit it must be said that in lifting to a higher plane of life the communities of his day and place, he achieved that which neither the Judaism nor the Christianity of mediaeval Arabia could accomplish. Nay more, in the fulfillment of that civilizing work Mohammed rendered invaluable service, not only to Arabia, but also to the entire world.*[215]

Danny Richmond, Faith Act Manager, Tony Blair Faith Foundation, feels that there was altruism about Prophet Muhammad (ﷺ) which gave rise to a genuine concern for those outside his inner circle. Prophet Muhammad's prophethood was not restricted to his own people and religious community. The selflessness is characteristic of Prophet Muhammad (ﷺ):

> *From the stories I know of his life, he seems like someone who was deeply committed to the other, whether the other was someone outside his family or someone outside his faith or the most vulnerable in his community. Many of the teachings of his life were about showing compassion and concern for the other and I think that reflects deeply upon the type of person he was and his teachings about what it is to be a person in a society.*[216]

Part Two:

The Simplicity of Prophet Muhammad

Simple

The great Indian politician Mohandas Karamchand Gandhi, also known as Mahatma Gandhi, was so inspired and enamoured by Prophet Muhammad (ﷺ), that he even kept a black blanket and simple attire as a tribute to the simple living which Prophet Muhammad (ﷺ) preferred. According to Gandhi, it would have been impossible to know that Prophet Muhammad (ﷺ) was a man of tremendous power and influence, because of his simplicity. This characteristic was also reflected in Prophet Muhammad's companion, the second Caliph of Islam, Umar al-Khattab, whom Gandhi used as an example for the Indian Congress as a good model of behaviour and conduct. He remarked:

> *I am only surprised when some Muslim asks me as to why I always use black blankets; I tell them that I do as a token of my personal homage to Prophet Muhammad who was the greatest man the world has ever produced. He was so simple in his day to day life that one could hardly imagine that he was the man who was ruling over the hearts of the millions all over the world. I instructed Congress Governments, immediately after they assumed power after the elections of 1936 that they should follow the footsteps of Hazrat Umar who thoroughly implemented every preaching of Prophet Muhammad and thus bettered the lot of the common man.*[217]

The debt which we owe to Prophet Muhammad (ﷺ) and his followers can never be truly realised. Prophet Muhammad's frugal lifestyle is most worthy of praise, especially when we consider the temptations and material riches that were offered to him. Instead of indulging in the pomp of this world, he would maintain simplicity and an everyday casual demeanour, attending to household chores. Alfred Martin acknowledges these traits of character of Prophet Muhammad (ﷺ). He notes:

> *To-day we decorate our walls and floors with fabrics that Mohammedans taught us to weave. We regale our senses with*

perfumes they taught us to make, we teach our children the algebra and higher mathematics which they taught the fathers.[218]

According to Alfred Martin:

His was the simple life, lived at times to the point of severe austerity. For we read that he would sometimes go for months without eating a single hearty meal, lighting his own fire, cooking his own food, mending his clothes and shoes in order that his slaves might enjoy a larger share of freedom.[219]

It is astonishing to discover how rooted Prophet Muhammad (ﷺ) was in his time and how he delivered his message in a manner that was conducive to the climate. When other religions and belief systems had failed in their attempts to civilise primitive folk, Prophet Muhammad (ﷺ) is given a unique distinction in this regard for succeeding where they failed. Alfred Martin goes on to say:

Nor is anything in religious history more remarkable than the way in which Muhammad fitted his transfiguring ideas into the existing social system of Arabia. To his everlasting credit, it must be said that in lifting to a higher place of life the communities of his day and place, he achieved that which neither the Judaism nor Christianity of Medieval Arabia could accomplish. Nay more, in the fulfillment of that civilising work Muhammad rendered valuable service, not only to Arabia, but also to the entire world.[220]

Davenport affirms that Prophet Muhammad (ﷺ) won the hearts and minds of the people – enemies as well as friends – by the simplicity of his behaviour, dealings, speech, etc. His lifestyle was was like that of an ordinary person. Although he became the supreme power of Arabia, he did all his own housework. Davenport explains:

His politeness to the great, his affability to the humble, and his dignified bearing to the presumptuous, procured him respect, admiration and applause. His talents were equally fitted for persuasion or command. Deeply read in the volume of nature, though entirely ignorant of letters, his mind could expand into controversy with the acutest of his enemies, or contract itself to the apprehension of the meanest of his disciples. His simple eloquence, rendered impressive by the expression of a countenance wherein awfulness of majesty was tempered by an amiable sweetness, excited emotions of veneration and love; and he was gifted with that authoritative air of genius which alike influences the learned and commands the illiterate. As a friend and a parent, he exhibited the softest feelings of our nature; but, while in possession of the kind and generous emotions of the heart, and engaged in the discharge of most of the social and domestic duties, he disgraced not his assumed title of an apostle of God. With all that simplicity which is so natural to a great mind, he performed the humbler offices whose homeliness it would be idle to conceal with pompous diction; even while Lord of Arabia, he mended his own shoes and coarse woollen garments, milked the ewes, swept the hearth, and kindled the fire.[221]

Muhammad could have assumed control over vast amounts of territory and become hell-bent purely on cementing and consolidating his power. But he preferred the simple, austere life instead, despite the success which came his way. He was living in a part of Arabia which was commercially thriving and all the pleasures of this world were easily accessible to him. Yet he had the moral strength and discipline to resist these temptations. This could have been due to his belief and the belief of prophets before him that too much luxury was the enemy of genuine spirituality. Until his very last moments on this earth, Muhammad (ﷺ) preferred the frugal life and never strayed from it. In the words of K.S. Ramkrishna Rao:

After the fall of Makkah, more than one million square miles of land lay at his feet. Lord of Arabia, he mended his own shoes and coarse woolen garments, milked the goats, swept the earth, kindled the fire and attended the other menial offices of the family. The entire town of Madinah where he lived grew in wealth in the later

> *days of his life. Everywhere there was gold and silver in plenty and yet in those days of prosperity many weeks would elapse without a fire being kindled in the hearth of the king of Arabia; his food being dates and water. His family would go hungry many nights successively because they could not get anything to eat in the evening. He slept on no soft bed but on a palm mat, after a long busy day to spend most of his night in prayer, often bursting into tears before his Creator to grant him strength to discharge his duties. As the reports go, his voice would get choked with weeping and it would appear as if a cooking pot was on fire and boiling had commenced. On the very day of his death his only assets were a few coins, a part of which went to satisfy a debt and the rest was given to a needy person who came to his house for charity. The clothes in which he breathed his last breath had many patches. The house from where light had spread to the world was in darkness because there was no oil in the lamp. Circumstance changed, but the Prophet of God did not. In victory or in defeat, in power or in adversity, in affluence or in indigence, he is the same man, disclosed the same character. Like all the ways and laws of God, Prophets of God are unchangeable.*[222]

Prophet Muhammad's lifestyle was similar to that of his fellows. At the wedding of the Prophet's disciple Ali, the feast, the clothing, the utensils etc., were very simple. Washington Irving observes:

> *A more reliable account states that the wedding feast was of dates and olives; that the nuptial couch was a sheep-skin; that the portion of the bride consisted of two skirts, one head-tire, two silver armlets, one leathern pillow stuffed with palm-leaves, one beaker or drinking cup, one hand mill, two large jars for water, and one pitcher. All this was in unison with the simplicity of Arab housekeeping, and with the circumstances of the married couple; and to raise the dowry required of him, Ali, it is said, had to sell several camels and some shirts of mail. The style of living of the prophet himself was not superior to that of his disciple.*[223]

Prophet Muhammad (ﷺ) lived a very simple life. Being a Prophet, a leader and a governor, he could lead the life of an aristocrat, but he was the opposite of all of these. Washington Irving notices:

> *He was sober and abstemious in his diet, and a rigorous observer of fasts. He indulged in no magnificence of apparel, the ostentation of a petty mind; neither was his simplicity in dress affected; but the result of a real disregard to distinction from so trivial a source. His garments were sometimes of wool; sometimes of the striped cotton of Yemen, and were often patched.*[224]

Pierce De Lacy Johnstone says that simplicity was a great attribute of Prophet Muhammad (ﷺ) which helped him solve huge problems. His way of dealing with people was the same whether they were a socially well positioned man, a child or a slave:

> *He visited the sick, followed every bier he met, accepted even a slave's invitation to dinner, mended his own clothes, waited on himself. Never was he first to withdraw his hand from another's, nor to turn away ere the other had turned. His hand was the most generous, his heart the most courageous, his tongue the most truthful; staunchest was he of protectors, and sweetest in conversation; and he inspired all men with awe and reverence. He was taciturn of habit, yet playful with children but not given to jesting.*[225]

Simplicity was key to Prophet Muhammad(ﷺ)'s life, his popularity and success with others. He never distanced himself from the rest of the society. Dr Samuel Johnson maintains:

> *His purely historical character, his simple humanity, claiming to be a man among men, his intense realism avoiding all mystical remoteness; the thoroughly democratic and universal form under which his idea of divine monarchy led him to conceive the relation of man, the force of ethical appeal all affiliate Muhammad with the modern world.*[226]

Saviour of Humanity

George Bernard Shaw, Irish playwright and a co-founder of the London School of Economics, affirms that the strength of Islam lies in its dynamism. Unlike other belief systems, the religion propagated by Prophet Muhammad (ﷺ) is very versatile and can adapt itself to any context, time and period in history. As a result, it appeals to all, irrespective of where and when it is being taught and implemented. According to Shaw, the age-old myths about Prophet Muhammad (ﷺ) are far from the truth. He goes as far as to view Prophet Muhammad (ﷺ) as a salvation to mankind. He continues by suggesting that any of the dictatorships prevailing in the world would be corrected and led to a just and peaceful path, if a man like Prophet Muhammad (ﷺ) was to lead it from the front. Shaw believes that there was nothing to prevent a warm reception and adoption of Islam in the modern age:

> *I have always held the religion of Muhammad in high estimation because of its wonderful vitality. It is the only religion which appears to me to possess that assimilating capacity to the changing phase of existence which can make itself appeal to every age. I have studied him – the wonderful man, and in my opinion far from being an anti-Christ, he must be called the Saviour of Humanity.*[227]

One of the main factors which led Prophet Muhammad (ﷺ) to victory was his teaching to his army and the companions. He always advised people not to deceive others, to have pity for children, the sick, women, orphans, the helpless and the disabled. and when fighting a war not to damage any houses, property or agricultural products. Prophet Muhammad (ﷺ) also advised his people to honour the clauses of any treaty, and behave well towards worshippers and their churches. His successors also guided their followers with the teachings of the Prophet.

Raymond Le Rouge, a French author, reiterates the above statement, saying that Prophet Muhammad was a man of peace and he preached peace to his followers. He taught them to have pity for the poor, woman, children, oppressed, helpless etc:

> *"Do not use frauds nor deceptions", said Muhammad to his soldiers. "Do not kill children. When you fight against the army of an enemy in his own territory, do not oppress the peaceful inhabitants of the country. Spare weak women. Have pity on suckling infants and the sick. Do not destroy the houses, do not overrun the fields. Do not devastate the orchards; do not cut down the date palm trees." And after him, his successor Abu Bakr guided his chiefs advising, "Do not oppress the populace, do not provoke them unnecessarily. Be good and just: success will be your recompense. When you encounter the enemy, attack him valorously. If you come out victorious from the battle, do not kill the women nor the children, spare the fields and houses. If you conclude a treaty, keep its clauses. In Christian countries you will encounter on the route holy men who serve God in the churches and monasteries. Do not molest them; do not destroy their churches nor their monasteries" ... Such are the words, never heard before, words which resounded in the 7th century, from the courtyard of the Mosque of Madinah.*[228]

Like Le Rouge, David George Hogarth, an English archeologist, author and the keeper of the Ashmolean Museum, admired the characteristics of Prophet Muhammad (ﷺ), noting that his daily habits have become standard behaviour to the present day. In comparison to other founders of religion, he has been unique and second to none:

> *Serious or trivial, his daily behaviour has instituted a canon which millions observe this day with conscious mimicry. No one regarded by any section of the human race as Perfect Man has been imitated so minutely. The conduct of the Founder of Christianity has not so governed the ordinary life of His followers. Moreover, no Founder of a religion has been left on so solitary an eminence as the Muslim Apostle.*[229]

Annemarie Schimmel, a German author, Orientalist and former

professor at Harvard University, describes the tremendous qualities of Prophet Muhammad (ﷺ). The most laudable of his qualities was his humility and kindness. He was very friendly with his followers and always smiled, filling them with great delight.[230]

Many scholars have admired the Prophet(ﷺ) because of his care and kindness for the weak. The Prophet(ﷺ) is said to have never beaten or ill-treated his servants or any of his wives.[231]

Schimmel goes on to say that Prophet Muhammad (ﷺ) had a well balanced form of kindness towards all. If anyone asked for any help, he never sent the person off without providing some support, or at least a pleasant word.[232]

Schimmel narrates a story regarding an Arab Bedouin who happened to visit the Prophet (ﷺ) and stayed as a guest overnight. Owing to eating too much, he had an upset stomach and he made the linen wet. He was ashamed of himself but left secretly before the dawn. However, he came back to collect his amulet which he had forgotten and found the Prophet (ﷺ) cleaning the room with his own hands. The Bedouin, who was till then a disbelieving idolater, was overwhelmed and embraced Islam.[233]

John Adair brings out the simplicity of the Prophet (ﷺ) who helped build his own mud-brick home, which that looked no better than any nomad's:

> *In Madinah, Muhammad lived in the long, low, mud-brick house with open windows with a palm-leaf roof that he had helped to build with his own hands. It was more of a Bedouin tent than a town house.*[234]

The Prophet (ﷺ) never liked to have a seat reserved for him when he attended a meeting. He also told his people that standing to show respect should be done only to honour humankind as a whole, and not an individual:

> *Muhammad would never allow a seat to be reserved for him when attending a meeting but would sit wherever there was an empty place. When men rose to their feet as he walked by, he would ask them to remain standing only if that was a way of showing their*

respect for humankind. If they were standing up to honour him, however, he always asked them to sit down.[235]

Compassion

At the core of Prophet Muhammad's personality and ministry was a humanity and love for all, be they rich or poor, healthy or sick. Maintaining healthy and warm social relations was something he gave priority to, and underlying this was compassion and mercy for others.

David De Santillan pays tribute to Prophet Muhammad (ﷺ) thus:

> *The prophet of Islam was a man with deepest human feelings and his heart always beat in unison with the suffered and the affected. Apart from all those things which he preached to his followers he said some golden and charming words with regard to neighborly relations. 'Be kind to your neighbor. Draw the veil over him. Avoid injury to him, look to him with kindness. If you see him doing evil, forgive him. If you see him doing good to you, proclaim your thankfulness'. These are words to be treasured and the Man who said them should be weighed in gold.*[236]

Dr Leitner remarks that to know about Prophet Muhammad (ﷺ) and his religion it is important to have some knowledge of the Arabic language, and sympathy is a vital element of knowledge. He claimed that the hostile Orientalist Sir William Muir, without having the knowledge of Arabic or any "sympathy", had made serious misjudgments about Prophet Muhammad (ﷺ) and his religion. Dr Leitner observes:

> *My special knowledge of Muhammadanism began in a mosque school at Constantinople in 1854, where I learnt considerable portions of the Qur'an by heart. I have associated with Muhammadans of different sects in Turkey, India and elsewhere, and have studied Arabic, the language in which their sacred literature is written. I may at once point out that without a*

knowledge of Arabic it is impossible to exercise any influence on the Muhammadan mind, but I would add that there is something better than mere knowledge, and that is sympathy: sympathy is the key to the meaning of knowledge – that which breathes life into what otherwise would be dead bones. There are instances of eminent scholars who, for want of sympathy, have greatly misjudged Muhammadanism. Sir William Muir, for example, has been led into very serious mistakes in dealing with this religion.[237]

Despite the fact that Muir was hostile to and critical of Prophet Muhammad (ﷺ), in his book *Life of Mahomet*, he admired him for his character and praised the way he dealt with others. Muir claimed that after Christianity, Prophet Muhammad (ﷺ) and Islam must be given the credit for awakening a religious fervour among people. Prophet Muhammad (ﷺ) and his followers had to endure considerable hardship in order for their message to prevail. The message was multidimensional, from promoting the oneness of God to encouraging brotherhood with equity and justice. Muir states:

For few and simple were the precepts of Muhammad. His teaching had wrought a marvellous and mighty work. Never since the days when the primitive Christianity startled the world from its sleep and waged moral combat with heathenism had men seen the like arousing of spiritual life, the like faith that suffered sacrifices and took joyfully the spoiling of goods for conscience's sake. Muhammad brought an end to idol worship. He preached Monotheism and infinite Mercy of God, human brotherhood, care of the orphan, emancipation of slaves, forbidding of wine. No religion achieved as much success as Islam did.[238]

Role Model

For Muslims, Prophet Muhammad (ﷺ) is the ultimate role model and is worthy of emulation in all spheres of life. Following the Prophet Muhammad (ﷺ) is a precondition for loving God, as ordained in the Qur'an. Such is the status of Muhammad (ﷺ) in the sight of God and the Muslims, who are required by faith to hold Prophet Muhammad (ﷺ) dearer to themselves than their own family members.[239]

One of the strong elements of the character of Muhammad (ﷺ) was to endure suffering and mistreatment from others without seeking revenge. He rather considered that the people were not aware of the wrong they were doing. However, he always cared and prayed for them. The Indian writer Dr N.K. Singh says:

> *People threw rubbish on his body and showered abuses. One particular lady adopted a novel technique: as the Prophet passed in front of her house every day, she threw rubbish, collected in her house, right on his body. This became such a regular practice that one day when rubbish was not thrown on him; he wanted to know the reason for it. On enquiry, he learnt that the old lady was sick. He then went into the hollow, sat by the bedside of the lady, consoled her and prayed for her early recovery.*[240]

It's interesting to note that Prophet Muhammad (ﷺ) did not define victory in terms of material success and military conquest. Rather, his mission was dedicated to winning the hearts and minds of his people. Love and compassion were essential hallmarks of his prophethood. The real proof that Prophet Muhammad (ﷺ) was not a war-hungry conqueror was that he insisted on the principle of non-compulsion in religion, and this teaching was practised by the many Muslim rulers and armies throughout history. As Singh notes:

> *The Prophet Muhammad's ultimate 'Victory' was great victory of love-force, heralded in Sura An-Nasr; and the memorable declaration contained in the Sura Al-Madinah verse is his supreme message of love and peace to mankind—the message of Islam: the*

Last Testament. Prophet's Message of Islam of non-violence and Truth and peace, soon reached the distant corners of the World — Spain, Africa, India, China, Russia and far beyond. No Army was ever dispatched for the propagation of Islam in these lands. What a miracle indeed! There is no compulsion (force) in religion, was the clarion call of Islam.[241]

There is a rational aspect of Islam which is a prerequisite for its adoption. As far as Prophet Muhammad (ﷺ) is concerned, his conduct is exemplary. He is especially known for his emotional resilience and discipline. Despite being the victim of persecution, he never resorted to senseless violence to accomplish his aims as he strove for his rights. Dr Singh claims:

With such broad concepts of religion, a Muslim cannot afford to be violent. Above all, Islam is a simple and scientific religion, which has to be understood before it is accepted. The life of the Prophet (may God's blessings be on him) is an illustrious model for all Muslims to emulate. He has shown the greatest restraint in the preaching and practice of Islam. His life in Makkah was full of examples where he suffered without a protest. Prophet Muhammad (ﷺ) was subject to many hardships and personal injuries while he was preaching Islam in Makkah. His reaction to these was nothing short of the true exposition of non-violence.[242]

Having conquered Makkah, Prophet Muhammad (ﷺ) had every opportunity to obtain revenge for all the sufferings, difficulties and pain he had received from the Makkan opponents, but he remained calm. Not only did he refrain from taking revenge, but he also ensured security for them all. He took no pride in his position or his achievements in life. British writer the Reverend Bosworth Smith asks all to read the story of how Prophet Muhammad (ﷺ) conquered Makkah, if someone desires to know about the greatness of Prophet Muhammad (ﷺ). He notes:

Now would have been the moment to gratify his ambition, to satiate his lust, to glut his revenge. Is there anything of the kind?

Read the account of the entry of Mohammed into Makkah, side by side with that of Marius or Sulla into Rome. Compare all the attendant circumstances, the outrages that preceded, and the use made by each of his recovered power, and we shall then be in a position better to appreciate the magnanimity and moderation of the Prophet of Arabia. There were no proscription lists, no plunder, no wanton revenge. The chief blots in his fame are not after his undisputed victory, but during his years of chequered warfare at Madinah, and, such as they are, are distributed very evenly over the whole of that time.[243]

Although Muhammad (ﷺ) assumed authority over his people and the religious institutions, and in this sense combined the functions of statesmanship with clerical rule, he did not command a huge following like the personalities mentioned above. Muhammad (ﷺ) did not possess the formidable military prowess, security apparatus or revenue of eminent statesmen throughout history and in this sense his claim to divine rule has the most credence. The influence he exerted was astonishing, considering that it was devoid of all the accessories and details which accompany the power of others. Muhammad (ﷺ) was not seeking status, opulence or honorific titles, which many in his position have become smitten by. He was content with whatever he had and lived an austere, understated life, brimming with modesty. Bosworth Smith adds:

Head of the State as well as of the Church, he was Caesar and Pope in one; but he was Pope without the Pope's pretensions, and Caesar without the legions of Caesar. Without a standing army, without a body guard, without a palace, without a fixed revenue, if ever any man had the right to say that he ruled by a right Divine, it was Mohammed; for he had all the power without its instruments and without its supports. He rose superior to the titles and ceremonies, the solemn trifling, and the proud humility of court etiquette. To hereditary kings, to princes born in the purple, these things are, naturally enough, as the breath of life; but those who ought to have known better, even self-made rulers, and those the foremost in the files of time – a Caesar, a Cromwell, a Napoleon – have been

> *unable to resist their tinsel attractions. Mohammed was content with the reality, he cared not for the dressings of power. The simplicity of his private life was in keeping with his public life.*[244]

Sir William Muir observes that Prophet was so kindhearted that he was easily moved by the sufferings of any people and always stood beside them:

> *He was a good friend, "kind and tender," says Sir William Muir, "weeping with those who wept, and thus bound to his person the hearts and lives of all around him ... as well as those who heard of his self-denying offices of love and friendship"; but where the Faith was at stake, he spared none, and was often misled by his supposed "inspirations." In a marvellous degree he united the peculiar excellences of the Christian and the pagan.*[245]

Annemarie Schimmel admired the personality of Prophet Muhammad (ﷺ). In her words,

> *The personality of Muhammad is indeed, besides the Koran, the center of the Muslims' life.*[246]

The fact that Prophet Muhammad (ﷺ) would spend long periods without eating his fill is a testimony to his austere living. Frugality was essential to his prophetic mission, as society during his time was laden with examples of wasteful indulgence. He would never overindulge and was very disciplined regarding food. He would often help his wife prepare the meal. Washington Irving highlights that Prophet Muhammad (ﷺ) behaved the same way towards those who were known, unknown, friends, and relatives, rich or poor. He paid attention to all. A servant who had worked for him since he was eight testified that he always kept his temper under great control. According to Irving,

> *In his private dealings he was just. He treated friends and strangers, the rich and poor, the powerful and the weak, with equity, and was beloved by the common people for the affability with which he*

> *received them, and listened to their complaints. He was naturally irritable, but had brought his temper under great control, so that even in the self-indulgent intercourse of domestic life he was kind and tolerant. "I served him from the time I was eight years old," said his servant Anas, "and he never scolded me for anything, though things were spoiled by me".*[247]

R.V.C. Bodley wrote in his book *The Messenger* that Prophet Muhammad's tremendous persona, simplicity and kindness were at the heart of his very being. He was wise and inspirational and showed a great degree of compassion for the less fortunate. In Bodley's words,

> *My attempt, has been to present Mohammed as he really was – an Arab like many I knew in the desert; a man of simple tastes, but of great personality, with the good of his people at heart; a man who was inspired, but thought out all he did logically; who had tolerance for the weakness of men and women, because he was often weak himself. Not a God by any means.*[248]

Bodley wrote that perhaps Prophet Muhammad (ﷺ)'s most tremendous feat was being able to achieve what he did within the confines of human capabilities. After all, he was not angelic – the only supernatural attribute that can be attributed to him was that of prophethood. The Qur'an and the prophetic traditions repeatedly point out that Prophet Muhammad (ﷺ) was a human being like others and was not beyond reproach, and was not entitled to any special or exclusive dispensation, simply on account of being a Prophet, because ultimately, he was a man:

> *Mohammed's unique position in religious history is due to the fact that he inspired all he did without being a saint or an angel, without having any attributes which were not strictly human. Outside his tremendous personality, he had nothing in life to distinguish him from other Moslems—neither titles, nor riches, nor a different mode of living. The mosque in Madinah, like the mosques in Damascus and Fez and Delhi, are as well-favoured*

works of art as any ecclesiastical architecture of the world, but they have nothing in common with Mohammed, the son of Abdullah and his wife Amina.[249]

Despite all his opportunities, Prophet Muhammad (ﷺ) lived the life of a very simple man. The world has countless examples of kings, queens, other rulers and generals who lived lives of great opulence. But although Prophet Muhammad (ﷺ), had many responsibilities, and great position and honour in the nation, he was just the opposite. He did not have a palace; he lived in a cottage with his wives. He did not have support for his domestic needs; he maintained everything on his own. His food and lifestyle were just like those of an ordinary man. Whatever little food his family owned was shared with others. His simplicity bears a great example in the history, as Bosworth Smith illustrates:

His ordinary dress was plain, even to coarseness; yet he was fastidious in arranging it to the best advantage. He was fond of ablutions, and fonder still of perfumes; and he prided himself on the neatness of his hair, and the pearly whiteness of his teeth. His life was simple in all its details. He lived with his wives in a row of humble cottages, separated from one another by palm branches, cemented together with mud. He would kindle the fire, sweep the floor, and milk the goats himself. Ayesha tells us that he slept upon a leathern mat, and that he mended his clothes, and even clouted his shoes, with his own hand. For months together, Ayesha is also our authority for saying that he did not get a sufficient meal. The little food that he had was always shared with those who dropped in to partake of it. Indeed, outside the Prophet's house was a bench or gallery, on which were always to be found a number of the poor who lived entirely on the Prophet's generosity, and were hence called the people of the bench. His ordinary food was dates and water, or barley bread; milk and honey were luxuries of which he was fond, but which he rarely allowed himself.[250]

The historian Edward Gibbon, like Bosworth Smith, says that Prophet Muhammad (ﷺ) did all his housekeeping himself and spent his days like an ordinary person. Many a time he did not have anything to eat or drink. Gibbon notes:

> *The good sense of Mahomet despised the pomp of royalty; the apostle of God submitted to the menial offices of the family; he kindled the fire, swept the floor, milked the ewes, and mended with his own hands his shoes and his woolen garment. Disdaining the penance and merit of a hermit, he observed, without effort or vanity, the abstemious diet of an Arab and a soldier. On solemn occasions he feasted his companions with rustic and hospitable plenty; but in his domestic life, many weeks would elapse without a fire being kindled on the hearth of the prophet.*[251]

Although Muhammad (ﷺ) had quickly won many military victories, this did not instil in him any feelings of pride or vanity. This was proof that his military endeavours were not motivated by any egotistical reasons. Even at the height of his power, Muhammad (ﷺ) maintained a very frugal inward and outward manner, and this remained with him from the time of his persecution all the way up to the point where he and his followers came to power. Washington Irving wrote in his book *The Life of Muhammad*:

> *His military triumphs awakened no pride nor vainglory as they would have done had they been effected by selfish purposes. In the time of his greatest power he maintained the same simplicity of manner and appearance as in the days of his adversity. So far from affecting regal state, he was displeased if, on entering a room, any unusual testimonial of respect was shown to him.*[252]

In her book *And Muhammad is His Messenger: The Veneration of the Prophet in Islamic Piety* Harvard University Professor Annemarie Schimmel included a chapter titled 'Prophet Muhammad (ﷺ) the Beautiful Model'. In it she notes that the Prophet was an ideal model in every sphere of life, be it at home, abroad, in work or during war. He was an example of moral perfection.[253]

The celebrated author John Alden Williams argues that Prophet

Muhammad (ﷺ) was the founder of the religion, a governor of state and also a role model:

The Prophet is not only the founder and legislator of the community: he is the model for Muslims.[254]

Peaceful

Dr E.B. Hocking speaks highly of the religion of Islam, preached by Prophet Muhammad (ﷺ). The manners, the behaviour, the calmness, the peacefulness and the friendliness etc. whatsoever Prophet Muhammad (ﷺ) taught deserve higher recognition in comparison with others. Dr Hocking said:

All religions, save the word of Muhammad, are broken boats. They cannot take humanity to the shore of serenity.[255]

Ruth Cranston, an American author, lecturer, and biographer claims that Prophet Muhammad (ﷺ) never instigated any violence, fights or killings. He never initiated any conflict with anybody. The battles in which he was involved were fought to protect himself or his people. He always took the defensive role to guard himself. Whenever he was required to fight for his existence in self-defence, he followed the technique, methodology and the technology of the day.[256]

Manners

Gibbon tells us how the good moral character, the manners and the greatness of the religion he preached made Prophet Muhammad (ﷺ) victorious in large parts of the globe throughout his life and beyond, leading even to the fall of the Eastern Roman Empire:

After pursuing above six hundred years the fleeting Caesars of

Constantinople and Germany, I now descend, in the reign of Heraclius, on the eastern borders of the Greek monarchy. While the state was exhausted by the Persian war, and the church was distracted by the Nestorian and Monophysite sects, Mahomet, with the sword in one hand and the Koran in the other, erected his throne on the ruins of Christianity and of Rome. The genius of the Arabian prophet, the manners of his nation, and the spirit of his religion, involve the causes of the decline and fall of the Eastern empire; and our eyes are curiously intent on one of the most memorable revolutions, which have impressed a new and lasting character on the nations of the globe.[257]

Davenport tells us that Prophet Muhammad (ﷺ) in his youth had beautiful physical attributes. His behaviour, way of talking, moving, looking, etc. pleased others. In Davenport's words,

At this time Mohammed was in the pride of manhood his figure was commanding, his aspect majestic, his features regular and most expressive, his eyes black and piercing, his nose slightly aquiline, his mouth well formed and furnished with pearly teeth, while his cheeks were ruddy with robust health. Art had imparted to his naturally black flowing hair and beard a lighter chestnut hue. His captivating smile, his rich and sonorous voice, the graceful dignity of his gestures, the apparent frankness and heartiness of his manner, gained him the favourable attention of all whom he addressed.[258]

The American author Elsa Marston states that people remembered Prophet Muhammad (ﷺ) as an understanding, kind, soft-hearted man who had a lot of respect and love for his companions, children and animals too:

Muhammad was remembered more, however, for his sympathetic, kind, and gentle nature. He treated his followers with courtesy and respect. Children, too, were drawn to him, and he loved playing with them.[259]

Washington Irving wrote in his book *The Life of Muhammad* that Prophet Muhammad's manners were peaceful and he was always level-headed. He had a sense of humour but was serious and distinguished and always wore a sweet smile.

> *His deportment, in general, was calm and equable; he sometimes indulged in pleasantry, but more commonly was grave and dignified, though he is said to have possessed a smile of captivating sweetness.*[260]

The British author Magsie Hamilton Little acknowledges that Prophet Muhammad (ﷺ) achieved the reputation for his character by dint of being trustworthy and honest. Many studies reveal that he was gentle and polite to all creatures, human or animal. It is a measure of his personality. The Prophet's manners were consistently kind towards children and animals.[261]

Respect

Edward Gibbon asserted that the great personality of Prophet Muhammad (ﷺ) was a divine gift. Members of the public were amazed even before he started speaking. They took his side. People respected his command, the topics he spoke about and the way he delivered his speeches. His body language was expressive. His physical attributes made people show regard to him and accept what he said. He was brave and always clear about what he should do and when. In Gibbon's words:

> *Before he spoke, the orator engaged on his side the affections of a public or private audience. They applauded his commanding presence, his majestic aspect, his piercing eye, his gracious smile, his flowing beard, his countenance that painted every sensation of the soul, and his gestures that enforced each expression of the tongue. In the familiar offices of life he scrupulously adhered to the grave and ceremonious politeness of his country: his respectful attention to the*

> *rich and powerful was dignified by his condescension and affability to the poorest citizens of Makkah: the frankness of his manner concealed the artifice of his views; and the habits of courtesy were imputed to personal friendship or universal benevolence. His memory was capacious and retentive; his wit easy and social; his imagination sublime; his judgment clear, rapid, and decisive. He possessed the courage both of thought and action; and, although his designs might gradually expand with his success, the first idea which he entertained of his divine mission bears the stamp of an original and superior genius...*[262]

Gibbon describes the simplicity of the character of Prophet Muhammad (ﷺ). He lived the life of a very simple man, doing his chores with his own hands. He never showed any pride; he ate the sparse diet of a simple Arab or a soldier:

> *The good sense of Mahomet despised the pomp of royalty: the apostle of God submitted to the menial offices of the family: he kindled the fire, swept the floor, milked the ewes, and mended with his own hands his shoes and his woolen garment. Disdaining the penance and merit of a hermit, he observed, without effort or vanity, the abstemious diet of an Arab and a soldier. The greatest success of Mohammad's life was affected by sheer moral force without the stroke of a sword.*[263]

Dr Daniel Peterson claims that in all respects Muhammad (ﷺ) even today can be regarded as a man with extraordinary personality who always made everyone felt that all his attention and care were reserved for that individual. He had deep respect for others.[264]

Qualities

William Montgomery Watt reports that Islam spread by leaps and bounds even beyond the Arabian lands. However, that spread was possible only because of the amazing qualities that Prophet Muhammad (ﷺ) possessed. Otherwise, such expansion could have never taken place.[265]

Davenport claims that Prophet Muhammad (ﷺ) was gifted with a sharp memory. He spoke very good Arabic with clear pronunciation. Davenport states:

> *He possessed talents of a superior order—his perception was quick and active, his memory capacious and retentive, his imagination lively and daring, his judgment clear and perspicuous, his courage dauntless, and whatever may be the opinion of some as to the sincerity of his convictions, his tenacity of purpose in the pursuit of the great object of his life, and his patient endurance, cannot but extort the admiration of all. His natural eloquence was enhanced by the use of the purest dialect of Arabia, and adorned by the charm of a graceful elocution.*[266]

Prophet Muhammad (ﷺ) was well known for his excellent character and extraordinary qualities, which won over public and private audiences alike. His respect for the rich as well as his affability with the poor was amazing. Edward Gibbon illustrates this:

> *Mohammed was distinguished by the beauty of his person, an outward gift which is seldom despised, except by those to whom it has been refused. Before he spoke, the orator engaged on his side the affections whether of a public or a private audience. They applauded his commanding presence, his majestic aspect, his piercing eye, his gracious smile, his flowing beard, his countenance which painted every sensation of his soul, and the gestures that enforced each expression of the tongue. In the familiar offices of life, he scrupulously adhered to the grave and ceremonious politeness of his country; his respectful attention to the rich and powerful was dignified by his condescension and affability to the poorest citizen of*

> *Makkah; the frankness of his manner concealed the artifice of his views, and the habits of courtesy were imputed to personal friendship or universal benevolence; his memory was capacious and retentive, his wit easy and social, his imagination sublime, his judgment clear, rapid and decisive. He possessed the courage both of thought and action; and although his designs might gradually expand with success, the first idea which he entertained of his divine mission bears the stamp of an original and superior genius.*[267]

Rowland George Allanson-Winn, 5th Baron Headley, was a British civil engineer by profession. He said that Prophet Muhammad (ﷺ) had very good qualities which were never seen in any other single individual in history:

> *No one can claim the quality of mercy who has never had anyone at his mercy, and there is no character in history which can be so safely held up for inspection and illustration of this particular quality as the Holy Prophet Mahomet.*[268]

R.V.C. Bodley points out that Prophet Muhammad (ﷺ) had certain qualities which pleased all. His smile was very charming and he never moved his hand off first from shaking hands with anybody. He maintained good relations with his friends. He loved children very much who flocked around him when he was walking. He loved animals and taught the followers to treat them well.[269]

Disciplined Character

Muhammad was not the type of person who would have others attending to his duties. He was a principled, disciplined character who would never place an undue burden on others and always dealt with his personal matters with the highest integrity. Not only could this be seen in his everyday routine, but also in his attire. Simplicity was something he would cling on to throughout his life and he never insisted on pompous living. Sir William Muir elaborates:

> *A patriarchal simplicity pervaded his life. Custom was to do everything for himself. If he gave alms he would place it with his own hand in that of the petitioner. He aided his wives in their household duties; he mended his own clothes; he tied up the goats; he even cobbled his sandals. His ordinary dress consisted of plain white cotton stuff; but on high and festive occasions, he wore garments of fine linen, striped or dyed in red. He never reclined at meals. He ate with his fingers; and when he had finished, he would lick them before he wiped his hands... Mahomet, with his wives, lived in a row of low and homely cottages built of unbaked bricks; the apartments were separated by walls of palm branches rudely daubed with mud; curtains of leather, or of black hair-cloth, supplied the place of doors and windows. His abode was to all easy of access.*[270]

Magsie Hamilton Little affirms that the aura of the Prophet Muhammad (ﷺ) and the influence he exerted on his contemporaries and followers was astounding. The charisma and appeal which he generated while alive was so great that long centuries after his death it is as if his presence and influence has never escaped from the Muslim conscience. Despite Prophet Muhammad's status as the leader and spiritual instructor of Muslims, he did not exploit his power and was never seen in domineering and bossy terms. The obedience which he commanded was not because people feared his punishment but out of love and affinity for the way he was.[271]

Pierce De Lacy Henry Johnstone marvels that even after 1400 years of the death of Prophet Muhammad (ﷺ) the followers of the religion far and wide are still very devoted to it. The main strength behind this is the power of the character of Prophet Muhammad (ﷺ):

> *It is nearly thirteen hundred years since the Prophet of Arabia died, but the religion which he founded still rules the hearts and lives of nearly one-sixth of the human race. To outward appearance Islam is one, though inwardly it is torn into many sects and schools. The*

magnetism of its founder's personality has endured through all generations, and the short symbol of his faith has lost none of its power.[272]

Patience

Prophet Muhammad (ﷺ) was a man of great patience. The saying 'Patience is a virtue' was reflected in his character. In spreading Islam, the struggles and persecution he he faced could not dissuade him from what he preached but made him more resolute. The lesson of 'No pain, no gain' is learnt through the degree of patience he had shown when preaching the message of Islam. According to Dr N.K. Singh,

> *When the Prophet went to the town of Taif and started preaching Islam, he was chased with stones by the people of Taif. He was badly hurt; bleeding, he fell down in a swoon. But he never scolded his abusers nor hated them. He calmly prayed that God lead them to the right path and pardon them as they did not know what they were doing. He felt that someday light would dawn — if not on them, then at least on their progeny — and they would accept the Truth. As such, he refused to curse these potential Muslims.*[273]

On many occasions Prophet Muhammad (ﷺ) had the opportunity to use military might to besiege a population, but he was above such ruthless ways of doing things and opted for peace at all times. His behaviour remains a shining example of how strength and numbers ought to be used without resorting to violence. Dr N.K. Singh continues:

> *The conquest of Makkah is unique in history, and is a glowing example of non-violent war. With an army ten thousand strong, the Prophet marched on Makkah. There was no opposition, no resistance, practically no blood was shed, and only handfuls were taken prisoners. The mode of entrance of the conqueror into the city is a lesson of humility and grace.*[274]

Muhammad was very passionate about changing and bettering the lot of his people. As far as his personal attributes were concerned, they were those which humanity generally considers the most desirable.

Dr Marcus Dods, a Scottish biblical scholar and minister of the Free Church of Scotland, stresses that Muhammad was a prophet who had vital qualities, which a prophet should have. He explains:

But is Muhammad in no sense a Prophet? Certainly he had two of the most important characteristics of the prophetic order. He saw truth about God which his fellowmen did not see, and he had an irresistible inward impulse to publish the Truth. In respect of the latter qualification, Muhammad may stand comparison with the most courageous of the heroic prophets of Israel. For the truth's sake he risked his life, he suffered daily persecutions for years, and eventually banishment, the loss of property, of the good-will of his fellow-citizens, and the confidence of his friends; he suffered in short as much as any man can suffer short of death, which he only escaped by flight and yet he unflinchingly proclaimed his message. No bride, treat or inducement could silence him. "Though they array against me the sun on the left, I cannot renounce my purpose." And it was this persistency, this belief in his call, to proclaim the Unity of God which was the making of Islam. Other men have been monotheists in the midst of idolaters but no other man has founded a strong and enduring monotheistic religion. The distinction in his case was his resolution that other men should believe.[275]

A noted Indian leader, Lala Har Dayal, testifies to the simplicity and patience of the Prophet of Islam:

Howsoever we may Judge, the character of this Man is a precious heritage for humanism. We can learn from his inspiring example. He was always very abstemious in his habits and contented himself with simple food, clothes and lodging. He was entirely free from avarice. He risked his life for his faith and had to flee from his native town. Rightly do the Muslims date their history from that night when Muhammad and Abu Bakr hid in the cave on the way from Makkah to Madinah. The Prophet was exemplar of patience and forbearance to the proud, hot tempered Arabs. His sweet patience was indeed his great virtue. His boundless charity and generosity to all flowed from his unworldly heart like a fountain in the Arabian desert. His greatness may be judged by the heroism and enthusiasm of his immediate disciples and the unquenchable vitality of his Movement after so many centuries.[276]

He further states:

Prophet Muhammad mended his own clothes, milked his own goats and waited upon himself. He shared his food, even in times of scarcity, with others. Dates and water were frequently his only food, even when he was the ruler of Arabia. He gave away his money to the poor or for public purposes.[277]

Carlyle further said that a man like Prophet Muhammad (ﷺ) was a man of true character; such a man is *what we call an original man.*[278]

Carlyle, in his speech, claimed that Prophet Muhammad (ﷺ), being born amongst the un-noticed Arabs of his times, guided people from various parts of the world, eventually. The great man had guided all by the heavenly light:

The history of a Nation becomes fruitful, soul-elevating, great, so soon as it believes. These Arabs, the man Muhammad, and that one century, it is not as if a spark had fallen, one spark, on a world of what seemed black unnoticeable sand; but lo, the sand proves explosive powder, blazes heaven-high from Delhi to Granada! I said, the Great Man was always as lightning out of Heaven; the rest of men waited for him like fuel, and then they too would flame.[279]

Part Three:

Honesty:

Truthful

Jawaharlal Nehru was an Indian statesman, a leader in the Indian Independence movement, and the first Prime Minister of independent India. In his book *Glimpses of World History* Nehru talks about Prophet Muhammad (ﷺ), Islam and its influence. He states that the religion of Islam was preached by Prophet Muhammad (ﷺ) who had a simple life and the highest degree of honesty in dealing with all, which contributed to him earning the title of Al-Ameen. His simplicity captured the minds and souls of his people.[280]

M.H. Hyndman, a British author and journalist, highlights that Prophet Muhammad (ﷺ), had a very high level of personal integrity. Because of his extraordinary qualities including honesty, sincerity, trustworthiness, honour, reliability, uprightness, humbleness etc. which worked like a touch stone, whoever came into contact with him was influenced by him. His self-confidence never abated, even when he was losing or suffering at the hands of enemies:

> *Even to-day, with all the details of his early life and subsequent career laid bare by men of our own race, who have studied the whole extraordinary story of the noble Arabian, it is no easy matter to comprehend the character, or to account for the marvellous success of Mohammed in the early part of the seventh century. Never claiming divine powers at any period of his mission, without a single miracle to his name, this very human prophet of God made his first converts in his own family, was able, after almost hopeless failure, to obtain control in his own aristocratic gens, and had such remarkable personal influence over all with whom he was brought into contact that, neither when a poverty-stricken and hunted fugitive, nor at the height of his prosperity, did he ever have to complain of treachery from those who had once embraced his faith.*[281]

Although Christianity had spread over vast territories, it could not resist the urge of co-opting the traditions of the people it conquered. In this sense, Christian theology could be said to have lost some of its staying power, and became somewhat abstract and theoretical. The dramatic overhaul which religion and culture underwent during this period is not so much owing to the success of Christianity, but to that of Islam and in particular, Prophet Muhammad (ﷺ). Prophet Muhammad's honesty and virtuousness were evident from his boyhood. He maintained a pure single life until the age of 25 years, when he married Khadijah (RA) ®. Major General Forlong states:

> *Naturally pious from boyhood, Mahamad had led a pure and single life to the age of twenty-five, when he married a devoted and good woman, aged forty, who had unselfishly befriended him from childhood and amid many troubles.* [282]

The famous Christian missionary and educator C. F. Andrews wrote in his article 'The Third Companion of the Prophet' that wherever we are, God is always with us. He praised the Prophet's teaching, saying that when Prophet Muhammad (ﷺ) and his very close associate Abu Bakr took shelter in a cave, Prophet Muhammad (ﷺ) told Abu Bakr about the presence of the third one with them, and the third Companion was God himself.[283]

By contrast François-Marie Arouet, known as Voltaire, was very hostile towards Prophet Muhammad (ﷺ), his prophethood and revelation, calling Muhammad an imposter and denouncing the revelation as fake (God forbid). Like Voltaire, Diderot, another French philosopher, had a negative opinion of the Prophet (ﷺ). However, Thomas Carlyle, in 1840, highlighted in his lecture, "Heroes and Hero-worship" that those hostile views were just their own reflections whereas 180,000,000 people accepted Islam as a true religion and Prophet Muhammad (ﷺ) as a brilliant guide of their lives. He found it strange to believe the opinions of a vast number of people could be so wrong! Carlyle claimed that the hypothesis that Muhammad was an imposter, fraud, and falsehood revealed the scepticism of the time and was an indicator of ill minds. According to Carlyle, Prophet Muhammad (ﷺ) was sincere, honest and a great man. He was sincere in the truest sense, others did not care for it and lived with false honour. But the life was real to Prophet Muhammad (ﷺ) and seemed extremely magnificent. This type of man was a great man. He would be called an original man, a true messenger of God.[284]

The celebrated British author and barrister Pringle Kennedy points out that the opinions abound throughout history regarding the legacy which Prophet Muhammad (ﷺ) left behind and the overall effects of his preaching and message. Superlatives and pejoratives have been deployed endlessly to capture the personality and character of Prophet Muhammad (ﷺ). But what is undeniable is that his legacy was groundbreaking. If there was ever an instance of the peak of human feats, it would be Prophet Muhammad (ﷺ) and his ministry.[285]

Kennedy goes on to say that whatever and whoever thinks about Prophet Muhammad (ﷺ), undoubtedly he is the brilliant example of what could be done by a single man.[286]

George Sale, a British Orientalist, author and practising solicitor, is best known for his 1734 translation of the Qur'an into English, *The Koran: Commonly called the Al-Koran of Mohammed.* He wrote on the 'Readers page' that, whatever the enemies of Prophet Muhammad (ﷺ) said about him, he could not afford to spare but highlighted the truth regarding the Prophet's charming behaviour, crystal like characteristics, free fair dealings with all, softness for the weak, strong for the injustice etc. Sale observes:

> *The praises due to his real virtues ought not to be denied him; nor can I do otherwise than applaud the candour of the pious and learned Spanhemius [a Dutch theologian] who, though he owned him to have been a wicked impostor, yet acknowledged him to have been richly furnished with natural endowments, beautiful in his person, of a subtle wit, agreeable behaviour, showing liberality to the poor, courtesy to everyone, fortitude against his enemies, and above all a high reverence for the name of God ; severe against the perjured, adulterers, murderers, slanderers, prodigals, covetous, false witnesses, &c., a great preacher of patience, charity, mercy,*

beneficence, gratitude, honouring of parents and superiors, and a frequent celebrator of the divine praises.[287]

Everything about Prophet Muhammad's demeanour suggested a man of simplicity and ease. He was very sociable and would often engage in lighthearted banter with his companions. As a man of integrity, he would never deceive others. Sir William Muir further elucidates:

His humility was shown by his riding upon asses accepting the invitation even of slaves, and when mounted, by his taking another behind him. He would say, "I sit at meals as a servant doeth, and I eat like a servant: for I really am a servant;" and he would sit as one that was always ready to rise. He discouraged (supererogatory) fasting, and works of mortification. When seated with his followers, he would remain long silent at a time. In the Mosque at Madinah, they used to repeat pieces of poetry, and tell stories regarding the incidents that occurred in the days of ignorance, and laugh; and Mahomet, listening to them, would smile at what they said. Mahomet hated nothing more than lying, and whenever he knew that any of his followers had erred in this respect, he would hold himself aloof from them until he was assured of their repentance.[288]

A famous Buddhist monk, Sangthong Phesrisai (Dhamacaro) admires Prophet Muhammad (ﷺ) and says that he was truthful to everybody in the community.

I am sure as a Prophet he was very truthful to himself and to other people around him.[289]

According to Reverend Rupert Hoare (April 2012), a former Dean of Liverpool, UK Cathedral and Chair of the Council of Faiths in Liverpool, UK, Muhammad urged his followers to be fair and trustworthy when dealing with others:

I know him to be a man of faith and trustworthy and who preached the necessity of faith in a merciful God who would reward faithfulness and who required honesty and justice in people's dealings.[290]

R.V.C. Bodley observed that the nature of trade and what was going on in the environment did not have any effect on the Prophet Muhammad's characteristics virtue, piousness, integrity, honesty, and truthfulness. He was known as *Al-Ameen* (trustworthy) from his early life.[291]

Many deduce from the characteristics of Muslims that Prophet Muhammad (ﷺ) would also have demonstrated similar qualities. A link is often made between the positive attributes of Muslims and their personalities with that of Prophet Muhammad(ﷺ)'s. According to Stephen Timms, a British MP:

What I would comment on is what I've seen reflected in Muslims, in the followers of Muhammad whose behaviour I've seen for myself. I see amongst Muslims very good and important qualities which in my view we need more of in our society. I'm thinking of things like truthfulness, that you've mentioned and also having a sense of responsibility, a sense of solidarity of mutual support, patience, compassion. All of those are things I observe amongst Muslims and which I take it to be reflecting the character of the Prophet himself.[292]

A spokesman from a Sikh Temple based in East London affirms that the Prophet was a very religious and honest person. In his words:

I think the prophet was very religious, honest and dedicated believer of God or messenger of God. He was like other prophets. He was verytrustworthy, that's why he had so many followers; no trust no followers.[293]

Learned Pandit Piyuskumar Mehta from Jalaram Hindu Mandir, Greenford, London echoes this view:

Honesty is the basis for every prophet in society. Honesty is the mother of all virtues. I believe Muhammad was a very honest person and I know that he worked as a merchant. Nowadays, businesses are conducted in a wrong way.[294]

Right Honourable Lord Neil Kinnock, the former leader of Labour Party, UK, testifies to Prophet Muhammad's significant role in imparting to his people more than simple religious edification. He positions Prophet Muhammad (ﷺ) as the most senior amongst the Prophets. He states:

These figures were responsible for providing a system of law, conduct and rewards and amongst these Muhammad would have been the most senior among the Prophets.[295]

Bhavin Tailor, an RE teacher at William Ellis School in London, felt that religious personalities should by default possess the principles of integrity and honesty. According to him:

When you think of leaders across religion, honesty and integrity always comes up as one of the first, because they are religious leaders, you expect them to be honest, and you expect them to be an integral part of the society which they originated from and the ones which we learn from now.[296]

Mehri Niknam MBE, Executive Director of the Joseph Interfaith Foundation, Camden, London, says that the integrity with which Prophet Muhammad (ﷺ) was characterised according to many, came from his honest dealings as a merchant and someone very heavily linked with the economic trade of his time. Although it was common for people to barter unscrupulously during his period, Prophet Muhammad (ﷺ) never succumbed to such practices and instead maintained a high level of honour in his exchanges with others:

I was giving a talk last week at an interfaith event organised by MCB at the House of Lords and I referred to this. I said, the Prophet of Islam was known as Muhammad Al-Ameen, (Muhammad the trustworthy one) and why was he called that?

Because for many years he was the leader of major merchandise caravans and in his financial dealings with people of other nations and also other faiths he was honest. Therefore, he came to be known as Muhammad Al-Ameen and that reputation remained with him. Therefore, I have always thought of him as an honest man.[297]

Reverend Thomas O'Brien, Our Lady of the Assumption Church, Tower Hamlets, London stated that Muhammad was a true representative of honest living and an advocate of justice who never sought antagonistic relations:

I believe Muhammad was trustworthy and wished to give God's will for people and saw the structure of faith as the best means of handing on God's will for the people. Muhammad would stand up for justice and speak out. His intent was never to provoke hostilities; rather, his intent was to speak truthfully and justly.[298]

British Conservative MP David Amess dismisses the popular view that Muhammad was bent upon the eradication of other belief systems and sought divisions with others. Amess claims that:

The history has been explained to me that just like God, he is totally honest, peace loving and his emphasis is on us all working together but not in conflict. The idea that Muhammad wants to destroy other religions, I think is nonsense.[299]

Jeremy Corbyn, who became Leader of the Labour Party in 2015, notes that Prophet Muhammad(ﷺ)'s honesty and integrity is observed by many, who suggest that his teachings presented a challenge to the prevailing thoughts and beliefs of his time. At a time when the Christian faith was gaining common currency in the European world, Prophet Muhammad's honest and sincere nature helped him to remain firm in his belief. Corbyn says:

I think he had a high level of integrity and was an honest person who was in some senses challenging the received wisdom at the time because Christianity was beginning to take hold in most of Europe at the time Muhammad was alive and they were themselves the derivation of Judaism up until Christ's time, beginning of the millennia and I think he was an honest person standing up for his beliefs.[300]

Prophet Muhammad's trustworthiness extended to all aspects of his teachings, including the code of conduct he imparted to others and the mutual tolerance and harmony he preached for dealing with non-Muslims. Jeremy Corbyn further states:

He was a person of high integrity and the teachings which include the question of honesty, lifestyle and living, respect for different faiths and people, but above all, it was a message of peace he was giving.[301]

Mike Stygal, Chairman, Camden Interfaith Foundation, London, declares that Prophet Muhammad (ﷺ) was a unifying force in a conflict-ridden Arabia and made a conscious effort to refrain from violence, despite this perception not being popularised in media circles. He says:

I think Muhammad was a man of great integrity who found himself in a very difficult period, with lots of warring factions and people seeking power, and Muhammad was trying to form a strong, respectful community that would listen to the message of Allah. He was trying to do this when there were many different factions who were in combat and who wanted to gain territory, etc. Muhammad's people were being attacked and he had to find the right way of saying you have to defend yourself but not in a way that meant violence for the sake of violence. It was always measured, but this does not come across in the media too often because I think the media does not deal with any faith community fairly. There is a lot of message of peace and accepting people's difference, e.g. there are messages from Muhammad that speak about people who have different religions and it doesn't say go out and convert them, etc.[302]

Stygal notes how the Prophet's trustworthiness was the key for him to establish good relations with others and that Prophet Muhammad (ﷺ) advocated peace during a period which was filled with hostilities. He states:

> *He was a man of incredible integrity in a difficult time and was trying to promote a message of peace in a world that was full of violence. Trustworthiness would have been key for him to prove that his message was true. If you can't show that you are trustworthy, you can't be trusted.*[303]

John Henry Haaren, an American educator and historian, in his *Famous Men of the Middle Ages*, insists that Prophet Muhammad (ﷺ) was an honest man. He never broke promises which he made to anybody:

> *Mohammed was very faithful and honest in all his works. He always spoke the truth and never broke a promise. "I have given my promise," he would say, "and I must keep it." He became so well known in Makkah for being truthful and trustworthy that people gave him the name of El Amin, which means "the truthful".*[304]

William Montgomery Watt, Professor of Arabic and Islamic Studies at the University of Edinburgh, maintains that Prophet Muhammad (ﷺ) had a great degree of fortitude and conviction in his beliefs, which led him to suffer and make sacrifice for the cause. In addition to his conviction was the uprightness of his companions, all of whom supported his call. The idea that Prophet Muhammad (ﷺ) was an impostor simply does not hold true and it is unfortunate that he has not been properly understood in the West.[305]

Encyclopaedia Britannica confirms that the Prophet's honesty and trustworthiness were frequently depicted in earlier studies. According to the Encyclopaedia,

> *[A] mass of detail in the early sources shows that he was an honest and upright man who had gained the respect and loyalty of others who were like-wise honest and upright men.*[306]

David Samuel Margoliouth, an Orientalist, minister of the Church of England and Professor of Arabic at Oxford University points out that the compassion of Prophet Muhammad (ﷺ) encompassed not only the mankind but also all sorts of creatures small or large. He did away with many Arabian superstitions associated with animals:

> *His humanity extended itself to the lower creation. He forbade the employment of living birds as targets for marksmen and remonstrated with those who ill-treated their camels... Foolish acts of cruelty which were connected with old superstitions were swept away by him... No more was a dead man's camel to be tied to his tomb to perish of thirst and hunger. No more was the evil eye to be propitiated by the bleeding of a certain proportion of the herd. No more was the rain to be conjured by tying burning torches to the tails of oxen; ... The manes and tails of horses were not to be cut, nor were asses to be branded.*[307]

Charles Stuart Mills, a British philosopher, political economist and civil servant extolled Prophet Muhammad (ﷺ) in his book, *History of Mohammadanism* saying:

> *Deeply read in the volume of nature, though extremely ignorant of letters, his mind could expand into controversy with the wisest of his enemies or contract itself to the apprehension of meanest of his disciples. His simple eloquence was rendered impressive by a manner of mixed dignity and elegance, by the expression of a countenance where the awfulness of his majesty was so well tempered by an amiable sweetness, that it exerted emotions of veneration and love. He was gifted with that authoritative air or genius which alike influences the learned and commands the illiterate.*[308]

The Scottish author Samuel Pearson Scott thought that the influence exerted by Islam was due to the superior characteristics of Prophet Muhammad (ﷺ):

> *The glories which invest the history of Islam may be entirely derived from the valor, the virtue, the intelligence, the genius, of one man. If this be conceded, the largest measure of credit is due to him who conceived its plan, promoted its impulse, and formulated the rules which insured its success. In any event, if the object of religion be the inculcation of morals, the diminution of evil, the promotion of human happiness, the expansion of the human intellect, if the performance of good works will avail in the great day when mankind shall be summoned to its final reckoning it is neither irreverent nor unreasonable to admit that Muhammad was indeed an Apostle of God.*[309]

William Cooke Taylor, a writer, journalist, historian and anti-Corn Law propagandist paid high tribute to Prophet Muhammad (ﷺ) in the book: *The History of Mohammedanism and its sects.* He declares the Prophet as a friend of the poor:

> *So great was his liberality to the poor that he often left his household unprovided, nor did he content himself with relieving their wants, he entered into conversation with them, and expressed a warm sympathy for their sufferings. He was a firm friend and a faithful ally.*[310]

Dr Gustav Weil, a German Orientalist, wrote about Prophet Muhammad (ﷺ) in his book *History of the Islamic Peoples* that, the Prophet was a man with a very good moral character. Anybody from anywhere had access to him irrespective of social status, colour or race:

> *Muhammad was a shining example to his people. His character was pure and stainless. His house, his dress, his food – they were characterized by a rare simplicity. So unpretentious was he that he would receive from his companions no special mark of reverence, nor would he accept any service from his slave which he could do for himself. He was accessible to all and at all times. He visited the sick and was full of sympathy for all. Unlimited was his benevolence and generosity as also was his anxious care for the welfare of the*

community.[311]

Prophet Muhammad's honest and frank nature can be clearly seen in his role as a mediator of disputes. The fact that he was given a judge's discretion testifies to his trustworthiness. According to the Reverend Stephen Williams, Senior Anglican Chaplain, University Chaplaincy, University of London,

> *I think one of the ways I would answer that question is by using the history of his role almost as a judge in deciding issues between conflicting parties and that therefore, if you go to somebody to whom people recognize that they are a person who can make a just judgement and right behaviour, then they must be very honest indeed.*[312]

The late Michael Meacher, Labour Party politician and academic, said in an interview that Prophet Muhammad (ﷺ) was very honest in the manner he went about conveying the message of the Qur'an to his people. His description of what happened to him and his presentation as a Prophet of God was communicated with the utmost sincerity:

> *When Muhammad had that vision in the cave, he very honestly became the channel through which the Qur'an [was received] – it is said that the Qur'an has immensely powerful language, very evocative, very rich and very meaningful ... and he honestly portrayed that. He was honest to his principles and I think he was a very honourable man.*[313]

Prophet Muhammad's trustworthy nature is evidenced by the way he became the founder of a faith that is today professed by over a billion people in the world. His frank nature was what helped him convey his divine message. Meacher went on to say:

> *I assume he was faithful, unquestionably yes. I have a very high regard for him – he was a strong driving force and he allowed himself to be the channel for communication with God which is*

> *extremely powerful and has won adherents for the last 1400 years. It is extraordinary.*[314]

British author Ruth Cranston voices something similar about Prophet Muhammad (ﷺ). She highlights that the Prophet, having been orphaned in childhood, was raised by his uncle. From his early life he showed evidence of being very honest, kind, calm and trustworthy to all around him. At a later stage he was given the title of *Al-Ameen* or 'the trustworthy' by the people of Makkah.[315]

The distinguished author Ruth Warren praises Prophet Muhammad (ﷺ) in her book *Muhammad: Prophet of Islam.* She claims that the Prophet gained the confidence of the people of Makkah by dint of his sincerity, truthfulness, and sound judgement. He was sensitive, polite, thoughtful and diplomatic.[316] Islam did not end at the fall of the Arab empire and Islam is glowing at the same intensity as ever; it is the second most followed religion in the world. The teachings of Islam, such as the daily prayers and fasting, establish unity among all believers. The basic ideology of Islam teaches that all men are brothers and equal before God.[317]

When assessing whether Prophet Muhammad (ﷺ) was an honest person, it is necessary to look into the circumstances prevailing at his time. There were people from various faiths living in his locality with whom he would have interacted, and exploring his relations with them can help understand to what extent Prophet Muhammad (ﷺ) was an upright and trustworthy person. Geoffrey Rowell, formerly Bishop of Gibraltar, affirmed:

> *We have the traditions of Muhammad and the holy Qur'an and the hadith and so on. Because I am a critical academic theologian, you look at the context. I have to ask was Muhammad honest in the context of his time? What did he know? Where did he gain knowledge of, for instance, Christianity? Where and who were the people that he drew that knowledge from? In the context of his time, certainly as far as I know, he was an honest person and not, as Christians have sometimes said in the past, 'the great deceiver'.*[318]

Jon Dal Din, Director of Westminster Interfaith Group, said in an interview that Prophet Muhammad (ﷺ) was an honest, intelligent and gifted person:

> *I will always assume he was completely an honest man; I have never doubted his integrity. He was very honest, outgoing and intelligent man. I think he was a gifted man.*[319]

Shiv Charan Singh Gill, in charge of the Sikh Temple in Southall, London, asserted in an interview that Prophet Muhammad (ﷺ) was one of the most honest persons in history and that his qualities led Khadija (RA) to marry him. He was a truthful businessman as well:

> *His honesty is known through that period of history. It was his honesty which won him his wife, Khadija. She married Muhammad because she found that young man honest. He was trusted by his trade when he used to take his goods out to the merchants trade, so throughout his work as a tradesperson for her he was quite honest with his accounts with his own labour, with his work.*[320]

David Blunkett the former British Home Secretary, expressed the view that honesty lay at the heart of Prophet Muhammad(ﷺ)'s prophetic mission and served as a model for communicating Islamic injunctions to others:

> *He made it an absolute article of his faith that honesty and openness should be the hallmark of anyone following him and obviously people have interpretations. I believe he saw his label of Al-Ameen in a symbolic light on these who wish to follow him. He was laying down a path which was about his way of demonstrating his way of living and beliefs.*[321]

Prophet Muhammad(ﷺ)'s honesty is acknowledged by Father Allen Green, Tower Hamlets Interfaith Forum, London, thus:

> *From what I've read, Muhammad was a very honest man with integrity.*[322]

Tolerance

Prophet Muhammad's actions and way of life demonstrated tolerance for those of other faiths. There are many incidents in his life which reflected fair treatment and respect for non-Muslims. Stephen Shashoua, Director, Three Faiths Foundation, Camden, London, notes:

> *I understand from Muslim friends I have spoken with that he had respect for other faiths, e.g. when a funeral service was passing, he stepped off the road and he showed humility towards death and when told that the funeral was not for a Muslim but for a Jewish person, he said that death is death and we respect all beings. By that action he shows there are no divisions between people and we have to develop respect. Even in his comments regarding the people of the book, he speaks about respecting all. These things illustrate that he respects 'otherness', which involves acceptance of other types of people, with whom we can live cohesively. He was known for being just to his first wife Khadija and as a salesman. My Muslim friends say he was known for being just.*[323]

Lord Norman Lamont, a former Chancellor of the Exchequer in the UK, is particularly sensitive to the cultural context of Prophet Muhammad's times, be it on matters such as women and war, and acknowledges his tolerant attitude to the members of different faith communities:

> *I think what Muhammad said and did has to be judged and interpreted in the context of the times. e.g. Muhammad's attitude to women might appear very conservative by today's standards but by the standards of his century, they were attitudes that advanced women's position and gave them a stronger position in society. Equally Muhammad's teachings on warfare might appear to us as rather warlike but in the context of the times, I think he actually preached compassion and mercy towards people who were captured in warfare. I think Muhammad preached a more tolerant attitude in the context of his time towards Christians and Jews.*[324]

Equality

HRH Prince Charles reminds us that it is worth noting that women were granted the rights of suffrage in Muslim majority states long before European countries. This is a fact that is often overlooked. Be it the right to own property, earn a living or receive inheritance, the Qur'an had stipulated these rights for women during a period when Europe was still in the dark ages. It is a fact that women in the West were not afforded the right to vote until the first quarter of the 20th century. Before Margaret Thatcher became the UK's first female Prime Minister, women were already elected to leadership in Muslim countries like Bangladesh and Pakistan. So it is unwise to suggest that all Muslim societies are misogynistic. Looking at the extreme practices of some Muslim states in regard to their treatment of women is not the best way of concluding what Islam has spelled out for them:

> *Remember, if you will, that Islamic countries like Turkey, Egypt, and Syria gave women the vote as early as Europe did its women – and much earlier than in Switzerland! In those countries women have long enjoyed equal pay, and the opportunity to play a full working role in their societies. The rights of Muslim women to property and inheritance, to some protection if divorced, and to the conducting of business, were rights prescribed by the Qur'an fourteen hundred years ago, even if they were not everywhere translated into practice. In Britain at least, some of these rights were novel even to my grandmother's generation! Benazir Bhutto and Begum Khaleda Zia became prime ministers in their own traditional societies when Britain had for the first time ever in its history elected a female prime minister. That, I think, does not necessarily smack of a medieval society. Women are not automatically second-class citizens because they live in Islamic countries. We cannot judge the position of women in Islam aright if we take the most conservative Islamic states as representative of the whole.*[325]

According to a teacher from a Church of England School (who

requested anonymity) Prophet Muhammad (ﷺ) was essentially a 'people person' who was very enthusiastic and motivated to have healthy relationships with others in the hope of developing close bonds with people through the principle of equality. His Prophetic mission had a didactic objective which at all times took into consideration the wider society. She says:

> *My understanding of Muhammad from studying his life and the information about him is that he was someone who cared deeply about people and built very good relationships and friendships with people, so the overarching theme I would take from my understanding of Muhammad is that he was someone who was there for the people, family, relationships and everything he was concerned with was building those relationships between each other through the equality of understanding each other in the eyes of Allah and also the understanding of God himself. The whole purpose of his life was to help people understand that key fact.*[326]

The teacher continues saying that Prophet Muhammad's dedication to fostering an atmosphere of equality speaks volumes for his just persona:

> *Again it's about people getting involved. This wasn't an elite – he lived in a situation where the elite ruled and they had ultimate power and he's bringing this new vision…it's all back to this concept of equality and equal rights to rule.*[327]

Prophet Muhammad (ﷺ) had established mutual trust and credibility with his people for a variety of reasons, after a period of uncertainty and scepticism on the part of many in society towards his message. His message of equality was troubling for the elite who wanted to maintain the *status quo* and monopolise economic advantages over the less fortunate, whereas those who were drawn to him were so because his message resonated with their aspirations of equality and justice. The teacher from the Church of England school went on to say:

There were two reasons why they trusted him. In the beginning not many people did trust him and that was difficult for him in terms of his furthering of Islam. They didn't trust him because he was preaching equality and for very rich people around the area they don't particularly want that, so it depends on your perspective. The majority who did trust him, they trusted him because he spoke something that was very clear and was very much about equality and being treated in a sense that they could have respect. The people who didn't trust him were people who were not very keen on that concept of equality and having respect for everybody, because they lived at a time where there were slaves, there were people you could treat differently and situations where you could make money out of it. They didn't trust him because they realised they would lose a lot out of the situation.[328]

Father Tom Quinn, Shadwell Catholic Church, East London, states:

From personal experience and interactions with the Muslim community at mosques, meeting places etc., I respect the Prophet's values.[329]

Washington Irving declares that Prophet Muhammad (ﷺ) dealt equally with everyone irrespective of whether they were friends, known or unknown, poor or rich:

In his private dealings he was just. He treated friends and strangers, the rich and poor, the powerful and the weak, with equity, and was beloved by the common people for the affability with which he received them, and listened to their complaints.[330]

CHAPTER THREE

Emancipation of Women and Equality

Prophet Muhammad (ﷺ) preached to the Arabs the significance of the equality of mankind. He said in his last sermon that humankind is the progeny of Adam and Eve. An Arab does not have superiority over a non-Arab and a non-Arab does not have have superiority over an Arab. Similarly, a white person does not have superiority over a non-white person or a non-white person over a white, except in the event of doing good. All Muslims are brothers to one another.

Slavery

The context in which Prophet Muhammad (ﷺ) lived must factor in our study of why Prophet Muhammad (ﷺ) permitted certain practices. A closer scrutiny of the circumstances prevailing during his time would reveal that Prophet Muhammad (ﷺ) was devoted to the principle of equality for all, be they women or slaves. British MP Frank Dobson says:

> *As I say, this all comes down to what sort of society he was born into and it clearly was a pretty intolerant society in which there were people who were regarded as less than human and were slaves ... and so he believes, as my understanding goes, that everybody, slave or free are equal in the eyes of Allah and so are all women and certainly under Islam as he advocated it, not as other people have interpreted it since. It gave rights to women in the Arabian Peninsula that they did not then have, so he was progressive in those senses.*[331]

The Italian Professor Laura Veccia Vaglieri, an Orientalist and a pioneer of Arabic and Islamic studies, points out that the freeing of a slave is a great virtue in Islam. According to the Qur'an, the freeing of a slave is expiation for certain sins, and this act is encouraged by God. God says that the person who frees a slave will be saved from the Hellfire:

> *In the Qur'an it is said several times that the freeing of slaves is the penalty for certain sins. And in traditions it is strongly affirmed that freeing of a slave is a deed most acceptable to God. "The one who frees a slave who believes, shall in the day of resurrection, be freed from Hell."*[332]

One of the oft-repeated accusations against Prophet Muhammad (ﷺ) was that he was a womaniser (God forbid), given his multiple marriages, as well as someone who endorsed slavery. It is unfair that these practices be considered Islamic as history reveals they predate Islam. Another important factor which goes overlooked is that Prophet Muhammad (ﷺ) did his best to improve the lot of women and slaves. The distinguished author Alfred Martin argues in his book *Great Religious Teachers of the East* that although there are charges against Prophet Muhammad (ﷺ) for supporting polygamy and slavery, the socio-economic situation of 7th-century Arabia should be taken into consideration. It was a time when there was no law to protect women from the ills of society or to abate slavery. Prophet Muhammad (ﷺ) was the first to try and establish law and order to combat polygamy and slavery. According to Alfred Martin:

> *The charge of advocating polygamy and slavery has been made against Mohammed many times. But it were well if his critics paused to remember that these evils existed for centuries before his time and that the most he could do was to improve the condition of slaves and the position of women. From several Suras (verses in the Qur'an) we learn that he inculcated kindly treatment of slaves and ranked their emancipation as a virtue for which the slaveholder would be abundantly rewarded in paradise. Certainly we to-day are too near the emancipation proclamation to dare to reproach Mohammed for not having abolished slavery.*[333]

David Blunkett noted that Muhammad did not treat those in subjugated positions as commodities which could be traded in the marketplace. He said:

> *As I understand it, Muhammad wished to liberate people from being owned by other people. In other words, they had rights and identities of their own, and were not chattels belonging to anyone else.*[334]

Despite the political climate and cultural norms of his time, it cannot be said that Muhammad promoted slavery. Father Allen Green says:

> *He was living in a polytheistic society – he was in political conflict with those who were ruling at that time. To my knowledge, he did not encourage slavery.*[335]

Far from practising slavery in its exploitative sense, Prophet Muhammad(ﷺ)'s practice, if anything, was just an extension or part and parcel of social convention. Lord Kinnock observes:

> *I always had the impression that Muhammad did not favour slavery but of course slavery was a strong social and economic convention in that age, practised by every single society.*[336]

It is interesting to note that Prophet Muhammad(ﷺ)'s promotion of the principle of equality was extended even to slaves. A fine demonstration of this value is seen in Prophet Muhammad(ﷺ)'s treatment of slaves and in particular, the freedom granted to a slave by Prophet Muhammad's companions. A teacher from a Church of England School (who requested anonymity) notes:

> *There was one situation of someone called Bilal, who was a key Muslim who refused to denounce his faith and was tortured and I believed it was Abu Bakr who bought him out and gave him freedom. That's one example of a slave who followed Islam who was seen as equal in the eyes of Islam and through that, Muhammad was promoting freedom and equality, and that's an example of*

freedom for a slave.[337]

Although the practice of slavery was still current during Prophet Muhammad's time, there is a remarkable example in his treatment of slaves which suggested that the institution of slavery was to depart from any notion of inequality since all are equal in the divine perspective. The warmth and friendliness with which Prophet Muhammad (ﷺ) treated slaves in Arabia on many occasions is not reproduced by Muslims in Muslim countries, many of whom exhibit discriminatory conduct towards their housekeepers. Niknam Mehri says:

> *[I]t seems to me – I may be wrong – that the Prophet by his own actions of bringing the slaves into Islam and treating them as equal, showed an example that really all human beings should be equal before God. Of course there was the longstanding tradition of slavery in Arabia, the slaves were badly treated, but perhaps the prophet did his best to show that if you own slaves, treat them humanely.*[338]

Polygamy

The cultural context of 7th-century Arabia must factor when analysing the rights which Prophet Muhammad (ﷺ) extended to females. Although Muslims are often criticised for their misogynistic attitudes and Muslim women are labelled as oppressed individuals with no voice, it is improper to attribute this state of affairs to the Islamic tradition and the Prophet(ﷺ)'s teachings in general. When asked about the Prophet(ﷺ)'s efforts to emancipate women from their oppression, British MP Frank Dobson noted in an interview (October 2011):

> *Yes, but that is against the circumstances in which they were living in that area at the time – as I understand it they had no rights at all and with Islam, they had very considerable rights and a lot of the criticism of Islam as I understand it, is really criticising what is*

a misinterpretation of what the Prophet said. And probably deliberately so, all over the world there are large numbers of people who want to have mainly dominant positions over women, so if you could then misinterpret religious belief to bolster the oppression of women, then people will misinterpret it that way. I don't think it's an accident that this misinterpretation suits the mentality of the people doing the misinterpreting.[339]

With polygamy being incongruous to the Western concept of relationships, Prophet Muhammad(ﷺ)'s polygamous marriages can be viewed contextually, as being a necessary union for women during their times. In this regard, Frank Dobson went to say:

Well I have to confess that I'm not very keen on multiple wives myself. I think again these things may be the product of the society and it may be a way of offering protection and help and finance to groups of women who would otherwise not be looked after, but nevertheless, broadly speaking, one man one woman is the best relationship.[340]

The fact that Prophet Muhammad (ﷺ) put an end to the atrocious practice of polygamy is testimony to his commitment to the principle of equality between the sexes. He was dedicated to liberating women from the shackles of oppressive laws and customs. However, Prophet Muhammad's multiple marriages are often the subject of criticism and in much literature on Prophet Muhammad (ﷺ) he is accused of harbouring chauvinistic tendencies. However, the polygamy which Prophet Muhammad (ﷺ) practised has often been misinterpreted and, as a result, misrepresented to non-Muslims. The critics of Prophet Muhammad (ﷺ) neglect the crucial fact that polygamy was a natural custom during his time and was practised by a considerable number of men. Therefore, such a practice needs to be examined in the context in which it took place. Furthermore, Islamic teachings shed new light on polygamy in a way which appears to curb its practice or at least prevent its abuse. The requirements for polygamy are strictly outlined by the Islamic dictates and these were adopted and practised by Prophet Muhammad (ﷺ). One of these requirements includes the ability of the male to provide financial support to his wives; if he cannot do so, polygamy is prohibited for him. Furthermore, the wider socio-economic circumstances and reasons behind polygamous unions have not been granted sufficient attention by those who are bent on condemning this practice and labelling Prophet Muhammad (ﷺ) a bigamist.

The conditions in Arabia during Prophet Muhammad's time were such that there were many wars which produced widows who would be left with no financial and physical security if left unmarried. A number of the marriages of the Prophet (ﷺ) were purely to promote peace and conciliation between tribes and nations. Except for Ayesha (pbuh) all the other wives of the Prophet (ﷺ) were either widowed or divorced. Then again, he remained faithfully committed to his first wife Khadiza (pbuh) till her death twenty-five years after their marriage. This is enough of a manifestation of the fact that the Prophet(ﷺ)'s marriages were not based on lust or sexual desires. Of course, there are some Muslims who violate the Islamic conditions of marrying only a maximum of four wives, but this has no legal basis in the Qur'anic tradition. Niknam Mehri says:

> *There are two matters I will refer to. One is, as I said before, the burying of the new born girls as practised by Makkan pagans, which was banned by the Prophet and is seen as a positive aspect of Islam. The second one is a negative one, namely that often Islam and the Prophet are attacked because of polygamy. I always explain the situation like this. At that time polygamy was the natural state of marriages almost everywhere. However, the laws that the Qur'an emphasises regarding polygamy for that time, were very advanced. First of all, the Qur'an limits it to 4 wives as opposed to as many wives as you want. That is already a way forward compared to what was happening at that time. Secondly, it tells you only if you can have equality of finance and your husbandly duties and everything else for your wives, then you may have more than one; if not, you're not obliged to have four wives.*
>
> *We know that the Prophet himself, while he was married to Khadijah, remained only with Khadijah. After he married his*

second wife, he had something like six or seven other wives. Now, several of those wives were widows who were unable to afford to keep themselves or their children and so the marriage was a type of support for those women. Several of his marriages were political alliances which were what was done at the time; if you made alliance with the head of a tribe you married into the tribe to consolidate the alliance. Although he did have several wives, as far as we know, he was never unjust to any of his wives.[341]

As far as polygamy is concerned, Reverend Thomas O'Brien, Our Lady of the Assumption Church, Tower Hamlets, notes that this was a social norm during Prophet Muhammad(ﷺ)'s time which in his words, necessitated such marriages:

In his day, there were wars and many men died and there would have been many more women than men. Polygamy was socially accepted at his time and at times it was socially necessary.[342]

Over the centuries, the permissibility of polygamy in Islam has been criticised by many Orientalists who are hostile to Prophet Muhammad (ﷺ). But if the social situation of the 7th century is looked into then one it becomes evident that there had been no law for marriage and divorce and adultery was taken as the norm of the time. There was no limit to the number of wives one could have. In such a barbaric period, Prophet Muhammad (ﷺ) restricted the number of wives to four only, which is again a Qur'anic ordainment. German Professor Max Muller viewed this as a progressive action with regard to the time of the Prophet (ﷺ):

Muhammadans "look upon polygamy as a remedy of many social evils and they are not far wrong," says Max Muller. In all that concerns that great leader we must remember the land, circumstances and ways of the desert, its rulers and wild men of the seventh century. Muhammad acted the part of a patriot and statesman by combating to such extent as he could the unlimited polygamy of the tribes, their common massacre or burial alive of female children, and the treatment of all women as mere chattels;

> *they could like cattle be seized by the strongest. Their fate as slaves in his day was indeed worse than that of cattle; any polygamy was to them an unspeakable benefit. He, therefore, ruled that "men might marry even up to four wives each, provided they could have and do justly by them."*[343]

Muhammad's Marriages

Professor Laura Vaglieri noted that the enemies of Islam have tried to condemn Prophet Muhammad (ﷺ) as a weak, sensual and dissolute individual, giving his polygamy as evidence. This is illogical because such behaviour would be expected to be strongest during someone's youth, when sexual affinity is stronger. But during that time Prophet Muhammad (ﷺ) had only one wife, who was 15 years older than him and previously married twice. The Prophet Muhammad (ﷺ) considered re-marrying only when his wife Khadijah (RA) died at the age of 65 when he was 50 years old! Vaglieri asserts:

> *Enemies of Islam have insisted in depicting Muhammad as a sensual individual and a dissolute man, trying to find in his marriages evidence of a weak character not consistent with his mission. They refuse to take into consideration the fad that during those years of his life when by nature the sexual urge is strongest, although he lived in a society like that of the Arabs where the institution of marriage was almost non-existent, where polygamy was the rule, and where divorce was very easy indeed, he was married to one woman alone, Khadijah, who was much older than himself, and that for twenty-five years he was her faithful, loving husband. Only when she died and when he was already fifty years old did he marry again and more than once. Each of these marriages add a social or a political reason.... With the sole exception of Ayesha, he married women who were neither virgins, nor young nor beautiful. Was this sensuality?*[344]

Shiv Charan Singh Gill, Gurdwara, Southall, Middlesex, England, believes that Prophet Muhammad(ﷺ)'s multiple marriages were mostly due to social and political reasons; providing protection to women from the ills of society as well as poverty and also for bridging the divide between tribes.[345]

A similar view on the marriages of Prophet Muhammad (ﷺ) is expressed by the American author Elsa Marston.[346]

Pandit Piyuskumar Mehta, Jalaram Hindu Mandir, Greenford, London, also argues that polygamy was a tradition at that time and the female population outnumbered men, which also contributed to multiple marriages. However, the Pandit claimed that as the Prophet (ﷺ) was so amiable, humble and well behaved, many parents were perhaps interested in marrying off their daughters to him:

> *At that time the circumstances were different and I heard that the numbers of women were bigger than men, so it was traditional to marry multiple times. There could be other purposes for why he married more than one wife but I think his personality was nice and honest. Due to his niceness, others liked him, others may have requested that he marry their daughter and because Muhammad was humble, he may have accepted, so there could be many reasons.*[347]

According to John L. Esposito, Professor of Religion and Director of the Centre for International Studies at the College of the Holy Cross, the Prophet Muhammad (ﷺ) had one wife, Khadijah (RA) who died after twenty four years of their marriage. After her death the Prophet contracted some other marriages all to widows (except one), some due to political factors and others for the protection of women who were widowed. In his words:

> *After her death Muhammad started to contract other marriages, all but one of them with widows. As was customary for Arab chiefs, some of these marriages were contracted to cement political alliances. Others were marriages to wives of his companions who had fallen in combat, women who were in need of protection.*

Remarriage for widow was difficult in a society that placed a high value on a bride's virginity.[348]

On the issue of marriages of the Prophet (ﷺ), Anita Rai argued that he did not marry again during the life of his first wife Khadijah (RA). If Khadijah (RA) had not died before him, Prophet Muhammad (ﷺ) would not have married again.[349]

Rai further says that Prophet Muhammad (ﷺ) spent the best part of his life with Khadijah (RA), his first wife. The other marriages he performed after her death, however, were due to social, economic, and political reasons and most certainly not for sexual desires. His marriages, after his first wife died, were contracted mainly for moral and spiritual obligations to protect the war-widowed, poor and helpless women from the barbarous society and also to mitigate the conflict between tribes. Rai clarified that for individual woman, marrying the Messenger of God was for protection.[350]

Caesar E. Farah, Professor of history at the University of Minnesota, holds that the reason Prophet Muhammad (ﷺ) conducted multiple marriages was due to the prevailing social and political situation – he married to protect widows from the evil society and also married some women to resolve tribal conflicts. Prophet Muhammad (ﷺ) had spent the best time of his life with his wife Khadijah (RA) who was 15 years older than him and twice married before and he did not marry any other woman until she died at 65 years and he was 50 years old. During his time, multiple marriages were acceptable in the society. It was known that David had six wives and many concubines (2 Samuel 5:13; 1 Chronicles 3:1-9, 14:3) and also Solomon had about 700 wives and 300 concubines (1 Kings 11:3) and Rehoboam (Solomon's son) had 18 wives and 60 concubines (2 Chronicles 11:2 1). Numerous marriages were the tradition amongst the Jews and the Christians. Professor Farah observed that multiple marriages of Prophet Muhammad (ﷺ) were based on the social and economic factors.[351]

The comments of Professors Esposito and Farah are also re-echoed by a spokesman from a Sikh Temple in East London:

Muhammad had only one marriage; he married Khadija. All other marriages were for the protection of women from the evil society. In order to provide shelter and security he married the widows of his companions who died in the battle, and or who were divorced. People have made wrong interpretations of his marriages providing incorrect information on the reason for several marriages.[352]

Reverend John Cowie of the English Reformed Church, Amsterdam, Holland, points out that Prophet Muhammad's practice of polygamy – often misunderstood – was in response to the cultural context in which he lived:

My contact with polygamy is very limited. I understand the prophet married a few times. These would be cultural circumstances in the time, where a man who could afford it, would support wives and family. I think that's not appropriate in our times…It was the necessary circumstances which compelled Muhammad to take more than one wife. Although some participants dismiss polygamy as an adequate institution in today's world, they are sensitive to the socio-political climate prevailing during Muhammad's life that drove him to multiple marriages.[353]

David Blunkett also holds that despite the male dominated society which was characteristic of his time, Prophet Muhammad (ﷺ) was someone who looked beyond these conventionalities, extending an equal status to women:

During that time, society was patriarchal so the main decisions were made by men, but this did not stop him viewing women in equal terms.[354]

Blunkett acknowledges that the deteriorating security situation during Prophet Muhammad(ﷺ)'s time would have led many, like him, to marry more than once:

I think it was part of the culture at his time, I think it was a given

> *... If Muhammad was granting security to these women then marrying multiple times would be understandable.*[355]

According to Father Tom Quinn, Prophet Muhammad (ﷺ) had designated an esteemed position for women in society. He goes on to say:

> *I believe within the family, Muhammad said that women had a special role which is honourable and important. From what I know, Muhammad would be open to women having an important role*[356].

Father Allen Green stated that Prophet Muhammad's polygamous unions were testament to his practical nature and his intentions to extend security to the vulnerable women during his time:

> *Polygamy can be used as a means of protecting women at a given society at a particular time. What I understand about Muhammad is that he was deeply practical. He wants to see how his relationship with God can work itself out in the practical world. I think he married all those women because of protection in society.*[357]

In an interesting admission, Father Green concedes that Prophet Muhammad(ﷺ)'s exhortations on the equality of women are more concrete than the instructions of Jesus:

> *The central tenet of Islam is that people are created equally. I think Muhammad was very clear about the equality of women. I think Muhammad is clearer about the equality of women than Jesus is.*[358]

Karen Armstrong feels that Prophet Muhammad (ﷺ) was an adoring person who married Khadijah (RA) ®, a lady 15 years older than him and previously married twice. However, he did not take a younger wife during the life of Khadijah (RA) ®. Of course Prophet Muhammad (ﷺ) married after the death of Khadija ® but he continued praising her compared to the other wives. Karen Armstrong explains that Prophet Muhammad (ﷺ) did not have any marriage of convenience. He distributed the majority of his income to the poor and lived life like a very simple person.[359]

According to Neil Kinnock, Prophet Muhammad's polygamous unions must be seen in the context of of the fact that women needed security and protection at that time. He mentions how Prophet Muhammad's multiple marriages must be viewed in the context of the conditions prevailing during that time, where many women were left protection ans support:

> *It was a social convention. When men were fundamentally the protectors, because of the insecurity and tension in every society, there are many instances amongst the Judaic and Christian Prophets of polygamy. I think he had many wives because he like many men of that age accepted a duty of care, responsibility and protection. I don't think he made the religious principle that polygamy represented the faith.*[360]

Prophet Muhammad (ﷺ) afforded women the full rights and responsibilities of citizenship and asserted their equal status with men, despite this particular bit of prophetic instruction not being adhered to by many Muslims. Kinnock continues:

> *Muslim friends of mine have always made the case that Muhammad recognised a full and socially and economically equal position for women and girls and showed particular enlightenment. What's unfortunate is that so many of his followers have been unable to accept the same teaching, because I don't think there is any doubt at all from his repetitive sayings that he considered humans to be equal in the sight of God.*[361]

Stephen Shashoua, Director, Three Faiths Foundation, Camden stated that Prophet Muhammad(ﷺ)'s marriage to Khadijah (RA) was an example of his attitude towards women and their status in society. It provides us with an insight into his motivations behind marrying who he did. Shashoua observes:

> *First, he married a woman that was older than him, so it can be*

said that he promoted the view that women could be quite old and marry. He also married the widow. I think many cultures have seen the widow as people with no life and Muhammad through marrying Khadija showed that life can still continue and from my understanding, Khadija is seen as the most important example in Islam of women. I understand it was a very strong example of how husband and wife should behave.[362]

The Qur'an allows a man to marry more than one woman but to the maximum of four provided that the husband treats all of them with justice and equality. However, if the husband is doubtful of being able to treat them equally, then the Qur'an instructs him to marry only one woman. Italian Professor Laura VecciaVaglieri writes:

The Qur'an has allowed a man to marry two, three and even four women. But, at the same time, it has specified a qualifying condition which is indispensable for such marriages by insisting upon the husband exercising the most perfect and complete justice towards each wife, meaning by "justice" not only equal treatment in material provisions but also equal love: "...marry but two, or three, or four; and if you fear that you will not deal justly, then marry only one."[363]

Dr Annie Besant (1847-1933) was a British theosophist, nationalist leader of India and the President of the Indian National Congress in 1917. She could not accept that Prophet Muhammad (ﷺ) married more than once due to physical needs. She stresses that there were good social and political reasons behind each marriage. She expressed the view:

But do you mean to tell me that the man who in the full flush of youthful vigor, a young man of four and twenty (24), married a woman much his senior, and remained faithful to her for six and twenty years (26), at fifty years of age when the passions are dying, married for lust and sexual passion? Not thus are men's lives to be judged. And you look at the women whom he married, you will find that by every one of them an alliance was made for his people, or something was gained for his followers, or the woman was in sore need of protection.[364]

A teacher from a Church of England School (who requested anonymity) believes that Prophet Muhammad(ﷺ)'s life was a fine demonstration of the principle of equality for women. This is seen from his wife Khadijah (RA) and her status as a merchant with an independent career, something which Prophet Muhammad (ﷺ) accepted and was pleased to live with. It is significant that Prophet Muhammad (ﷺ) considered women as equal to men in the eyes of God:

I think this links greatly with his life and how he grew up and the link with him being an orphan. He had a very strong wife. Khadija was older than him, she was a merchant, she was able to earn her own living and therefore that had a huge impact on his teaching – he did treat women as equals and he did see them as being included in worship and religion. I think that's where that name comes from the idea that he is bringing about freedom for women.[365]

Jeremy Corbyn feels that the motivation behind Prophet Muhammad(ﷺ)'s multiple marriages is often misunderstood and is the subject of much prejudice and misinformation about Prophet Muhammad (ﷺ). The fact that Prophet Muhammad (ﷺ) had many wives due to the untold loss many women suffered during his time as a result of war often goes unmentioned in Western circles. Corbyn states:

The question of polygamy is a huge debate. The Western world makes polygamy absolutely illegal and I think that personally, polygamy is not a good idea. The teaching of Muhammad was that if a woman had lost her husband or lost her family support then it was a responsibility to support her and continue to support her and this is a narrative that runs through many communities including Muslim communities – of support for women who have lost the breadwinner in their family, in the case of the man.[366]

Mike Stygal, Chairman, Camden Interfaith Foundation, believes that

Prophet Muhammad (ﷺ) denounced the objectification of women and in this way liberated them from conventions which treated them as commodities. According to him, the prevailing cultural practices– caused by a misreading of the Scripture – may deny Muslim women some rights, but this is not to be conflated with the authentic Islamic viewpoint on women. He states:

> *Given the historical time and the different cultural rules of that period, I do think he was an emancipator of women. The modesty rules can be seen as a way of emancipating women because they could not be seen as objects of sex but they would be seen as human beings. I know that in some Islamic cultures today, it may not seem emancipating for women, where women are prevented from being equal, which it should not be. The nature of religions is that they get interpreted and people manipulate and use religions – this does not represent the message in Islam.*[367]

Stygal also sheds some interesting light on Prophet Muhammad(ﷺ)'s multiple marriages. He mentions one of the motivations of Prophet Muhammad (ﷺ) for marrying many times was to provide economic security and their general welfare, given that such a practice was a norm at the time. He continues saying:

> *Sometimes he would marry to prevent women from being destitute and having no means of support etc. His other marriages were a love match. I understand he married some women because their husbands had died, they were widowed and they would not have had a means for support and protection so he did this to take them in and make sure they were provided for and safe. And given the society at that time, this was the way of doing things.*[368]

The motivations behind Prophet Muhammad(ﷺ)'s multiple marriages speak volumes about the general concern he had for women's welfare and status in society. Reverend Dr Harriet Harris, the Chaplain and honorary Fellow at the school of divinity, Edinburgh University and former Chaplain and tutor at Oxford University and lecturer of theology at

Sussex University observes:

> *This background presents a very socially compassionate and faithful understanding of the Prophet's marriages.*[369]

Mako Nagasawa, Area director, advisor to the Harvard-Radcliffe Christian Fellowship (HRCF), and a staff member with Inter Varsity Christian Fellowship at Harvard University says that societal factors must be acknowledged and taken into consideration when concluding what compelled Prophet Muhammad (ﷺ) to marry multiple times:

> *Yes. I know that he himself had a number of wives, over 10 if not 12 or something like that. I know that on the one hand, there were social reasons for that. Some of his Muslim followers might have died and left a widow. That was his way of caring for them. That seems to have been the case a couple of times.*[370]

Prophet Muhammad(ﷺ)'s objective in marrying more than one wife was deeply connected to the cultural context of his time. An interplay of socio-economic and political factors lay at the heart of his decision to form polygamous unions. Also of concern to Prophet Muhammad (ﷺ) was the precarious position many women would be left in in the context of his time, unless they decided to settle on a marriage which could grant them financial and physical security. According to Reverend Stephen Coles, St Thomas Church, North London,

> *I imagine that there can be a number of possible reasons. One is, I know he married some people because they became widows, so it would be to protect them and I know that if you're living in a tribal society, the likelihood is that because of fighting between tribes, men will get killed. Therefore, you can have more women than men; therefore, two things happen. One is, the women need to be kept within the social structure, so they might need be married to somebody, rather than just left to one side with nobody to look after them. The other is that you have to keep having children because you have to build up your society. Biologically, a man can father*

many children – in a tribe, where there is conflict with other tribe, it needs to have more people because they're also getting killed, so there's a very practical basis to all this.[371]

One of the most frequently misunderstood aspects of Prophet Muhammad(ﷺ)'s life is his multiple marriages. The reason and motivation behind his several marriages is often ignored or at best receives cursory treatment. Although marriage to one woman may be considered the more emotionally fulfilling arrangement, it is interesting to note what can prompt polygamous marriages. Father Alban McCoy of the Cambridge University Catholic Chaplaincy says:

I can see how under some social conditions polygamy can be a social necessity. I think it's a stage on the way to something better and I think monogamy is more respectful to the integrity of each human being and less apt to lead to discrimination among women.[372]

The renowned author Annemarie Schimmel points out that there were no limits to marriages and divorces in the pre-Islamic Arab society. Therefore, limiting to four marriages was a significant development in Arabian society. However, Prophet Muhammad(ﷺ)'s several marriages were due to the social, political and economic situation of that time. He did not marry again until the death of his first wife when he was 50 years old, and by then the best time of his life had already been passed.[373]

Equality in general

Anita Rai notes that Prophet Muhammad's preaching on the issue of equality was crystal clear, easy to understand and simple. He made laws stating that the disadvantaged, helpless, the poor, the rich, people of any abilities, colour and gender are equal to God. So, the discrimination should not exist there.[374]

Dr Leitner observes that Islam teaches equality amongst all. There can be no difference between the rich and poor or any kind of discrimination. Anybody can sit anywhere in the mosque and also lead the prayer as Imam. In his words,

> *In a mosque there is perfect equality among worshippers: there are no pews; the imam of the place or any other worshipper may lead the prayers, and nothing can be a more devotional sight than a crowd of Muslim worshippers going through their various genuflexions with perfect regularity and silence.*[375]

Islam affords non-Muslims a high level of religious tolerance. With the exception of one or two incidents during Prophet Muhammad(ﷺ)'s life, he clearly demonstrated how the places of worship belonging to people of other faiths ought to be respected. This practice continued throughout the Caliphates of his companions. According to Dr N.K. Singh,

> *The Islamic doctrine of tolerance categorically prohibits desecrating any place of worship, or forcibly using it for Islamic worship; however, the Prophet did remove the idols from the Ka'aba at Makkah on the ground that the Ka'aba was, originally, a mosque built by Abraham. The Prophet viewed the 'cleansing' of the Ka'baa from idols as the restoration of a monotheistic place of worship to its original status. This is a solitary instance of a house of worship having been 'cleansed' in the life of the Prophet or the pious Caliphs.*[376]

Professor Vaglieri highlights that man is the servant of God alone and free from submission to all others. Islam stressed equality in all aspects of life. People had suffered from discrimination in many social issues. The superiority of a Muslim over another of his Muslim brothers will be determined only by his God-consciousness, and his moral and intellectual qualities. She adds:

> *Man became the servant of God alone and towards the other men he had only the obligations of one free man towards other free men. While previously men had suffered from the injustices of social*

> *differences, Islam proclaimed equality among human beings. Each Muslim was distinguished from other Muslims not by reason of birth or any other factor not connected with his personality, but only by fear of God, his good deeds, his moral and intellectual qualities.*[377]

Karen Armstrong claims that inheriting wealth or giving testimony in legal disputes would have been unheard of in Arab society before Islam's introduction of these practices. The rights extended to women in Europe came at a much later stage, which should prompt one to exercise caution before pointing the finger at Islam for women's maltreatment.[378]

Ruth Cranston notes that Prophet Muhammad (ﷺ) made policies for women to be more liberal 1400 hundred years ago. In contrast, women in England or America have only recently got the same right.[379]

The situation of women was worse in the 7th-century Arabia. Author Anita Rai expresses her gratefulness to the Prophet Muhammad (ﷺ) for bringing significant change in the lives of women who were used to be exploited and were valued less in the society. Prophet Muhammad (ﷺ) eliminated their plight and alleviated their suffering.[380]

Rai further reminds us that the Qur'an, revealed to Muhammad, is the guide book for the whole of mankind until the last day of the universe. One should not forget the Islamic instructions as laid down by Muhammad.[381]

Pandit Gopal Krishna is an Indian astrologer and palmist who claims that Prophet Muhammad (ﷺ) was sent with special skills, power and morals to benefit mankind. He was an emancipator of women and he treated the rich and the poor equally. In his work, *Glory of Prophet Muhammad* (ﷺ), Krishna notes:

> *God had sent him to reform the world. He had been endowed with the strength of character and moral qualities of a great reformer and of a great man. He was responsible for the emancipation of woman and he made no distinction between rich and poor.*[382]

According to Reverend Rupert Hoare there is an understanding that the social circumstances prevailing at his time warranted Prophet

Muhammad(ﷺ)'s polygamous marriages. Furthermore, it is acknowledged that Prophet Muhammad (ﷺ) had elevated the rank of women to a higher degree compared to their existing status in tribal Arabia and granted them a considerable number of rights. Reverend Hoare says:

> *The position of women in his day in surrounding tribes was much worse, very bad. He gave women a much higher position in society and in the faith then they had in the tribal religions of the area from which he came. I assume he treated his wives well. They were certainly given many more rights than they were given before.*[383]

Prophet Muhammad (ﷺ) had instructed others to honour women and treat them as sanctified human beings. Danny Richmond, Faith Act Manager, Tony Blair Faith Foundation says:

> *I know that the respect for women was part of the Prophet's life and stating that women were an equal half of men, you know, demonstrates his commitment to women's rights.*[384]

Sir John Glubb explains that women have different role than men in the theoretical perspective of Islam. It is to be accepted that women are physically weaker than men; however, the general Western view of the place of women in Muslim culture is repellently twisted.[385]

Solidarity among human beings is one of the essential hallmarks of the Islamic faith. This extends to relations between Muslims and non-Muslims and is never intended to be among Muslims exclusively. As far as the Qur'an is concerned, its message is not limited to the Arab population but to all of mankind, thus its global people. In fact, Prophet Muhammad (ﷺ) is not a messenger just for the Arabs but for the world, and this is in tandem with Islam being the final revelation. This was one of the reasons which explain why Islam spread fast and was accepted quickly by others. Of course, it cannot be denied that there were incidents and periods in Islam's history which halted the momentum, but this has nothing to do with the Islamic faith. Dr N.K. Singh notes:

> *The religion of Islam puts great emphasis on brotherhood and*

equality. The brotherhood between the Muslim and equal treatment of non-Muslim are its two basic principles. The Qur'an, which contains the commandments of the Islamic religion, is not addressed to one single nation belonging to one single age, but to all nations belonging to all ages and, therefore, the moral code it embodies is universal. Because of this feeling of equality, Islam spread rapidly and was met with sympathy by the followers of other religions.[386]

Prophet Muhammad (ﷺ) had promoted a role for women which was complementary to men's, and his vision for women's responsibilities was liberating and helped to foster the concept of equality between the sexes. According to a Christian priest from a church in East London,

Muhammad's teaching at the time was emancipating for women, all equal under God and yet with different roles with what they could do and not do.[387]

The cultural context during Prophet Muhammad(ﷺ)'s time must be evaluated when coming to any conclusion on his practice and endorsement of polygamy. Christianity has a long tradition of polygamy as well as concubinage, and this can be gathered from a reading of Christian scriptures and history. However, as was the case with Prophet Muhammad (ﷺ), the Christian practice viewed multiple marriages as a way of safeguarding the welfare of women who would otherwise be left in a vulnerable position.Prophet Muhammad(ﷺ)'s overtures to women have sometimes received mixed responses but it cannot be denied that he made huge strides in guaranteeing women's rights. According to the Reverend Stephen Williams,

I think modern feminists are forced to recognize this that in fact he was one of the first legislators on behalf of women's independence and rights and also the care of unwanted children.[388]

Shiv Charan Singh feels that Prophet Muhammad(ﷺ)'s crusade against slavery is a great lesson for mankind, and the wars he waged were all in self-defence:

> *Slavery has a long history and he fought against slavery. I understand the rudiments of Islam but I am not a scholar. He had to fight, when he left Makkah to Madinah, he had to fight even in Madinah, so many battles. So that was a battle for liberation.*[389]

The reforms which Prophet Muhammad (ﷺ) introduced for slaves were progressive and demonstrated how he wanted to establish a fair and equal society, as far as his capabilities would permit. Mr. Bhavin Tailor, a secondary school teacher, William Ellis School, London, says:

> *It's something we should strive to do because to have a slave almost creates a hierarchy in society, where one person dominates another, for reasons that are only selfish. Surely the freeing of slaves will give them liberty and surely that must be a good thing. Slavery creates disparity and inequality – anybody in a cohesive society should want to break that barrier.*[390]

Contrary to popular belief, Muhammad(ﷺ) was not an advocate of slavery and championed the cause of equality, according to British Conservative politician David Amess, who comments:

> *He denounced the slavery system. Muhammad was concerned about equal opportunity and was against manipulation to force others to do things against their judgement. He thought it was wrong to oppress people. He didn't believe in the superiority of any race or group over others.*[391]

Professor Vaglieri states that in Islam there is no discrimination against race, gender, colour, tribe, and rich, poor, literate or illiterate, ruler or subject etc. It treats everyone equally. The lessons of Islam are reflected not only in theory but in practice as well. An incident involving the Second Caliph of Islam, Umar Al Khattab is one of the brilliant examples of the practices.

> *Islam, which has never made any distinction of race or colour*

among men, which considered the white and the black, the nomad and the settled farmer, the ruler and the subject as all alike, not only in theory but also in practice (and as a matter of fact in the tent, in the palace, in the mosque, in the market, they all mingled together without reserve and with no sign of contempt or arrogance towards each other), never countenanced any humiliating treatment for slaves. Is it not fitting to remember here … the beautiful episode of King Jabale, who, having become a Muslim, went in great state to Makkah. While he was making the ritual tour around the Ka'bah, he struck a Bedouin who had accidentally trodden on his rich mantle. The Caliph Umar ruled that he was to receive a similar blow from the Bedouin because in Islam all men are alike.[392]

Major General Forlong notices that Prophet Muhammad (ﷺ) implemented an equal opportunities policy which uplifted the position of slaves. He encouraged all to free their slaves and said tht in the case of female slaves, if they become mothers, they should be treated as family members and their children should receive all benefits from the home like others. Forlong clarifies:

Muhammad also raised vastly the position of the slave, always freeing his own, and doing the best he could for others. As to female slaves, he enacted that when they became mothers they were to be recognized as members of the family; and that their children were to have all the rights of legitimacy. The result is that no young mothers commit murder and suicide as in Christian lands. Of course slavery could not be put down, so the statesman had to restrain any wish he may have had to go further in this respect.[393]

On the topic of women's right Forlong adds:

Muhammad insisted that "without four witnesses no woman may be maligned; that none might touch a woman's property, be she widow, maid or wife, without her free consent; that whoever wronged the orphan, Allah would broil in hell fire … It was

> *declared that not even the legal heir of a woman was to succeed to her estate except by her consent; and that as much belief was to be placed on her word as that of the male accuser, even though he were her husband.*[394]

Equality was a principle for which Muhammad (ﷺ) constantly strived. Stephen Shashoua says:

> *I understand that he had a strong sense of equality for all people and that's between men and women and it would be for slaves or others. As for what followers of Islam have taken forward, that's a different thing.*[395]

The equal treatment of slaves is an important step creating a cohesive society, as it sets a precedent that there can be no discrimination on the basis of class. A teacher from a Church of England School, North London (who requested anonymity) says:

> *Well I presume that's a direct link to a cohesive society because it's saying people shouldn't be treated differently depending on their social status in life.*[396]

Given the importance Prophet Muhammad (ﷺ) afforded to the respect of others, Mike Stygal cannot conceive of him consenting to practices which exploited human beings:

> *From what I understand about Muhammad, I cannot think that he would be in favour of slavery because he cared about humans being treated with respect. I cannot see Muhammad approving of a system that did not respect human beings.*[397]

Muhammad (ﷺ) was truly a people's person and showed the utmost care and concern for others. He would never shut anyone out and included everyone in his circle, irrespective of race, class etc. Stanley Lane-Poole affirms:

> *He visited the sick, followed any bier he met, accepted the*

invitation of a slave to dinner, mended his own clothes, milked the goats, and waited upon himself... He never first withdrew his hand out of another man's palm and turned before the other had turned.[398]

Another charge against Prophet Muhammad (ﷺ) which has persisted for centuries is that he was bent on violence and intimidation as a means to expand his religion. Once again, this kind of thinking reflects ignorance about Prophet Muhammad(ﷺ)'s life. According to Gandhi,

I wanted to know the best of one who holds today's undisputed sway over the hearts of millions of mankind....I became more than convinced that it was not the sword that won a place for Islam in those days in the scheme of life. It was the rigid simplicity, the utter self-effacement of the Prophet, the scrupulous regard for his pledges, his intense devotion to his friends and followers, his intrepidity, his fearlessness, his absolute trust in God and in his own mission. These and not the sword carried everything before them and surmounted every obstacle. When I closed the 2nd volume (of the Prophet's biography), I was sorry there was not more for me to read of the great life.[399]

Prophet Muhammad(ﷺ)'s rise to power did not lead to any material excesses and he did not oppress anyone when he reached a lofty position. His concern was for the betterment of people and he lived a frugal life. British civil servant and Arabist Bertram Thomas noted:

His moral teachings sprang from a pure and exalted mind aflame with religious enthusiasm. From being a persecuted preacher exiled to Madinah, he rose to political power. This he enjoyed only in the last few years of his life, and this he used for the spiritual and material welfare of Muslims. Such indeed was the magnificence of his good works that he died in debt, some of his belongings in pawn with a Jew – among them his only shield for which he obtained three measures of meal.[400]

He would often perform labour intensive tasks himself and was dedicated to improving the condition of slaves during his time. Ruth Cranston says that Prophet Muhammad (ﷺ) did almost all of his work manually with his own hands, including kindling the fire, sweeping the floor, milking goats, sewing his own garments and mending his shoes.[401]

Muhammad (ﷺ) is noted for his unprejudiced nature and he sought to redress the unfair disadvantage which any in his society were subject to. The socio-economic class of any individual would have no bearing on how they would be treated; rather, equal treatment was a key ingredient to his message. British MP Frank Dobson appreciates this quality of Muhammad (ﷺ), when he says:

> *In so far as I understand what's in the Qur'an, the Prophet was in favour, not just of equal opportunities, but he was in favour of equality, in the sense that nobody is going to be in a superior position in the eyes of God as a result of any human status or human wealth.*[402]

Prophet Muhammad's democratic spirit is noted by Father Tom Quinn, who appreciates Prophet Muhammad's example of sharing with others:

> *He was democratic in the sense that he shared everything with his disciples.*[403]

Jon Dal Din claims that Prophet Muhammad's eagerness to obtain equal rights for women do not go unnoticed. He observes:

> *My understanding is he was actually quite keen on women's rights and he wanted to treat people equally… he valued all equally.*[404]

The principle of equality is one which recurs in the Prophetic traditions and is enshrined in the Islamic scripture. Many of the rituals Islam prescribes reinforce this equality; in particular, the equality which is God-ordained. There is a fraternity that can be discerned from many Muslim actions and at the same time, there are social roles and responsibilities which may differ among men and women but not for discriminatory purposes. This is a common thread in most faiths. When one ponders on the social circumstances prevailing in Prophet Muhammad(ﷺ)'s time, it can be said that he made significant strides to reverse women's second class status. Furthermore, we cannot discount the misinterpretation of scripture and cultural forces which have paved way to the subjugation of women in some Muslim circles. It may be that the choice of interpretations-some being liberal while others more restrictive-have a great bearing on the freedom and social mobility of Muslim women but this is not to be confused with the generally positive teachings which Prophet Muhammad (ﷺ) had for women and equality as a whole. Niknam Mehri argues:

> *What I understand is that based on the way that Muslims pray in sufoof (lines of prayer) when they go to mosque, the most important ones should not be in the front and the rest in the back. It is equal. All Muslims stand next to each other and the only one who has the place in front of the jama'a (congregation) is the Imam, and that is only because he is leading the prayers. Otherwise, when Muslims pray, they pray as equals before God.*[405]

H.G. Wells mentioned some of the important points from the Prophet Muhammad(ﷺ)'s sermon during the last pilgrimage. The Prophet (ﷺ) stressed the fact that human life on earth is sanctified; wives have equal rights to their husbands; slaves should be treated as other members of the family. He also stressed the brotherhood amongst Muslims; that they are brothers to each other and that everybody is equal in the sight of God. He declares:

> *Your lives and property are sacred and inviolable amongst one another until the end of time...The Lord hath ordained to every man the share of his inheritance; a testament is not lawful to the prejudice of heirs...Ye people! Ye have rights demandable of your wives, and they have rights demandable of you...And your slaves, see that ye feed them with such food as ye eat yourselves, and clothe them with the stuff ye wear. And if they commit a fault which ye*

> *are not inclined to forgive, then sell them, for they are the servants of the Lord, and are not to be tormented... Ye people! hearken to my speech and comprehend the same. Know that every Moslem is the brother of every other Moslem. All of you are on the same equality.*[406]

Reuben Levy, Professor of Persian at the University of Cambridge, in his book, *The Social Structure of Islam* refers to the fair treatment of slaves by the Prophet of Islam. The slavery system existed in Arabian society before Prophet Muhammad (ﷺ). He was against this social element. He taught people the equality of human beings and did his best to get rid of slavery.[407]

Emancipation of Women

Though the misinformed West holds the Qur'anic teachings responsible for substandard dealings with the women in some parts of the Muslim world, Prophet Muhammad (ﷺ) was indeed a protector of the women. Karen Armstrong says that the Western critics often make mistake of holding the Qur'an responsible for the treatment of women which they think is improper. However, the truth is that Prophet Muhammad (ﷺ) was the real emancipator of women.

> *Western critics often blame the Qur'an for its treatment of women, which they see as iniquitous, but in fact that the emancipation of women was dear to the prophet's heart.*[408]

In the pre-Islamic days, the ways the women were treated, were more than deplorable. In comparison, Prophet Muhammad (ﷺ) took a good number of significant steps towards achieving women's equality. Armstrong notes that in pre-Islamic times in Arabia, baby girls were not valued and were buried alive, and women had no legal rights whatsoever in society. They were treated no better than household possessions. Considering this situation, what Prophet Muhammad (ﷺ) did was amazing.[409]

Sir H.A.R. Gibb, the Scottish historian and Orientalist has claimed that Islamic societies of the past have a great track record of guaranteeing rights and freedoms to women. According to him, Islam is the only religion to have a successful record of providing equality to women and Islam still has the power to unite many conflicting groups and religions.[410]

Slavery existed in Arabia before the advent of Islam, yet Muhammad introduced and promoted the practice of freeing slaves as a virtuous act in the eyes of God. Major General Forlong paid high tributes to Prophet Muhammad (ﷺ) who led a very simple life. Having Married Khadija ®, he remained lovingly attached and faithful to her till her death. After her death, while he was 50 years old and beyond the youthful years, he married a few other women, the sole purpose of which was to address social and political issues. Major General opines:

> *He was sincerely attached to Khadijah and absolutely faithful to her for twenty years; only after her death did he marry again, and with others, mostly widows and orphans of persecuted followers, who would have perished had he not received them into his quiet frugal household. None could protect these but by marriage, and they abounded in his restless troubled land, the laws and circumstances of which must never be forgotten in judging this great militant prophet* .[411]

According to American author Pierre Crabitès, as far as women's rights is concerned, there is no doubt that Prophet Muhammad (ﷺ) fought long and hard to achieve rights for women. Just a cursory glance at the rights which Islam extends to women is enough to prove that Prophet Muhammad (ﷺ) was committed to this end. Crabitès further notes that Islam offers equal rights to wife and husband.[412]

Culture is in many cases responsible for marginalising women and denying them their rights. The absence of equality in many parts of the Muslim world has no connection with the rules and regulations stipulated by Prophet Muhammad (ﷺ) regarding women's status. In fact, many have argued that Prophet Muhammad (ﷺ) was ahead of his time and had a modernising influence and contrary to popular belief, was not oppressive towards women. According to Reverend Jennifer Potter, Minister, Wesley's Chapel, London:

> *I know Muhammad's wife Khadija was a strong woman and she was allowed to be a strong woman. I think the view in Britain and parts of the non-Muslim world that Islam is very repressive towards women, but I think this is because of the culture of some societies into which Islam has been accepted and the culture has overridden the message of the prophet. I believe that the Prophet was by the standards of his day and the place where he lived, a rather emancipating man in regards to women*[413].

Annie Besant observed that the tired cliché that Islam was oppressive to women and stifles their rights was an incorrect view, and history bears testimony to how Islam elevated the ranks of women by affording them privileges which in the West had only been granted in much later times. Writing in 1932, Besant stated:

> *I often think that woman is freer in Islam than in Christianity. Woman is more protected by Islam than by the faith which preaches monogamy. In Al-Qur'an the law about woman is more just and liberal. It is only in the last twenty years that Christian England has recognized the right of woman to property, while Islam has allowed this right from all times.* [414]

The marriage contract in Islam is another example of how faith seeks to establish equality for both men and women. When contrasted with other country's rights for women during the same time, the rights offered by Islam were far greater than the rights of women in other countries. According to
R.V.C. Bodley:

> *The contract covered everything: the man's dowry, the woman's dowry, and what should be done with dowries in case of divorce.*

These regulations gave more consideration to womankind than in any occidental country of the period. In fact, today a Moslem has fewer claims over his wife's property than husbands in many European communities. Thirteen hundred years ago Islam made a woman free and independent of her husband in the enjoyment of her rights of possession.[415]

It was Islam's emphasis on equality that saw it spread and become popular among the masses. Islam compares favourably to other faiths and armies which conquered territories and people in an oppressive manner. M.N. Roy, an Indian author, said:

Still one more historian bears testimony to the fact that the spectacular triumph of Islam was rather due to its liberating and equalitarian principles than to the military valour of its early adherents. In almost every case in which the Saracens conquered a Christian nation, history unfortunately reveals that they owed their success chiefly to the favour with which this progress was regarded by the masses of the conquered people... The inhabitants of Syria welcomed the followers of Mahomet; the Copts of Egypt contributed to place their country under the domination of the Arabs; All these nations were induced, by the hatred for the government of Constantinople, to place themselves under the sway of the Mohammedans. The treachery of the nobles and the indifference of the people made Spain and the South of France easy prey to the Saracens.[416]

The author Malise Ruthven says that Islam's insistence on the equality between men and women cannot be denied. This can be gleaned from passages in the Qur'an which condemn evil practices towards women, as well as the improvement of women's conditions. The husband must treat the wife with justice and they are all equal in the eyes of God. Women were treated very badly before Prophet Muhammad (ﷺ). The Prophet (ﷺ) brought changes endorsing women's rights through legislation. Many Orientalists agree on this statement although nowadays there is a debate on the issue of the veil.[417]

Consensus was a characteristic of Prophet Muhammad's practices in Madinah. Lord Norman Lamont (Baron Lamont of Lerwick) is a British politician and former Conservative MP and Chancellor of the Exchequer. Lamont (January, 2012) says that:

> *The community in Madinah might have been argued as quite a democratic consensual society.*[418]

Lord Lamont acknowledged that Prophet Muhammad(ﷺ)'s efforts in bettering the status of women:

> *I think Muhammad was an advocate of improving the condition of women relatively.*[419]

Prophet Muhammad (ﷺ) had instructed others to honour and revere women and treat them as sanctified human beings. Danny Richmond, Faith Act Manager, Tony Blair Faith Foundation says:

> *I know that the respect for women was part of the Prophet's life and stating that women were an equal half of men, you know … demonstrates his commitment to women's rights.*[420]

Prophet Muhammad(ﷺ)'s emphasis on shared values and social justice was very democratic in nature. Common goals are mutually reinforcing and help establish stronger ties between individuals. There are verses in the Qur'an which allude to such a principle, namely, celebrating differences. Danny Richmond notes:

> *I think fundamental to the Prophet's teaching was a sense of responsibility to the other. I think that's at the heart of democracy because at the end of the day, we live in a society where we are both responsible for each other but also we're responsible for the society we can build together.*[421]

Lord Headley observed that a true Muslim leave no stone unturned to make his wife's life happy. With a similar vision in mind he wrote a poem and believed others could like to share his thoughts:

The true Muslim regards his woman folk as sacred, and he spares no pain to make them happy and comfortable. Some years ago I wrote the following lines in praise of a really good woman, and I am sure that most Muslims will agree with the sentiment when they think of their mothers and their wives:

A Good Woman
Sweet offering of our Maker's care
To crown my life thou didst appear
And give my joy untold:
A ray divine
Of sweet sunshine
Turned all life's dross to gold.
To fill an aching void thou gav'st
A treasured promise – an thou mad'st
My soul to dance with joy.[422]

CHAPTER FOUR

Islam – Influence and Impact

Islam Means Peace

Dr N.K. Singh wrote in the preface to his book *Islam: A Religion of Peace* that Islam is not a religion of violence and the spirit of Islam does not have any association with violence; rather it is opposed to violence. Islam means, firstly, to give in to God's will and secondly, it means establishing peace. Muslims greet each other by saying 'salaam', which means 'peace'. Dr Singh explains:

> *In this study, I have tried to make it clear with the reference to Islamic scriptures that Islam is neither a religion of violence, nor is violence integral to this religion. The very word "Islam" is the negation of the concept of violence. Islam means surrender to the will of God on the one hand, and establishing peace on the other. The word for peace in Arabic is 'salaam'. When Muslims greet each other, they invoke peace — 'Salem alaykum' (peace be on you). Thus, it is a religious duty of a Muslim to strive for establishment of peace in society. A Muslim is one who surrenders to the will of Allah and an establisher of peace. Thus Islam means establishment of peace and Muslim means establisher of peace through his action and conduct. A true Muslim lives and dies in submission to God and in the establishment of peace in this world.*[423]

Influence of Islam

Karen Armstrong notes that the 18th century was a period when reflections on and the presentation of Islam in the West started to move away from the tired stereotypes and come closer to an objective understanding of the faith.[424]

Sir Archibald Watkin Hamilton, Baronet, was also a Lieutenant in the Royal Defence Corps. He commented that although he was born and raised as a Christian, the essence of Islam always attracted him and he did not believe in the blind teachings of the Church. Hamilton said that an attractive feature of Islam is its simplicity. As a Christian by birth, he found the anti-rational tendencies of the Church difficult to reconcile with his predilection for reason and logic, which for him took priority over blind belief. Claiming Islam to be the most misrepresented faith by the misinformed, he also says that Islam is universal in its reach and application. According to Hamilton:

> *There is no religion that is so maligned by the ignorant and the biased as is Islam; yet if people only knew; it is the religion of strong for the weak, the rich for the poor. Humanity is divided into three classes. First, those on whom God has, out of His bounty, bestowed possessions and wealth; secondly, those who have to work to earn their living; and lastly, the great army of the unemployed, or those who have fallen by the wayside through no fault of their own.*[425]

He compares Islam with Christianity in relation to supervising and regulating life day by day. He states:

> *I would like to say that where as Islam guides humanity in the daily workday life, the present-day so-called Christianity, indirectly in theory and invariably in practice, teaches its follower, it would see, 'to pray' to God on Sundays and 'to prey' on His creatures for the rest of the week.*[426]

The subject of war is a fiercely contested one, especially in light of the Islamic faith. In Islam's history, wars were often waged to defend the lives of Muslims and others and were rarely offensive in nature. The motivation for war was to establish justice and peace and to get rid of oppression and injustice. Islam emphasises the fact that as humans, we are naturally disposed against fighting and warfare, and there are verses in the Qur'an which testify to this. In the words of Dr N.K. Singh:

> *The basic object of war, defensive wars of Islam in the cause of Allah, is to restore peace and freedom of religion and worship. To fight in the cause of truth is one of the highest forms of charity — a fard (compulsory religious duty). ... In fact, Islam is fundamentally an anti-war religion of peace. Peace is the basic root of Islam. The Prophet's Hadith is:*
>
> *"The ink of the scholar is holier than the blood of the martyr." The jihad of peace is holier and mightier than the jihad of war.*[427]

Dr Gottleib Leitner claims that the Christians have adopted many laws of eastern faiths (Muhammadanism) into their daily life, but, he was surprised that, this was not recognised. He maintains:

> *We do not seem to recognise that laws are laid down for general guidance and that the letter of such laws is not to be the lord but the servant of our interpretation of them. Above all, our abstract charities, our abstract religion, our hard-and-fast rules, are in contrast to the personal, individual, concrete, dramatic, allegorical and imaginative which characterise the Eastern faiths and forms that have been adapted by us. There would be no Nihilists and no Socialist in Europe were Western society constituted on the basis of Muhammadanism; for in it a man is not taught to be dissatisfied, as is the great effort, aim and result of our civilization.*[428]

Edward Montet, a French intellectual, notes that Islam is fundamentally a faith which relies on reason as the best guide for belief and action. Its origin is with the teachings of Prophet Muhammad (ﷺ) and the Qur'an, where the doctrine of unity has been emphasised. He states:

> *Islam is a religion that is essentially rationalistic in the widest sense of this term considered etymologically and historically....the teachings of the Prophet, the Qur'an has invariably kept its place as the fundamental starting point, and the dogma of unity of God has always been proclaimed therein with a grandeur, a majesty, an invariable purity and with a note of sure conviction, which it is hard to find surpassed outside the pale of Islam....A creed so precise, so stripped of all theological complexities and consequently so accessible to the ordinary understanding might be expected to possess and does indeed possess a marvelous power of winning its way into the consciences of men.*[429]

The Chinese Emperor Hong-Wu (also known as Zhū Yuánzhāng, 1368–1398) was greatly influenced by Islam. He built several mosques in the country and recruited a number of Muslims who served in the army as generals.[430]

Indian author M.N. Roy wrote an essay on Islamic culture: "The Historical Role of Islam", in which he claimed that the sudden growth and spread of Islam was an amazing part of history. The contribution of Islam to human culture became a great political element:

> *The apparently sudden rise and the dramatic expansion of Mohammedanism constitute a most fascinating chapter in the history of mankind. A dispassionate study of this chapter is of great importance in the present fateful period of the history of India. The scientific value of the study by itself is great, and the meritorious quest for knowledge is sure to be handsomely rewarded. But with us, to-day in India, particularly with the Hindu, a proper understanding of the historical role of Islam and the contribution it has made to human culture has acquired a supreme political importance*[431].

Roy went on to say that there is no link between Islam and militarism. Islam means peace, which is necessary to be established in this world:

> *It is a gross misreading of history to confound Islam with militarism. Mohammad was the Prophet not of the Saracen warriors, but of the Arab merchants. The very name with which he baptized his creed contradicts the current notion about its aim. Etymologically, Islam means to make peace, or the making of peace: to make peace with God by doing homage to his Oneness, repudiating the fraudulent divinity of idols which had usurped His sole claim to the devotion of man; and to make peace on earth through the union of the Arabian tribes. The peace on earth was of immediate importance, and greater consequence.*[432]

Roy further noted that Islam is an essential element for human progress on earth. In his words,

> *Islam was a necessary product of history,—an instrument of human progress. It rose as the ideology of a new social relation which, in its turn, revolutionized the mind of man.*[433]

On an everyday level, Muslims and non-Muslims mutually interact with one another, and there is little proof to suggest that relations between the two are acrimonious. Amit Pal, the author of the book *Islam Means Peace* says that the society in which he was raised included both Muslims and Hindus. He has never found Muslims to be aggressive. He says:

> *I spent much of my childhood in India, where Hindus and Muslims live and work together at numerous levels. The idea of Muslims being inherently violent goes against a lifetime of my observations. I had Muslim neighbors, friends, and classmates, and the notion that they somehow were more disposed toward violence was ridiculous*[434]

Pal goes on to say that in many cases, pondering on the Qur'an leads one to the conclusion that it is certainly not violent. In fact, it would reveal that in essence the book advocates for peace and encourages mankind to live harmoniously with each other. Pal says that the great

Indian leader Mahatma Gandhi read the Qur'an and concluded that there is no violence in Islam; rather it means peace.

> *Gandhi, the ultimate icon of nonviolence, said, "My reading of the Qur'an has (convinced me that the basis of Islam is not violence, but is unadulterated peace. It regards forbearance as a superior to vengeance. The very word 'Islam' means peace, which is nonviolence."*[435]

To emphasise Islam's commitment to peace, Muslims are required to greet each other wishing peace, i.e. non-violence, for each other. Amit Pal says:

> *The standard Muslim greeting is Salaam ale-kum, or "peace be upon you."*[436]

Reverend Edwin R. Stephenson of the Methodist Episcopal Church holds that the religion of Islam is a blessing from God for human beings. It guides people from darkness to light. According to him:

> *The message of Mohammad, Islam, is nothing but a blessing for mankind - The usher from darkness to light and from Satan to God.*[437]

Major-General Charles George Gordon, CB also known as Chinese Gordon, Gordon Pasha, and Gordon of Khartoum, was sympathetic towards Islam as preached by Prophet Muhammad (ﷺ). In response to a reporter claiming the religion to be imperiled, he said:

> *Not so, I find the Mussulman quite as good as Christian, as many a Christian, and do not believe he is in any peril. All of us are more or less pagans, I like the Mussulman; he is not ashamed of his God, his life is a fairly pure one; certainly he gives himself a good margin in the wife line, but, at any rate, he never poaches on others. Can our Christian people say the same?*[438]

George Bernard Shaw said that such was the weight and influence of

Islam that it has the potential to become the majority faith in Europe. In his words:

> *If any religion had the chance of ruling over England, nay Europe within the next hundred years, it could be Islam.*[439]

Edward Gibbon and Simon Oakley point out the religion of Islam as preached by Prophet Muhammad (ﷺ) is still the same, even after many centuries:

> *It is not the propagation but the permanency of his religion that deserves our wonder, the same pure and perfect impression which he engraved at Makkah and Madinah is preserved after the revolutions of twelve centuries by the Indian, the African and the Turkish proselytes of the Koran.... The Mahometans have uniformly withstood the temptation of reducing the object of their faith and devotion to a level with the senses and imagination of man. 'I believe in One God and Mahomet the Apostle of God' is the simple and invariable profession of Islam. The intellectual image of the Deity has never been degraded by any visible idol; the honours of the prophet have never transgressed the measure of human virtue, and his living precepts have restrained the gratitude of his disciples within the bounds of reason and religion.*[440]

Sir Thomas Walker Arnold, a British Orientalist and scholar of Islamic art, said that Islam became a missionary religion in the early days of Islam and Prophet Muhammad (ﷺ) is still able to attract many non-Muslims into the folds of Islam. Arnold observed:

> *Thus from its very inception Islam has been a missionary religion, both in theory and in practice, for the life of Muhammad exemplifies the same teaching, and the Prophet himself stands at the head of a long series of Muslim missionaries who have won an entrance for their faith into the hearts of unbelievers.*[441]

R.V.C. Bodley observed that Islam was expanding more rapidly than any other religion and that caused fear amongst Christians and Jews. He compared Islam with other religions and raised a series of questions in an attempt to clarify this phenomenon:

> *What had Muhammad evolved in his mind in those ten years since the first revelation in the Mount Hira which was so disturbing? Why did his doctrine spread more rapidly than those of the Jews and Christians? What was the difference between Prophet Muhammad's teaching and that of Moses and Jesus? Why is the ratio of practicing Moslems greater than the ration of practicing Jews and Christians?*[442]

Balbir Singh, an Indian journalist, highlights that Islam was not spread by force and those who believe this are ignorant of affairs of the world:

> *Those who believe Islam was spread by force are fools who neither know the ways of Islam nor the ways of the world.*[443]

H.G. Wells also affirmed that the religion of Islam has urged its followers to deal amicably and ethically with each other. The emphasis on this aspect of human behaviour is essential to a healthy social order and is necessary if humans are dedicated to eradicating corrupt and unethical practices. In the estimation of President Eliot of Harvard University:

> *Mohammedanism has been a vastly better thing for many of the tribes of Africa, habitually drunk, than Christianity could have been.*[444]

Dr Tor Andrae was a Swedish scholar who understood the sacred power of Islam; he claimed that Islam's significance would be obvious once followed and put into action widely. In his words:

> *Islam is a forceful spiritual energy. Its true meaning will manifest itself when it will be implemented on a large scale.*[445]

Islam is the complete code of human life on earth. It provides a comprehensive explanation of man's purpose in this life and imparts a code of conduct which will facilitate a pious life that will prevent its adherents from torment in the afterlife and help them obtain salvation in the hereafter. In simple terms, Islam is about submitting to the will of Allah. The Muslim is the one who practises Islam, i.e. the one who submits to the will of God. It has been the fastest-growing religion in the world.[446]

Bernard Lewis was a British-American historian, scholar in Oriental studies, and political commentator. He wrote in his book: *The Crisis of Islam – Holy war and Unholy Terror* about the influence of Islam as the most civilised religion.[447]

Lewis continues noted that the struggle between good and evil in Islam was manifest in many different ways, including politics and armed forces. Muhammad was not just a Prophet and teacher but also an administrator and soldier.[448]

A common perception is that Prophet Muhammad (ﷺ) extracted wisdom from Christian scriptures, although a historical assessment will find that such an opportunity was beyond his reach as he was an unlettered person. Dr Angus Nicolson says:

> *In Muhammad's day there was no Arabic version of the Bible from which he could obtain accurate knowledge of Christ ... Therefore some maintain that the very existence of Islam is due to the failure of the Church.*[449]

William Montgomery Watt said that, although he was not a Muslim, he believed that the Qur'an is the divine truth from which many scholars can learn and it would be the leading religion in days to come:

> *I am not a Muslim in the usual sense, though I hope I am a "Muslim" as "one surrendered to God," but I believe that embedded in the Qur'an and other expressions of the Islamic vision are vast stores of divine truth from which I and other occidentals have still much to learn, and Islam is certainly a strong contender for the supplying of the basic framework of the one religion of the future.*[450]

Major Arthur Leonard observed that Islam began with a genuine strength and morality which has lasted over time.

> *Launched upon the world of Arabia in no false and unreal spirit, but with the spirit of grim sincerity and earnestness, Islam has proved its stability spiritually and materially, the present result of which speaks for itself.*[451]

Frederick Hamilton, the 1st Marquess of Dufferin and Ava, was a British public servant and prominent member of Victorian society. He pointed out that Europe should be grateful to the Muslims for their contributions towards science, art and literature which helped bring them out of the middle ages. In his words:

> *It is to Muslims science, to Muslims art and to Muslims literature that Europe has been in a great measure indebted for its extrication from the darkness of the Middle Ages.*[452]

A.M. Theodore Lothrop Stoddard, an American historian, journalist, racial anthropologist, eugenicist, political theorist and anti-immigration advocate, thought that the rise of Islam was a key part of history. He was astonished that Islam, having emerged from an insignificant land and people, had extended throughout the earth in the span of a century:

> *The rise of Islam is perhaps the most amazing event in human history. Springing from a land and a people alike previously negligible, Islam spread within a century over half the earth, shattering great empires, overthrowing long established religions, remoulding the souls of races, and building up a whole new world – the world of Islam.*[453]

Islam's growth was astonishing. Many other religions, such as Christianity, Buddhism and Zoroastrianism spread slowly through long periods of struggle. But this was not the case with Islam. The victory of Islam was apparently with phenomenal ease and no difficulty, from the Pyrenees to the Himalayas and from the deserts of Central Asia to the deserts of Central Africa. Stoddard continues:

> *Arising in a desert land sparsely inhabited by a nomad race previously undistinguished in human annals, Islam sallied forth on its great adventure with the slenderest human backing and against the heaviest material odds. Yet Islam triumphed with seemingly miraculous ease, and a couple of generations saw the Fiery Crescent borne victorious from the Pyrenees to the Himalayas and from the deserts of Central Asia to the deserts of Central Africa...* [454]

The Vatican City paid tribute to the practice of 'Fasting' by the Muslims, one of the five pillars of Islam. On the occasion of Eid, a speech delivered by the Vatican admired the teachings of the religion of Islam:

> *We rejoice with you for this privileged time which gives you the opportunity to deepen obedience to God, by fasting and other pious practices, a value equally dear to us.* [455]

Sir William Muir, although hostile to Islam, admitted the greatness of Prophet Muhammad (ﷺ) in his book, *Life of Mahomet*, in these words:

> *There can be no question but that, with its pure monotheism, and a code founded in the main on justice and humanity, Islam succeeds in raising to a higher level races sunk in idolatry and fetishism, like those of Central Africa, and that in some respects, notably in that of temperance, it materially improves the morality of such peoples.* [456]

The beauty of Islam comes by living very close to God which results in peace and contentment for mankind. M.S. Baboona thought that unlike Islam, Christianity is materialistic and businesslike. According to Baboona:

> *Christianity is commercialism. It says, God must have His pound of flesh and then forgive. Islam is Universalism. It says, God's love knows no measure, on metre. It is unqualified, unbounded, and*

wide as the wide world.[457]

Fossey John Cobb Hearnshaw, an English Professor of history specialising in medieval history acknowledges the contributions of Islam, particularly in the transition of Europe from the dark ages to a more enlightened era:

They were spellbound to see that Muslims were owners of a culture that was far superior to their own. The Dark Ages of Europe were illuminated by nothing but the beacon of Muslim civilization.[458]

Duncan Greenlees, a writer, theosophist and educationist, admits that the teachings of Islam amply prove that a perfect world religion can be established:

The nobility and the broad tolerance of this creed, which accepts as God-inspired all the real religions of the world, will always be a glorious heritage for mankind. On it could be built a perfect world religion.[459]

Dr A. Bertherand, a French scholar, observes that a Muslims are told to acquire knowledge even they have to travel far. Prophet Muhammad(ﷺ)'s encouragement towards cultivating knowledge suffices to refute the claim that Islam had stifled progress and civilisation, when in fact, the opposite is true. A scrutiny of the Prophet's teachings reveals the emphasis he placed on being contemplative of life and the world – the purpose of the creation of both. Although there are many detractors of Prophet Muhammad (ﷺ) who insist that he had a regressive influence, many Muslims have been the beneficiaries of his teachings:

To seek knowledge is a duty of every Muslim man and woman. 'Seek knowledge even though it be in China'. 'The savants are the heirs of the Prophets.' These profound words of the great reformer are an indisputable contradiction to those who seek and exert themselves in putting the responsibility of the intellectual degradation of Muslims upon the spirit of the Qur'an. Let them read and meditate upon this great Book and they will read that the Prophet incessantly called the attention and the meditation of his people to the splendid marvels, to the mysterious phenomenon of creation. The incredulous, sceptical and unbelieving may convince themselves that the importance of this Book and its doctrine was not to throw back, eventually, the intellectual and moral faculties of a whole people. On the contrary, those who have followed its counsels have been, as we have described in the course of this study, the creators of a civilisation which is astounding unto this day.[460]

Charles R. Watson noted that the Muslims are more religious minded than others:

It may be boldly asserted that no people in the world give the impression of being as religious-minded as do Moslems. All of life is saturated with the consciousness of God.[461]

Lancelot Lawton, a prolific British author, said about polygamy that it was not only limited to the East (Muslims). Rather, the West was ahead of them; and also that the West used more violence in propagating their beliefs. He was sure that the Muslim faith enjoyed superiority before the others.[462]

Reverend Bosworth Smith considers that Islam is a spiritual religion and there is no mediator between humans and God:

Again, Mohammedanism is essentially a spiritual religion. As instituted by Mohammed it had no priest and no sacrifice; in other words, no caste of sacrificing priests were ever to be allowed to come between the human soul and God: forbidding the representation of all living things alike, whether as objects of use or of admiration, of veneration or of worship, Mohammedanism is more opposed to idolatry even than we are ourselves.[463]

Smith further declares that Islam is the revitalisation of the previous religions:

I admitted above that the religion of Mohammed was in its essence not original. Mohammed never said it was: he called it a revival of the old one.[464]

Smith goes on to say that only the religion of Islam has had a permanent effect on mankind as compared to other belief systems:

One of the most philosophical of historians has remarked that of all the revolutions which have had a permanent influence upon the civil history of mankind, none could so little be anticipated by human prudence as that effected by the religion of Arabia. And at first sight it must be confessed that the Science of History, if indeed there be such a science, is at a loss to find that sequence of cause and effect which it is the object and the test of all history, which is worthy of the name, to trace out.[465]

Wilfred Cantwell Smith, a Canadian professor of comparative religion, claims that one of the unique features of Islam which distinguishes it from Christianity is its social dimension. Its survival until the current period is a testimony to some of its social characteristics which have a broad application that resonates with people, irrespective of their social class.[466]

The lack of spirituality in Western civilisation continues to plague societies, and this is something which the implementation of Islam in one's everyday life can help redress. No amount of cultural pressure and legal stipulation can exert the same effect and influence of religious decree, and this is particularly true of Muslim societies and persons, where much of everyday life is dictated by religion. More importantly, this sense of spirituality, if exerted on the Western sensibility, may help it to fill the spiritual void that currently characterises Western societies. A.J. Toynbee, a British historian, notes:

If ever the 'natives' of these regions (Central Africa and Indonesia) succeed in recapturing a spiritual state in which they are able to call their souls their own, it may prove to have been the Islamic spirit that has given fresh form to the void. This spirit may be expected to manifest itself in many practical ways; and one of these manifestations might be a liberation from alcohol, which was inspired by religious conviction and which was, therefore, able to accomplish what could never be enforced by the external sanction of an alien law...Here, then, in the foreground of the future, we can remark two valuable influences which Islam may exert upon the cosmopolitan proletariat of a Western society that has cast its net round the world and embraced the whole of mankind.[467]

Napoleon Bonaparte pointed out that the distinction between Prophet Muhammad (ﷺ) and previous prophets was that his message was intended for a universal audience and not restricted to a specific part of the world populace. Bonaparte stated:

Moses has revealed the existence of God to his nation, Jesus Christ to the Roman world, & Muhammad to the old continent.[468]

If one considers how the various denominations among the Christians fought amongst themselves, it appears even more surprising that Europeans were not more favourably disposed to the Islamic faith. Despite the corrupt bureaucracy, tyranny of clerical institutes and the general social and political breakdown in Christian quarters, the Europeans turned a blind eye to their own decadence prevailing for centuries and instead stigmatised the Islamic faith. The depths of European ignorance are striking, seeing how Europe's degraded state was a continuing phenomenon which showed signs of little improvement until a much later period. Commenting on the European lethargy, Major Leonard said:

Is it not obvious that in her outlook on Islam, Europe has overlooked her own Dark Ages – that awful period of intellectual oblivion which commenced with the decline of classical learning subsequent to the establishment of the barbarians in Europe in the fifth century, and continued down to the Renaissance, i.e., towards the end of the fourteenth century? Is it, too, not evident that she has lost all recollection of the torn and disturbed state of Christendom even in the middle of the fifteenth century when the renaissance was in full swing, or had at least run half its course?[469]

Professor Arnold argued that Islam is not only for Muslims but for the whole of mankind and is a universal religion. There is no god but one God and Islam is the religion for all. This belief of a Moslem is not in theory only but is in practice as well. As the Messenger of God Prophet Muhammad (ﷺ) wrote letters to the leaders of other nations inviting them to accept Islam. For instance, he wrote to the Emperor of Rome (Heraclius), king of Persia, governor of Egypt, etc. Professor Arnold relates:

But the message of Islam was not for Arabia only; the whole world was to share in it. As there was but one God, so there was to be but one religion into which all men were to be invited. This claim to be universal, to hold sway over all men and all nations, found a practical illustration in the letters which Muhammad is said to have sent in the year A.D. 688 (A.H. 6) to the great potentates of that time. An invitation to embrace Islam was sent in this year to the Emperor Heraclius, the king of Persia, the governor of Yaman, the governor of Egypt and the king of Abyssinia. The letter to Heraclius is said to have been as follows : – "In the name of God, the Merciful, the Compassionate, Muhammad, who is the servant of God and His apostle, to Hiraql the Qaysar of Rūm. Peace be on whoever has gone on the straight road. After this I say, verily I call you to Islam. Embrace Islam, and God will reward you twofold. If you turn away from the offer of Islam, then on you be the sins of your people. O people of the Book, come towards a creed which is fit both for us and for you. It is this - to worship none but God, and not to associate anything with God, and not to call others God. Therefore, O ye people of the Book, if ye refuse, beware. We are Muslims and our religion is Islam.[470]

Professor Arnold adds:

The proof of the universality of Islam, of its claim on the acceptance of all men, lay in the fact that it was the religion divinely appointed for the whole human race and was now revealed to them anew through Prophet Muhammad (ﷺ), the seal of the prophets as it had been to former generations by other prophets.[471]

The renowned author and Harvard Professor Annemarie Schimmel affirms that Prophet Muhammad (ﷺ) was the last amongst the Prophets of God.[472]

The Christians of Europe would only be doing themselves a favour by owning up to their misdemeanours and recognising how Islam had imparted to its own civilisation much benefit and progress. The concealed antagonism and suspicion between the two faiths can be mitigated to a great extent if Christians assume an apologetic stance towards the Muslim world, insofar as it realises the mistakes it made in its representation and treatment of the Muslim world. Such a feat would help reinstate the credibility of Christians in the hearts of many Muslims who, still to this day, cannot forget the Christian stigmatisation of the Islamic faith. On this subject, Major Leonard comments:

Let Europe – Christendom rather – confess and acknowledge her fault. Let her proclaim aloud to her own ignorant masses, and to the world at large, the ingratitude she has displayed, and the eternal debt she owes to, the Islam she no longer despises. Open confession is good for the soul, and only a confession such as this can wipe off the black stain which has for so long besmirched her fair name. Let Christendom once and for all recognise that the greatest of all faults is to be conscious of none – that acknowledging a fault is saying, only in other words, we are wiser today than we were yesterday. Only through magnanimity such as this can she claim redemption. For, she must surely know that injustice founded on religious sources and national conceit cannot be perpetrated forever.[473]

Dr Gustave E. Von Grunebaum, an Austrian historian and Arabist, wrote in his book *Muhammadan Festivals* that Islam is the last religion of the world. It is an independent religion although it is very close to Christianity and Judaism. The basic beliefs of Islam are few and simple.

Malise Ruthven claims that only the religion of Islam had advanced and continued to exist in the modern times but no other religion was able to with the same degree of success and impact. Islam has a range of thoughts, codes and saintly principles by means of which the followers maintain distinctiveness and contact with God.[474]

Ruthven further says that Islam is flexible and accepted different cultural principles within its structure. For instance, the Abrahamic family of Western Asian monotheism encompasses Islam, Judaism and Christianity.[475]

Dr Leitner highlights that he was using the term Muhammadanism to mean the religion of Prophet Muhammad (ﷺ); but he argued that if he would address the great religion with the term 'Islam' then a great attention would be required which was not possible in a short time.

> *As regards the great religion with which we are dealing today, I have adopted the term Muhammadanism in order to limit this address to the creed as now professed by Muhammadans. If I had used the better heading Islam, which means the creed of resignation to the Divine Will, a more extensive treatment would have been necessary that can be afforded in the course of an hour.*[476]

Dr Leitner admired the mission of Prophet Muhammad (ﷺ). Having acquired the knowledge of Judaism and Christianity, he said that the religion of Islam is not a mere copy of other religions, rather a true inspiration from the Goodness itself deep within. In his words:

> *But so far as I know either of Judaism or of Christianity, the system preached by Muhammad was not merely imitative or eclectic; it was also inspired - if there be such a process as inspiration from the source of all goodness. Indeed, I venture to state in all humility that if self-sacrifice, honesty of purpose, unswerving belief in one's mission, a marvelous insight into existing wrong or error, and the perception and use of the best means for its removal are among the outward and visible signs of inspiration, the mission of Muhammad was inspired.*[477]

Dr Leitner argues that the Christians criticised Prophet Muhammad (ﷺ) in a very undeserving method that included Dante and many others. However, whoever and whatever they said, the proclamation at the Mount Hera had been achieved in daily life. Dr Leitner explains:

> *The founder of Muhammadanism has been talked of by Christians in the most unworthy manner. Still, at first, he was regarded as a Quasi-Christian Sectarian. Dante refers to Muhammad as a heretic in his Inferno; and indeed, in another sense, he was only a dissenter from one of he many forms which have adopted the appellation of Christian. Some authors alleged that his religion was taken from the Talmud: but it seems to me that the question of what Muhammadanism really is cannot be summed up better than in stating it to be pure Judaism plus proselytism, and original Christianity minus the teaching of St Paul. This as regards its theory; in practice it is far more than modern Christianity in it artificial European aspect - the Sermon on the Mount translated into daily life*[478].

H.A.R. Gibb, a Scottish historian and Orientalist remarks that the continuous spreading and victory of Islam in a short time over various parts of the world signifies how strong and influential the message of this religion is![479]

A Misrepresented Religion

Jon Dal Din, the Director of Westminster Interfaith Group opines that adequate respect is not being given to Islam as Prophet Muhammad (ﷺ) had asked and possibly the religion is misinterpreted for political reasons. In his words:

> *My understanding would be that the prophet has asked for more respect than perhaps some people would have given Islam credit for...Islam is perhaps being misrepresented by few people...whether*

they are using it for political reason....we are talking about political things ...when we are talking about community, we are talking about community –fundamentally; I think-our perceptions of Islam and its teachings are secured by some fairly.[480]

British MP Frank Dobson comments that Islam is a universal religion; there are groupings within Islam, as is true for other religions, and due differences of opinions, and many people have been killed also as a result of differences:

It's a large worldwide religion. Within it there are many different groupings as there are in all large organisations-in a sense it is not a large organisation, because it does not have any pyramidal structure and it clearly gives great inspiration and sustenance for large numbers of people who believe. There are large differences of opinion. I think it's always worth noting that just as most Christians have been killed by fellow Christians in history, most Muslims who have been killed, have been killed by fellow Muslims and that shows the dangers of theological differences, although again I think the theological differences may frequently have been exploited by people who wanted to use them as an excuse to get their own bit of territory.[481]

Although Islam is essentially a religion of peace, misconceptions about the faith, as with other fails, are many. According to Singh:

The meaning of Islam is 'peace' but the religion has been misunderstood because of two main reasons: (1) Lack of proper exploration i.e. without studying, understanding and evaluating the real standpoints of Islam. (2) An imperfect and partial conception of non-violence.[482]

Carl Heinrich Becker, a German scholar of Islam, pointed out that the enmity between Christianity and Islam worsened because of the Crusades, the Turkish wars and the huge expansion of Europe, and not because of any hatred of Christianity by the Muslim conquerors:

The Crusades, the Turkish wars, and the great expansion of Europe widened the gulf between Christianity and Islam, while as the East was gradually brought under ecclesiastical influence the contrast grew deeper. The theory, however, that the Muhammadan conquerors and their successors were inspired by a fanatical hatred of Christianity is a fiction invented by Christians.[483]

M.N. Roy gives the various reasons why and how the religion of Islam was established in India:

A critical investigation of the internal as well as the external causes of the Muslim conquest of India is of practical value today. It will remove the prejudice that makes the orthodox Hindu look upon his Muslim neighbor as an Inferior being. Freed from preconceived ideas, the Hindus will be in a position to appreciate the constructive consequences of the Muslim conquest of India. That will enable them to live down the hatred of the conquered for the conquerors. Unless a radical change of attitude is brought about by a sober sense of history, the communal question will never be solved. The Hindus will never be able to look upon the Muslims as integral parts of the Indian nation until they come to appreciate the contribution they made towards the emergence of Indian society out of the chaos caused by the breakdown of the antique civilisation. Besides, a proper understanding of history derived from a correct understanding of the successful advent of the Muslims in India will enable us to ascertain and stamp out the deeper causes of our present misfortune.[484]

Professor Kaltner highlights that it would be a great mistake to think that Muslims have only abhorrence for non-Muslims and see them as foes. But the real message is that there is no such aspect in the Islamic institution; rather Islam teaches to the contrary of this understanding.[485]

HRH Prince Charles explained that not only do many in the West have an incorrect understanding of Islam, but there also exists a lack of awareness of Islam's contribution to human civilisation. In addition to this, there is general ignorance about the golden age of Islamic civilisation and how Muslims have, in the past, contributed intellectually for the benefit of mankind and in a way from which Western civilisation tremendously benefited. Again, our historical prejudice plays a large part in this ignorance. The idea that Muslims and the Islamic faith are a threat to the West has undermined perceptions of the significance of early Muslims. A large part of history which we in the West have virtually ignored and pay little respect to is that Andalusia – Muslim Spain, one of history's greatest civilisations, which went on to influence the renaissance and ensuing enlightenment of modern Europe. According to Prince Charles:

> *If there is much misunderstanding in the West about the nature of Islam, there is also much ignorance about the debt our own culture and civilization owe to the Islamic world. It is a failure which stems, I think, from the straightjacket of history which we have inherited. The medieval Islamic world, from Central Asia to the shores of the Atlantic, was a world where scholars and men of learning flourished. But because we have tended to see Islam as the enemy of the West, as an alien culture, society, and system of belief, we have tended to ignore or erase its great relevance to our own history. For example, we have underestimated the importance of eight hundred years of Islamic society and culture in Spain between the eighth and fifteenth centuries. The contribution of Muslim Spain to the preservation of classical learning during the Dark Ages, and to the first flowerings of the Renaissance, has long been recognized. But Islamic Spain was much more than a mere larder where Hellenistic knowledge was kept for later consumption by the emerging modern Western world. Not only did Muslim Spain gather and preserve the intellectual content of ancient Greek and Roman civilization, it also interpreted and expanded upon that civilization, and made a vital contribution of its own in so many fields of human endeavour—in science, astronomy, mathematics, algebra (itself an Arabic word), law, history, medicine, pharmacology, optics, agriculture, architecture, theology, music. Averroes and Avenzoor, like their counterparts Avicenna and*

> *Rhazes in the East, contributed to the study and practice of medicine in ways from which Europe benefited for centuries afterwards.*[486]

Teachings of Islam

Dr Leitner explains some of the teachings of Islam in relation to the socio-economic situation. In Islam the rich, as guardians, should take care of the poor. There is no unpleasant distinction between the rich and the poor. A great teaching about slaves is that they are not just a member of the household, but they have the option to take part even in the governance of the state. Dr Leitner elaborates:

> *With regard to social gradation, the rich man is considered to be the natural protector of the poor, and the poor man takes his place at the table of the rich. Nowhere in Muhammadan society is there any invidious distinction between rich and poor; and even a Muhammadan slave is not only a member of the household but also has far greater chances of rising to a position in government or in society than an English pauper.*[487]

The Bishop of London wrote in the *Times* on 17 April 1893, paying tribute to the followers of Prophet Muhammad (ﷺ). He compared the behaviour of the Muslims after conquering a land to what the Christians did. According to him, the activities of the Muslims did not seem to increase any of the existing vices in the land they conquered while the opposite was true for the conquering Christians. The Bishop wrote:

> *Mahamadans never make any addition to the vices already prevalent among those whom they reach or conquer as do Christians. The approach of these is almost everywhere the introduction of drunkenness, previously all but unknown.*[488]

British writer John Hick stated that although Islam started with difficulties, its teachings were very realistic in forming community brotherhood, fair dealings, truth-telling, keeping promises, donating to the poor, and sympathy for the helpless, widows, orphans and slaves.[489]

The teachings of Islam are simple and appeal to the common man as they are relevant to his daily life. These teachings require him to be generous, kind, considerate and brotherly to his fellow human beings. Islam gives man a way of worship that is scrupulous but easy to follow and gratifying. The monotheistic concept of God in Islam is fundamental. It liberates him from slavery to any deity but God. This theological stance of Islam is distinctly different from the idea of the Creator in Christianity. H.G. Wells observes:

> *This insistence upon kindliness and consideration in the daily life is one of the main virtues of Islam, but it is not the only one. Equally important is uncompromising monotheism, void of any Jewish exclusiveness, which is sustained by the Koran. Islam from the outset was fairly proof against the theological elaborations that have perplexed and divided Christianity and smothered the spirit of Jesus. And its third source of strength has been in the meticulous prescription of methods of prayer and worship and its clear statement of the limited and conventional significance of the importance ascribed to Makkah. It was full of the spirit of kindliness, generosity and brotherhood; it was a simple and understandable religion; it was instinct with the chivalrous sentiment of the desert; and it made its appeal straight to the commonest instincts in the composition of ordinary men.*[490]

As far as tolerance is concerned, this is clearly advocated in the Qur'an and exemplified in the character of Prophet Muhammad (ﷺ). The overwhelming number of Islamic traditions which support the principle of tolerance prove that compulsion has never been something endorsed in Islam. According to Dr N.K. Singh:

> *The Islamic philosophy of tolerance is derived from the Qur'an and the practice of the Prophet. The Qur'an teaches that "Religion is only for Allah": Ya kunuddinu lillaht. The basis of Islamic*

toleration is firmly laid in the teaching of the Qur'an, "toleration" means "the recognition of free thought and practice in religious matters" (Oxford Dictionary). Toleration is a law, not of Coercion but of Love, not one of violence but of peace.[491]

Professor Max Muller likewise admired the teachings of Islam. In February 1894, he wrote how Islam helped people turned their back on a cursed life, immersed in drinking and immorality.

Professor Max Muller bears similar testimony in the Nineteenth Century of Feb. '94, written on his return from Constantinople. He finds Islam has "cured the two cancers that eat into the flesh of our modern society – drunkenness and immorality; no Mahamadan woman leading an openly immoral life." This, which is too emphatic, is perhaps more owing to our injudicious laws and customs, founded, it is erroneously believed, on New Testament teaching; though this only prescribes to bishops one wife, but urges Paul's example of none at all.[492]

Michael Cook, an English-Scottish historian and scholar of Islamic history and Lecturer at the School of Oriental and African Studies, in comparing Islam with other religions, i.e. Christianity and Judaism, wrote that he was overwhelmed with the excellence of Islam as a way of life. He felt that Prophet Muhammad made an immense contribution for the good of mankind. His preached religion of Islam showed the world the relationship between God andmankind which is so natural and genuine.[493]

The great Indian politician Jawaharlal Nehru claimed that the religion of Islam was accepted in the neighbouring countries because of its simplicity, sincerity and equality.[494]

Oneness and Unity of God is the first and foremost teaching of Islam; other religions also have more or less the same basic theme but not with such strong emphasis on the Unity of God. According to James A. Spronle:

Islam teaches the Unity of God. Other religions have taught the

> *same, but not so emphatically and persistently as in simple confession of the followers of Muhammad.*[495]

Reverend Canon Isaac Taylor, a philologist and Anglican canon of York, in a speech delivered at the Church Congress of England, admired the teachings of Islam:

> *When Muhammadanism is embraced by a Negro tribe, paganism, devil worship, fetishism, cannibalism, human sacrifice, Infanticide, witchcraft disappears. The natives begin to dress, filth is replaced by cleanliness and they acquire personal dignity and self-respect. Hospitality becomes a religious duty, drunkenness becomes rare, gambling is forbidden, Immodest dances and promiscuous Intercourse of the sexes cease, female chastity is rewarded as a virtue. Industry replaces Idleness, license gives place to law, order and sobriety prevail, blood-feuds, cruelty to animals and slaves are forbidden. A freeing of humanity, benevolence and brotherhood is inculcated. Polygamy and slavery is regulated and all their evils are restrained. Islam above all is the most powerful total abstinence Association in the world.... Islam is cosmopolitan and not like Judaism confined to one race but extended to the world ...Islam swept away corruptions and superstitions...*[496]

Islam is not a barrier to ethical conduct or performing good deeds. In Islam, all deeds of goodness, mercy, forgiveness, perseverance and well-being are liable to be amply rewarded by God. These are strong incentives for noble deeds and pious actions for the sake of God. Professor Vaglieri explained:

> *Islam was not only not an obstacle to moral perfection; since it possessed in itself an efficient strength directed towards good deeds, it succeeded, earlier than other religions, in educating and raising men towards God. Islam succeeded because it was not less concerned for the moral responsibility of its members than other monotheistic religions whose prophets Muhammad recognised as his teachers, but in certain respects it was even more concerned than they, because it*

counted on human weakness and exhorted its believers towards ideals within their reach. The same virtues which Judaism and Christianity present as the supreme end of the moral life of man, are not only set forth but are even prescribed as ideals in Islam. This is true of the ideals of mercy towards all creatures, understanding, forgiveness, simplicity, fitness in social contacts, acceptance of misfortunes, and so on.[497]

Major General Forlong believes that the spread of Islam in Europe contributed immensely towards the continent's development in education and enlightenment, as if it were a light in darkness:

As soon as its rule was firmly established in Western Asia, Africa and Southern Europe, its rulers did their best to upraise the people intellectually. It was they, says the author of the 'History of European Civilisation' who kindled the lamp of learning which illumined the dark pages of European History; which but for the Arabs might never have become a centre of civilization and progress. They established seats of learning from Spain to Baghdad. There teachers and scholars arose, bright and shining lights, the cultured saviours of Europe when Christians were ignorant gloomy, pessimists, busy only in darkening the land with all the devout senility which characterised our dark middle ages.[498]

Prophet Muhammad (ﷺ) emigrated from the place of his birth to avoid conflict and confrontation with his adversaries in faith, to a place where it should be possible to preach and practise the way of life he was entrusted to propagate. Eventually, this became a precedent for Muslims to follow. Amit Pal says:

The notion of emigration as a form of nonviolent protest is central to Islam and is hallowed among Muslims since they believe that by doing so they are following in the footsteps of Muhammad and his companions.[499]

The teachings of Islam leave Muslims with no option but to pursue the most peaceful means in everyday life. J. Patout Burns, an expert in comparative religion, declares that there is nothing in Islam that prescribes violence.[500]

The principal declaration of Islam is the oneness of God and surrendering to His will. This is the nucleus of the religion of Islam. Edward Arnold echoes this:

> *The soul of Islam is its declaration of the Unity of God, its heart is the inculcation of an absolute resignation to His will.*[501]

Sadhu T. Vaswani highlighted the contributions of Islam in Europe and explained how Christian scholars were fascinated with its teachings. Islam showed light in the dark days of Europe and it contributed to the development of many disciplines of science and arts including medicine, mathematics, chemistry, history, philosophy, fine arts etc. Vaswani explains:

> *Islam founded the great University of Cordova which attracted Christian scholars from different parts of Europe. One of these scholars became, in due course, the Pope of Rome .... At a time when Europe was in darkness, the Muslim scholars of Spain held high the torch of science and literature. They taught medicine and mathematics, chemistry and natural history, philosophy and fine arts. And it is no exaggeration to say that Islam has made several contributions to the thought and life of India. Islam has been one of the nationalising forces in India. Islam has enriched the art and architecture, the geometry and philosophy of India. The Taj is perhaps the most imaginative architecture in the world.* [502]

Julius Germanus, a Hungarian professor of Oriental studies and Islamologist of Jewish origin, member of the Hungarian Parliament and member of multiple Arabic academies of science, observed that Islam does not require an arbitrator between God and man to relate and communicate. It is a religion that offers entry to one and all:

> *Muhammad the Prophet had broken the spell of priesthood before*

long; Islam did not need a mediator between God and man. It was a democratic religion from the beginning. No institution stood between the Creator and created. Through the knowledge of the Qur'an every body had access to the revelation, which would be expounded freely, without any synod putting limitations upon it. In this respect Islam did not need a reformation similar to that in Christianity, and as a matter of fact the democratic spirit which has reigned in Islam, began in Christianity only with the rise of nationalism and the Reformation.[503]

The claim that Islam is attracting a considerable number of followers is reflected by the statistics on the ground. Be they new members to the faith or newly arriving Muslims to a country, helping to swell the numbers of Muslims, it can be said that Islam enjoys regular growth in its number of adherents due to its universality.

The American politician Hillary Clinton notes that Islam is the fastest growing faith in America and it provides directions and support appropriate to the people of the country. She says:

Islam is the fastest-growing religion in America, a guide and pillar of stability for many of our people...[504]

Islam teaches mankind to submit to God only and to dispense with the mediator between God and man. The place of worship for a Muslim is where he finds himself to be. Dr Leitner notes:

Every Muhammadan is a church in himself: everyone is allowed to give an opinion on a religious matter, on the basis of the belief common to his co-religionists. They are not slaves to priests; they pray to God without an intermediary, and their place of worship is wherever they happen to be at the appointed hours of prayer.[505]

M.N. Roy says:

Mohammad's religion was rigorously monotheistic; and as a Monotheism It was uncompromising, which outstanding characteristic won for it the distinction of the highest form of religion.[506]

The author Kerena Marchant admires the Muslim family bond:

Family is the corner stone to Islam. Muslims look to the example of Muhammad's family, particularly to the example of his wife, Khadijah, and daughter, Fatimah. Muslims believe that people are born Muslims but the family determines whether they are true Muslims.[507]

Islam offers guidance in every sector of life for whatever we do on a daily basis. According to Marchant:

Islam governs every aspect of life; worship and the family. It affects everything in life; even eating, drinking and washing.[508]

She notes that Prophet(ﷺ)'s teachings were inspired by God himself. She further adds:

Muhammad's teaching was not his own, it was God's, because it came direct from God. This teaching covers all aspects of life: a person's relationship with God, relationship to others, family life and everyday life.[509]

E. Alexander Powell, an American war correspondent during World War I wrote in his book *The struggle for Power in Muslim Asia* that the Muslims showed a higher level of tolerance than many Christian nations. Powell said:

In their wars of conquest, however, the Muslims exhibited a degree of toleration which puts many Christian nations to shame.[510]

The author Magsie Hamilton Little explains in her book *The thing about Islam: Exposing the myths, facts and controversies* that Islam teaches us not to treat work as a burden, but rather to accept it as the essential criterion of daily life. She says that the Muslims thank God for whatever they achieve by using their fullest potential and they should never look down upon the status of work they do. In the eyes of Allah the job of a labourer is 'just as praiseworthy as that of a white-collar worker'.[511]

Hamilton Little further says that Islam has established laws for business and other transactions. Muslims are to abide by government law and the instructions of the Qur'an. Islam teaches people to respect all works so long as the Qur'anic laws are not violated. The Qur'an clarifies the distinction between lawful (*halal*) and unlawful (*haram*) work).[512]

> *In resignation to God's will, in temperance, chastity, veracity and in brotherhood of believers they (Muslims) set up a pattern which we should do well to follow. Islam has abolished drunkenness, gambling and prostitution, the three curses of Christian lands ... Islam has done more for civilization than Christianity.*[513]

Contributions of Islam

HRH Prince Charles highlighted that the UK of the twentieth century is a prime example of where the values of tolerance and mutual respect have been applied with good effect and success. Despite the misunderstanding and confusion which surrounds the nations Muslim minorities, Muslims have established themselves across all aspects of business and trade and are a welcome addition to society. Much of this is of course due to the multiracial policies which the country is so keen to preserve. In his words:

> *If this need for tolerance and exchange is true internationally, it applies with special force within Britain itself. Britain is a multi-racial and multi-cultural society. I have already mentioned the size of our own Muslim communities who live throughout Britain, both in large towns like Bradford and in tiny communities in places as remote as Stornaway in Western Scotland. These people are an asset of Britain. They contribute to all parts of our economy - to industry, the public services, the professions, and the private sector.*

We find them as teachers, as doctors, as engineers, and as scientists. They contribute to our economic well-being as a country, and add to the cultural richness of our nation. Of course, tolerance and understanding must be two-way.[514]

The Prince added that the European civilisation inherited a vast intellectual legacy from its Muslim predecessors. In the intellectual disciplines, state organisation and other fields, the Muslim influence on European thought is unmistakable. As far as religious tolerance is concerned, the idea of members of different faiths living harmoniously enjoying mutual respect was reflected in Muslim Spain centuries before it was encountered in the rest of Europe. What we may refer to as purely 'Western' politics, society etc. were derived in part from the systems which Muslims had put in place in the medieval ages. According to Prince Charles:

Many of the traits on which modern Europe prides itself came to it from Muslim Spain. Diplomacy, free trade, open borders, the techniques of academic research, of anthropology, etiquette, fashion, various types of medicine, hospitals, all came from this great city of cities. Medieval Islam was a religion of remarkable tolerance for its time, allowing Jews and Christians the right to practice their inherited beliefs, and setting an example which was not, unfortunately, copied for many centuries in the West. The surprise is the extent to which Islam has been a part of Europe for so long, first in Spain, then in the Balkans, and the extent to which it has contributed so much towards the civilization which we all too often think of, wrongly, as entirely Western. Islam is part of our past and our present, in all fields of human endeavor. It has helped to create modern Europe. It is part of our own inheritance, not a thing apart.[515]

Prince Charles added that the pursuit of knowledge was deemed obligatory for Muslims and there are many prophetic sayings to the effect that knowledge and its acquisition is one of the loftiest ideals for a Muslim. History also bears witness how Muslims put this principle into practice. In particular, the example of Andalusia, Muslim Spain, is a revealing one. Europeans ought to note that the Muslim civilisation originated earlier and progressed way before theirs:

> *Islam nurtured and preserved the quest for learning. In the words of the tradition, 'the ink of the scholar is more sacred than the blood of the martyr'. Cordoba in the tenth century was by far the most civilized city of Europe. We know of leading libraries in Spain at the time King Alfred was making terrible blunders with the culinary arts in this country. It is said that the 400,000 volumes in its ruler's library amounted to more books than all the libraries of the rest of Europe put together. That was made possible because the Muslim world acquired from China the skill of making paper more than four hundred years before the rest of non-Muslim Europe.*[516]

H.G. Armstrong notes that Islam unified the Arabs and within about a decade, Prophet Muhammad (ﷺ) was soon able to control the entire Arab lands:

> *Islam united the Arabs, purified and bound them into one people. Muhammad filled them with great faith. His power increased rapidly. Within ten years he controlled all Arabia.*[517]

The Reverend Stephens found that Islam, having spread outside of Arabia to different parts of the world, abolished inhuman practices and led the people towards the right path, the way of Islam:

> *As Islam gradually extended its conquest beyond the boundaries of Arabia, many barbarous races whom it absorbed became in like manner participators in its benefits. The Turk, the Indian, the Negro, and the Moor were compelled to cast away their idols, to abandon their licentious rites and customs, to turn to the worship of one god, to a decent ceremonial and an orderly way of life. The faith even of the more enlightened Persians was purified – he taught that good and evil are not coordinate powers, but that just and unjust are alike under the sway of one All-wise Ruler, who ordereth*

all things in heaven and earth. For barbarous nations, then, especially nations which were more or less in the condition of Arabia itself at the time of Mohammad; nations in the condition of Africa at the present day with little or no civilisation, and without a reasonable religion, Islam certainly comes as a blessing as a turning from darkness" to light and from the power of Satan unto God. [518]

Alfred Martin admires the contributions of Islam in the field of education:

To-day we decorate our walls and floors with fabrics that Mohammedans taught us to weave. We regale our senses with perfumes they taught us to make, we teach our children the algebra and higher mathematics which they taught the fathers. [519]

Martin added that the teachings of Islam brought many parts of the world from anarchy to the rule of law:

In the ethical legislation that Mohammed provided for his theocracy, prominence was given to total abstinence from intoxicating liquor and to humaneness. Drunkenness is the vice most to be feared in tropical countries and was generally condemned as a violation of Divine Law. Mohammed's opposition to Christianity was based, in part, upon its failure to put an absolute veto on the use of intoxicants. General Lew Wallace, after twenty years' residence in Constantinople, declared that while Christian drunkards were to be seen daily in the city streets, he never once saw a drunken Mohammedan. In the estimation of President Eliot of Harvard University Mohammedanism has been a vastly better thing for many of the tribes of Africa, habitually drunk, than Christianity could have been[520].

Professor Arnold observes that there were proofs that the spread of Islam was carried out not only by men, but also involved women in various walks of life. He provides some examples of how Muslim women took part in the propagation of the faith:

> *It is interesting to note that the propagation of Islam has not been the work of men only, but that Muslim women have also taken their part in this pious task. Several of the Mongol princes owed their conversion to the influence of a Muslim wife, and the same was probably the case with many of the pagan Turks when they had carried their raids into Muhammadan countries. The Sanusiyyah missionaries who came to work among the Tubu, to the north of Lake Chad, opened schools for girls, and took advantage of the powerful influence exercised by the women among these tribes (as among their neighbours, the Berbers), in their efforts to win them over to Islam. In German East Africa, the pagan natives who leave their homes for six months or more, to work on the railways or plantations, are converted by the Muhammadan women with whom they contract temporary alliances.*[521]

Islam is a religion which appeals to reason. For the Muslims the Qur'an is the source of knowledge and justification. The religious beliefs of Islam are based on a plausible rationale. Professor Edward Montet explains:

> *Islam is a religion that is essentially rationalistic in the widest sense of this term considered etymologically and historically. The definition of rationalism as a system that bases religious beliefs on principles famished by the reason, applies to it exactly. It is true that Muhammad, who was an enthusiast and possessed, too, the ardour of faith and the fire of conviction, that precious quality he transmitted to so many of his disciples,—brought forward his reform as a revelation... To believers, the Muhammadan creed is summed up in belief in the unity of God and in the mission of His Prophet, and to ourselves who coldly analyse his doctrines, to belief in God and a future life; these two dogmas, the minimum of religious belief, statements that to the religious man rest on the firm basis of reason, sum up the whole doctrinal teaching of the Qur'an.*[522]

The main teachings of Islam contain 'simplicity' and 'directness' which turned out to be strong forces in the spreading of the religion. According to Montet:

> *[I]n spite of the rich development, in every sense of the term, of the teachings of the Prophet, the Qur'an has invariably kept its place as the fundamental starting-point, and the dogma of the unity of God has always been proclaimed therein with a grandeur, a majesty, an invariable purity and with a note of sure conviction, which it is hard to find surpassed outside the pale of Islam. This fidelity to the fundamental dogma of the religion, the elemental simplicity of the formula in which it is enunciated, the proof that it gains from the fervid conviction of the missionaries who propagate it, are so many causes to explain the success of Muhammadan missionary efforts. A creed so precise, so stripped of all theological complexities and consequently so accessible to the ordinary understanding, might be expected to possess and does indeed possess a marvelous power of winning its way into the consciences of men.*[523]

Sadu Vaswani affirms that Islam brought significant cultural reforms in different parts of the world and guided people to the right path as instructed in the Qur'an:

> *Islam introduced a vigorous Puritanism into Asia and Europe, deprecating even dancing and card playing. Who is Muslim, says the Qur'an, he seeketh after the right way. Islam moved out with its great message of Allah the Rahman, the merciful, and became the torch bearer of culture and civilisation in Africa, in China, in Central Asia, in Europe, in Persia, in India; of the achievements of Islam in the days of the Baghdad Khilafat every Muslim may be proud and every Sindhi too: for Sindhis had their share in the intellectual life of the Baghdad Court. Of the achievements of Islam in Europe, less is known to the Muslims and Hindus in Sindh; yet even a rapid sketch will show how much Islam did for Europe in the Middle ages.*[524]

The British journalist Lancelot Lawton commented in *The Sphere* that Islam was suited not only to the part of the world where it arose, but to many other lands. Lawton said:

> *As a religion the Mohammedan religion, it must be confessed, is more suited to Africa than is the Christian religion; indeed, I would even say that it is more suited to the world as whole...*[525]

Author Ruth Cranston notices that Muhammad (ﷺ) says there is but one religion: Islam. But what does it mean – and how does he use the word? Islam means bowing to, or surrendering to, i.e. religiously submitting to the will of God. All men of all faiths who surrender themselves to the will of God and who are the seekers of righteousness are truly children of Islam in the sense of which the Prophet of Islam spoke.[526]

Cranston felt that the creed of Islam is rather simple:

> *There is no God but one and Mohammed is His Messenger. This declaration takes on new significance when we understand this in relation to the idolatry and the many gods of the time – the then prevalent way of life that subjugated humans to others besides the true God. In Islam the giving of alms to the needy and the poor is a virtue as this evokes in men fellow feeling. One's relation to one's fellow man is second in importance only to one's relation to God. From your provisions, a portion of these be given to the wayfarers, the orphans, the destitute and the poor, the seekers of help and for freeing humans from bondage – enjoins the Qur'an and ordered the Prophet.*[527]

M.K. Gandhi stated that the religion of Islam received respect from all everywhere and worked as a torch in the days of darkness in the Western world not long ago. It is not a fake religion; a close study of this will make people, including the Hindus, change their opinions regarding Islam:

> *In its glorious days Islam was not intolerant. It commanded the*

admiration of the world. When the West was sunk in darkness, a bright star rose in the Eastern firmament and gave light and comfort to a. groaning world. Islam is not a false religion. Let Hindus study it reverently and they will love it even as I do.[528]

A point that is frequently ignored is that the popular stereotypes regarding Prophet Muhammad (ﷺ) are something to which many audiences have been preconditioned, given the abundance of European literature which stigmatises Prophet Muhammad (ﷺ). This is ironic when we acknowledge the contributions Muslims have made to the arts and sciences. In this regard, Michener states:

Many Westerners, accustomed by their history books to believe that Muslims were barbarous infidels, find it difficult to comprehend how profoundly our intellectual life has been influenced by Muslim scholars in the field of science, medicine, mathematics, geography and philosophy. Crusaders who invaded the Holy Land to fight Muslims returned to Europe with new ideas of love, poetry, chivalry, warfare and government. Our concept of what a university should be was deeply modified by Muslim scholars, who perfected the writing of history and who brought to Europe much Greek learning.[529]

The Arabs were not intent on death and destruction, particularly after becoming Muslims. Countries like Rome, Greece, and Persia were overwhelmed with their preaching of the new belief. Islam was the most progressive religion during the centuries from 650 to 1000 AD. The Muslim world offered a striking contrast to the Christian West by building mosques, beautiful cities and universities. A.M. Stoddard elaborates:

The Arabs, in their turn, knew how to consolidate their rule. They were no bloodthirsty savages, bent solely on loot and destruction. On the contrary, they were an innately gifted race, eager to learn and appreciative of the cultural gifts which older civilizations had to bestow. Intermarrying freely and professing a common belief, conquerors and conquered rapidly fused, and from this fusion arose a new civilization—the Saracenic civilization, in which the ancient cultures of Greece, Rome, and Persia were revitalized by Arab vigour and synthesized by the Arab genius and the Islamic spirit. For the first three centuries of its existence (circ. a.d. 650-1000) the realm of Islam was the most civilized and progressive portion of the world. Studded with splendid cities, gracious mosques, and quiet universities where the wisdom of the ancient world was preserved and appreciated, the Moslem East offered a striking contrast to the Christian West, then sunk in the night of the Dark Ages.[530]

John Davenport states that Muslims show higher respect to the Qur'an than Christians do towards the Bible. The Qur'an, a manual with complete guidance for the whole of mankind, consists of two parts: The faith (*iman*) and the practice (*din*). He illustrates the differences between Christianity and Islam as below:

Such is the Koran which has been received by Mohammedans with a degree of reverence rarely witnessed among Christians towards the Holy Scriptures. In it they view the whole code of religious belief, civil law, and moral obligation. The belief which they generally profess as drawn from the Koran consists in the following leading points. Religion is divided into two branches, Iman (faith) and Din (practice). Faith includes belief in God, his angels, his revelations in the Koran, his prophets, the resurrection and Day of Judgment, and God's absolute decrees. Practice includes prayer, comprehending under this head the purifications necessary before prayer, alms-giving, fasting, and the pilgrimage to Makkah. In order fully to appreciate the difference between Christianity and Mohammedanism, it must be borne in mind that whereas the hold which the former has over its professors is naturally referred by them to its dogmas, thus causing religion and morals to be regarded as distinct from each other in the latter it is, on the contrary, not the dogmatic, but the practical portion which has influenced the moral, social, legal, and political ideas and circumstances of its believers.

So that to the Mohammedan mind, patriotism, legality, tradition, constitution, right, are all included in that one word - Islam![531]

The theological predicament which many Christians faced was to some extent given more clarity with the advent of Islam. The ritual obligations of Islam provide its followers with a form of discipline. It can be argued that the social order prevalent in Muslim societies throughout history made remarkable efforts to rid social vices and corruption compared to other traditions. The English novelist H.G. Wells said:

Islam from the outset was a fair proof against the theological elaborations that have perplexed and divided Christianity and smothered the spirit of Jesus. And its third source of strength has been in the meticulous prescriptions of methods of prayer and worship and its clear statement of the limited and conventional significance of the importance ascribed to Makkah ... Islam created a society more free from widespread cruelty and social oppression than any society had ever been in the world before.[532]

Julius Germanus said that a point which often goes unnoticed is how the European world to a great extent inherited the intellectual legacy of Muslim civilization. The principle of politics and religious ferment in much of Christian society owed a considerable debt to Muslims and much of the intellectual rigor sustained in the West was linked to the achievement of Muslims who excelled academically. Undeniably, this influence exerted itself in the non-Muslim world. According to Germanus:

We may safely say that Islam, its force and extensive power has contributed to a self-awakening of Europe from its lethargy. ... Christian spiritual culture and even political organization was influenced and moulded by Islam. There was a time when learning in Europe could be derived only through the medium of the Arabic tongue, which was the language of Islam, and European scholars went to Spain to enrich their minds with the treasures of knowledge, amassed in its schools and libraries. Arts and crafts flourished in Islamic countries to such perfection, town life developed to such a height that when the industrious Arabs were driven out of Spain, manufacturing skill suddenly relapsed in Spain in the XVI Century.[533]

Jawaharlal Nehru did not believe that the Arabs destroyed the library of Alexandria, as he found them to be fond of literature. They were very friendly with the people of India. He noticed the Arabs had a higher level of tolerance than other nations.[534]

Some people at the time did resist intellectual advancement and knowledge, but it is incorrect to claim that Prophet Muhammad (ﷺ) and his followers exhibited a similar hostile trait to knowledge and progress. The importance to Muslims of progress in these fields can be seen by their efforts throughout history to provide their own audience with the learning and knowledge derived from cultures before Islam and helping to establish educational institutes so that this type of learning could be broadly disseminated. Be it in the natural sciences or the arts, the Muslims proved themselves to be proficient in all areas of life and contributed to establishing flourishing fields of thought. During the golden age of Islam and under the auspices of an Islamic state, the Muslims of Spain and Egypt produced libraries of the highest intellectual calibre. According to Napoleon:

He wrote on the flyleaf of the Qur'an: 'There is no god but God.' The Parthians, the Scythians, the Mongols, the Tartars and the Turks have generally shown themselves enemies of science and arts, but this reproach cannot be fastened on to the Arabs, no more than upon Muhammad.

The Muslims attached so much value to this art that they regarded it as equal to bravery. Al-Mansur, Harun al-Rashid and Al-Mamun cultivated arts and sciences. They were fond of literature, chemistry and mathematics; they lived with savants, caused the Greek and Latin authors – the Iliad, the Odyssey, Euclid, etc. – to be translated into Arabic, and founded schools and colleges for medicine, astronomy and moral science. Ahmad corrected the tables of Ptolemy; Abbas was a distinguished mathematician; Costa,

Alicude, Thabit and Ahmad measured one degree of meridian from Saana to Kufa. Chemistry, alembics, sun-dial, clocks and the numerical signs owe their existence to Arab invention. Nothing is more elegant than their moral tales; their poetry is full of fervour. Muhammad extolled everywhere the savants and such men as devoted themselves to a speculative life and cultivated letters.
In the library of Cairo there were 6000 volumes on astronomy, and more than 100,000 on other subjects; in the library of Cordava there were 300,000 volumes. Sciences and arts reigned five hundred years under the Caliphs and made great progress, which was brought to naught by the invasion of the Mongols.[535]

The unifying potential of Islam and its ability to lead others into a state of peace and tranquillity has been acknowledged by many throughout history including Napoleon, who said:

I hope the time is not far off when I shall be able to unite all the wise and educated men of all the countries and establish a uniform regime based on the principles of the Qur'an which alone are true and which alone can lead men to happiness.[536]

There was much intellectual dishonesty and a host of misguided attitudes cultivated in the West regarding Islam and the Muslims. This was ironic when we consider how the Muslims had risen to the pinnacle of civilisation, progress and achievement at a time when Europe was steeped in its own ignorance and intellectual torpor. The truthfulness of this reality tends to be obscured; particularly how Europe had benefited from the Muslims' remarkable feats. It was often arrogantly presumed that Western civilisation as it stood at that time, owed everything to its own merit and not to anything else. However, the educational and cultural fabric woven by Islamic societies was certainly a feature which helped the West recover from its helpless state. In fact, some would argue that the approach to higher learning differed considerably between the Muslim world and Europe. Major Arthur Glyn Leonard states:

But apart from all these weighty considerations, the attitude of

Europe towards Islam should be one of eternal gratitude, instead of base ingratitude and forgetfulness. Never to this day has Europe acknowledged in an honest and wholehearted manner the great and everlasting debt she owes to Islamic culture and civilization. Only in a lukewarm and perfunctory way has she recognised that when, during the Dark Ages, her people were sunk in feudalism and ignorance, Moslem civilization under the Arabs reached a high standard of social and scientific splendour that kept alive the flickering members of European society from utter decadence. Do not we, who now consider ourselves on the topmost pinnacle ever reached by culture and civilization, recognize that had it not been for the high culture, the civilization and intellectual as well as the social splendour of the Arabs, and to the soundness of the school system, Europe would to this day have remained sunk in the darkness of ignorance? Have we forgotten that the Mohammedan maxim was that the real learning of a man is of more public importance than any particular religious opinion we may entertain – that Moslem liberality was in striking contrast with the intolerant state of Europe? Have we forgotten that the Khalifate arose in the most degenerate period of Rome and Persia, also that the greater part of Europe lay under the dark cloud of barbarism? Does the magnificent valour of the Arabs, inspired as it was by a theism as lofty as it was pure, not appeal to us?[537]

Bernard Lewis wrote in his book *The Crisis of Islam. Holy war and Unholy Terror* that Prophet Muhammad (ﷺ) was not only a religious leader but also a statesman who governed the land and its people, offered justice, collected taxes, commanded soldiers, and worked towards establishing peace in the land.[538]

Philip K. Hitti acknowledged the greatness of Arab culture when he wrote in his *History of the Arabs:*

Moslem Spain wrote one of the brightest chapters in the intellectual history of medieval Europe. Between the middle of the 8th and the beginning of the 13th centuries, as we have noted before, the Arabic-speaking peoples were the main bearers of the torch of culture and civilization throughout the world. Moreover, they were the medium through which ancient science and philosophy were recovered, supplemented and transmitted in such a way as to make possible the renaissance of Western Europe. In all this Arabic Spain had a large share.[539]

Professor Vaglieri in her famous work *An Interpretation of Islam* clarifies that there is no mediator between God and man in Islam. The pretending mediators who believed that they had authority on the will of others, had also been displaced from their positions. In her words:

The spirit was liberated from prejudice; man's will was set free from the ties which had kept it bound to the will of other men or other so-called hidden power. Priests, false guardians of mysteries, brokers of salvation, all those who pretended to be mediators between God and man and consequently believed they had authority over other people's will fell from their pedestals.[540]

The intellectual heavyweights of Islamic history are hardly given adulation and praise in European circles. Be it those who made instrumental progress in the field of medicine, or luminaries of literature, it seems as though their influential work and efforts has been discarded to the dustbin of history, no longer deserving mention. The overwhelming European ignorance of what the Muslim world had contributed defies belief, as does the unrecognised fact that there was a monumental loss to the world's intellectual heritage when Muslim libraries were set alight in Cordoba or Baghdad by the unjustifiable envies and jealousies of intolerant people. A very important juncture in history is overlooked if the European debt to the Muslim world is not appreciated and if many Christian Europeans do not accept culpability for the injustice they have done to the Muslim world. Major Leonard adds:

Is it possible that Europe is unmindful of, and has the ingratitude to ignore, the splendid services of the scientists and philosophers of Arabia? Are the names of Assamh, Abu Othman, Albernin Albeithar, Abu Ali Ibn Sina (Avicenna) the great physician and philosopher Ibn Rushd (Averroes) of Cordova the chief commentator on Aristotle, Ibn Bajja (Avempace) besides a host of others, but dead letters? Is the great work which they have done and the fame they have left behind them in their books, to be consigned to the limbo of oblivion, by an ungrateful because antipathetic Europe? Does the work of Alhazen, author of optical treatises, who understood the weight of air, corrected the Greek misconception or theory of vision, and determined the function of the retina, count for nothing? Do we owe no tribute to a great thinker such as Ghazali, who in speaking of his attempts to detach himself from his youthful opinions says: 'I said to myself, my aim is simply to know the truth of things, consequently it is indispensable for me to ascertain what knowledge is?' It cannot be that already we have lost sight of the amazing intellectual activity of the Moslem world, during the earlier part of the 'Abbasid' period more especially? It cannot be that we have quite forgotten the irrecoverable loss that was inflicted on Arabian literature and on the world at large by the wanton destruction of thousands of books that was prompted by Christian bigotry and fanaticism? It cannot surely be said of Christian Europe that for centuries she has done her best to hide her obligations to the Arabs? Yet, most assuredly obligations such as these are far too sacred to lie much longer hidden![541]

John William Draper explains how Islam was spread in Asia and Africa:

He raised his own nation from Fetichism, the adoration of a meteoric stone, and from the basest idol-worship; he preached a monotheism which quickly scattered to the winds the empty disputes of the Arians and Catholics, and irrevocably wrenched from Christianity more than half, and that by far the best half of her possessions, since it included the Holy Land, the birth-place of our faith, and Africa, which had imparted to it its Latin form. That continent and a very large part of Asia, after the lapse of more than a thousand years, still remains permanently attached to the Arabian doctrine. With the utmost difficulty, and as if by miracle, Europe itself escaped.[542]

The spread of Islam beyond its early frontiers and the rate of its growth is an unprecedented feat in human history. Misconceptions abound about how this spread was easily facilitated by the use of force and violence. However, such a view is often dismissed by those familiar with Islam's history. A study of Islamic history substantiates the view that Muslims openly embraced multi-faith communities to settle within their territory provided some conditions were satisfied. It was common for the Prophet of Islam to urge followers to establish close ties with other religious groups. It cannot be denied that wars were fought between Muslims and members of other faiths but a more exhaustive analysis of these events and that particular historical juncture reveals that Muslims extended civil liberties to others. According to the American author James Albert Michener,

> *No other religion in history spread so rapidly as Islam... The West has widely believed that this surge of religion was made possible by the sword. But no modern scholar accepts that idea, and the Qur'an is explicit in support of the freedom of conscience. The evidence is strong that Islam welcomed the peoples of many diverse religions, so long as they behaved themselves and paid extra taxes. Muhammad constantly taught that Muslims should co-operate with the 'People of the Book' (Jews and Christians). ...True, there were often wars between Muslims and either Christians or Jews (sometimes because the older religions insisted on battle), and the Qur'an contains passages of primitive violence relating to those wars. But testimony is overwhelming that "followers of the Book" were usually given decent treatment, sanctuary and freedom to worship as they wished.*[543]

Popularity of Islam

Michael Cook notes in his book *Muhammad* that Islam spread outside of Arabia within a couple of centuries after the death of Prophet Muhammad (ﷺ). Due to the spiritual influence of Islam and its social benefits, the people of conquered territories were converted in great numbers and thus Islam spread rapidly beyond Arabia.[544]

In a similar vein the celebrated author Arthur Naylor Wollaston remarks that Islam has established a notable history in the world and has occupied the deepest part of the hearts and minds of many people:

> *Such is the history of Islam, with its quaint ceremonies its fatiguing devotions, and its trying hardships. It forms a remarkable chapter in the history of the world ...it is, at any rate, a creed which has taken deep root in the minds of a large mass of the peoples of the earth.*[545]

R.M. Savory of the University of Toronto points out that after the death of Muhammad (ﷺ), Islam expanded in various parts of the world. The people of the conquered land accepted Islam as they were able to improve their social situations.[546]

Professor Laura Veccia Vaglieri wrote in her book *An Interpretation of Islam* that Islam spread over different parts of the world in a short time, which surprised many people:

> *It is difficult to appreciate the speed with which Islam accomplished its conquests and changed from the religion of a few enthusiasts to that of millions. It is still a puzzle to the human mind to discover what were the secret forces which enabled the rough warriors to triumph over people so far their superiors in civilization, wealth, experience and ability to wage war? It is surprising how these people could occupy so much territory, and consolidate their conquests in such a way that even centuries of warfare did not succeed in dislodging them ; how they could inspire their followers with so much zeal for their ideals, preserve a pulsating vitality unknown to other religions, even ten centuries after the death of Muhammad;*

and infuse into the minds of their followers, although of an age and culture quite different from that of the first Muslims, a burning faith capable of any sacrifice.[547]

Christopher Dawson identifies the influence of Islam on the Western Mediterranean during the dark ages. He claimed that the Western Mediterranean, having lost support from Christian Europe, received significant cultural developments from the Islamic world. The Spanish scholars translated into Latin the valuable works of Muslim philosophers, including al-Kindi al-Farabi, al-Battani, Avicenna, Ibn Gebiral and al-Ghazali. That helped the religion of Islam reach every corner of the world.[548]

John Kaltner, the author of *Islam: What the non-Muslims should know* has written in his book that immediately after the death of Muhammad (ﷺ), Islam expanded to many parts of the world and that popularity is continuing. People from diverse cultures are embracing Islam.[549]

The late Indian Prime Minister Indira Gandhi praised the Prophet Muhammad (ﷺ) for spreading the message of Islam over a great part of the world in a short time. The Prime Minister remarked that:[550]

Prophet Muhammad extols his message in the desert and within half century it reverberates over three continents. (23 December, 1972)

The Reverend Bosworth Smith stated that Islam encompassed the best policies in the system and it is the latest and most historical religion of the world. He said:

Is a religion less true because it recognises itself in other garbs, because it incorporates in itself all that is best in the system which it expands or supplants? What if we found the whole Sermon on the Mount dispersed about the writings of the Jewish Rabbis, as we unquestionably find some part of it? Christ himself was always the first to assert that He came, not to destroy, but to fulfil. But it is strange that the avowed relation of Christianity to Judaism has not protected Islam from the assaults of Christian apologists, grounded

> *on its avowed relation to the two together! But what of interest, I am free to admit, the religion of Mohammed loses on the score of originality, it gains in the greater fullness of our knowledge of its origin. It is the latest and most historical of the great religions of the world.*[551]

Michael Hart has chosen Prophet Muhammad (ﷺ) as the most influential person in history, adding that Islam spread rapidly all over the world even after the death of the Prophet (ﷺ). In 711 AD, the Arab armies conquered North Africa as far as the Atlantic Ocean. Then they crossed the Straits of Gibraltar and overpowered the empire of Spain.[552]

Ruth Cranston was confused after studying some religions, but was amazed with the simplicity of the teachings of Islam.[553]

Dr Germanus highlights that the powerful religion of Islam had worked very well in raising awareness among the Europeans. Islam influenced the Christian social and political policies. Thus the Arabic language and culture was accepted in different parts of Europe. Dr Germanus said:

> *We may safely say that Islam, its force and extensive power, has contributed to a self-awakening of Europe from its lethargy and shaped it into a steady spiritual power. So, while Islam and Christianity stood as two hostile bodies against one another, Christian spiritual culture and even political organisation was influenced and moulded by Islam. There was a time when learning in Europe could be derived only through the medium of the Arabic tongue, which was the language of Islam, and European scholars went to Spain to enrich their minds with the treasures of knowledge, amassed in its schools and libraries. Arts and crafts flourished in Islamic countries to such perfection, town life developed to such a height that when the industrious Arabs were driven out of Spain, manufacturing skill suddenly relapsed in Spain in the XVI Century. These things are too well known to need arguments, but they must be mentioned to put down forever the assumption that Islam could not create a culture. Nothing is more absurd. Islam has brought forth tremendous armies which in equipment, strategy and discipline surpassed the armies of the then*

inhabited world; it created and preserved a learning and advanced science from which all European nations have learned.[554]

Equality in Islam

Anglican Canon Isaac Tailor finds Islam as an end to the slavery system, as a pioneer of friendliness and acceptance of all truths that mankind require.

It (Islam) replaced monkishness by manliness. It gives hope to the slave, brotherhood to mankind, and recognition of the fundamental facts of human nature.[555]

There is no place for discrimination in Islam and it treats everybody equally as brothers, irrespective of colour, creed, nationality or ability, etc. According to S.H. Leeder,

How, for instance, can any other appeal stand against that of the Moslem who, in approaching the pagan, says to him, however obscure or degraded he may be 'Embrace the faith, and you are at once equal and a brother.' Islam knows no color line.[556]

A similar theme is voiced by Elsa Marston that everyone is equal in Islam.[557]

Sarojini Naidu, also known by the sobriquet 'The Nightingale of India', was an Indian Independence activist and poet. She believed that social equality was applied in Islam before any other religion. Its practices abolish the distinctions between the rich and the poor who pray side by side in mosques. She was struck by the policy of brotherhood of the religion of Islam which is put into practice also by the Muslims. Naidu notes:

It was the first religion that preached and practised democracy; for, in the mosque when the call from the minaret is sounded and the worshippers are gathered together, the democracy of Islam is

embodied five times a day when the peasant and the king kneel side by side and proclaim: "God Alone is Great". I have been struck over and over again by this indivisible unity of Islam that makes a man distinctively a brother. When you meet an Egyptian, an Algerian, an Indian and a Turk in London it matters not that Egypt was the motherland of one and India the motherland of another.[558]

Having read the Qur'an, she praises the Islamic principles as very suitable for day-to day-life. She states:

Sense of justice is one of the most wonderful ideals of Islam, because as I read in the Qur'an I find those dynamic principles of life, not mystic but practical ethics for the daily conduct of life suited to the whole world.[559]

Islam is a religion of great value and consequence. The elimination of racial distinction in Islam is a great virtue. Arnold Joseph Toynbee recognised the merits of Islam thus:

The extinction of race consciousness as between Muslims is one of the outstanding achievements of Islam, and in the contemporary world there is, as it happens, a crying need for the propagation of this Islamic virtue.[560]

Toynbee carried on to say that global problems would be solved by accepting Islam as it is the one religion that goes beyond nationalism. He expected all human beings to unite together. According to him:

The solution to all international conflicts lies only in embracing Islam en masse because Islam is the only religion that can transcend nationalism. I see, with great dismay, that nationalism is gaining grounds even among the bearers of the Qur'an. I will hope for the day when all humanity will break this idol and unite all as the children of God.[561]

Dr R.L. Mellema, a Dutch anthropologist, writer and scholar notes that the brotherliness imbibed by the followers of Islam helps eliminate the differences of ethnicity, colour, race or religion. Islam is the only religion on the earth that teaches the principle of inclusion of all as brothers.[562]

Equality and brotherhood are hallmarks of the Islamic faith. Speaking on the aspect of equality before God in Islam, the famous poet of India, Sarojini Naidu said:

> *It was the first religion that preached and practiced democracy; for, in the mosque, when the call for prayer is sounded and worshippers are gathered together, the democracy of Islam is embodied five times a day when the peasant and king kneel side by side and proclaim: 'God Alone is Great'... I have been struck over and over again by this indivisible unity of Islam that makes man instinctively a brother.*[563]

Muhammad (ﷺ) was an advocate of ruling based on consensus and shared agreement as opposed to exclusive rule. There is a popular misconception that Muhammad (ﷺ) was bent on one-man rule and exhibited autocratic tendencies. However, a reading of Muhammad (ﷺ) reveals otherwise. Reverend Jennifer Potter, Minister, Wesley's Chapel, London, observes:

> *I think Muhammad tried to be democratic in an undemocratic context. When it came to decision making, I don't think Muhammad was acting as a dictator or with a small inner circle but tried to get a wider agreement for things. e.g. the move to Madinah - I don't think he just said to people that we are going, rather, there was a consultation process.*[564]

The Islamic brotherhood is a new theme in the Eastern countries which teaches true unity amongst mankind. Dr Laurence E. Browne, a former ophthalmologist in the US Air Force is not sure if a similar spirit of brotherhood existed among Christian Syrians and Christian Persians. Browne says:

> *The Islamic brotherhood which they proclaimed was a real thing,*

and a new thing, and a new thing among Eastern nations. It is doubtful whether Christian Syrians ever felt the same sense of brotherhood with Christian Persians as Muslim Syrians did with Muslim Persians.[565]

According to S.H. Leeder, in Islam all are equal, regardless of the colour of one's skin or race, and it teaches people to judge a person by his personality and his deeds:

"Take away that black man! I can have no discussion with him," exclaimed the Christian Archbishop Cyrus when the Arab conquerors had sent a deputation of their ablest men to discuss terms of surrender of the capital of Egypt headed by 'Ubaadah as the ablest of them all....To the sacred Archbishop's astonishment, he was told that this man was commissioned by General 'Amr, that the Muslims held black and white men in equal respect – judging a man by his character and not by his colour.[566]

Like the author, Leeder, there are thousands of black persons who love to fight the enemies of God and submit to His will. Their desires were not the resources of this world, but rather of the next. One of the significant teachings of Islam is that there is no place for discrimination in Islam. Leeder adds:

There are a thousand blacks, as black as myself, amongst our companions. I and they would be ready to meet and fight a hundred enemies together. We live only to fight for God, and to follow His Will. We care naught for wealth, so long as we have the wherewithal to stay our hunger and to clothe our bodies. This world is naught for us, the next world is all... Such a spirit of class distinction is certainly the greatest hindrance to missionary work in the East, as every impartial observer has noted. How, for instance, can any other appeal stand against that of the Muslim who, in approaching the pagan, says to him, however obscure or degraded he may be: 'Embrace the faith, and you are at once an equal and a brother.' Islam knows no colour line.[567]

Sir Hamilton Alexander Rosskeen Gibb felt that Islam had to extend its services further for humankind. Islam stands very closely in the East than Europe and its wonderful teachings on equality had helped succeed in uniting people. Gibb thought that Islam's role would be vital in establishing collaboration between communities of the East and the West as there is no parallel to Islam in uniting societies on the issue of equality. [568]

Islam is by no means a phenomenon unique to the Arabs. Rather, its universality can be gauged when we reflect on the statistical representation of Muslims in the Arab and non-Arab world. Perhaps this can be attributed to Islam's emphasis on ethnic diversity and cultural pluralism – both of which the early Muslims readily accepted. James Michener brought home this point:

> *Although Islam originated in Arabia today only a small percentage (7 percent) of the world's Muslims are Arabians, and less than a quarter (20 percent) speak Arabic as their native language...More than most religions, Islam preaches the brotherhood of all races, colours and nations within its fold. Muhammad himself probably had exactly the same skin colouring as Jesus – a very suntanned white – but today his followers embrace all colours: black men from Africa, yellow men from China brown men from Malaya, white men from Turkey...Islam permits no priesthood, and because Muhammad had to fight so bitterly against idols, his religion discourages portraiture. Mosques are decorated with geometrical patterns only.* [569]

According to Victor Robinson, a physician and medical journalist, a very popular misconception was that Islam was not a host to civilisation and actively militated against intellectual progress. This is far from the truth, as an examination of the history of Muslims reveals their relative ascendancy compared to other European states:

> *Europe was darkened at sunset, Cordova shone with public lamps: Europe was covered with vermin, Cordova changed its undergarments daily: Europe lay in mud, Cordova's streets were*

paved; Europe's palaces had smoke-holes in the ceiling, Cordova's arabesques were exquisite; Europe's nobility could not sign its name, Cordova's children went to school; Europe's monks could not read the baptismal service, Cordova's teachers created a library of Alexandrian dimensions.[570]

Amit Pal highlights that the equality of mankind and the rejection of racial superiority is emphasised in Prophet Muhammad(ﷺ)'s famous sayings:

"All people are equal, as equal as the teeth of a comb," says a Hadith line." "There is no claim of merit of an Arab over a Persian, or of a white over a black person, or of male over female. Only God-fearing people merit a preference with God."[571]

Professor T.L. Vaswani wrote in the preface of his book *The Spirit and Struggle of Islam* that there was no longer any excuse to hold incorrect ideas about Islam. Islam has already conquered the Eastern and Western hemispheres of the world. Many world leaders have accepted that Islam reformed social systems and provided freedom and equal opportunities long before the French Revolution.

It is time to abandon crude conceptions of the Islamic ideal – an ideal which has been a shaping power in East and West. Guizot and Draper had the frankness to admit that Islam freed Europe from feudalism. And did not Islam exert an uplifting influence on mediaeval Europe? Long before the French Revolution, Islam gave to the nations a message of liberty, equality and fraternity.[572]

Monotheism in Islam

Historian Edward Gibbon commented that the notion of God in the Islamic tradition was not influenced by any pagan considerations and that the Prophets of God measured up to the highest standard of humanity:

'I believe in One God and Mohammed the Apostle of God,' is the

simple and invariable profession of Islam. The intellectual image of the Deity has never been degraded by any visible idol; the honours of the prophet have never transgressed the measure of human virtue, and his living precepts have restrained the gratitude of his disciples within the bounds of reason and religion.[573]

Prophet Muhammad (ﷺ) was a revolutionary as far as his theological teachings were concerned. He introduced the monotheism preached by the Prophets of the Old and New Testaments and made a concerted effort to purify the monotheistic concept from accretions. In this regard, Napoleon states:

Arabia was idolatrous when, six centuries after Jesus, Muhammad introduced the worship of the God of Abraham, of Ishmael, of Moses and of Jesus. The Ayrians and some other sect had disturbed the tranquillity of the East by agitating the question of the nature of the Father, the Son, and the Holy Ghost. Muhammad declared that there was none but One God Who had no father, no son and that the Trinity imported the idea of idolatry.[574]

Simplicity of Worship in Islam

Dr Shireen Hunter, a distinguished scholar, Director Center for Strategic and International Studies, USA says in praising Islam that one of its beauties is that anyone can perform the rituals anywhere on Earth, which is created by God:

It is one of the glories of Islam that temples are not made with hands and that its ceremonies can be performed anywhere upon God's earth or under His heaven.[575]

Major Arthur Glyn Leonard extols Islam for two principles – Idea of God and Islam's indisputable authenticity – which engrossed him. He regarded it as a huge asset:

Two features in the Creed of Islam have always specially attracted me. One is the God conception, the other is its unquestionable sincerity – a tremendous asset in human affairs, the religious aspect of them especially. After all, sincerity is almost divine and like love covers a multitude of sins.[576]

Professor Vaglieri made it clear that the religion of Islam is straightforward and simple. That was one of the main reasons for its speedy expansion across the world. It is still expanding in Asia and Africa:

Islam is a religion of marvellous easiness and crystal clear simplicity... This was also another cause of its speedy diffusion at the time of the early conquests among people who had fallen into deep confusion on account of the uncertainty of some of their religious dogmas. It is also the cause of its continuous diffusion today among uncivilized peoples of Asia and Africa.[577]

The famous historian and author George Sarton described in a Symposium at Princeton how swiftly the development of Arabian culture and science took place. He compared it with the Greek development. Some key factors, according to him, which contributed to this rapid development, included the simplicity of the religion and its accessibility to others.[578]

Lord Headley affirms that Islam is a religion with great straightforwardness and does not contradict the basic teachings of the Prophets Moses and Christ. Lord Headley declares:

Islam is the religion of grand simplicity; it satisfies the noblest longings of the soul, and no way contravenes the teachings of Moses and Christ.[579]

CHAPTER FIVE

The Qur'an and its Teachings

The Qur'an is the Holy Book of guidance revealed by God to Prophet Muhammad (ﷺ) through the angel Gabriel (pbuh). As the Qur'an was revealed to the Prophet (ﷺ), in bits and pieces, as the time and context deserved, he memorised the verses and presented them to his disciples. The holy Qur'an is the collection of these divinely inspired words. The Qur'an is the Book sent down from on high by God through His Messenger for the guidance of humanity. This is in Arabic, a human language, to make it comprehensible and intelligible to humans. The Qur'an is composed of 114 chapters, long and short, and contains more than six thousand verses. Some of the chapters were revealed in Makkah and others in Madinah.

The Qur'an is Universal

God said in the Qur'an that He is the Lord of the universe and the Qur'an is the guideline for mankind. Dr N.K. Singh explains that God said in the Qur'an that He is the '*Rabb-ul-Alameen*', i.e. the Lord of all creation and of the universe. It is to be noted that God did not say that He is the '*Rabb-ul-Muslimeen*', *i.e.* for the Muslims (only).[580]

According to the Qur'an, Prophet Muhammad (ﷺ) was sent as a blessing for the universe (i.e. the whole of mankind). Dr Singh continues saying that:

> The Qur'an says, '*Inna Arsalnaka Rahmatul Lil Al-Ameen*' that is the Prophet came as the blessing of mankind.[581]

The Holy Qur'an is the guideline for the whole of mankind. Professor Vaglieri affirms that the Qur'an is the word of God revealed to Prophet Muhammad (ﷺ) as a mercy to the mankind. Prophet Muhammad (ﷺ) preached the message of God with the conviction that it is to go beyond the Arab frontiers to all other parts of the world:

> *The passage in the Qur'an which refers to the universality of Islam as the religion sent by God to His Prophet as "a mercy for all peoples" is a direct appeal to the worlds. This is definite proof that the Prophet felt with an absolute certainty that his mission was to go beyond the limits of the Arab nation and that he was to convey the new Word to people of different races and languages. Evidence of the same consciousness is also found in the tradition which mentions that it was a custom of Muhammad's to address himself to "the red and to the black ones", or to employ other similar expressions. Further evidence is furnished by the mention of future conquests beyond the boundaries of Arabia, and finally in the contacts which Muhammad himself began to make with foreign countries.*[582]

Goethe claimed that the teachings of Islam cannot be unsuccessful in any circumstances. According to him:

> *The teachings of Islam can fail under no circumstances. With all our systems of culture and civilization, we cannot go beyond Islam and, as a matter of fact, no human mind can go beyond the Qur'an.*[583]

Dr Herbert Udny Weitbrecht Stanton, a German author, notes that Islam means 'submission to God'. Islam was the religion of the prophets including Noah, Abraham, Moses and Jesus. Islam does not distinguish among any of them. Stanton said:

> *Islam is the word chosen by Muhammad to sum up his idea of the true religion which is offered by Allah and accepted by man if he is wise. The word signifies submission, resignation or acceptance, in*

each shade of meaning denoting the true attitude of man towards Allah. Islam is the faith of Noah, Abraham, Moses and Jesus; the sons of Jacob at his death confessed themselves Muslims; believers have been called Muslims by Allah ever since Abraham; acceptance of Islam is demanded by the Law and the Evangel; faithful Jews and Christians were Muslims before the Qur'an was given: now they and the Sabeans have only to add faith in the Qur'an. Islam has belief in all the prophets... [584]

Teachings of the Qur'an

The legendary Indian actor Amitabh Bachchan reads the Qur'an for peace, calmness of mind and for finding the real meaning of life. He was advised to do so by a member of Twitter family (TwFmXt). He said:

A member of TwFmXt here asked me to read the Koran, for peace and tranquillity, for essence of life ... I did. [585]

He also picked up a quotation from the Qur'an in which God said that He does not change anybody if the person first does not change themselves.[586]

God Changes not what is in a people until they change what is in themselves. (Chapter 13, verse 11)

He later added another quote:

"Walk not on the earth exultantly, for thou canst not cleave the earth, neither shalt thou reach to the mountains in height".

He showed high respect for the Qur'an and apologised for spelling the word wrongly as 'Koran' which is how it was written in a book he was reading[587]:

Correction; Qur'an and not KORAN!...however the book I was reading from had it as 'KORAN' so I mentioned it so...apologies.

Professor Vaglieri claimed that with the advent of Islam, people recanted earlier religions and accepted Islam, which they found easy and simple. The new law and order was far superior. When it was promulgated the richshould give alms to the poor, a new equilibrium started to take shape between the rich and the poor in an Islamic society. Equality was established in many aspects of life:

> *Two civilizations and two religions having been demolished, a new stream of intense life began to flow in the veins of these exhausted peoples. They unfolded before the eyes of an astonished world, a new religion, simple, easy, one which speaks to the heart and to the brain, a new form of government, far superior in its moral principles and qualities to those existing at that time, was established; gold that had been hidden in the safes of plutocrats began changing hands and going to the poor, starting a system of healthy circulation once again; the educated, capable, intelligent under the guidance of a government ruled by honest, democratic ideals found encouragement in the new order and were able to rise to the highest public offices ... A new era of prosperity and wealth was ushered in, a richness which Asia had not witnessed for centuries. The life of the conquered people, their civil rights and their wealth received a degree of protection approximating to that enjoyed by the Muslims themselves.*[588]

The Indian author Deepak Chopra explains some noteworthy teachings of the Qur'an. Although the aim of all religions is to take their followers close to God, the Qur'an is exemplary in being more open and clear in its goal. The five pillars of Islam, i.e. faith, daily five times prayers, fasting, charity and pilgrimage embody the practice and responsibilities of the followers.[589]

Chopra says that the Qur'an, like the previous book of Jesus, informs about the salvation and the doom; but in addition, the Qur'an offers hopes for mercy and forgiveness and the guidelines for all to follow in everyday life.[590]

A British politician (requested to be anonymous) revealed that he makes a habit of reading Holy Scriptures on a daily basis, including the Qur'an, due to its enlightening effects. According to him:

> *I read the Bible every day. I read the Qur'an every day, partly to understand some of the things happening in the world, but mainly just because it is immensely instructive.* [591]

What inspired him to read the Qur'an and be conversant with its teachings was the urgent need to understand religions in general at a time of great religious strife. Reciting the Qur'an kept him 'faith-literate'. An understanding about Islam serves as a guiding principle for him. On several occasions, the said politician has heaped praise on the Islamic faith and its scripture. Some years back, he commended the Qur'an owing to its emphasis on cohesion and rationality.[592]

On matters relating to gender and politics, the Qur'an has articulated a framework which is progressive and applicable to any period. He noted that it is inclusive, extols science and knowledge and abhors superstition. It is practical and way ahead of its time in attitudes to marriage, women and governance. In his words, the Qur'an is a:

> *Reforming book, it is inclusive. It extols science and knowledge and abhors superstition. It is practical and way ahead of its time in attitudes to marriage, women and governance.*[593]

Karen Armstrong argues that the Qur'an does not encourage one to generate an abundance of personal wealth at the expense of others. Rather, it teaches us to distribute wealth equitably among the poor and the needy.[594]

Pandit Thillai K Ranganathan, the Chairman of Britannia Hindu Temple Trust, Highgate, London believes that the right meaning of the Qur'an is lost in English translation (and for that matter in any language) and it is liable to be wrongly interpreted. He also highlights that the Qur'an never supports vengeful retaliation against others. The Qur'an is the authentic book from Allah (God) and it neither provokes chaos, struggle, killings nor forces the non-believers to accept Islam. He states:

> *Qur'anic teaching never encourages the policy of "eye for eye" revenge. It is a wrong interpretation of the Qur'an, it is misleading. The English translation of the Qur'an was not right which approves "eye for eye" revenge. The Qur'an emphasises one (same) thing about believer and non-believer. If you are a believer of Allah, this is what the Qur'an says is perfectly true, if you do not believe, nobody can force you to do something. This is what I have gathered from the Qur'an. The Qur'an is against harming people, against fighting, against killing, it is clearly stated in the Qur'an. Killing is not appreciated.*[595]

Ruth Cranston wrote in her book *World Faith* that the Qur'an teaches that Muslims should not differentiate among any prophets and should respect them all equally. It also instructs that they should use a prefix of 'Hazrat' or 'His Holiness' before the name of any prophet, including Jesus(pbuh) and Moses(pbuh). Prophet Muhammad (ﷺ) taught that the prophets are sent to their people by God to carry out certain missions.[596]

The real path of Islam is not the one which some of the Muslims are following now. The teaching of the Qur'an is authentic, but some people have interpreted it in ways which are wrong and unfortunate. A Muslim in the true sense must follow what the Qur'an instructs. According to a spokesman from Sikh Temple, East London,

> *Present religion is man-made not the real religion. The Qur'an's teachings are perfect, but people have made them according to their choice which is not right. But the Qur'an's teaching cannot be changed. You cannot change any of Allah's words. If you are a real Muslim and if you follow the Qur'an, you will never be wrong – it is the principle of life – a good way of life.*[597]

The Qur'an's ethical teachings are of paramount significance in today's life of consumerism. The conditions it stipulates for fair trade impart a very commendable economic ethos. Magsie Hamilton Little says the Qur'an provides instructions which can be used to formulate business deals. It requires that business has to be fair and transparent and one be true to his promises and deals. The Qur'an pays tribute to those who run business successfully and honestly and are good to the clients and others who are involved in it.[598]

Bosworth Smith wrote in his book *Muhammad and Islam* that Islam had a revolutionary impact on mankind. Such was the importance given to learning that it was considered more valorous than physical sacrifice. The significance which Muslims attached to education and learning gave birth to scholars of the highest calibre. All of this had a beneficial impact on humanity.

> *The teachings of the Qur'an, which mentions knowledge and the pen in its opening verses, brought about a tremendous transformation. Islam proclaimed study to be a religious duty, and made the black ink of the scribe and the scholar to be superior to the red blood of the martyr. Thanks to the teachings of the Qur'an and its emphasis on the cultivation of knowledge, countless scholars made their appearance and wrote innumerable books. Different scientific disciplines were derived from the Qur'an and spread across the world by Muslim thinkers. The world was illumined with the light of the Qur'an and the culture of Islam.* [599]

Europeans are indebted to the intellectual contributions of Muslims for the panoply of achievements across multiple fields. An argument could be made that

if it was not for the Muslim input into science, the Europeans would not have had such a flourishing civilization. Robert Stephen Briffault, a surgeon and also a social anthropologist and novelist, says:

> *For although there is not a single aspect of European growth in which the decisive influence of Islamic culture is not traceable, nowhere is it so clear and momentous as in the genesis of that power which constitutes the paramount distinctive force of the modern world and the supreme source ofits victory natural science and the scientific spirit ... Arab astronomy did not forestall Copernicus or Newton, though without it there would have been no Copernicus and no Newton ... The debt of our science to that of the Arabs does*

> *not consist in startling discoveries or revolutionary theories; science owes a great deal more to Arab culture, it owes its existence.*[600]

Briffault further notes that the real renaissance took place under Arab rule and not in the 15th century. In his words:

> *It was under the influence of Arabian and Moorish revival of culture, and not in the 15th century, that the real renaissance took place. Spain and not Italy was the cradle of the rebirth of Europe. After sinking lower and lower in barbarism, it had reached the darkest depths of ignorance and degradation when the cities of the Saracenic world—Baghdad, Cairo, Cordova, Toledo, were growing centres of civilization and intellectual activity. It was there that the new life arose which was to grow into a new phase of human evolution. From the time when the influence of their culture made itself felt, began the stirrings of a new life.*[601]

The Qur'an's monumental impact on humanity can be gauged by the rational thought and disciplines which it gave rise to. After bringing civilisation to a previously primitive people, it resulted in a social revolution which reverberated across continents. According to Margoliouth:

> *The Koran (Qur'an) admittedly occupies an important position among the great religious books of the world. Though it is the youngest of the epoch-making works belonging to this class of literature, it yields to hardly any in the wonderful effect which it has produced on large masses of men. It has created an all but new phase of human thought and a fresh type of character. It first transformed a number of heterogeneous desert tribes of the Arabian Peninsula into a nation of heroes, and then proceeded to create the vast politico-religious organizations of Muslims world wide which are one of the great forces with which Europe and the East have to reckon with today.*[602]

Compared to other religions, it can be said that Islam has had the biggest influence on the intellectual advancement of the world. In its absence, the potential for widespread violence and savagery to take hold of the world would have been very likely. Sir Philip Gibbs says in the *Glory of Prophet Muhammad*:

> *Islam (meaning resignation), as the religion of Muhammad is properly called, has done more for the progress of civilisation and morality than any other faith which has animated the souls of men since the creation of this world. Through many centuries and at the present day it has been, and is, a power for good among hundreds of millions of the human race, and without its high moral code there is no doubt that the blackest barbarism and the most idolatrous worship would reign omnipotent where Allah and faith of nobility lead men to light.*[603]

The Qur'an's teachings can be applied to personal life as well as to the external order. Sir Richard Arman Gregory, Baronet, was a British astronomer and promoter of science and author. He wrote in his book *Religion in Science and Civilization* that the book given to Muhammad was an unchangeable one and for all mankind.[604]

Although Islam's vast territorial expansion is often attributed to the sword, this argument does not stand ground with the Qur'an's unequivocal statements regarding the prohibition of forced conversions. James Michener endorses the above:

> *No other religion in history spread so rapidly as Islam. The West has widely believed that this surge of religion was made possible by the sword. But no modern scholar accepts this idea, and the Qur'an is explicit in the support of the freedom of conscience.* [605]

Professor R.M. Savory, Toronto University, Canada, notes that some parts of the Qur'an teach a social law and order, some deal with obligatory religious principles, and others address general issues:

> *What were the bases on which the law of the new Islamic community was built? First and foremost, there was the Qur'an, the*

> *word of God as revealed to His Prophet, Muhammad. Only a small portion of the Qur'an, however, takes the form of legal prescriptions – some six hundred verses in all, and of this number only about eighty can be considered legislation in the strict sense. The remainder deal with religious duties, with the rituals of fasting, prayer and pilgrimage, and so on. Much of the so-called Qur'anic 'legislation' consists of general ethical principles: for instance, the Qur'an urges compassion toward the weaker members of society, and calls for good faith in commercial transactions, and for up-right conduct in the administration of justice. The Qur'an also gives evidence of a desire to upgrade the status of women.*[606]

Former United States President Bill Clinton paid high tribute to the Qur'an. The president invited some Muslim guests in the month of Ramadan (2007) and gave a speech on how he was influenced by the Qur'an. The meeting started with the recitation from the holy Qur'an. President Clinton used the Qur'anic verses in his address and expressed his eagerness to study the holy book. He said:

> *I thought it was particularly moving that Imam read the passage from the Koran that said that Allah created nations and tribes that we might know one another, not that we might despise one another. There's a wonderful passage in the Hebrew Torah, which warns people never to turn aside the stranger, for it is like turning aside the most high God. And the Christian Bible says that people should love their neighbor as themselves. But it's quite wonderful to say that Allah created the nations and tribes that they might know one another better... Let me say, also, that there is much that the world can learn from Islam. It is now practiced by one of every four people on Earth. Americans are learning more in our schools and universities. Indeed, I remember that our daughter took a course on Islamic history in high school and read large portions of the Koran, and came home at night and educated her parents about it, and later asked us questions about it... So I ask you again to rededicate yourselves in this coming year to making sure that others in this country truly understand and appreciate the faith you embrace, its*

> *practices, its beliefs, its precepts and its inclusive humanity... The Koran also teaches, in addition, to the fact that we should do unto others as we wish to have done to us, and reject for others what we would reject for ourselves, but we should also make a commitment to live in peace...*[607]

The Encyclopaedia Britannica notes that the Qur'an is a book on many topics and chapters. There are verses with theological and ethical contents. It confirms the oneness of God and the messengership of Muhammad (ﷺ), and condemns idolatry. According to the *Encyclopaedia Britannica*:

> *The contents of the different parts of the Qur'an are extremely varied. Many passages consist of theological and moral reflection. We are reminded of the greatness the goodness, the righteousness of God, as manifested in nature, in history, and in revelations through the prophets especially through Muhammad. God is magnified as the one, the All-powerful. Idolatry, and all deification of created beings, such as the Worship of Christ, as the son of God, are unsparingly condemned.*[608]

High tribute has been paid towards Islam and the Qur'an in the *Chambers Cyclopaedia* Volume 6. It notes the high ethics of the Qur'an, brighter than those found in any other lawbook, and says that with revelation of the Qur'an the darkness surrounding mankind has been lifted and light poured down on humanity.[609]

The Qur'an's literary composition cannot be matched by man, and this is in itself a testimony to its divine origin. Achieving the eloquence of the Qur'anic language and the accuracy of the information, historical or scientific, provided therein was certainly beyond the capability of Prophet Muhammad (ﷺ) who was but a human being. According to Harry Gaylord Dorman, a biographer of the Prophet:

> *It (the Qur'an) is a literal revelation of Allah, dictated to [Prophet] Muhammad [saas] by Gabriel, perfect in every letter. It is an ever-present miracle witnessing to itself and to [Prophet] Muhammad*

> *[saas], the Prophet of Allah. Its miraculous quality resides partly in its style, so perfect and lofty that neither men nor Jinn could produce a single chapter to compare with its briefest chapter, and partly in its content of teachings, prophecies about the future, and amazingly accurate information such as [Prophet] Muhammad [saas] could never have gathered of his own accord.*[610]

The cadence of the Qur'an is one of its unique traits. Such was its sophistication and grace that many of its first listeners dismissed it as the work of a magician or a witch. George Sale says:

> *The Koran is universally allowed to be written with the utmost elegance and purity of language, in the dialect of Koreish, the most noble and polite of all Arabians... The style of the Qur'an is generally beautiful and fluent... and in many places, specifically where the majesty and attributes of God are described, sublime and magnificent... He succeeded so well, and so strangely captivated the minds of his audience, that several of his opponents thought it the effect of witchcraft and enchantment.*[611]

Carlyle observed that the merits of the Qur'an are unlimited:

> *Sincerity, in all senses, seems to me the merit of the Qur'an; what had rendered it precious to the wild Arab men. It is after all first and last merit in a book; gives rise to merits of all kinds, nay, at bottom, it alone can give rise to merit of any kind.*[612]

The Qur'an opposes violence. When dealing with the sensitive topic of the Qur'an and violence, we need to take an important point into consideration. In principle, the Qur'an is against all violence and urges its followers always to seek peaceful solutions to any conflicts that may arise. However, bearing in mind the context in which the Qur'an was revealed and propagated, there may be circumstances which call for what can be said to be a violent approach. However, any sanction for violence is context-laden and warranted out of necessity. Dr N.K. Singh says:

What is the place of violence in Islam? Is Islam a non-violent religion, then? The answer, to be honest and to be truthful to life is, both yes and no. Islam does not advocate violence but does not shut it altogether. Life is full of contradictions and these contradictions do reflect themselves in what we can call a contextual theology, if it wishes to be true to life. The Qur'an does not advocate mere abstract theological and metaphysical doctrines. The Qur'anic theology does not neglect the concrete socio-political context. All scriptures, on close scrutiny, would be found to contain contextual contradictions. The Qur'an is no exception to that. In fact, the scriptures provide both normative as well as contextual answers. Normatively speaking, the Qur'an opposes violence but permits it contextually.[613]

There are many factors which are at play when trying to make sense of why a religion and scripture may permit violent means to resolve a conflict. This is the case with any faith, be it Islam, Christianity, Hinduism, etc. We must be sensitive once again to the context of a situation and resist the temptation to make crass generalisations. If those who are committing the injustice in the first place are doing so purely for personal and ruthless reasons, then they must be met with force, if force is the only way of repelling their aggression. However, the idea of propagating faith through the sword is never a plausible means and cannot be justified. Dr N.K. Singh notes:

When it comes to the context, we must take the socio-political and socio-economic conditions of the society in which a particular religion originates. Hinduism is non-violent religion in the ideal sense. However, in the midst of the Mahabharat war, the conditions were different and even Lord Krishna had to urge Arjuna to fight even if it meant shedding the blood of his near and dear ones, in fact, his own cousins. War has justification in certain circumstances, especially if inflicted by exploitative and oppressive forces. But war can have no justification for spread of religion. Even the concept of jihad in Islam has to be seen in this light. Jihad has nothing to do with the spread of religion; it is only a war

> *against oppression and exploitation. The Qur'an sanctions war if the weaker sections of the society are being persecuted and there is no way left out to rescue them. Thus the Qur'an says:*
> *"And what reason have you not to fight in the way of Allah, and of the weak among the men and the women and children, who say our Lord, take us out of this town, whose people are oppressors, and grant us from Thee a friend, and grant us from Thee a helper?"*
> *It can, thus, be clearly seen that the Qur'an urges upon believers to fight against oppression being perpetrated against men, women, and children, who are weak.*[614]

Author Amit Pal states that Islam obliges Muslims not to transgress limits when seeking revenge and that justice should be maintained at all times. The Qur'an states that clemency and patience is more desirable than revenge, even when revenge is sanctioned by law. Pal says:

> *The Qur'an exhorts that revenge should be proportional to the wrong inflicted and that patience (sabr) is always superior to revenge: "If ye take vengeance on any, take a vengeance proportional to the wrong which hath been done to you; but if ye suffer wrong patiently, verily this will be better for the patient."*[615]

Inappropriate Translation and its Consequences

British MP Frank Dobson pointed towards the distortion of the meaning of the Qur'an and its translation. He believes that in order to find the real meaning of the Qur'an, it should be translated by only the knowledgeable and learned, as in the case of the English King James Bible:

> *Well I've read bits of it from time to time and I suspect it loses a lot in translation in terms of its impact and the way things are expressed is important and this year, marks the 400th anniversary of the King James Bible in English, much of which is almost poetry.*

I believe the quality of the English in the King James Bible has been a major contributor to both the prospering of Christian belief in the English speaking world and its also been a major contribution to large parts of the world speaking English, because it is such good English. I suspect that the English translations of the Qur'an leave a lot to be desired compared to the original Arabic, because the modern translations of the Christian Bible are generally speaking, tend to be written by management consultants.[616]

Influence of the Qur'an

Arthur John Arberry was a respected British Orientalist, a famous scholar of Islamic studies, Arabic and Persian. He translated the Qur'an into English as *The Koran Interpreted* in 1955: one of the most prominent translations written by a non-Muslim scholar:

In making the present attempt to improve on the performance of my predecessors, and to produce something which might be accepted as echoing however faintly the sublime rhetoric of the Arabic Koran, I have been at pain to study the intricate and richly varied rhythms which – apart from the message itself – constitute the Koran's undeniable claim to rank amongst the greatest literary masterpieces of mankind. This very characteristic feature – 'that inimitable symphony', as the believing Pickthall described his Holy Book, 'the very sounds of which move men to tears and ecstasy' has been almost totally ignored by previous translators; it is therefore not surprising that what they have wrought sounds dull and flat indeed in comparison with the splendidly decorated origina.l[617]

Arberry adds:

Whenever I hear the Qur'an chanted, it is as though I am listening to music, underneath the following melody, there is sounding all the time the instant beat of a drum, it is like the beating of my heart.[618]

William Draper points out that the Qur'an has greatly influenced mankind and continues to provide laws relating to life:

> *The Koran, which is that basis, has exercised a great control over the destinies of mankind, and still serves as a rule of life to a very large portion of our race.*[619]

Draper maintains that the Qur'an, though small in size, is large in action. Its excellent moral suggestions require a special mention of guidelines for daily life and are very helpful in many socio-economic situations. According to him:

> *An impartial reader of the Koran may doubtless be surprised that so feeble a production should serve its purpose so well. But the theory of religion is one thing, the practice another. The Koran abounds in excellent moral suggestions and precepts; its composition is so fragmentary that we cannot turn to a single page without finding maxims of which all men must approve. This fragmentary construction yields texts, and mottoes, and rules complete in themselves, suitable for common men in any of the incidents of life. There is a perpetual insisting on the necessity of prayer, an inculcation of mercy, almsgiving, justice, fasting, pilgrimage, and other good works; institutions respecting conduct, both social and domestic, debts, witnesses, marriage, children, wine, and the like;*[620]

Draper further argues that many scholars who studied the Qur'an have been greatly influenced by its teaching:

> *But the great Mohammedan philosophers, simply accepting the doctrine of the Oneness of God as the only thing of which man can be certain, look upon all the rest as idle fables, having, however, this political use, that they furnish contention, and therefore occupation to disputatious sectarians, and consolation to illiterate minds.*[621]

Edward Gibbon and Simon Ockley admired the Qur'an for its laws for mankind, covering a wider part of the world. They state:

> *From the Atlantic to the Ganges, the Koran is acknowledged as the fundamental code, not only of theology but of civil and criminal jurisprudence; the laws which regulate the actions and the property of mankind, are guarded by the infallible and immutable sanction of the will of God.*[622]

Arabic literature was greatly enriched by the Qur'an. Its rhymes are melodious. H.A.R Gibb says that the Qur'an has tremendous influence on the development of Arabic literature. The Qur'anic idea, language and rhymes permeate many other works on literature.[623]

Arthur Naylor Wollaston notes that the Qur'an is widely used in educational institutes as well as various contexts in social life and is a unique work:

> *Further, as the Qur'an is widely used in schools and generally in private life, it may be said with truth to be the most widely read book in existence, and as the more orthodox believe, and are taught by the book itself, inimitable by any human pen.*[624]

The Qur'an's stylistic effect is a notable phenomenon and a large part of its appeal. This also explains the reasons why it is regarded with admiration and veneration, and this is not restricted to a particular generation. Johann Wolfgang von Goethe (1749–1832) a German writer, poet, pictorial artist, biologist, physicist, scientist and a local politician comments:

> *Whenever I read the Qur'an, I feel something has shaken my spirit. .It soon attracts, astounds, and in the end enforces our reverence... Its style, in accordance with its contents and aim is stern, grand – ever and always, truly sublime – So, this book will go on exercising through all ages a most potent influence.*[625]

Dr F. Steingass, a professor at the University of Munich and the author of English-Arabic and Arabic-English dictionaries, said that the

Qur'an's emotive and evocative nature had been acknowledged by many scholars and commentators. Its mystical ability to exert an influence and impression on people in the remotest parts of the earth, irrespective of time and place, could be credited to the powerful effect it produces,; it is undoubtedly a masterpiece among literary works:

> *A work, then, which calls forth so powerful and seemingly incompatible emotions even in the distant reader – distant as to time, and still more so as mental development – a work which not only conquers the repugnance which he may begin its perusal, but changes this adverse feeling into astonishment and admiration, such a work must be a wonderful production...indeed and a problem of the highest interest to every thoughtful observer of the destinies of mankind.*[626], [627]

An adequate way of gauging the Qur'an's efficacy is by critically observing how it proved compelling to its initial audience in 7th- century Arabia, many of whom harboured hatred and hostility for Islam. The Qur'an definitely had a progressive effect on its hearers, changing those who were unreceptive to it to become among its most faithful patrons. In this regard, Dr Steingass further comments:

> *Here, therefore, its merits as a literary production should perhaps not be measured by some preconceived maxims of subjective and aesthetic taste, but by the effects which it produced in Muhammad's contemporaries and fellow countrymen. If it spoke so powerfully and convincingly to the hearts of his hearers as to weld hitherto centrifugal and antagonistic elements into one compact and well organized body, animated by ideas far beyond those which had until now ruled the Arabian mind, then its eloquence was perfect, simply because it created a civilized nation out of savage tribes, and shot a fresh woof into the old warp of history.*[628]

According to the former British pop star Cat Stevens (Yusuf Islam), one of the Qur'an's attractive elements is its encouragement to participate in deeds which mutually benefit humanity. He says:

Everything made so much sense. This is the beauty of the Qur'an; it asks you to reflect and reason.... When I read the Qur'an further, it talked about prayer, kindness and charity. I was not a Muslim yet, but I felt the only answer for me was the Qur'an and God had sent it to me.[629]

The conviction in the Qur'an's uniqueness is arrived at when it is compared with other holy books. With this profound sense of objectivity and critical study, Saifuddin Dirk Walter Mosig, an American born in a German Christian family in 1943, states:

I have read the Sacred Scriptures of every religion; nowhere have I found what I encountered in Islam: perfection. The Holy Qur'an, compared to any other scripture I have read, is like the Sun compared to that of a match. I firmly believe that anybody who reads the Word of Allah with a mind that is not completely closed to Truth, will become a Muslim.[630]

A prolific politician (requested to be anonymous) made some comments about the Qur'an as the final immaculate revelation sent to mankind from God Almighty. He claimed that the Qur'an is a practical book and ahead of its time. There is something which is socially relevant and common-sense about the Qur'an's teachings, which moves it away from being a scripture which commands only rituals. The Qur'an has often been credited for having a modernising impact on its followers and civilisation in general.[631]

The details of Islam's exponential growth and expansion into what can aptly be described as a progressive civilisation are an outstanding chapter in Islam's history.[632]

He also said that he reads the Qur'an every day so as to become faith literate. He expressed the view:

'To be faith-literate is crucial in a globalised world, I believe. 'I read the Qur'an [Koran] every day; partly to understand some of the things happening in the world, but mainly just because it is immensely instructive.'[633]

He further paid tribute to the religion of Islam, saying that the Qur'an is a reforming and inclusive book and also Prophet Muhammad (ﷺ) was 'an enormously civilizing force'.[634]

John Naish, a Christian clergyman, was familiar with the originality of the Qur'an – its attractive nature that made people devoted to it. Naish says about the Qur'an:

> *The Qur'an in its original Arabic dress has a seductive beauty and charm of its own. Couched in concise and exalted style, its brief pregnant sentences, often rhymed, possess an expressive force and explosive energy which it is extremely difficult to convey by literal word for word translation.*[635]

The Popular Encyclopaedia noted that the Arabic language used in the Qur'an is pure and its poetic beauty is enormous. If anyone follows it carefully, they will lead an honest life. According to the *Popular Encyclopaedia*:

> *The language of the Qur'an is considered the purest Arabic, and contains such charms of style and poetic beauties, that it remains inimitable. Its moral precepts are pure. A man who should observe them strictly would lead a virtuous life.*[636]

Alfred Martin wrote in his book: *Great Religious Teachers of the East'* that the Qur'an is the most widely read of all the sacred scriptures of the world. It is more extensively and frequently read among Moslems than is the New Testament among Christians.[637]

Despite the Qur'an being the last Scripture of the major religions on earth, it is held in reverence by over a billion people in the world today. Its impact can be measured when we consider how Islam generated transformation in the fields of culture and intellect. It most certainly had a civilising effect on its early followers and went to help establish a state. According to Margoliouth:

> *The Koran (Qur'an) admittedly occupies an important position among the great religious books of the world. Though it is the*

> *youngest of the epoch making works belonging to this class of literature, it yields to hardly any in the wonderful effect which it has produced on large masses of men. It has created an all but new phase of human thought and a fresh type of character. It first transformed a number of heterogeneous desert tribes of the Arabian Peninsula into a nation of heroes, and then proceeded to create the vast politico-religious organizations of Muslims world wide which are one of the great forces with which Europe and the East have to reckon with today.* [638]

Reverend Bosworth Smith challenges those who said that the Qur'an was not the work of Prophet Muhammad (ﷺ). He said:

> *The Arabs said that the Koran could not be Mohammed's work because it was too good. Mohammed replied to the effect that they were both right and wrong. They were right, for it was too good for Mohammed uninspired; they were wrong, for it was too good to have come originally from any one but the All-Merciful.* [639]

William Montgomery Watt remarks that the Qur'an, revealed through Muhammad, provided the Arab world with guidelines which resolved the social anarchy and unrest. The guidelines provided insight into the social depression and also the talent to put across such insight in a way that stirred the minds and souls of others.[640]

Scientific Information in the Qur'an

Once again, Prophet Muhammad's illiteracy is recognised as a factor which precludes the possibility of him producing the Qur'an and stating principles of concrete scientific facts. The resources prevailing in his time would not have allowed him to achieve such a tremendous feat. When the Qur'an was revealed, many non-believers claimed that the Qur'an has been authored by Prophet Muhammad (ﷺ), but on the contrary, there are also many opinions by those who have conducted investigations in studying the Qur'an, life of Prophet Muhammad (ﷺ) and his sayings. One of them was Maurice Bucaille (1920–1998).

Bucaille was a French medical doctor, member of the French Society of Egyptology, former chief of the surgical clinic, University of Paris and author of *The Bible, the Qur'an and Science.* He had a longstanding interest in the correspondence between the teachings of the Holy Scriptures and modern secular knowledge. Having studied for ten years, he gave a lecture in the French Academy of Medicine in 1976 concerning the existence of some statements in the Qur'an about physiology and reproduction. He argued:

> *It is impossible that Muhammad (peace be upon him) authored the Qur'an. How could a man, from being illiterate, become the most important author, in terms of literary merits, in the whole of Arabic literature? How could he then pronounce truths of a scientific nature that no other human- being could possibly have developed at that time, and all this without once making the slightest error in his pronouncement on the subject?* [641]

He added:

> *A totally objective examination of it [the Qur'an] in the light of modern knowledge leads us to recognize the agreement between the two, as has been already noted on repeated occasions. It makes us deem it quite unthinkable for a man of Muhammad's time to have been the author of such statements, on account of the state of knowledge in his day. Such considerations are part of what gives the Qur'anic Revelation its unique place, and forces the impartial scientist to admit his inability to provide and explanation which calls solely upon materialistic reasoning.* [642]

Muslims have often maintained that the authenticity of the Qur'an has remained intact all along. When we consider how the Qur'an was compiled and preserved, this claim has credence. Not only was the Qur'an written on tablets, gazelle skin and other material, but it was committed to memory and recited in front of Prophet Muhammad (ﷺ),

so he could authenticate whether the recitals by his companions were genuine and correct or not. On this subject, Bucaille says:

> *About fourteen centuries ago at a meditation retreat near Makkah, Muhammad received the first message through the Archangel Gabriel. After a long period of silence, the first message was followed by successive revelations spanning a period of some twenty years. They were not only transcribed while the Prophet was still alive, but also recited by heart by his early followers and later by the many believers who had gathered around him. After his death (i.e. 632 A.D.), the various elements were brought together in a book, henceforth known as The Qur'an. It contains the Word of God to the exclusion of any human addition. The manuscripts we possess from the first century of Islam authenticate today's text.*
> *[O]ur knowledge of these disciplines is such that it is impossible to explain how a text produced at the time of the Qur'an could have contained ideas that have only been discovered in modern times...The above observation makes the hypothesis advanced by those who see Muhammad as the author of the Qur'an untenable. How could a man, from being illiterate, become the most important author, in terms of literary merits, in the whole of Arabic literature?*[643]

Bucaille compared the sayings of Prophet Muhammad (ﷺ) with the sayings of Jesus. The sayings of Prophet Muhammad (ﷺ), known as Hadith, were written decades after his death; similarly, the Gospel, known as the sayings of Jesus was written decades after his death.[644]

The renowned British Orientalist Marmaduke Pickthall, in his well-known work *Islamic Culture*, deals briefly with the contribution of Muslim Spain to the advancement of sciences and arts and he observes:

> *The Qur'an undoubtedly gave a great impetus to learning, especially in the field of natural science: and, If, as some modern writers have declared, the inductive method, to which all the practical modern discoveries are chiefly owing, can be traced to it, then it may be called the cause of modern scientific and material*

progress.[645]

J. Christy Wilson, an American author, wrote about the power of the Qur'an in *Introducing Islam*, published in New York in 1950. Considering that Christianity and Islam are the two most dominant and popularly followed religions today, the Qur'an's impact on the hearts of its followers cannot be underestimated.[646]

The Qur'an may be said to have a more enduring impact on the sensibilities of its followers, judging by the number of Muslims who partake in rituals mandated by their faith. In relation to the readership of the Qur'an, Charles Francis Potter, an American philosopher and author said:

> *It is (the Qur'an) more read than any other book in the world. The Christian Bible may be a world best-seller, but nearly 250 million followers of the Prophet Muhammad read or recite long sections of Alcoran (The Qur'an) five times a day, every day of their lives, from the time they can ta*[647]

The aspects of science in the Qur'an and the achievements in the field of science by the Arabs are well accepted. The celebrated professor and historian Edward Montet regards their achievement as a miracle which he found hard to believe! He did not find an example comparable to the Arabian development in science in the world except for the Japanese adoption of science and technology. Montet observes:

> *This Introduces what might be called the miracle of Arabic science, using the word miracle once more as a symbol of our liability to explain achievements which were almost incredible. There is nothing like it in the whole history of the world, except the Japanese assimilation of modern science and technology during the Meiji era. The comparison is useful, because the situation was fundamentally the same in both cases; the intellectual leaders of the Arabs realized the need of Greek science as urgently as the Japanese of two generations ago that of European science. Both had the will and the kind of spiritual energy which overcomes insuperable difficulties;*

indeed they had not sufficient experience nor enough patience to consider difficulties and be frightened by them; they simply rushed through. Everything becomes easier if you don't even imagine how difficult it is![648]

The contributions of the Qur'an in relation to science are huge. However, the development of Arabic science took place after the Prophet. The real miracle of the Qur'anic scientific development did not take place in Madinah, Makkah or even in Syria; rather, it was in Baghdad. Professor Montet adds:

It should be noted that the almost unbelievable development of Arabic science did not begin until the second half of the second century of the Hijrah. The Prophet was too deeply concerned in the hereafter and, as far as this life was concerned, stoical and religious issues, to be interested in science. Some modern apologists have tried to read scientific ideas in the Qur'an, but they can do this only by giving some words of it connotations which could never have occurred to the Prophet or to anybody else for centuries. The orthodox caliphs were not more scientifically-minded than he was; it is probable that the Greek clerks whom they employed were more familiar with business administration than with science, and that they were no longer capable of appreciating the intellectual achievements of their own ancestors. In short, there was no science to speak of in Madinah or Makkah, or even in Damascus. The miracle of the Arabic renaissance did not manifest itself before the establishment of the Caliphate in Baghdad. What happened there? The Arabic genius was actuated by the Iranian ferment; the Arabic and Persian qualities (and defects) were complimentary. The miracle of Arabic Science was largely due to the catalyzation of Arabic vigor and earnestness and of Islamic faith by Persian curiosity and sophistication. To put it in more general terms, Arabic science was the fruit of the Semitic genius fertilized by the Iranian genius. This may be too general a statement for strict accuracy, but it helps us to understand roughly what happened in Baghdad. Within a couple of centuries (c.750-950) the Islamic

> *rulers, using their polyglot subjects, most of them Christians and Jews, caused the best of Greek knowledge to become available in the Arabic language.*[649]

Historically, Islam was host to a civilisation which enshrined the principle of progress. Its rate of growth exceeded other societies and it was receptive to the intellectual legacies of non-Islamic civilisations. Much of the intellectual achievements of Muslims owe a legacy to others, yet Muslims used this to their advantage and embarked on a phase of modernisation unprecedented for its time. According to Jared Diamond, prizewinning author of the book *Guns, Germs, and Steel: The Fates of Human Societies* (1998),

> *Medieval Islam was technologically advanced and open to innovation. It achieved far higher literacy rates than in contemporary Europe; it assimilated the legacy of classical Greek civilization to such a degree that many classical books are now known to us only through Arabic copies. It invented windmills, trigonometry, lateen sails and made major advances in metallurgy, mechanical and chemical engineering and irrigation methods. In the middle-ages the flow of technology was overwhelmingly from Islam to Europe rather than from Europe to Islam. Only after the 1500s did the net direction of flow begin to reverse.* [650]

The length at which the Qur'an describes some aspects of scientific knowledge amazes the mind. Professor Dorja Rao, a specialist marine geologist, pays tribute to the Qur'an. He was surprised that such knowledge as described in the Qur'an was at that time, 1400 years ago! He exclaims:

> *It is difficult to imagine that this type of knowledge existed at that time, around 1400 years back. Maybe some of the things they had a simple idea about, but to describe those things in great detail is very difficult. So, this is definitely not simple human knowledge.*[651]

Many were drawn to the Qur'an's teachings and spirituality due to its intellectual rigour. They were intellectually satisfied with its contents, particularly in the realm of scientific thought. According to Dr Ali Selman Benoist, what the Qur'an revealed 1400 years ago, is consistent with modern science.[652]

Arthur Penrhyn, also known as Dean Stanley, an author, English churchman, and Dean of Westminster paid huge tribute to the Qur'an. He compared the Qur'an with the Bible and stated that the Qur'an, without question, has more in-depth thought than the Bible. In his words,

> *Within a confined circle the code of the Qur'an makes doubtless a deeper impression than has been made on Christianity by the code of the Bible.*[653]

Karen Armstrong states that the Qur'an is not the life story of Prophet Muhammad; rather it is the early Islamic history. The Qur'an reveals God and not His messenger. However, it providesinformation about early Islamic history.[654]

The Qur'an as a Miracle

A pioneer of Arabic and Islamic studies in Italy, Veccia Vaglieri served as Professor at Naples Eastern University and is the author of books on the historical and institutional analysis of the Arab and Muslim world. Professor Vaglieri notes that there is purity about the Qur'an's composition and profoundness regarding its contents, such as the numerous prophecies and the scientific information it stores. The Qur'an also possesses a code of conduct for everyday living and its tenets are not just restricted to the personal and ritual realm. The immensity of the topics it covers and the accuracy with which it reports data is inconceivable for its period and striking even by modern standards. The Qur'an's authorship is unlikely to be the product of an unlettered individual. Rather, its source must be of a supremely high intelligence which transcends human limitations:

For the book, besides its perfection in form and method, proved itself beyond irritation even in its substance. In it, among other things, we read a forecast of future events, and a description of events which had taken place centuries before but were generally ignored. There are frequent references to the laws of nature, to various sciences, both religious and secular. We find there vast stores of knowledge which are beyond the capacity of the most intelligent of men, the greatest of philosophers and the ablest of politicians. For all these reasons the Qur'an could not be the work of an uneducated man, who had spent all his life in the midst of an unrefined society far away from men of learning and religion, a man who always insisted that he was but a man just like any others, and, as such, unable to perform miracles unless he had the help of Almighty God. The Qur'an could have its source only in Him Whose knowledge comprehends everything in heaven and earth.[655]

Prophet Muhammad (ﷺ) would often refer to the Qur'an's linguistic style and calibre to prove its miraculous origins. Its language, pace and rhythmic expressions are a feat which even non-Muslims are compelled to admire. The profundity of its expressions and gracious style is of the highest calibre and is acknowledged by many non-Muslims.

A celebrated French author Paul Casanova relates in the article "L'Enseignement de I'Arabe au College de France" (The Arab Teaching at the College of France) how Prophet Muhammad (ﷺ) would answer when he was asked by his people to perform a miracle as proof of his doctrines. According to Casanova:

Whenever Muhammad was asked a miracle, as a proof of the authenticity of his mission, he quoted the composition of the Qur'an and its incomparable excellence as proof of its divine origin. And, in fact, even for those who are non-Muslims nothing is more marvellous than its language ... with such apprehensible plenitude and a grasping sonority... The ampleness of its syllables with a grandiose cadence and with a remarkable rhythm have been of much momentum in the conversion of the most hostile and the most sceptic.[656]

Washington Irving stated that Prophet Muhammad (ﷺ) never claimed to have any miracle other than the Qur'an:

> *The miracles ascribed to him are all fabrications of Moslem zealots. He expressly and repeatedly disclaimed all miracles excepting the Koran - which, considering its incomparable merit, and the way in which it had come down to him from heaven, he pronounced the greatest of miracles.*[657]

The fact that Prophet Muhammad (ﷺ) was unlettered continues to provoke mystery in the minds of thinkers. Living in a period where cultural and intellectual avenues were foreclosed to him from the very start, Prophet Muhammad (ﷺ) had to make do with the very little he had. Carlyle says:

> *One other circumstance we must not forget: that he had no school-learning; of the thing we call school-learning none at all. The art of writing was but just introduced into Arabia; it seems to be the true opinion that Muhammad never could write! Life in the Desert, with its experiences, was all his education. What of this infinite Universe he, from his dim place, with his own eyes and thoughts, could take in, so much and no more of it was he to know. Curious, if we will reflect on it, this of having no books. Except by what he could see for himself, or hear of by uncertain rumor of speech in the obscure Arabian Desert, he could know nothing. The wisdom that had been before him or at a distance from him in the world was in a manner as good as not there for him. Of the great brother souls, flame-beacons through so many lands and times, no one directly communicates with this great soul. He is alone there, deep down in the bosom of the Wilderness; has to grow up so, – alone with Nature and his own Thoughts...*[658]

There is a great deal of information about Prophet Muhammad (ﷺ) available today, from authentic sources and criteria; in fact it is available in far greater abundance than the facts of the lives of many other historical personalities. The fact that our assessment of him is not based on fragmentary information gives us greater clarity about his character. R.V.C. Bodley observes:

> *While we have no contemporary records of Moses or Confucius or Buddha, while we know some fragments of a fragment of Christ's life, but nothing of the thirty years which prepared the way for the culminating three, the story of Mohammed is extremely clear. Here, instead of the shadowy and the mysterious, we have history. We know as much of Mohammed as we do of men who lived much closer to our epoch. His external record, his youth, his relatives, his habits are neither legendary nor hearsay. His internal record, after his mission had been proclaimed, is no hazy tradition of some obscure or perplexed preacher. We have a contemporaneous book, absolutely unique in its origin and in its preservation, on the authenticity of which no one has ever been able to cast a serious doubt. This book, known as the Koran, is available today as it was first written under Mohammed's supervision.*[659]

The Qur'an is Original

According to Basanta Coomar Bose (1931), an Indian author, one of the unique aspects of the Islamic Scripture is its authenticity and the absence of any genuine evidence showing it to be tampered with. A stranger phenomenon is the Qur'an's literary prowess, albeit initiated by an unlettered Prophet:

> *So there has been no opportunity for forgery or pious fraud in the Koran, which distinguishes it from almost all other religious works of ancient times…it is exceedingly strange that this illiterate person should have composed the best book in the language.*[660]

Smith claims that the world knew the full history of Prophet Muhammad (ﷺ) from his early life, through the revelation till his death; mankind has a book, the Qur'an, and there was no doubt about its originality. He remarks:

> *But we know everything of the external history of Mohammed his youth, his appearance, his relations, his habits; the first idea and the gradual growth, intermittent though it was, of his great revelation; while for his internal history, after his mission had been proclaimed, we have a book absolutely unique in its origin, in its reservation, and in the chaos of its contents, but on the authenticity of which no one has ever been able to cast a serious doubt.*[661]

Washington Irving admired the pure contents of the Qur'an and re-echoed what had been commended by Dr Stengass and Goethe:

> *The Qur'an contains the pure, elevated and benignant precepts, which in the words of Dr Stengass 'is one of the grandest Books ever written' and in the words of Goethe 'attracts, astounds and enforces our reverence'.*[662]

The fact that the Qur'an is unchanged is one of its most remarkable traits. Unlike the other Abrahamic faiths, Islam alone can claim this unique distinction. The evocative nature of the Arabic language in which the Qur'an was revealed adds to its splendour; just one of its many magnificent qualities. R.V.C Bodley remarks:

> *What is important is that the Koran is the only work which has survived for twelve hundred years with an unadulterated text. Neither in the Jewish religion nor in the Christian is there anything which faintly compares to this.*[663]

Bodley continues:

> *To anyone who has not heard the sonorous majesty of an Arab reciting the Koran or listened to the call to prayer from minaret of a mosque, it is impossible to convey what the book lacks in English or French or German. It is like Shakespeare in a foreign tongue or Wagner in Italian.*[664]

It is Divine

One of Islam's unique characteristics is its ability to assimilate with the progressive forces of time. Muslims had a yearning to know more than they did and to transcend the boundaries of knowledge and capability, and this precedent can be found in their religion, which invoked its followers to be contemplative. In her book *The Thing about Islam* Magsie Hamilton Little reinforces this view. She feels that Islam encourages the acquiring of knowledge. Everything on the earth is God's creation and in order to understand it human beings need to gain knowledge, whatever their age.[665]

Hamilton Little points out that as a result of the accumulation of knowledge, Muslims gained competence in multiple disciplines. The disintegration of the Islamic body politic in no way sapped the Muslim potential and the desire to work for the betterment of their societies. She says that by following Prophet Muhammad's message, the Muslims achieved great things. The Muslim advancement in art, science, mathematics and literature extended to South East Asia. The message of Prophet Muhammad (ﷺ) inspired the Muslims; it is still working in the minds of the people and will work in the centuries ahead, the teachings of the Holy Book Qur'an bear the great message of God sent to the Prophet(ﷺ).[666]

Hamilton Little claims that the Qur'an's effects are not simply restricted to the fields of science. Its influence can also be gleaned in the realm of linguistics, as many contend that it sparked a renaissance in language and linguistic forms. The word of God, its spirits and power as laid in the Qur'an has affected language too; Grammar and syntax were advanced. After Prophet Muhammad (ﷺ), the study of the Qur'an extended the Arabic language beyond the Arab lands. That had contributed to the introduction of Persian, Urdu, Turkish and Indonesian languages.[667]

Otto von Bismarck, was a conservative German statesman who dominated European affairs from the 1860s until his dismissal in 1890. He highlighted that something that has favourably disposed many to the Qur'an, is its pristine purity, the fact that unlike other religious scriptures it remains unadulterated and unchanged since its very revelation. Coupled with the Qur'an's erudition and scientific information, its authorship has been attributed to the Divine. Bismarck said:

> *I looked into and studied all holy and heavenly books. Due to some amendments and modifications made in all could not find the true wisdom capable to provide happiness and welfare and prosperity to human beings. However, I found the holy Qur'an of the Muhammad extremely superior to other books. I found divine wisdom in each word of the holy Qur'an. Such an excellent work could not be the words of a human being...Those who claim that the Qur'an is the words of Muhammad are in the position of denying the necessity of science. In another words, it is very clear and obvious that the holy Qur'an conveys the words of God.*[668]

The Scottish historian H.A.R. Gibb said that it was often claimed in Orientalist literature that Prophet Muhammad (ﷺ) was credited with authorship of the Qur'an. However, the failure to reproduce something remotely similar to the Qur'an's literary magnitude could suggest its authorship to be miraculous. Gibb disagreed with those who think that the Qur'an is Mohammad(ﷺ)'s own composition. He, too, challenged the unbelievers to produce only ten verses similar to those of the Qur'an and if they failed, he suggested that they accept the Qur'an as the outstanding miracle.[669]

Goethe argued that the Qur'an is not an ordinary book but is of divine provenance:

> *He is a prophet and not a poet and therefore his Koran is to be seen as Divine Law, and not as a book of a human being made for education or entertainment.*[670]

Ruth Cranston wrote in *World Faith* that it is impossible in brief to give an adequate idea of the variety, profundity and the practical help of the teachings of the Koran. It contains the rulings on marriage and divorce, health, money lending and property. But in every section and every instruction, the majesty of God runs like a golden thread on which all the rest is hung.[671]

The Qur'an is the reconfirmation of monotheism – worship of one God Who has created everything in the universe. He is the Almighty, the Supreme, the Omniscient, the Compassionate and the Just. The creation signifies His power and knowledge. Whatever He has created is for the advantage of mankind. Michael E. Marmura of Toronto University elaborates:

> *The Qur'an is an ardent reaffirmation of monotheism. It declares that the world and all that there is in it is created by God, omnipotent, omniscient, merciful and just. The creation is a 'sign': a manifestation of His power and wisdom. It is also manifestation of His bounty and goodness; for He has created things for man's benefit. Men are enjoined to consider God's handiwork, to reflect the wonders of his creations.*[672]

The Qur'an's divine provenance is attested to by Jaims Jenz, an astronomical scientist, who said that the Qur'an is a brilliant book 'but of God'[673]

The Qur'an's pronouncements on embryological development have prompted many to believe in its divine nature. The Japanese Professor Yoshido Kozan, head of Tokyo planetarium, says:

> *I don't find any difficulties in accepting the Qur'an as a true word of God – because the explanation of the growth of the fetus in the womb of his mother which the Qur'an gives, 14 hundred years ago, is typically what science knew recently.*[674]

Since Prophet Muhammad (ﷺ) was so ahead of his time as far as scientific information is concerned, it confirms the belief about the Qur'an's origin as Divine. According to Prof. Alfred Kroner:

> *It is impossible that Muhammad could have known about the common origin of the universe, scientists only found this out in the last few years using complicated and advanced technology.*[675]

Deepak Chopra says that Prophet Muhammad (ﷺ) appealed to him most because the Prophet reformed humankind by reaching into the inner level of divine. Such an achievement was only possible due to his being chosen by God. The Qur'an will keep its place in the hearts of people as a hymn of the soul.[676]

Marshall B. Broomhall, a British Protestant Christian missionary to China with the China Inland Mission and an author declared that the Qur'an is the true book of God which was revealed to Prophet Muhammad (ﷺ). The author says:

> *As to the meritorious work of stooping to learn and comprehend, there is nothing more explicit than the Koran, which the True Lord revealed to Mohammed.*[677]

CHAPTER SIX

The Prophet's Teachings and Link to Terrorism

Charges are levelled against Islam that it provokes violence and terrorism. It is alleged that many were compelled to accept Islam at the point of the sword and Prophet Muhammad (ﷺ) had conquered the world by the use of force. This chapter seeks to find out whether such charges are tenable.

No Link to Terrorism

A genuine study of Prophet Muhammad(ﷺ)'s life would reveal that it was not the sword, but his personality, his unique character, his sincerity of purpose that earned him the trust and loyalty of his followers which helped Islam to spread far and wide. The late Michael Meacher, Labour Party politician and academic, in an interview in 2012 said that the terrorist activities being committed today in the name of Islam are the result of gross misunderstanding and misinterpretation of the religion which would not have been corroborated by Prophet Muhammad (ﷺ). Often, the considerations of power and other motivations incite a person to perpetrate violence and hostility. The true religion, be it Islam or Christianity, approves no such acts. Prophet Muhammad (ﷺ) did not ever endorse terrorism as the means to propagate faith. The Qur'an declares in the clearest term that "There shall be no coercion in matters of faith" [Al-Qur'an 2:256].

Unfortunately, terrorism that smears the image of Islam today is due to some heinous acts of a handful of individuals misguided and misled in the name of Islam. Behind this are the nefarious designs of others, too.

One cannot discount the fall outs of the colonial and military operations in the Muslim world, spearheaded by the West. This, many would explain, compel those, oppressed and violated, to commit terrorist acts. According to the late Michael Meacher, Labour Party politician and academic:

> *I don't think there is a link between Muhammad's teachings and terrorism. I think if Muhammad came back today, he would deeply disapprove of terrorist acts just as if Jesus Christ came back today he would disapprove of attacking Iraq or Afghanistan. What is done in the name of the prophets and founders of our religion is dreadful; it is distorted and corrupted by the lust for power. Muhammad didn't support terrorism. He wanted to win people over his faith through the revelation he received through the angel Gabriel and he wanted to protect his own people. I think the idea that somehow Islam is a terrorist religion is a deliberate caricature and falsity which is spread by the West and particularly by the Americans. It is true that some Muslim people do undertake terrorism. Most of us disapprove of it but the reason I think is because the West has behaved extremely badly towards the Muslim countries. It has occupied them. It has forced them into subjugation and as we know in Iraq, probably killed more than a 100,000 Iraqis, the vast majority of whom were civilians. So it is not surprising that Muslims in other countries feel extremely angry and bitter about this and themselves then commit terrorist acts. They shouldn't but it's entirely understandable why they do, but Muhammad would not have approved.*[678]

When asked about links between Prophet Muhammad(ﷺ)'s teachings and terrorism, some participants in this reseach recounted personal stories and real life experiences to shed light on the question. Although one cannot deny that terrorist activities are committed by some in the name of Islam, it is generally maintained that Prophet Muhammad's (ﷺ) teaching has no connection with these actions and the majority of Prophet Muhammad(ﷺ)'s followers are law abiding peaceful citizens. According to British MP Stephen Timms:

> *I'm certainly not aware of any link. It is true that almost two years ago I was stabbed by a young woman and she told the police that she was doing it because of her faith. After that happened to me, I had hundreds of cards and letters and messages from Muslims, telling me they were praying for me for a speedy recovery. So I think those people were reflecting the teachings of the Prophet more faithfully than the young woman who stabbed me but it can't be denied that there are some people apparently who believe they should commit acts of terrorism because of their faith that is an unfortunate fact.*[679]

The source of terrorism is never and can never be religion. Islam has no link with terrorism. Jon Dal Din, the Director of Westminster Interfaith, London thinks that Islam has no link with terrorism. He says:

> *No link.... Terrorism has political and cultural roots and I make very clear distinction between terrorists who are labelled as Muslims and the tenets is Islam itself. I don't have problem in that direction...I don't see the Muslims are potential terrorists*[680].

Ram Dev was the editor of a Vedic magazine during the Arya Samaj movement in Lahore in 1915. He admired Prophet Muhammad (ﷺ), saying how the Prophet managed to control the Arabs in Madinah, preaching the religion of monotheism. He stressed that religion cannot be spread by force and that Islam was not spread by the sword:

> *Sitting in Madinah, Muhammad Sahib (peace be to him) held the Arabs spellbound; he filled them with spiritual strength; strength that makes devtas [gods] out of men... it is incorrect to say that Islam spread with the force of the sword. It is a fact that the sword was never wielded to propagate Islam. If religion can be spread by force then let anyone try it today.*[681]

Professor of religion John Kaltner has claimed that many non-Muslims perceive that Islam was spread through violence, but this is wrong. Islam does not endorse forcible conversion. There is a Qur'anic verse saying: "There is no compulsion in religion". Kaltner goes on to say that, once the Muslims had conquered a land, they offered several options for the resident of the land which included invitation to join the fold of Islam but no forcible conversion[682].

Lord Headley claims that Islam is not a religion of violence as the Qur'an did not advocate coercion in religion, either. According to him:

> *I am certain that the Muslims – who are all loyally inclined – would never attempt to establish Islam by any violent methods. Sedition and rebellion are absolutely forbidden by the Koran. "Let there be no violence in the religion" is one of the maxims of the Muslim faith.*[683]

British Tony Benn MP strongly believes that there is no link between terrorism and the teachings of Prophet Muhammad (ﷺ). He observes:

> *No. I think acts of terrorism are committed by people and then they say it is because I have been taught this, but they never take responsibility for it themselves and I don't believe terrorism was an instrument of Islam, because I think it is anti-Islamic propaganda.*[684]

The Sikh Temple of East London also thinks that there is no link between Prophet Muhammad's teachings and terrorism. A spokesman from the Temple says:

> *There is no link between the prophet's teaching and terrorism. It is power why some people are terrorising others; Jihad means killing one's own ego.*[685]

For some participants like the school teacher Bhavin Tailor, terrorism and religion are not interchangeable terms and Prophet Muhammad(ﷺ)'s teachings have no correlation with terrorism:

> *From the teachings that I know, no [link between Islam and terrorism]. Historically from my knowledge, terrorism wasn't in a*

> *religious context, yet immediately in the modern world, we have the word terrorism and immediately people think religion, Islamic fundamentalism, Christian fundamentalism etc. so my knowledge about Prophet Muhammad's teachings and his life, I see no link.*[686]

Anita Rai relates that a war broke out between the tribe of Prophet Muhammad (ﷺ) and Hawazin. At that time Prophet Muhammad was 20 years old and although he was present at the battle, he did not take part in the war. The author Anita Rai feels that the Prophet Muhammad (ﷺ) had an innate dislike of atrocities.[687]

The association of Prophet Muhammad(ﷺ)'s teachings with terrorism has been categorically rejected by British MP David Amess, who feels that violence perpetrated in the name of Islam is no different to that committed in the name of any other religion, with both representing a hijacking of faith and in no way connected to Prophet Muhammad(ﷺ)'s teachings:

> *I don't think there is a link. I don't understand how these groups have seized on his teachings and become terrorists, just like I can tell you as a Catholic that I can't understand in God's teachings how the Catholic IRA decided they could embrace violence, murdering people to take over a country. The terrorism has nothing to do with the teachings of the Prophet.*[688]

Terrorism is not even remotely associated with Prophet Muhammad(ﷺ)'s teachings according to Mike Stygal, who insists that violent actions being committed in the name of Islam is a disservice to the religion and its people:

> *I don't find any correlation between Muhammad's teachings and terrorism because Islam is without a doubt … a religion of peace. The people who commit acts of terrorism in the name of Islam are so grossly misrepresenting Islam that anybody who knows anything in the slightest about Islam cannot see them as being good Muslims. I cannot see how anyone with the slightest knowledge about Islam could believe they are representing Muslims and Islam.*[689]

Prophet Muhammad(ﷺ)'s message was essentially inclusive and demonstrated remarkable tolerance for the difference between various faiths. Terrorism, therefore, bears no relation to Islam's intentions. A Christian priest from a church in East London comments:

> *I don't think there are any links from what I know of the prophet. There is no link with terrorism at all. His message is one of acceptance of different faiths although they may be considered of different faiths, although it may not be considered the true path by him, they are accepted. I see terrorism happening due to man's wickedness that I want to do it my way.*[690]

Terrorism is a distortion of the genuine teachings of Prophet Muhammad (ﷺ) and like the abuse of other faiths, is committed by violating the religion's core principles. Jeremy Corbyn says:

> *None whatsoever. Those that seek to practise terrorism on behalf of any faith are denying the basic tenets and honesty of that faith. I draw the parallel with Christianity.*[691]

Many are quick to dismiss the allegation that Prophet Muhammad(ﷺ)'s teachings are associated with terrorism. Islam, like other peaceful and tolerant religions like Christianity have been misappropriated and exploited to justify evil ends which neither Prophet Muhammad (ﷺ) nor Jesus(pbuh) could ever endorse. The perception that Prophet Muhammad(ﷺ)'s teachings and the Islamic religion intrinsically harbour terrorist inclinations is according to a substantial number of participants, a deliberate agenda of some Western states. The wider context behind terrorism is also considered, in particular the foreign policy of some countries which has led to the victimisation and oppression of Muslims the world over. Although this does not justify acts of murder, it provides some much needed perspective on the motivation behind these acts. Nonetheless, it has been observed that Prophet Muhammad (ﷺ) would find such actions to be of a criminal nature and would never support such atrocities.

Dr Julian Fulbrook is a Councillor of London Borough of Camden for over three decades; a primary school governor and Dean of Graduate studies in the London School of Economics (LSE), University of London, and formerly he has held numerous posts such as Mayor of Camden, Chair of Housing, Chair of Education and Chair of Social Services. According to him, denying a person his right can often lead to despair and actions we may describe as terrorist. In Fulbrook's (February, 2012) words:

> *Terrorism is an outflow of people who are oppressed.*[692]

Many dismiss any link between Prophet Muhammad(ﷺ)'s message and the phenomenon of terrorism today. Despite the reality of some Muslims invoking Islam to justify certain acts, it must be kept in mind that terrorism is not the sole preserve of any religious group. Councillor Fallbrook (February, 2012) adds:

> *I don't find any relationship at all in fact quite the reverse. I think that's why Tony Blair sent the Qur'an around to all local councilors because at the time there was some scurrilous versions in the gutter press suggesting that terrorism was a feature of Islamic life but sad to say, terrorism is a feature of many people who may or may not have religious viewpoints.*[693]

Former British Chancellor of the Exchequer Norman Lamont said that terrorism and Prophet Muhammad(ﷺ)'s teachings are unrelated and he observes how the subject of *Jihad* has been hijacked and given wrong connotations:

> *I don't think there is a link and I think the word Jihad is misunderstood and misinterpreted. Jihad could mean two things. It could mean a war in defence of Islam when Islam is under threat and secondly, Jihad can be an internal thing about conquering oneself and struggling to be a better person.*[694]

It is Simplicity, Not the Sword

Mohandas Karamchand Gandhi was favourably disposed to Prophet Muhammad(ﷺ)'s contributions to humanity and made genuine efforts to debunk the myth that Prophet (ﷺ) spread Islam at the point of the sword. It was his noble personal characteristics that had won him such praise and support from Muslims and non-Muslims alike. Prophet Muhammad (ﷺ) had an unwavering conviction in God and his mission and was not distracted from fulfilling its aims. The Qur'an was the guidance he followed that proscribed violence and enjoined that coercion be not resorted to in matters of religion. Therefore, the idea that Prophet Muhammad (ﷺ) compelled others to embrace Islam and resorted to violence to achieve this end is not true at all. In Gandhi's words:

> *I wanted to know the best of one who holds today's undisputed sway over the hearts of millions of mankind. I became more than convinced that it was not the sword that won a place for Islam in those days in the scheme of life. It was the rigid simplicity, the utter self-effacement of the Prophet, the scrupulous regard for his pledges, his intense devotion to this friends and followers, his intrepidity, his fearlessness, his absolute trust in God and in his own mission. These and not the sword carried everything before them and surmounted every obstacle. When I closed the 2nd volume (of the Prophet's biography), I was sorry there was not more for me to read of the great life.*[695]

Gandhi argued that it was not the sword or violence or terrorism by which Islam conquered parts of the world. Rather, it was the Prophet's humbleness, simplicity, caring for people and pledges that he maintained, his trust in God and conviction in his mission which won a position for Islam:

> *I passed from the Companions to the Prophet himself. ... I became more than ever convinced that it was not the sword that won a place for Islam in those days in the scheme of life. It was the rigid simplicity, the utter self-effacement of the Prophet, the scrupulous*

regard for pledges, his intense devotion to his friends and followers, his intrepidity, his fearlessness, his absolute trust in God and in his own mission. These and not the sword carried everything before them and surmounted every obstacle. [696]

Prophet Muhammad(ﷺ)'s teachings on ethics and life were enough to gain the loyalties of people as opposed to the use of force. Edward Gibbon says:

The greatest success of Mohammad's life was effected by sheer moral force without the stroke of a sword.[697]

A very popular assumption among Christian writers is that the Muslims applied force to convert people to Islam. But like many authors, philosophers, leaders and writers, Dr Laurence E. Browne, who was the chief ophthalmologist in the US Airforce, feels differently:

Incidentally these well-established facts dispose of the idea so widely fostered in Christian writings that the Muslims, wherever they went, forced people to accept Islam at the point of the sword.[698]

Laurence E Browne further claims:

Under his influence people became united in one bond which they knew not, the bond of true monotheism.[699]

Uri Avnery, Jewish journalist and peace activist, said in response to Pope Benedict's attack on Prophet Muhammad (ﷺ) that, historically, Muslim communities safeguarded the rights and freedom of Jews, although it is assumed in many quarters that non-Muslims did not fare well under Muslim rule. The contrast with the Jewish treatment and subordination by Christian authorities is truly striking. When the Pope came out in condemnation of Islam's aversion to reason and propensity for violence, many non-Muslims took exception to his comments, particularly in relation to the age-old bias that Prophet Muhammad (ﷺ) and the early Muslims were intent on violence and spread Islam yielding the sword. According to Uri Avnery, a German-born Israeli journalist:

Every honest Jew who knows the history of his people cannot but feel a deep sense of gratitude to Islam, which has protected the Jews for fifty generations, while the Christian world persecuted the Jews and tried many times 'by the sword' to get them to abandon their faith.
In his lecture at a German university, the 265th Pope described what he sees as a huge difference between Christianity and Islam: while Christianity is based on reason, Islam denies it. While Christians see the logic of God's actions, Muslims deny that there is any such logic in the actions of Allah.
As a Jewish atheist, I do not intend to enter the fray of this debate. It is much beyond my humble abilities to understand the logic of the Pope. But I cannot overlook one passage, which concerns me too, as an Israeli living near the fault-line of this "war of civilizations".
In order to prove the lack of reason in Islam, the Pope asserts that the prophet Muhammad ordered his followers to spread their religion by the sword. According to the Pope, that is unreasonable, because faith is born of the soul, not of the body. How can the sword influence the soul?[700]

The Editor of 'Sat Updesh', Lahore, Pakistan did not agree that Islam was spread at the point of the sword. He argued:

They say that Islam was spread by means of sword but we cannot agree with this view, because whatever is forcibly propagated is speedily lost. Had the propagation of Islam been through compulsion there would not have been any trace of it to-day. But no it is not so. On the other hand we see that Islam is progressing day by day. Why is it so? Because the Founder of Islam had spiritual power within him. He was all love for mankind, in him the sacred passions of love and mercy were at work all the time. His righteous thoughts guided him.[701]

As many commentators have rightly stated, Islam would not have become a global and popular religion if initially it had been propagated through force. Rather, it was Prophet Muhammad(ﷺ)'s personality which acquired converts. The very nature of Prophet Muhammad(ﷺ)'s message precludes the possibility of forcing others to embrace Islam and compromise the prophetic creed. According to Reverend Jennifer Potter, Minister, Wesley Chapel, London:

> *Islam means submitting to the teaching of the Prophet and Allah, so it's a contradiction in terms. If you force someone to do that, then they are not submitting but are being forced to do it.*[702]

Ram Dev, editor of Vedic Magazine during Arya Samaj in Lahore in 1915 admired Prophet Muhammad (ﷺ), noting how the Prophet controlled the Arabs living in Madinah and preached the religion of monotheism. He stressed that religion cannot be spread by force and that Islam was not spread by the sword. He claimed that Prophet Muhammad (ﷺ) did not need to use his sword; rather, it was spiritual force that helped the spread of Islam. [703]

The religion of Islam which was preached by Prophet Muhammad (ﷺ) does not have any elements of terrorism. Aumie, a prominent and senior personality and a follower of Jewish religion from North West London insists that terrorism is against the teachings of Islam:

> *I have found that in true Islamic thinking, terrorism is something which they object to and is not acceptable to Islam.*[704]

One of the prevailing characteristics of the Islamic faith and something which was evident through the behaviour and practice of Prophet Muhammad (ﷺ) is the abhorrence of violence. The misconception, however, that Islam is a violent religion and that Muslims are violent people persists. There are many non-Muslim thinkers who also share the same view that Islam was not spread by sword. According to Dr N.K. Singh:

> *It can be clearly seen that non-violence exists as a dominant element in Islam as an individual Dharma and as a comprehensive and perfect Dharma. Simply because Muslims are non-vegetarians and because Islam permits the USE of the Sword in times of need, Islam should not be misunderstood to be a religion of Himsa or violence.*

> *If anyone claims that Islam was spread with the sword, the only reply is to ask with Carlyle, how could Islam get the first few who wielded not the sword?*[705]

Author Anita Rai says that the history of Islam recorded the most important achievement of the Prophet(ﷺ), which was the victory of Makkah. The victory by the Muslims was extraordinary, without bloodshed and won primarily through magnanimity, forbearance and simplicity of manners that captured the hearts and souls of the Makkans amongst whom there had been many of Prophet(ﷺ)'s deadly and avowed enemies of the past. History records the strength of this show of mercy and simplicity.[706]

Prophet Muhammad (ﷺ) and terrorism have no link according to Father O'Brien, who attributes it to the misinterpretation of the Scripture, by some:

> *I don't. But even in our scripture, there are Christians who take part of our scripture and they use that to purse some aim which is fundamentally not Christian. I think certain passages in the Qur'an have been taken out ofcontext and associated it with other passages in the Qur'an. I would say it has been wrongly interpreted.*[707]

Ira Lapidus, Emeritus Professor of History, Islamic Social History at the University of California at Berkeley declares that as far as what motivated people to convert to Islam are concerned, the reasons and motivations are many. Many non-Muslims felt that by becoming Muslim, it would provide them with a more civilised way of life and a progressive future. Others meshed in with the new political systems which Muslims had brought with them.[708]

Violence is Not the Way of Islam

According to Reverend Rupert Hoare the alleged link between Prophet Muhammad(ﷺ)'s teachings and terrorist activities is rebuffed by many on the basis that other religious traditions feature verses and injunctions which on face value appear to be an incitement to arms against disbelieving communities, yet upon closer inspection, it emerges that terrorism is bred through a misinterpretation of such decrees. Terrorism is also said to be a method adopted to pursue agendas which do not have any religious credibility. In answer to the question whether Prophet Muhammad(ﷺ)'s teachings are connected to terrorism, the reverend replied:

> *No. I find a parallel in the New Testament which speaks quite a lot about struggle as if one were in an army. But this does not mean terrorism. It is a use of language which in Christian history has been misunderstood as if it was a direct use of force to gain one's way. I imagine the same thing has been true from time to time in Islam. To gain ones ends by terrorism, the use of violence, is not the way of Islam – it's not the way of peace.*[709]

A closer scrutiny of history will help dispel misconceptions regarding the alleged Muslim tendency towards nihilism and violence. Rather, according to M.N. Roy:

> *There is no end of testimonies to prove that even in the predominantly martial period of their history, the Saracens were far from being barbaric bands of fanatical marauders, spreading pillage and rapine, death and destruction in the name of religion. Then, the period of conquest was short, as compared to the long era of learning and culture that flourished subsequently under the patronage of the Khalifs as well as of the tributary and independent Empire.*[710]

Father Tom Quinn does not see in Prophet Muhammad(ﷺ)'s teachings any promotion of terrorism but remarks that every faith has members who lean towards extremism:

> *I wouldn't see it being encouraged. Amongst extremists in any group, whether its Christianity or Islam, you will always have fundamentalists and terrorists.*[711]

According to Reverend Hoare, the Qur'anic provision forbidding forced conversion to Islam is recognised by many as a categorical prohibition of such an act. According to Reverend Rupert:

> *I'm sure there is a passage in the Qur'an that makes it clear that force is not to be used to convert people to Islam.*[712]

The Reverend Dr De Lacy Evans O'Leary, a British Orientalist who lectured at the University of Bristol and wrote a number of books on the early history of Arabs and Copts, said that the notion that some Muslims forced Islam on others at the point of the sword, thus helping the faith to expand, is a blatant distortion which has persisted throughout history:

> *History makes it clear, however, that the legend of fanatical Muslims sweeping through the world and forcing Islam at the point of the sword upon conquered races is one of the most fantastically absurd myths that historians have ever repeated.*[713]

One of Islam's principles regarding warfare is that the deliberate targeting of non-combatants is prohibited. Force can only be used to resist those who commit violence. Dr N.K. Singh says:

> *Islam does not permit Muslim to take up sword against those who are unarmed. It only permits them to fight against aggressions. It is obvious from the Qur'anic verse:*
> *"Fight in the way of Allah those who fight you but be not aggressive. Surely, Allah loves not aggressors".*[714]

Prophet Muhammad's main objective was to purge Arabia of its polytheism and establish the supremacy of monotheism. This, however, did not entail the use of violence to achieve what he set out to. According to Henry Stubbe:

> *I do not find that Mahomet proceeded any further in Arabia the desert then to exterminate Idolatry, but not to force men to the profession of Islamism. He himself gave Letters of security and protection to the Jews and Christians in Arabia, and never used any Violence to them upon the Account of religion.*[715]

Mike Stygal is careful not to associate Prophet Muhammad (ﷺ) with the forcible conversion of others to Islam. Like others, he is aware that personal interpretations can easily distort genuine teachings and insists that Prophet Muhammad (ﷺ) never promoted the use of arms to win converts:

> *One of the problems of religion is that they are manipulated by people and there may have been a point in Islamic history where some Muslims did use the sword for conversions. From what I understand of Muhammad, that was never part of his message.*[716]

Professor Arnold did not believe that Islam was preached by violence. According to him, the religion reached different parts of the world very peacefully:

> *Moreover it is not in the cruelties of the persecutor or the fury of the fanatic that we should look for the evidences of the missionary spirit of Islam, any more than in the exploits of that mythical personage, the Muslim warrior with sword in one hand and Qur'an in the other, - but in the quiet, unobtrusive labours of the preacher and the trader who have carried their faith into every quarter of the globe. Such peaceful methods of preaching and persuasion were not adopted, as some would have us believe, only when political circumstances made force and violence impossible or impolitic, but were most strictly enjoined in numerous passages of the Qur'an.*[717]

Muslims follow the guidance of the Prophet Muhammad (ﷺ) in all aspects of life, including how to deal with friends and enemies and have never provoked violence. The only time Islam permits its followers to use force is to protect the community from aggression. Professor John Esposito observes:

> *Islam, like all world religions, neither supports nor requires illegitimate violence. The Qur'an does not advocate or condone terrorism. The God of the Qur'an is consistently portrayed as a God of mercy and compassion as well as a just judge. Every chapter of the Qur'an begins with the reference to God's mercy and compassion; throughout the Qur'an in many contexts, Muslims are reminded to be merciful and just. Indeed, whenever a pious Muslim begins an activity such as meal, writing a letter, or driving a car, he or she says, 'Bismillahir Rahmanir Rahim' (in the name of God the merciful and compassionate). However, Islam does permit, indeed at times requires, Muslims to defend themselves and their families, religion, and community from aggression.*[718]

Dr N.K. Singh states that forcing others to become Muslim is prohibited and is well known in Islam. When a land comes under the legal authority of Islam, non-Muslim citizens of that region have the freedom and right to remain as non-Muslims and are granted the full rights of citizenship:

> *The Islamic doctrine of tolerance prohibited force as an instrument of conversion. The doctrine held that once a territory became part of 'the land of Islam' (dar ul Islam) those inhabitants who were not willing to embrace Islam, though willing to give up fighting (open as well as concealed) were entitled to full protection of life and property and to freedom of belief and of practice of their religion, and the carrying on of their normal means of livelihood, provided they paid 'jizya', a special discriminatory tax on an annual per capita basis. Women, children, the aged and the infirm were exempted.*[719]

Former British Home Secretary David Blunkett dispels any link between terrorism and Prophet Muhammad (ﷺ) and welcomes Muslim scholars to denounce those who advocate violence:

> *His teachings are against terrorism and the taking of innocent life. That's why I think it's important that Islamic scholars have this debate publicly and are able to thrash out these issues so they can put a very clear message and strike down verbally those who try and root their terrorist action within the faith. There is nothing I read in the teachings of Muhammad that actually gave and signal to succour to any justification for terrorism.*[720]

Islam's original meaning and intention for mankind has unfortunately been clouded by a fringe minority who have manipulated the pure teachings to justify terrorist acts. Certain teachings of Prophet Muhammad (ﷺ) have been grossly misinterpreted and only reinforce the prejudices which are widely circulating about the Islamic faith and the character of Prophet Muhammad (ﷺ) himself. The West's historical encounter with Islam and the Muslims has also contributed to this false perception. Professor John Eade says:

> *As many Muslim representatives have pointed out, there is no link. As far as I can understand, Islam in its origins is a religion of peace. The word Jihad has been interpreted by many people as about violence, force against other people but as we know, it's a struggle for wisdom, a struggle for learning, struggle for faith. Those who wish to interpret it in terms of violence and distort the ritual meaning of jihad…it's difficult because in the Western world, because of the crusades, jihad has become associated with violence so there has to be quite a lot of work to say that it is not.*[721]

There is no terrorism in Islam as claimed by many scholars. However, the Prophets were allowed to use arms for their defence. George Sale observed that great persons in the history including Moses, Cyrus, Theseus and the like used arms to protect themselves and their communities from harm. Similarly, Prophet Muhammad (ﷺ) was also required to use arms in self-defence. Sale explains:

> *[A]ll the armed prophets have succeeded, and the unarmed ones have failed. Moses, Cyrus, Theseus, and Romulus would not have been able to establish the observance of their institutions for any length of time had they not been armed. The first passage of the Koran which gave Mohammed the permission of defending himself by arms, is said to have been that in the twenty-second chapter; after which a great number to the same purpose were revealed.*[722]

H.A.R. Gibb stated that more surprising aspect of Islam is not only its rapid expansion but its character. The Arabs, the followers of Prophet Muhammad (ﷺ), adopted the law and culture of the land whichever they conquered and there were no forced conversions. By its strong character Islam entered the far-flung areas and commanded respect far and wide.[723]

Arms Only for Self-Defence

John Esposito notes that the Qur'an provides detailed guidelines and regulations regarding the conduct of war: who is to fight and who is to be exempted, when hostilities must cease, and how prisoners should be treated … permission to fight the enemy is balanced by a strong mandate for making peace: if your enemy inclines towards peace, then you too, should seek peace and put your trust in God (The Qur'an 8:61) It is forbidden in Islam to kill non-combatants as well as women and children and monks and rabbis, who are given immunity unless they took part in the fighting.[724]

Professor Laura Vaglieri wrote in the introduction of her book *An Interpretation of Islam* that Islam has given the guidelines for how human beings ought to live their lives. Islam allows using arms only to defend oneself and forbids violence.

> *We thus observe that not only Islam lays down correct principles for the beneficent regulation of all aspects of human relations and conduct but that the Prophet of Islam was, through the Divine Mercy, also vouchsafed the opportunity to illustrate in his own life*

> *their successful application. Islam permits the taking up of arms only in defence and expressly forbids aggression. The Qur'an designates war as a conflagration which must be put out as speedily as possible, as often as it breaks out. Islam condemns and forbids all brutal and savage practices and customs of war and has instituted a set of rules designed to render even war humane.*[725]

Sangthong Phesrisai, Dhamacaro, a Buddhist monk from Wimbledon Buddhist Temple, London says, that much of what Prophet Muhammad (ﷺ) said and did has unfortunately been misrepresented and perversely interpreted. This may be due to personal agenda of people in high positions:

> *I think no... maybe some people have taken his teaching on the wrong side or in the wrong way... this is my understanding...because what he taught people you know ... love your neighbour, live together in peace and harmony, but at the present time people might take the teaching in the wrong way... maybe they have some power and when they have power they just use the power in the wrong way. They misunderstand the teaching and take it the wrong way. This is what I understand.*[726]

Prophet Muhammad(ﷺ)'s sanctioning of force must be understood in its context. It was never intended as an end in itself and he always opted for a peaceful solution. A study of his life and teachings would reveal that he condemned actions of gratuitous violence. According to British MP Frank Dobson:

> *Well I think that there are aspects of his teachings which suggest that you are entitled to resort to force, if there is no other way of being dealt with justly but there are constraints the other way in that-certainly with things like suicide bombings-there is, I'm fairly clear, there is no justification in the works of the Prophet for suicide, quite the reverse, whatever the benefits people may think may flow to them after they are no longer mortal beings on planet earth.*[727]

According to Leo Tolstoy, the Prophet(ﷺ)'s capacity to affect human change for the benefit of the community granted him the status of a reformer, who had brought about an operative change in the social values obtaining during his time, in an ordered manner. His instruction to his followers and humanity at large to cease warfare and strife and encouragement of upward mobility and development was unique to him. Tolstoy observes: "He forbade acts of bloodshed or human sacrifice. He opened up for his nation the way to progress and civilization. That was a great feat which nobody - no matter how powerful he may be – is able to achieve".[728]

Prophet Muhammad(ﷺ)'s teachings have been often manipulated to suit the twisted ends of some individuals and groups, who use it to justify terrorist actions. Reverend John Cowie of the English Reformed Church, Amsterdamsays:

> *I think some people use the prophet's teachings to support terrorism. Muslim authorities I read say that this is a wrong use of what the prophet wrote and I'm quite willing to accept that. Some people will use any means to support what they want even if they are illegitimate. I hope that it's an inappropriate use of what the Prophet wrote.*[729]

According to a Sikh journalist, Prophet Muhammad (ﷺ) used force only as a last resort. When all other options had been exhausted and his enemies failed to incline towards peaceful methods, he had no option. Here is what this objective Sikh has to say on the subject:

> *In the beginning the Prophet's enemies made life difficult for him and his followers. So the Prophet asked his followers to leave their homes and migrate to Madinah. He preferred migration to fighting his own people, but when oppression went beyond the pale of tolerance he took up his sword in self- defence. Those who believe religion can be spread by force are fools who neither know the ways of religion nor the ways of the world. They are proud of this belief because they are a long, long way away from the Truth.*[730]

Amit Pal says that Islam has allowed war for the sake of self-defence but never instructs Muslims to initiate hostilities and be the aggressor. There are many examples when Prophet Muhammad ( ) took arms only for self defence.[731]

Wrong Presentation of Islam

The widespread conflict which today is often given a religious twist is caused by misinterpreting the teachings of Islam. Rev Jennifer Potter says:

> *Muslims can do what Christians do. They can go to the Qur'an and select the passages that support their point of view if they could find them. Any scripture can be applied selectively.*[732]

Niknam Mehri notes that, as with any other religion and Scripture, there are always going to be verses and legal injunctions which at face value appear to be sanctioning harsh and threatening acts. This is owing to a fundamental misreading of the Scripture. Unfortunately, much of the Qur'an's content has been taken out of context and deployed as a pretext for terrorist actions. The misinterpretation is particularly the case with the Islamic concept of Jihad which has been abused by some Muslims factions to such an extent to mean the legal permissibility of slaying non-Muslims in general. It is a travesty to know that the original usage of these terms and concepts were as a response to social and political factors during the Prophet(ﷺ)'s time but this is not factored in the reasoning and interpretations by many Muslims today, many of whom are not qualified to issue religious verdicts and answers to pressing questions. As a result, the misinterpretation of passages in the Qur'an has led many to incorrectly assume that Prophet Muhammad(ﷺ)'s teachings endorse terrorism whereas in reality, nothing could be further from the truth:

> *There are some verses in the Qur'an which are difficult but that is*

not just in Islam. There are difficult verses also in Christianity and in Judaism. There are always statements which are difficult to interpret. It seems to me that what has happened in the 20th century is that the interpretations of certain verses of the Qur'an have been promoted as means of physical fighting only and by extension, violence and terrorism. This to my understanding is a misunderstanding of the original interpretation of the verses. 'You shall not murder' is one of the Ten Commandments in the Tora (Hebrew Bible) and there is no religion as far as I am aware that says go and murder... When one is using those interpretations for today, one should put them in their historical context. Why were they interpreted in this way? Who was saying this interpretation? What was the political situation at the time? What was the sociological situation? Who was the leader of the Muslims at the time? Was he a just and true leader? ... What I am saying is that in my understanding those who promote and encourage and commit acts of terrorism today are in error and are not truly representing the best of Islam.[733]

Islam had a revitalising effect in the regions it penetrated. It gave birth to culturally rich societies, with Spain being one of the most prominent examples of Islam's civilising effect. Dr John Clark Archer, Professor of Comparative Religion at Yale University, wrote in an article entitled 'Our Debt to the Muslim World':

Islam was more than military invasion, it was a cultural invasion. Even as Islamic art came into being in the East amidst mutually hostile Saracenic and Hellenistic cultures, so also in the West amidst hostilities, through the instrumentality of the enemies of Christendom, came new cultural forms of art, architecture, science, literature and philosophy. By the tenth century, the whole basis of life throughout Spain was profoundly influenced by Islam, and with the capture of Toledo in 1085, by the Christian forces, the path was effectively opened for the spread of that influence to the rest of Europe.[734]

Many philosophers, historians and thinkers including Leo Tolstoy have affirmed that an inaccurate portrait of Prophet Muhammad (ﷺ) has been created. Aumie shares the same view:

Yes I agree. … Many in the West think Islam is a religion of terror which is wrong.[735]

The idea that the sword was to account for the expansion and progress of Arabian civilisation is one that many Orientalists have put forward. A simple way of reflecting on this absurd explanation is that violence can never touch the hearts and the inner conscience of man. It would have taken something more persuasive, more gripping than the mere resort to violence for a faith to claim huge number of followers outside its borders, with such quick succession. John William Draper remarks:

It is altogether a misconception that the Arabian progress was due to the sword alone. The sword may change an acknowledged national creed, but it cannot affect the consciences of men. Profound though its argument is, something far more profound was demanded before Mohammedanism pervaded the domestic life of Asia and Africa, before Arabic became the language of so many different nations.[736]

Father Green dismisses any link between Prophet Muhammad (ﷺ) and terrorist activities and comments that the Qur'anic injunctions can be manipulated just as the Bible can also be. Responsibility lies, according to Father Green, with those in leadership positions:

In the sense that Muhammad is an active proponent of terrorism, I see no link. However, it is the case that it is possible to interpret verses of the Qur'an in particular ways, in the same way the verses from the old and new testaments can be interpreted. I think there are a few who are consciously Islamophobic but I think on a broader scale, the real failure is for Western leadership to understand the role of faith.[737]

Lord Kinnock observes that the issue of terrorism is a highly complex and multi-layered phenomenon, and needs to be explored in the wider geopolitical and socio-economic context, which may fuel and exacerbate tensions. It is these tensions and not the teachings of Prophet Muhammad (ﷺ) which result in unrest or terrorist activities.

> *No link. It's just used as an excuse. Those who act violently need some preconditions. There needs to be a sense of grievance – the grievance can be an outrage at offence against a religious belief, or poverty. There needs to be an environment of resentment for terrorism to occur. They have to feel aggrieved. When this component is there, the next task for fundamentalists is to persuade people to find a way out of their condition by committing atrocities.*[738]

The diversity of Muslims precludes any possibility of anyone sanctioning violence in the name of Islam and claiming such an interpretation to be the most authoritative and closest to the truth. Stephen Shashoua, Director, Three Faiths Foundation, Camden, London, points out:

> *Links are made by terrorists to his teachings, but the jury is still out because the Ummah is such a spectrum of differences, interpretations are as different as people are. There are differences in understanding of what people have said. I think a wrong portrait of Muhammad has been created but who do you blame?*[739]

Often, Prophet Muhammad(ﷺ)'s teachings are implicated in terrorism and the various terrorist activities committed in the name of Islam. The Islamic concept of Jihad, translated as 'Holy War', is associated with a violent strand in the Islamic faith. However, there are misconceptions about this concept, which often lead misinformed people to link Prophet Muhammad(ﷺ)'s teachings with violence and terrorism. According to a teacher from a Church of England School in North London:

From my understanding, there are two forms of Jihad and jihad is struggle. And the greatest of those is your spiritual struggle to do what is right and follow Allah. The second is only in defence and defence of the religion. None of those promote violence in any way. My understanding of Islam is that it does not promote violence, therefore terrorism will not be acceptable.[740]

The alleged link between Prophet Muhammad(ﷺ)'s teachings and terrorism is a distortion of the reality. Such a link can and has been made by the followers of various religions, who manipulate scriptural passages to suit their own ends. Reverend Dr Harriet Harris, the Chaplain and honorary Fellow at the school of divinity at Edinburgh University and former Chaplain and tutor at Oxford University and lecturer of theology at Sussex University says:

I don't see a direct link. I can see how people will make that direct leap, as they do in Christianity too, making a leap from scriptures and sayings to endorsing certain violent acts which would seem to be a long way from the genuine teaching. People can use scriptures to make any point they want to.[741]

The human interpretation of religion can unfortunately lead to indiscretions which religion in its original state had never licensed. There has been a phenomenon whereby Prophet Muhammad's words and practices have been skewed to suit the agenda of a few, but that in no way implies that Prophet Muhammad (ﷺ) preached terrorism. Danny Richmond, Faith Act Manager, Tony Blair Faith Foundation, says:

I think a challenge for any faith tradition is to put teachings out into the world and how people can use those. Religion, like anything, can be a force for good and for bad, much like the internet can be a force for good or bad. So, I know that there are many who would connect the Prophet's teachings and use and manipulate them to give the basis for a violent non-pluralistic view of the world.[742]

It is unfortunate that historians have opted not to study and document the positive aspects of Prophet Muhammad(ﷺ)'s teachings and how they contributed to the good of humanity. Instead, they focus on those parts of his teachings which can be spinned to look controversial and tarnish his reputation. In the words of Pandit Gyanandra Dev Sharma Shastri:

> *They [Muhammad's critics] see fire instead of light, ugliness instead of good. They distort and present every good quality as a great vice. It reflects their own depravity…The critics are blind. They cannot see that the only 'sword' Muhammad wielded was the sword of mercy, compassion, friendship and forgiveness – the sword that conquers enemies and purifies their hearts. His sword was sharper than the sword of steel. But the biased critics of Islam are prejudicial and partisan; they are narrow minded and their eyes are covered by a veil of ignorance. They see fire instead of light, ugliness instead of beauty and evil instead of good. They distort and present every good quality as a great vice. It reflects their own depravity.*[743]

While Prophet Muhammad (ﷺ) did exert force on some occasions, it was warranted, considering that there were many tribes and groups in his society who were hell-bent on violence and plunder. Frank Dobson says:

> *I don't know about that. He certainly could be warlike and that's at variance with what I think of as being at the heart of Islam but again he was living in a period where people were as likely to be bloody and cruel towards him as he was towards them. It was that sort of society.*[744]

There are many parts of Prophet Muhammad(ﷺ)'s biography which suggest that he did not condone or participate in forced conversions. Again, it all comes down to interpretations. Dobson continues:

> *Well I'm not sure that there is evidence that he tried to force people on pain of death to become a Muslim because certainly other parts of his writing clearly are tolerant of other people's religions. I am*

sure a lot of other people are well capable of misinterpreting what he said and did attempt to and in some cases succeeded in forcing people to change their religious beliefs.[745]

The idea that the Arabs flourished because of the fanatic zeal of early Muslims is false. Ultimately, force cannot win the hearts and minds of people. M.N. Roy has observed:

It is altogether a misconception that the Arabian progress was due to the sword alone. The sword may change an acknowledged national creed, but it cannot affect the consciences of men. Profound though its argument is, something far more profound was demanded before Mohammedanism pervading the domestic life of Asia and Africa... The explanation of this political phenomenon is to be found in the social condition of the conquered countries. The influences of religion in them had long ago ceased; it had become supplanted by theology... How was it possible that unlettered men, who with difficulty can be made to apprehend obvious things, should understand such mysteries?[746]

Prophet Muhammad(ﷺ)'s social and political circumstances sometimes compelled him to use force, but it was only as a last resort. But force was never used to win converts. Pandit Lalit Kumar Sharma, Hindu Temple, East London, argues:

No, it is not true. It was a requirement at that time and this happened according to the demands of the time. For example, in Hinduism, there are many groups – people came in different time according the necessity of that time. So it is not true that the people were converted at sword point.[747]

Tolstoy noted that despite the hardship and trials which the Prophet (ﷺ) suffered he continued with his efforts to disseminate Islamic teachings:

[H]e endured in his first years of inviting people to Islam

tremendous tyranny and persecution from the pagans and others, just like every Prophet before him. He invited people to the truth, without these massive adversities undermining him and his cause, but instead strengthened his determination to carry on with his propagation.[748]

Another aspect of the Prophet(ﷺ)'s mission which Tolstoy cites is his celebration of religious pluralism and the principle of religious freedom, as he never compelled people from other faiths to embrace Islam:

He also said that the Jews and Christians must not be coerced to leave their religions, but he said that they should fulfill the commandments of their prophets.[749]

Father Thomas O'Brien agrees that Prophet Muhammad (ﷺ) never compelled anyone to embrace Islam:

From what I know, he never used coercion. With all religions, this is a subsequent consequence.[750]

It is unfair to claim that Islam expanded due to the violent actions of its followers. This ignores the fact that many were attracted to Islam out of their own will and saw it as a way of emancipating themselves from oppressive social and political conditions. Wars were fought by Prophet Muhammad(ﷺ)'s companions and rarely were there forced conversions, but this cannot be attributed to Prophet Muhammad(ﷺ)'s teachings or doings, as many throughout history have distorted peaceful messages. According to Mehri Niknam:

I do not agree that Islam spread by the sword only. Islam did spread in many ways by invitation and by people seeing the religion of Islam as a means of freedom because of the concepts of equality that it had in it. However, the Muslims under the leadership of Ali did fight and later under the leadership of Umar who was a great general of the army. Most of the Islamic expansion took place under the leadership of the second Caliph Umar... At the time of the prophet himself, as far as I am aware, we don't have historical evidence that people were converted forcefully. What happened was that the condition for the non-Muslims became so difficult that it if they would convert, they would be in a much better position socially than they would be as non-Muslims. However, many people became Muslims willingly and not because they were forced. Later on, there were forced conversions, as late as 19th-century in Iran.[751]

Prophet Muhammad(ﷺ)'s teachings reflected a healthy respect towards Jesus and Christians. Everything rests upon the interpretation of Qur'anic injunctions. Ifleniency is preferred, then interpretations which pave the way to freedom of religion can be fostered. Otherwise, there will be tight religious control on a person's freedom to choose their faith. Reverend Cowie of the English Reformed Church, Amsterdam, says:

My understanding of the Qur'an and what the Prophet taught is that Muslims were to respect Christians. I think the problem is when people decide they would rather be Christians than Muslims, then there are harsh passages in the Qur'an that lead to persecution of people who become Christians. If they're interpreted harshly – that may not have been the prophet's fault – but I think there are problems there.[752]

The RE teacher Bhavin Taylor is not of the view that Prophet Muhammad (ﷺ) coerced others to accept the message of Islam. He says:

No I don't think he did. I think any teaching that is shared like a story, if people like it, they would follow it. So it wasn't forced but it was out there for people to follow.[753]

David Blunkett is quick to disassociate the forceful conversions by later Muslims from Prophet Muhammad(ﷺ)'s teachings. He says:

I think some of his followers did; that's not the same thing as Muhammad forcing others.[754]

The oft-cited sword thesis as an explanation for conversions to Islam, during and after Prophet Muhammad(ﷺ)'s lifetime, is not endorsed by the former Labour Party leader Neil Kinnock, who believes that Prophet Muhammad(ﷺ)'s proselytisation was without coercion. He says:

> *Muhammad didn't force anyone, just like Christ did not force anyone to be a Christian, but followers have done by force of savage oppression, certainly in the case of Christianity, Islam, etc., they became military and governing religions.*[755]

That Prophet Muhammad (ﷺ) co-existed with a Jewish tribe is sufficient evidence for Shashoua that he did not coerce anyone to embrace Islam:

> *He was close with one of the Jewish tribes, so by having that relationship, it means he is saying that you have your way and we have ours. So at least for them, I know there was not a forcing.*[756]

The idea that Prophet Muhammad (ﷺ) forced others to accept Islam is rejected by many scholars. The essence of faith and religion in general is that its acceptance must be voluntary and not compulsory. While many have interpreted Prophet Muhammad(ﷺ)'s expeditions in a way which substantiates the view that he forced others at the point of the sword to accept Islam, other interpretations may see his military battles as defensive acts to protect the Muslim community from harm, oppression and extinction. Historically, there is no evidence that Prophet Muhammad (ﷺ) forced others to embrace Islam. When asked whether Prophet Muhammad (ﷺ) forced others to become Muslims, a teacher from a Church of England School in North London replied:

> *I would say no. He didn't ever force someone to convert to Islam. The idea is that it's meant to be a choice of their own. I think sometimes it can be perceived that he did because of the battles that took place but I think if you spin that in one way, it was defence. The unfortunate thing is that it makes a big grey area when understanding why something which stems from peace and the understanding that we have to resort to violence. I think that's the*

> *only thing I would find difficult to match up in that situation. But there are no records of Muhammad ever forcing someone into following Islam.*[757]

George Bernard Shaw regarded Prophet Muhammad (ﷺ) as a shining light for mankind, who has been wrongly presented by fellow Christians. Bernard Shaw claimed:

> *The Christians and their missionaries have presented a horrible picture of Islam. Not only that: they also carried out an organized and planned propaganda against the personality of Prophet Mohammad and the religion he preached. I have very carefully studied Islam and the life of its Prophet. I have done so both as a student of history and as a critic. And I have come to the conclusion that Mohammad was indeed a great man and a deliverer and benefactor of mankind which was till then writhing under a most agonising pain.*[758]

CHAPTER SEVEN

Western Perceptions of Prophet Muhammad (ﷺ) and His Wrong Image

In the earlier chapters I have discussed the issue of falsely portraying Prophet Muhammad (ﷺ), Islam and the Qur'an. The chapter is divided in two parts.

Part One

Misunderstandings: The Islamic World and the West

HRH Prince Charles, a patron of the Oxford Centre of Islamic Studies, delivered a lecture on 'Islam and West' in 1993. Despite his claim not to have a deep knowledge on the subject, he felt it necessary to address the topic in order to promote a healthier understanding between Muslims and Westerners in general. In particular, he noted the pressing need to foster dialogue between the West and Islam due to the misconceptions which abound regarding both, and due to the fact that in today's interconnected world, a genuine appreciation and knowledge of others is paramount. Prince Charles said:

> *I believe wholeheartedly that the links between these two worlds matter more today than ever before, because the degree of misunderstanding between the Islamic and Western worlds remains dangerously high, and because the need for the two to live and work together in our increasingly interdependent world has never been greater.*[759]

Prince Charles further observed that although there has been a proliferation of technology, communication and interaction between the global communities, this has not done much to dispel the confusion which surrounds Islam and the West. Incorrect interpretations and perceptions about each other seem to be more common than before. It is unlikely that ignorance is the main cause for misconceptions about Islam in the West, as millions of Muslims live in the West, and there is hardly a shortage of Muslims in European countries like the UK, where mosques and Islamic centres are found throughout. However, an atmosphere of mistrust and suspicion continues and Muslims and non-Muslims are yet to build many more bridges to close the gaps:

> *The depressing fact is that, despite the advances in technology and mass communications of the second half of the twentieth century,*

despite mass travel, the intermingling of races, the ever-growing reduction – or so we believe – of the mysteries of our world, misunderstandings between Islam and the West continue. Indeed, they may be growing. As far as the West is concerned, this cannot be because of ignorance. There are one billion Muslims worldwide. Many millions of them live in countries of the Commonwealth. Ten million or more live in the West, and around one million in Britain. Our own Islamic community has been growing and flourishing for decades. There are nearly 500 mosques in Britain. Popular interest in Islamic culture in Britain is growing fast. Many of you will recall – and I think some of you took part in – the wonderful Festival of Islam which Her Majesty the Queen opened in 1976. Islam is all around us. And yet distrust, even fear, persist.[760]

Wrong Western Attitudes

Pandit Gyanandra Dev Sharma Shastri, a member of the staunch anti-Islam Arya Samaj community, thinks that there is a lot of misrepresentation regarding the history of Prophet Muhammad's life and his actions. Most of this malicious propaganda aims to discredit Prophet Muhammad (ﷺ), and claim that he was a Machiavellian despot. Some of the hackneyed, age-old prejudices about Prophet Muhammad (ﷺ) have unfortunately survived down the ages and continue to affect people's perceptions of him to this very day. This wilful distortion of Prophet Muhammad's life does no one any good and is a blatant piece of political propaganda which has only one thing in mind: to sow seeds of dissension among between Muslims and non-Muslims.

Biased critics of Islam and especially those who want to provoke Hindu–Muslim riots in the country say that Hazrat Muhammad after acquiring power in Madinah could not maintain his facade of mercy and kindness. There he used force and violence and became a murderous prophet to achieve his life-long aim of power, status and wealth. He fell short of his own ideal of patience, moderation and endurance. But this is the view of those observers who are prejudicial and partisan, who are narrow minded and whose eyes are covered by a veil of ignorance. They see fire instead of light, ugliness instead of beauty and evil instead of good. They distort and present every good quality as a great vice. It reflects their own depravity... The critics are blind. They cannot see that the only 'sword' Muhammad wielded was the sword of mercy, compassion, friendship and forgiveness—the sword that conquers enemies and purifies their hearts. His sword was sharper than the sword of steel.[761]

The West has fought many wars with the Muslims, leading them to think that the Muslims may occupy the West sooner or later. The British politician Tony Benn argues that this is a wrong idea. He says:

This is partly for historic reasons as we have had many wars with Muslims in the past and it's partly because we are insecure because our own economic situation is dangerous and therefore people are frightened – they are frightened that anyone may come in and threaten them, and they say Muslims can threaten us therefore we are going to protect ourselves. We have to rid ourselves of these ideas. Islam has a very important educational role, working with other faiths.[762]

John Glubb reminds us that the Muslims and the Christians had fought for centuries for political gains and not for religion or theological issues. The long-standing war between them in Europe gave rise to strong hatred and intense discrimination against Prophet Muhammad (ﷺ).[763]

However, Glubb pointed out that Christians continued to live in Muslim countries for many years without being ill-treated.[764]

Glubb noted another important fact: that the Arab historians started to write their informative and scholarly books on Prophet Muhammad (ﷺ) well over a century after his death from Baghdad, a much more developed region than 7th-century Arabia. That may have led some historians to overlook facts and events of the time, and even led them to condemn the

Arabs as robbers. These mistaken themes have been continued, unfortunately, over the centuries by a few Western historians.[765]

Glubb further noted that Prophet Muhammad (ﷺ) was known as an imposter in the West for many years. However, the scholars, authors and biographers have in the recent years tried to uncover the truth about Prophet Muhammad (ﷺ) and Islam.[766]

According to Reverend Rupert Hoare, a former Dean of Liverpool, UK Cathedral and Chair of the Council of Faiths in Liverpool, misconceptions abound about Prophet Muhammad (ﷺ) and his supposed militant tendencies. Such ignorance is self-inflicted, and not as a result of a genuine appraisal of Prophet Muhammad(ﷺ)'s life and teachings. According to Reverend Hoare:

> *Quite a lot of people will regard him as a leader of the Muslim people in a fight to gain territory. I think a lot of Western people do not have a good impression of his leadership and I think they are wrong. When I compare Muhammad with Jesus, I would say that the situation which Muhammad found himself in with his followers was different to the situation of Jesus. I think a lot of people don't think much about it at all. For those who do not know Muslims and don't have Muslim friends, there is an equation of Muslims with armed struggle. But I think the West has brought a lot of that upon itself.*[767]

Karen Armstrong says the West has formed an incorrect image of the Qur'an, Islam and the Prophet Muhammad (ﷺ). The accusation by Western Orientalists that the Qur'an endorses the mistreatment of women is incorrect. The truth is that the protection of women was at the heart of the Prophet (ﷺ), and he introduced legislation which ensured equal rights for women.[768]

In an interview in March 2012 Tory politician and academic Michael Meacher noted that a dilemma some religious followers face is the increasing politicisation of their religion, and the purity of religion sometimes gets tied up with the political agenda being pursued by those whose main interests do not lie in religion. This is a common trait when we observe politicians in the contemporary period, be they Muslim or Christian. Once again, the notion of power and war is inextricably tied with religion and sometimes this has the effect of emotionally swaying religious devotees. A study of Prophet Muhammad (ﷺ)'s life, however, establishes that he advanced his prophetic mission without resorting to deliberate acts of provocation and violence, unless it was essential for the survival of the community at large.[769]

Dr Henry Stubbe highlighted that the representation of Muslims in Middle Ages by Christendom was remorseless, to say the least. Christian legends from this period were unrelenting in their demonic depiction of Muslims and their much-revered Prophet (ﷺ). Dr Stubbe said that the influence which these portrayals exercised on European minds and literature was a lingering phenomenon. Muslims were referred to by a catalogue of pejoratives, such as: "Infidels, Miscreants, Paynims, Pagans, Heathens, heathen hounds, Enemies of God, Turks, Allophili, Hagerenes, Ishmaelites, Canes, Moabites, Aliens, Gentiles etc., and occasionally Goths and Vandals". The disparaging label which obtained popular currency was 'Saracens'. Contrary to the belief – promulgated by Muslim-hating Christians – that the term Saracens was adopted by Muslims who "claimed to be descended from Sarah, with the object of concealing their low birth", subsequent Orientalist scholarship on the etymology of the word 'Saracens' concluded it to be a derivative of the Arabic word 'Serq', meaning to 'steal'; hence the Saracens, according to Christian scholarship, were equated with thieves. The 'Turks' – another in the list of sneering descriptors for Muslims – were invariably identified with 'Magog', which in Christian and Muslim doctrine refers to one half of the promethean, Godless force, which will be unleashed to wreak havoc as a prelude to the final day of judgement. With the Arabs frequently equated with the other sacrilegious half, known as 'Gog', early Christian notions spared no Muslim in their quest to brandish the Islamic faith and its adherents as a bulwark against the forces of good.[770]

The falsehood propagated about Muslims became popular currency and ultimately led to a much skewed understanding of Prophet Muhammad (ﷺ). These perceptions were thoroughly ingrained in scholarly circles, which also demonised prominent Muslim intellectuals and thinkers. Dr Stubbe continues:

> *The myths surrounding Muslims went unabated and a consensus emerged from the Christian clerical class that Muslims harboured polytheistic tendencies, culminating in the veneration of Muhammad. These opinions were touted by historians who would note the Muslim adulation of Muhammad, reflected in the content of the hymns they would recite. To compound the Muslim incredulity, Christian notions of the Saracens attached to them the associations of incantation, with prominent sages such as Al-Kindy and Ibn Sina represented as the custodians of witchcraft and magic. Thus, the characterization of Muslims in medieval Christian reports is replete with fabricated and insubstantial generalizations, which upon further inspection, reveal the invidious abuse which many Christian scholars set about hurling at Muslims.*[771]

A teacher from a Church of England School, North London (who requested anonymity) observed that an effective way of countering false impressions about Prophet Muhammad (ﷺ) is to present people who harbour incorrect perceptions of him with historically supported and incontrovertible facts about Prophet Muhammad (ﷺ), which are abundantly available, and to try to make light of the gloomy but false image of him. The RE teacher said:

> *I would go and get the facts for them, present it to them and then say what can we find out from this.*[772]

The Muslims had left behind a very rich intellectual legacy which was absorbed by Europe for centuries. Jeremy Corbyn says:

> *If you think of the political history of Europe from the 9th century through to the establishment of Europe as an identifiable continent in the 16th to 18th – that sort of period, it was the period of the crusades in the 11th and 12th centuries which was unsuccessful' it was then the battles [took place] between what was seen as the expansion of Islam into Spain and north into what is now*

> *Czechoslovakia and Poland in the 15th century and then the expulsion of the Moors from Spain. They left behind them not only the buildings of Cordoba and Grenada but they also left behind them a whole narrative of law and civilisation which is quite interesting. That is still there in modern Spain.*[773]

The image of Prophet Muhammad (ﷺ) in the west worsened in the period of conflicts between Western powers and Muslims in Ottoman Empire, the expansion of Christianity in Spain and the rest of Europe. Corbyn notes:

> [The hostile attitude towards the Prophet] *was built in the battles with the Ottomans and the expansion of the Christian church in Spain and central Europe.*[774]

There was an element of medieval scholarship on Prophet Muhammad (ﷺ) that was predisposed to the prejudicial stereotyping of Islam and, in particular, the reputation of Prophet Muhammad (ﷺ). Many of these base generalisations were unfounded and became a hallmark of the 12th-century scholarship on Prophet Muhammad (ﷺ), and these misguided perceptions were inherited by many Western scholars in later centuries.[775]

Therefore, implanting an image of the Muslims as brutes in the consciousness of the masses served as a defence mechanism; as Watt notes, "In deadly fear Christendom had to bolster confidence by placing the enemy in the most unfavourable light".[776]

The studies on Prophet Muhammad (ﷺ) have historically tended to be biased, lacking impartiality. Most of them appear to have been conducted through a distinctly Western lens and adopting a Western attitude that is prejudiced towards the Prophet (ﷺ). Selective readings of Prophet Muhammad (ﷺ) and non-objective accounts were a standard feature of medieval standpoints on his personality and character. The influence which these perceptions exercised on the Western views on Prophet Muhammad (ﷺ) cannot be underestimated. Norman Daniel is of the view that the non-Western peoples are inferior to their Western counterparts and this has continued to be a theme in much of Western scholarship. There was a predisposition among Europeans to perceive the Orient in lesser terms in contrast to the Europeans' progress and civility.[777]

This theme of discrimination has been identified by a Sikh spokesman from a Sikh temple based in East London thus:

> *Prophet Muhammad's teachings were right, but now, in the present world, the politicians tell lies for their power and establish discrimination among us. This is not what Prophet Muhammad (ﷺ) taught in Islam.*[778]

The Right Reverend Geoffery Rowell, formerly Bishop of Gibraltar, said that one cannot approach the term West in a reductive sense. Many countries and cultures fit into this category, and opinions about Prophet Muhammad (ﷺ) differ across the board. Opinions abound, positive and negative, and we cannot dismiss the fact that the majority of negative stereotypes about Prophet Muhammad (ﷺ) persist because of the medieval polemics against him and the Islamic faith:

> *The West is a very large and rather vague concept. There are many different perceptions, some informed and others ill-informed. There is a little bit inherited from Christian things in the past, of Muhammad as an impostor and so on. But there are also people like myself who have stood in the places of the great mosques which are wonderful spiritual places and these are part of that tradition which came from Muhammad. The deep pattern of the life of regular prayer is something that is good. I think the West need to hold that against the distortions. Just as there were terrible inquisitions in the name of Christianity, there are also interpretations of Islam, some of which have contributed to terrorist actions.*[779]

On the issue of the incorrect image Rowell further feels that there is definitely an urgent need to refute those who have tarnished the image of Prophet Muhammad (ﷺ). Dr Rowell says:

I think this is true. We can only combat that with a presentation of what is the truth about Prophet Muhammad.[780].

Philosopher Leo Tolstoy drew attention to the fact that serious discrimination has taken place against Prophet Muhammad (ﷺ). According to him, many unfounded and unjustified claims had been made about the Prophet(ﷺ) which contributed to painting a tarnished image of him. In order to bring a correct picture of the Prophet to the Russians, Tolstoy learnt about him and wrote a book with the title *Selected Sayings of the Prophet* and encouraged them to find out the truth about the Prophet (ﷺ) by using their fullest potential. The revelation of the Qur'an through which God enjoined men to stick together and hold onto His guidance is stressed by Tolstoy in the following words:

Anyone who wants to verify the tolerance in Islam should only read the Qur'an carefully. Its verses are indicative of the high spirit of Islam, such as: [And hold fast, all together, by the rope which Allah (stretches out for you), and be not divided among your-selves; and remember with gratitude Allah's favor on you; for ye were enemies and He joined your hearts in love, so that by His Grace, ye became brethren; and ye were on the brink of the pit of Fire, and He saved you from it. Thus doth Allah make His Signs clear to you: That ye may be guided.[781]

Father Allen Green, Tower Hamlets Interfaith Forum, London believes that Prophet Muhammad(ﷺ)'s perceptions and teachings in the West have been deliberately distorted by those who seek to tarnish his reputation, and this explains the somewhat blinkered outlook many have of Prophet Muhammad (ﷺ):

The cheap and popular version that is represented in its worst, extreme forms, with groups such as the English Defence League, and a slightly more polite view that Muhammad was a conqueror who wanted to subjugate others and sought world domination. According to narrow views, Muhammad is seen in all sorts of very unfortunate ways, many of them simply manufactured by those who want to show that he was not a great person at all.[782]

As the followers of Islam and Christianity have not always seen eye to eye, the onus on both to bridge the divide and dispel any misconceptions is greater than ever before. In particular, Prophet Muhammad(ﷺ)'s personality and the authenticity of the Qur'an has been maligned to a great degree and these perceptions must be corrected for the benefit of all. Jane Smith notes:

Muslims face a formidable task in presenting Prophet Muhammad as not only the vehicle through which the words of God were communicated to humanity and recorded in what we know as the Qur'an, but as the very model for human piety. The history of Christian-Muslim relations has some very bleak aspects, among them the consistent Christian disparaging of the Prophet as a warmonger, a charlatan, and a libertine, and ridicule of the Qur'an as a sadly lacking and misguided attempt to duplicate Jewish and Christian scriptures. This legacy of misunderstanding remains deep in the psyche of the West, and the chore of disentangling it from the good intentions of Christian evangelism or from assumptions implicit in Western foreign policies is formidable.[783]

The fabrications which European Christians have propagated about Prophet Muhammad (ﷺ), Islam and the Muslims run deep and have led to much injustice throughout history. After all this undeserving malice and antagonism shown towards Islam by those hostile towards it the misconceptions, the untruth about it must have to be corrected to foster better relations between the Muslims and the Christians. Dr Henry Stubbe says:

Painful as is the inquiry into Christian misrepresentations, it has been necessary to enter upon it at length in order to know the true state of affairs and to understand the general demeanour of Europe towards us. It is beyond my present scope to examine the extent to which the malignant influence of these misrepresentations has gone against the true interests and spirit of Islam. Besides the original estrangement between Islam and Christianity, it has caused a number of deplorable events in history, such as the Crusades, the expulsion of the Moors from Spain, and last, but not least, the modern attempt to rob the Muslims of their faith, in order to lure them on to belief in the doctrines of Trinitarianism. Is it not time that we should show at least equal activity, instead of contemplating this hostile propaganda with indolent indifference and letting judgment go by default?[784]

It is generally agreed that Prophet Muhammad (ﷺ) has been misrepresented in the West. The historical reasons for this misrepresentation are many, given the spread of Muslim dominion over Christian territories and the crusades which ensued. The view of Islam and Muslims as the aggressor remains firmly lodged in the conscience of many Western Christians. Reverend John Cowie of the English Reformed Church, Amsterdam, said in an interview in February 2012:

I think cultural portraits have cast the Prophet in a different light. I think the problem is that in the Christian world, Islam came onto the stage as a warrior group that dominated previously Christian areas militarily and for several hundred years; that was the dominant impression of Islam. And the Christian crusades took up arms. Christians became associated in the Muslim world with military might as well, so you have these two opposing camps. We have to move away from the idea that we can impose our will militarily.[785]

According to Reverend Rupert Hoare, age-old clichés about Prophet Muhammad (ﷺ) are still believed, as evidenced by the general ignorance that persists about Prophet Muhammad(ﷺ)'s character and what he stood for. Christian-Muslim encounters factor prominently when trying to understand why misconceptions of Prophet Muhammad (ﷺ) are so mainstream.[786]

The inaccurate portrayal of Prophet Muhammad (ﷺ) owes a lot to the erroneous representations of him by Western writers. The authentic material based on Prophet Muhammad(ﷺ)'s life has on many occasions been rejected and those aspects of his life which can easily foster wrong interpretations have been considered instead. Alfred Von Kremer, an Austrian Orientalist, author of works on Islamic studies and the cultural history of Eastern countries said that European authors do not make constructive criticism of Prophet Muhammad(ﷺ)'s life and actions. Kremer blames them for concealing the original Arabic texts and information and depending on the Orientalist works of the present period. He says that the Western readers of Prophet Muhammad (ﷺ) tend to like more fantastic stories written by the recent authors.[787]

Sir William Muir, an Orientalist hostile to the Prophet Muhammad (ﷺ), was nevertheless also critical of the biographers who were omitting the truth and genuine facts about the Prophet(ﷺ) and instead recording imaginary stories about him.[788]

Sir Charles James Lyall, an English civil servant working in India during the period of the British Raj, and also an Arabic scholar, claimed that Muir's works on Prophet Muhammad (ﷺ) were a standard for that period; but he argued that it was still very much an anti-Islamic discourse.[789]

The prejudice against Prophet Muhammad (ﷺ) and his generally negative portrayal is a historical phenomenon, and not just a contemporary one. There was evidently an Orientalist bias against Islam and the Prophet(ﷺ) and this prejudice sadly still survives till today. It is also the case that the wounds of Muslims are self-inflicted, since many of them fail to live following Prophet Muhammad(ﷺ)'s teachings. Niknam Mehri says:

> *It also seems to me that the Muslims themselves must bear some responsibility by not presenting the best of the Prophet's teachings in their actions. In short, the responsibility is multi-layered.*[790]

According to Karen Armstrong, the idea that Islam has been distorted in the popular imagination is true, but is worsened by how some Muslims are antagonising Western communities. Islam was never a religion bent on violence and anarchy but unfortunately this is the understanding which many Europeans had cultivated in the minds of ignorant folk. Also, fundamentalism is not the preserve of Muslims, but many belief systems have fostered movements and followers who share fundamentalist traits. Colonialism also precluded the possibility of a genuine scrutiny into the Islamic faith, with the intention of omitting prejudice. All this has further divided faiths and turned religious communities against each other.[791]

According to Professor John Eade, the historical encounters and the recent cultural exchange and interaction between the West and the Muslim world go a long way to explaining why a certain image of Prophet Muhammad (ﷺ) persists in the Western mind. Orientalist scholarship has contributed to a large extent to providing a false view of Muslims, and this has engendered racial stereotypes that require urgent addressing.[792]

No single entity or movement can be blamed for distorting Prophet Muhammad(ﷺ)'s image. An analysis of history and socio-political factors will prove this to be the case. Professor Eade adds:

> *Well I think a variety of people [were responsible].... I think the colonial project had to be justified somehow...they tried to bring civilising projects to others and therefore to some extent, Christian missionaries etc...*[793]

Historical facts and exchanges between the Muslims and the Western world/Europe go a long way in explaining why an incorrect perception of Prophet Muhammad (ﷺ) characterises much of the Western discourse. This can only be dispelled and clarified through genuine attempts to foster good relations between religions and their followers. Otherwise, misinformation will become widespread and bigotry will reign. Father Alban McCoy of the Cambridge University Catholic Chaplaincy, says (May, 2012):

> *I think a part of the problem is ancient hostility between east and West. Even as late as the 18th century, the West in the form of the Austro-Hungarian empire, and Turkey, were at war...There is no substitute for face to face dialogue and familiarity. You can write as*

many books as you like, you can have as many community schemes as you like, but until people meet each other face to face on the grounds of their common humanity, then there will always be fear, ignorance and therefore prejudiced.[794]

Lord Norman Lamont remarks that one of the reasons for Islam's wrong presentation has been the increasing secularisation of life and society at the expense of religion. He says:

I think one of the reasons for the distortion of Islam and Muslims in Europe, is that Europe has become very secular and because religion has declined, people don't comprehend so easily how deeply and how strongly millions of people in the world feel about religion. America is obviously different. 9/11 and religion have played their part in forming attitudes.[795]

Amit Pal states that the Western historiography of Islam is filled with accounts of how Islam spread by the sword. If history was studied objectively, then it would become clear that violence did not feature as much as some historians insist:

The history of Islam has been caricatured as one of blood thirsty warfare and conversion by the sword. This has been a trope in the West since medieval times. However, reality was much more complicated, and violence has played a much lesser role in the formation and spread of Islam than is commonly imagined.[796]

Sir Lepel Henry Griffin was a British administrator, diplomat during the British Raj in India and a writer who commented on the paper, 'Pan-Islam', which was presented by Sir Ignatius Valentine Chirol, a journalist, prolific author, and historian and British diplomat. The paper looks into the spread of Islam and future of Europe. Having perceived the teachings of Prophet

Muhammad (ﷺ), Sir Griffin claimed in his discussion that, although Islamic movements were operating in different parts of the world, the Muslims posed no threat, and the British would be well advised to view the movement in non-threatening terms:

> *There is no doubt to-day a great revival of Islam in all parts of the world. But if this movement be looked upon with sympathy and generosity by the British Government and the English people, there will be in it no danger to the British Empire. Indeed, I think the tendency will be in the reverse direction.*[797]

Lack of Knowledge about Prophet Muhammad (ﷺ)

Danny Richmond, Faith Act Manager, Tony Blair Faith Foundation (February 2012) says that the misrepresentation of Prophet Muhammad (ﷺ) can only be deconstructed by the efforts and attempts of those who are committed to living in a world where understanding and tolerance are premier values. Only through such an enterprise can people rework and revise the tainted understanding about Prophet Muhammad (ﷺ).[798]

Gaining an understanding of different belief systems is a very good way of becoming more tolerant and less prejudiced about others. Since many are of the view that single interpretations of Islam are not the be all and end all, different strategies need be employed in order to exploit the plurality of understandings. Richmond adds:

> *We should all learn more about faith traditions. If you look at social cohesion on a global level, we have 1.3 billion Muslims today, so when a sixth of the world is Muslim, it's essential, both living in our communities but also at a global level that we understand the influences in each other's life. I also know there is an incredible amount of diversity within Islamic thought and various communities, particularly on how they viewed the life and teachings of the Prophet (ﷺ) and so it would be helpful to explore that as well.*[799]

The more informed and erudite in Western societies have been favourably disposed to Prophet Muhammad (ﷺ), considering him an influential personality. Unfortunately, this level of enlightenment is not the case with the rank-and-file, among whom misconceptions about Prophet Muhammad (ﷺ) thrive. The Reverend Stephen Williams, Senior Anglican Chaplain, University of London observes:

> *Thomas Carlyle wrote a book called "Heroes and hero worship" and the Prophet Muhammad is one of the historical people looked at in that. There was a time in 19th-century Britain where the study of Prophet Muhammad's life was one from which people derived a great deal of inspiration, as an ideal to be followed, emulated and appreciated, a historical figure who encapsulated heroic virtues. That comes from a tiny majority of people who are educated, read etc. The vast majority of people have no idea.*[800]

Bhavin Tailor emphasises how a minority of Muslims can affect positive perceptions about Prophet (ﷺ) owing to their misinterpretation of Islam and his teachings:

> *Some Muslims would argue in such an extreme way using Islam in a way which is not helpful to other people. That's all they may know. Likewise, other people who are not Muslim can see a perception of Islam that might be only very narrow. Since Islam is such a diverse religion, why should one small group be allowed to speak for everyone else?*[801]

Academic research and interest in Prophet Muhammad(ﷺ)'s life and teachings can certainly help dispel the commonplace misconceptions which abound about Prophet Muhammad (ﷺ) in the West. Such endeavours can help bring to light the relevance of Prophet Muhammad(ﷺ)'s teachings in our contemporary lives and can be instrumental in imparting to even Muslims, a critical and comprehensive viewpoint about Prophet Muhammad (ﷺ). According to Michael Meacher:

> *By producing on the basis of historical research which shows that our view of Muhammad is very wrong. You have to produce the actual evidence yourself to justify that view and you can do it.*

When you have produced the evidence about the nature of his life, that's the central part. Then the question will arise, does this have lessons for us today? And I'm absolutely convinced it does. Even Muslims need to have a deepening of their understanding. Sometimes there are Muslims who do not want to hear anything which might interfere with their perfect view of Muhammad. But the best way is to understand very deeply what happened and why.[802]

The reason why a distorted perception of Islam became commonplace is because of the lack of education about the Prophet (ﷺ)'s teachings and message. In many cases, teaching about Prophet Muhammad (ﷺ) in the West has been virtually non-existent. As a result, prejudices and perceptions are formed with no prior knowledge about Prophet Muhammad (ﷺ), thus hampering attempts to create a socially cohesive society. A teacher from a Church of England School, North London observes:

It's not that people have a completely wrong perception of Muhammad, I think ... they don't have a perception based on facts because they haven't learned about it. Most people who have a misconception about something, it's not because they've been taught wrong, it's because they haven't been taught at all. They form this view based on no knowledge. If we're going to live in a cohesive society with different religions and races, we actually have to understand each others religions' and races.[803]

Travesties of justice continue to occur in Muslim circles, primarily due to a gross misunderstanding of Prophet Muhammad's teachings. There are always wider contextual reasons as to why individuals arrive at erroneous and problematic conclusions which do nothing but generate concern for others. Prophet Muhammad(ﷺ)'s character and personality need be examined from various angles so that a sound appraisal of his teachings can be made. Mehri says:

Firstly... there are many misinterpretations and misunderstandings of the sayings and actions of the Prophet which need to be pointed out to the Muslims. Secondly, ... we are human beings and we are subject to all kinds of political circumstances, economic circumstances, social circumstances, educational circumstances. Respectfully, also allow me to say this again, you have to present a realistic profile of the Prophet for the non-Muslims. I acknowledge that from the Muslim perspective he is the example par excellence of a human being. I do not agree in any way that we should be disrespectful to him, but with respect, there were a few actions of the Prophet that need to be looked at from more than just the Muslim perspective. These have been a matter of non-Muslim scholarly debate for a long time, but I only know of a couple of Muslim scholars who are just beginning to look at them from a scholarly perspective. So it seems to me that instead of always glossing over these few incidents and always insisting that only the Muslim perspective which maintains that all was perfect should be accepted, it would actually help to clarify the situation and lead to a better understanding of those incidents. This would be very helpful because it would remove the negative exaggerations that are made against the Prophet, but it would also allow other scholarly perspectives to be heard. We need to be realistic and accept the good and the not so good and then we can move forward.[804]

Prophet Muhammad (ﷺ) or his teachings cannot be held to account for the violence in the world today. Rather, politicians, absence of learning and a subversion of religious teachings are prime reasons to explain the phenomena of fundamentalism, as a Sikh spokesman says:

I think there is lack of education and some people are fundamentalists who perceived his teaching wrongly...that's why there are so many confusions...if they would follow the right teachings of Prophet Muhammad (ﷺ), there would not be problems... some people take his name as excuse ... no religion teaches to kill people ... but they are doing on their own and they are using Islam or Muhammad as a cover... which has created a very bad image of Islam specially in the West – America and

Europe.... Politicians are behind all these works, these are politically driven.[805]

The social and political conflicts which involve some degree of Muslim involvement in the world today cannot be attributed to Prophet Muhammad(ﷺ)'s message, but rather to our failure to observe what he brought to mankind, as Pandit Lalit Kumar from East London Temple suggests:

The main cause behind this is money. For money we become ready to die even, we think that for the good cause of family it does not make difference even to face death. For a substantial amount of money we can die. Our family will have prosperous life. The think is that we are not following the teachings of Prophet Muhammad properly, that is why this is happening within the societies. Otherwise these conflicts could never take place.[806]

An appreciation of history is necessary, however, if our present condition is to render any meaning to our lives and this can be applied in the realm of scholarship on Prophet Muhammad (ﷺ). Sirah or the biography of Prophet Muhammad (ﷺ) is an important source when investigating his life and times, and the early biographical accounts of Prophet Muhammad (ﷺ) must engage the attention of Western scholars, so that his image may be rebuilt as it was portrayed incorrectly. Edward Hallett Carr, a British historian, journalist and international relations theorist also thought in similar vein. According to Carr, the past is 'as a key to understanding the present'.[807]

The idea that Prophet Muhammad (ﷺ) promoted polytheism is utter falsehood and has unfortunately helped contribute to a much distorted understanding of his teachings and legacy. According to Alfred Martin:

No authentic portrait of Mohammed has come down to us, chiefly because of that abhorrence of idolatry and image-worship which the prophet instilled into the hearts of his followers. All the portraits that have come down to us are outright fabrications, in the production of which imagination and prejudice have proven powerful creative agencies.[808]

According to Karen Armstrong, there is a mutual relationship between the West and Islam, although this reality has by and large not been acknowledged by the West. An unfortunate consequence of this is that a bigoted and intolerant trend has emerged among some Muslims, who incorrectly use Islam to justify their hatred of the West. Certain moments in our recent history have made this hostility even more apparent. If Muslims are to develop a more favourable and sympathetic understanding of the West, then the West has some responsibility to shed stereotypes of Islam and Muslims to make such a forthcoming relationship achievable. A very good starting point is a thorough examination in the West of the life of Prophet Muhammad (ﷺ).[809]

Due to globalisation and a host of other factors, there is no way of excluding religions such as Islam from one's consciousness. In fact, many feel obliged or at least have some sort of commitment to understand Islam from its authentic sources. Karen Armstrong says that although there are many demonstrations of religions currently on main doctrines, Islam still has the leading role worldwide.[810]

It was Islam's swift expansion into territories which most of the world would find inconceivable that played on the minds of many Europeans and non-Muslims, leading to a biased view of Prophet Muhammad (ﷺ), the Muslims and Islam. Armstrong continues that although humanity has made significant strides to learn from other spiritualties, this mutual engagement appears to be ambivalent in the case of Islam. Armstrong takes note of the age-old antagonism which the West has harboured against Muslims and states the cause of this hatred to be Islam's territorial expansion and swallowing of vast Christian territories, from the Middle East to North Africa (Armstrong, 11). Muslims' militant tendencies, the ease with which they vanquished other nations politically and militarily, the encounters with the Christian crusades and their encroachments against Europeans, evidenced by the strength of the Ottomans, helped create a collective trauma in the European minds and stance towards Islam.[811]

Islam became associated with war and aggressive conquest; this hindered the possibility, by the West, of an accurate study and portrayal of Muslims and their religion. According to Armstrong, the consequences of associating Islam with impending military conquest and subduing of Christian populations made any rational and impartial assessment of Islam a remote possibility. This is reflected in the biased Western scholarship on Islam and the portrait of Prophet Muhammad (ﷺ) as an impostor, bent on battering the non-Muslim world into submission.[812]

Islam is definitely a potent force today and its infusion with political thinking makes this the case. British politician Tony Benn noted:

> *Islam is a powerful and rapidly growing religion and it gives its followers guidance and strength. It is associated with some political movements, so I think it has to be treated as a major force in the world.*[813]

It is unfortunate that Islam has been stigmatised and maligned in many circles, simply to suit the agenda of some. In this regard, Benn states:

> *People who are not Muslims don't understand much about it. Political leaders engaged in war blame Islam for this in order to justify what they're doing and they try to build up support for themselves by identifying Islam as a bad thing and this is very dangerous and undesirable*[814].

Some of the teachings of Islam have been manipulated and used as a pretext by some to further their ambitions against Muslim countries and suspected individuals. Benn adds:

> *Perception of Jihad in Britain is that it is a violent movement which is a threat to our security, presenting Islam as an enemy and Jihad as an instrument of that enemy…I don't know but I will be very surprised. I think the political forces in Britain try to establish their strength by saying we will defend Britain from all these other*

ideas, including the ideas of Islam and Jihad.[815]

The problem which some Muslim communities or groups may be causing in Europe is not an accurate reflection of Prophet Muhammad(ﷺ)'s teachings. Prophet Muhammad (ﷺ) would never have wanted to encourgae hostilities between his people and the host community, so those Muslims involved in such a practice are betraying the Prophetic examples. Shiv Charan Singh Gill says:

> *Now, Muslims themselves, they created such a situation in their countries and in the West, in France, here, or Holland, they are antagonising the host community. It is not Muhammad, it is the Muslim population, they say they are Muslims, in fact they do not follow the Islamic principles. If I follow the commandments in the Qur'an, I will call myself Muslim, but if I don't follow the commandments in the Qur'an, do you think I am Muslim? No. So that is what is happening. In the Western world, the Muslims are antagonising the host community at every step. They are a bad name for Muhammad and Muhammad has nothing to do with it.*[816]

RE teacher Bhavin Tailor notes that the 'West' is a multi-layered phenomenon and that Prophet Muhammad (ﷺ) has been received differently by different audiences:

> *The West is a wide range, it is diverse. If we remember the cartoon published in a Danish magazine – that was done by an individual taking out of context. In the West, the perception is diverse. I wouldn't say everyone has a negative or positive perception. I think it's mixed.*[817]

In regard to the terrorists who are claiming Islam as a justification for their actions, British politician David Amess views this as a perfect example of the ends justifying the means and once again, having no connection with Prophet Muhammad(ﷺ)'s teachings:

> *I think organised gangs of terrorists have hijacked the religion for their own ends.*[818]

The political atmosphere, according to Neil Kinnock, had brought Prophet Muhammad (ﷺ) to the fore of the West's political and general consciousness. He notes:

> *More people in the West know more about Muhammad now than they did 10 years ago, due to the interplay between grievance and politics. Issues 'said to be' related to Islam have been much nearer the front of the news than ever in history, over a prolonged period of time.*[819]

Misconceptions abound in the West regarding the perception of Prophet Muhammad (ﷺ). There is a great degree of ignorance about his teachings and what Prophet Muhammad (ﷺ) stood for. A teacher from a Church of England School, North London (who requested anonymity) says:

> *I think the main perception of the West would be misunderstanding. I think the greatest difficulty and one thing I strive in teaching Religious Studies, is for people to understand what he taught and why he taught it. To be honest, most people I ask about Muhammad wouldn't be able to tell me anything about him at all. Most of it is lack of knowledge.*[820]

The West remains blissfully unaware and ignorant of Prophet Muhammad(ﷺ)'s true persona and teachings. Owing to this lack of knowledge, and distortion in some cases, some genuine media representations of Prophet Muhammad (ﷺ) have the advantage of creating the positive type of public opinion and awareness about the life and teachings of Prophet Muhammad (ﷺ) and can help spark an interest which is essential and ultimately educational. Jeremy Corbyn observes:

> *I think it's one of quite sufficient ignorance about the life of Prophet Muhammad. When Rageh Omar did his programme on Prophet*

Muhammad, it got a big audience, and I noticed that after it, quite a lot of people were speaking about Islam for the first time and out of interest. I thought as a piece of television presentation, the programme was interesting, informative and excited people to learn more.[821]

Mako Nagasawa (May 2012) is an area director, advisor to the Harvard-Radcliffe Christian Fellowship (HRCF), and staff member at InterVarsity Christian Fellowship, University of Harvard. According to him, one must exercise caution before taking any view of Prophet Muhammad (ﷺ) at face value. With so much false knowledge circulating about Prophet Muhammad (ﷺ), a more balanced assessment is required to develop an objective opinion regarding him, just as one would expect of their own revered personalities. In his words:

I really do enjoy history and I am always for learning more and understanding more as a person as important as Prophet Muhammad. I feel as a Christian, there is a kind of care that we must take when we approach historical figures of great significance, obviously because the same would apply to Jesus and so I do find that it is important to try and be more educated and informed if there are popular historians or people who are mischaracterising the Prophet Muhammad, then I think that should definitely be discussed.[822]

There is no single, uniform understanding of Prophet Muhammad (ﷺ) in the West, although it would be of great benefit if it was transmitted to the Western audience that much of the theology propagated by Prophet Muhammad (ﷺ) is similar to our Judaeo-Christian heritage. Unfortunately, the trepidation with which many people regard Prophet Muhammad (ﷺ) prevents them from acknowledging a similarity between his teachings and those of Christendom. Nagasawa further adds:

I'm sure there's a range of perception. I'm sure there are some, probably fewer, who know that in general, monotheism and ethical

> *monotheism ... such as Judaism, Christianity and Islam, have a lot of similarities, and there are a lot of similar principles in ethical monotheism that come out of the idea that somehow there is a God who cares about our lives and behaviour and the way we relate to each other. In general, those monotheistic movements have improved the lives of people but I do think in the West there is a lack of knowledge and a general nervousness about Muhammad*[823].

According to Professor John Eade, one cannot reduce Western perceptions of Prophet Muhammad (ﷺ) to a uniform, single perception. Viewpoints on Prophet Muhammad (ﷺ) are strikingly diverse and different. There may be some scholarly perceptions which deem Prophet Muhammad's message to be inherently inimical to Western civilisation, but among enlightened and well informed individuals, this position is often dismissed for lacking the element of truth and objectivity.[824]

Karen Armstrong thinks that, despite common ground between the two, the relationship between Islam and the West has reached a sort of boiling point for many reasons. It is a worrying trend that some Muslims are antagonising communities, even though their faith forbids them to do so. But just as a minority of Muslims ought to rethink their practices, so should the non-Muslims who are biased in their perception of the Muslims and Islam.[825]

According to Armstrong, although the Muslims have accepted the common ground between Islam and the West since Prophet Muhammad (ﷺ) preached Islam, which was nothing but a renewal of the basic religions of the earlier prophets, the West cannot recognise these mutually beneficial aspects. Some Muslims have gone against the People of the Book. This has led them to being humiliated and unpopular in the West. If Muslims could appreciate Western cultures, then the West, for its part, could more easily rid itself of most prejudices. Armstrong feels that the beginnings of this 'give and take' could be found in the teachings of the great person, Prophet Muhammad (ﷺ) who founded the religion of Islam which means peace and understanding and which was not preached at the point of a sword – a Western charge.[826]

The West cannot be reduced to a single entity, as is sometimes mistakenly assumed. Those in the Western world harbour a plethora of opinions about Prophet Muhammad (ﷺ), reflecting sometimes realities on the ground or international news. Often, these have the potential of distorting an objective and fair take on Prophet Muhammad (ﷺ). Father Alban McCoy of Cambridge University Catholic Chaplaincy observes:

> *I think it varies. People are more ignorant than they should be. But you have a range of views from complete ignorance to thorough familiarity and scholarly acquaintance. In between, you have prejudice which is largely rooted in ignorance. The perception now is getting more and more muddied by world events. People are seeing through a prism of certain historical events.*[827]

Former British Chancellor of the Exchequer Norman Lamont noted in an interview that perceptions about Prophet Muhammad(ﷺ) in the West have been distorted, with people believing that Muslims are generally militant:

> *I think there is deep misunderstanding. People think Islam is a warlike religion which I don't think it is. They think Muslims are out to wage Jihad. I think the perceptions of Islam in America are ridiculous.*[828]

An understanding of different belief systems is a very good way of becoming more tolerant and less prejudiced about others. Since many are of the view that single interpretations of Islam are not the be all and end all, different strategies need to be employed in order to exploit the plurality of understandings. Danny Richmond, Faith Act Manager, Tony Blair Faith Foundation (February 2012) says:

> *We should all learn more about faith traditions. If you look at social cohesion on a global level, we have 1.3 billion Muslims today, so when a sixth of the world is Muslim, it's essential, both living in our communities but also at a global level that we understand the influences in each other's life. I also know there is an incredible amount of diversity within Islamic thought and*

various communities, particularly on how they viewed the life and teachings of the Prophet (ﷺ) and so it would be helpful to explore that as well.[829]

One must take into consideration the various motives and agenda people and organisations have for presenting a particular image of Prophet Muhammad (ﷺ). Misconceptions about what Prophet Muhammad (ﷺ) really called for and symbolised lie at the heart of this ignorant perception and a more bias-free understanding about Prophet Muhammad (ﷺ) is urgently required. Dr Julian Fulbrook notes:

I would think there are certain people with a vested interest in portraying the Prophet Muhammad in a very poor light. I think that there are people who do so out of ignorance. There are people who are certainly bigoted and prejudiced about anyone who is slightly strange, in terms of their own culture, and I think it's a shame. A sign of maturity is that you can get along with people of a different faith and a different background.[830]

Much of the information and conclusions reached on the character of Prophet Muhammad (ﷺ) fails to engage the primary sources of his teachings and instead relies on accounts which are mere hearsay. Reverend Stephen Coles of St Thomas Church, North London observes:

The problem is that most people's knowledge of Muhammad is so second hand. Very few people have looked at stuff...its all received information, worse than secondary data. ... I think this will actually be true for a lot of Muslims as well.[831]

Amit Pal declares that it has become a norm to criticise Islam and Muslims without finding out the facts and getting to know Muslims in a deeper, personal capacity. In this regard he says that it is essential to develop a better understanding about their religion and followers. [832]

According to Amit Pal, it is unfortunate that the actions of a minority of Muslims have received such disproportionate attention on national and media levels. The nonviolent potential in Islam has hardly been explored and it is assumed that the opposite is true.[833]

The Media's Responsibility

According to HRH Prince Charles, one of the most common misconceptions about Islamic law is that it is backward and very harsh. This view has been promoted by the media, but we need to look beyond such crass stereotypes. If we look at Islamic law as a whole, we can see that the values it espouses are those which can indeed benefit humanity. We need to make an important distinction between the laws of the Book and of Islam which advocate justice, equality, humanity and fair play, and those which are manipulated for political or other agenda, erroneously applied and thus bereft of the true Islamic spirit. Prince Charles comments:

> *[P]eople in this country frequently argue that the Shari'a law of the Islamic world is cruel, barbaric, and unjust. Our newspapers, above all, love to peddle those unthinking prejudices. The truth is, of course, different and always more complex. My own understanding is that extremes are rarely practised. The guiding principle and spirit of Islamic law, taken straight from the Qur'an, should be those of equity and compassion. We need to study its actual application before we make judgments. We must distinguish between systems of justice administered with integrity, and systems of justice as we may see them practised which have been deformed for political reasons into something no longer Islamic.*[834]

US politican Hilary Clinton said that the most tragic thing about the planned Qur'an burning incident was the amount of news coverage and attention which the actions of this pastor had generated.[835]

British politician David Amess holds the media largely responsible for the distortion of Islam: 'I feel that the media have a lot to answer for. They often get stories wrong'.[836]

The media should accept responsibility for producing a distorted version of Islam which subsequently affects the Western perception of Prophet Muhammad (ﷺ). According to Revd John Pritchard, Assistant Priest, All Saints Church, West London:

> *There is a lot of propaganda. You just have to look at the papers and there are stories about Islamic clerics who the papers create a sense of fear and loathing. With all religion, there is propaganda which is not good, which takes you away from the original tenets of the teaching.*[837]

Our institutions bear a great responsibility to ensure that faith communities are not hostile to one another. Reporting and coverage has to be partial with no bias and the media must resist the temptation to sneer at Muslims and to peddle – as many are – an Islamophobic agenda. Only then can we see a normalisation in relations between Muslims and non-Muslims. We must work towards these objectives, Muslims and non-Muslims, to achieve global understanding.[838]

Islam's message was so emancipating that people of all ranks in society were empowered by it, from rich to poor, the free man to the slave etc. Islam promotes values which both the privileged and underprivileged can espouse and use as a basis to get along with each other. Canon Isaac Taylor commended the teachings of Islam in a speech delivered at the Church Congress of England, noting:

> *It replaced monkishness by manliness. It gave hope to the slave, brotherhood to mankind, and recognition to the fundamental facts of human nature ....The virtues which Islam inculcates are what the lower races can be brought to understand temperance, cleanliness chastity, justice, fortitude, courage benevolence, hospitality veracity and resignation ... The Christian ideal of brotherhood of man is the highest but Islam preaches a practical brotherhood—the social equality of all Muslims. A Christian convert is not regarded as a social equal but the Muslim brotherhood is a reality ... Slavery is not part of the creed of Islam.*[839]

Reverend John Cowie of the English Reformed Church, Amsterdam, says that the West cannot be considered as a homogeneous entity which shares a monolithic understanding and perception about Prophet Muhammad (ﷺ). Within the West, it is common to find concerns about the militant tendency among some Muslims, while other Westerners will be concerned about other strands of the Islamic faith which may not correspond with Western values in general. This may be due to the fact that Islam itself cannot be reduced to a monolithic faith which produces a single unilateral response across different issues.[840]

The media have an instrumental role in the dissemination of information regarding Prophet Muhammad (ﷺ). On occasions, actions by a fringe group of Muslims have a detrimental effect on the overwhelmingly large number of peaceful and law abiding Muslims, who are stigmatised as a result. There are many cases around the world today to prove this point. According to Cowie:

> *If you live in an area with a few Muslims, you rely on the press for your understanding of what a Muslim is. For example, I lived in Pakistan for three years and I know that most Muslims are moderate there and open and friendly and hospitable. Unfortunately, the impression of Islam in Pakistan is now dominated by the publicity about madrassas and terrorism and support for the Taliban, which doesn't represent the majority but represents people who are willing to commit atrocities who are willing to take up violence. The minority gives the majority a bad publicity.*[841]

Blaming the media alone for Prophet Muhammad(ﷺ)'s distorted image in the West is somewhat of an oversimplification, according to Professor Eade:

> *I think it's too simple to say that the media simply distort and manipulate. I think to some extent they express quite powerful currents of belief in society.*[842]

Dr Julian Fulbrook observes that a reflection and study of the primary sources of Islam has led many to conclude that the media image of Islam is biased and a misrepresentation of the religion's true tenets. According to Fulbrook:

> *When I looked at the Qur'an, it was pretty obvious that some of the things I was reading in newspapers and magazines about Islam were not actually the reality but then that's true of quite a few things in life isn't it.*[843]

Pandit Jay Lakhan, Professor, Eaton College, London, has blamed the crusades for maligning Muhammad (ﷺ) and the media for not exploring the truth about Islam and the Muslims. Professor Lakhan says:

> *Due to the animosity between Islam and the Christians caused by the crusades, this has left an indelible mark, causing each other to vilify one another. Islamophobia is very much a result of the poor media presentation of Islam.*[844]

There is therefore a pressing need to provide a comprehensive and well-studied account of Prophet Muhammad(ﷺ)'s life to the general population in order to dispel the ignorance and biased views which often arise from ignorance about him. According to Mehri:

> *If we were to base our perception on the tabloids or biased media, or the right wing elements, or the extremists, or those who take atheism to the extreme, or those who are ignorant about Islam, Mohammad's image is definitely negative. But there are also many who do not have a negative view of him. They may not necessarily have a very positive view of him like the Muslims have, but they certainly don't have a negative view of him. But I think it is important to show the genuine Prophet Muhammad and that should not be propaganda or idealistic, it should be realistic. If you portray him realistically, it would be possible for people to see him as a real prophet and it would be positive. You cannot make others accept him as he is accepted by the Muslims, because for the Muslims he represents something else, the perfection of humankind.*

> *But if you portray him realistically and historically then I think a great deal of good can be achieved.*[845]

There is much distortion of Islam in the media in general and this view is shared by Shashoua, Director, Three Faiths Foundation, Camden, London:

> *Often our education is received from a misinformed media, who go for sensationalist stories: 'If it bleeds, it leads'.*[846]

The media is culpable for the distortion of Islam. Rev Thomas O'Brien, Our Lady of the Assumption Church, Tower Hamlets, London, says:

> *Unfortunately, in the context of terrorism, the media has badly presented Islam, completely falsely.*[847]

The media's tendency to exaggerate and report along sensationalist lines with no justification is mentioned as the main cause of distorted perceptions, by Father Tom Quinn, Shadwell Catholic Church, East London. According to him:

> *The media often go to extremes. The media have lost their integrity and truth. It is too sensationalist.*[848]

Stagal mentions how the perception of Prophet Muhammad (ﷺ) is very much determined by media references, which provide a distorted vision of Islam. In this age of the internet, information is prone to manipulation. Mike Stygal, Chairman, Camden Interfaith Foundation, London has criticised the media for their poor presentation of Islam. He says:

> *There are official organisations in the West and they have done the sensible thing and made a point of finding out about Islam, so government for example have invited Muslims to come and educate them about Islam. In terms of the general public, they are fed by the media which gives a false picture. One of the things which the*

media seems very scared of is the internet, as it is not controlled by the media. Also, social networkings, facebook, twitter, blogs-those sorts of things are really useful tools to start correcting misinformation. Really good quality websites which are good at correcting misinformation...I would tell people do not ever take what the media has to say about anybody, even if they say good things.[849]

The media to a large extent must shoulder responsibility for not broadcasting the positive effect which Islam has had on society and how it has contributed to bettering relations between Muslims and non-Muslims. According to Reverend Jennifer Potter, Minister, Wesley's Chapel, London:

For those who have the opportunity to interact with educated Muslims, for us the perception is a positive one. The problem I find is that the part of Islam we hear about is the negative aspect. Our newspapers don't report on the Islamic university in Cairo and their teachings and links with Christian groups and Interfaith issues, but that never gets on the papers.[850]

Owing to our recent political climate, Muslims the world over have unfortunately been on the receiving end of a biased media campaign which has wrongly linked their faith with terrorism. And this has distorted Islam's true nature. Falsehood about the Islamic faith persists, despite the overwhelming Muslim voice in condemnation of terrorist activities. Jane I Smith, Senior Lecturer in Divinity and Associate Dean for Faculty and Academic Affairs, wrote in the preface of the book,

The Qur'an and the sayings of Prophet Muhammad: Islam does not support violence, but is a religion of peace. The Qur'an does not condemn Christians and Jews as idolaters, but insists that all who follow the teachings of the Prophets are inheritors of the gardens of paradise. Muslims do not mistreat women, but consider them to be partners in their families, their communities, and their nations. In recent years and particularly since the tragic events of 9/11,

> *Muslims in the West have tried to affirm all of this and much more about the texts and traditions that guide their lives and rule their hearts. Listen, they say, and let us tell you about true Islam, its beauty and its power to give those who would listen to its call a guideline for life and a key to entering into the presence of God. Despite the many efforts to dissociate Islam from movements that support terror and hostility toward the West, fears and misunderstandings are difficult to dispel. Current polls and surveys suggest that prejudice against Islam, Prophet Muhammad, and the Holy Qur'an is not declining but is actually on the rise.*[851]

Far from pointing a finger at Prophet Muhammad(ﷺ)'s message to make sense of the terrorist activities in the world, a Buddhist monk comments that the media must share some culpability in perpetuating a biased perception about the Muslims:

> *There are so many terrorist activities under the name of Muslims. This is not good for Allah or Prophet Muhammad (ﷺ). I don't know who are leading these actions… in the media it is Muslims.*[852]

The injustice in the name of Islam, according to the RE teacher Bhavin Tailor, is motivated out of opportunism and selfishness and those responsible for perpetrating this image are a minority of Muslims and the media:

> *When you look at acts like 9/11 that seems to be almost like the stepping stone from which people have associated Islam with acts of terrorism. It was such a big act done by a few people that gave Islam a bad name, however, there is much disparate views, there's a very small number who have taken Islam as an excuse to do selfish acts. The perception given by the media didn't help the peaceful Islam which is the real Islam of many people.*[853]

Mike Stagal considers the media responsible for demonising the Islamic faith by giving it unwelcome associations. He says:

> *The media are very good in creating the wrong portrait. The media have given the impression that Islam is filled with radicals, extremists and potential terrorists.*[854]

Politics

The late Michael Meacher, Labour Party politician and academic, observed in an interview in 2012 that the abuse of religion and the distortion of its reality is a topic to which many people in general have given due consideration. Islam, like many other faiths, is often exploited as a political tool, to give political leaders and their campaigns the necessary leverage to consolidate their power base. This political use of religion exercises a strong influence on the imagination of many religious adherents but this cannot be applied to Prophet Muhammad(ﷺ)'s case as his political and military campaigns were warranted out of necessity, for the survival of him and his his followers.[855]

Part Two

Consequences of Demeaning the Qur'an

The act of burning the Qur'an reflects a deep-rooted ignorance about the life and teachings of Prophet Muhammad (ﷺ) and the Qur'an, the revelation sent down to mankind by God. Participants in this research, including many scholars, commented that the burning of the Qur'an is a grossly offensive and abhorrent practice which will only fuel further hatred and tension among communities.

A grossly offensive gesture

According to Reverend Rupert Hoare, a former Dean of Liverpool, UK Cathedral and Chair of the Council of Faiths in Liverpool, the burning of the Qur'an is a grossly offensive gesture towards the Muslims, and reflects a depraved state of mind:

> *I think the burning of any book is a dreadful thing to do and the burning of the Qur'an, it is blasphemy. It's an extraordinary, aggressive thing to do which should never be done, just as the Bible should never be burnt, or a book of prayers.*[856]

The Qur'an, the holy book of the Muslims, was revealed by God verse by verse through the angel 'Gabriel' (AS), to Prophet Muhammad (ﷺ), over a long period of time i.e. 23 years, guiding the Prophet (ﷺ) and the Muslims. It is thus a complete code of conduct for men for their lives on earth and is an array of glad tidings and promises of goodly rewards from God, in the hereafter, for those who would do good and adhere to its (Qur'an) guidance. Muslims respect it dearly and should follow its instructions at every step of their life. Every follower of a religion has respect for their holy books. Nobody should disrespect the holy book of other religions.[857]

According to John L. Esposito, Muslims believe that Prophet Muhammad (ﷺ) was known as the living Qur'an. Whatever he did in every aspect of his life, he followed strictly the Quranic guidance and teachings and encouraged, advised and trained others to do the same:

No group or the followers of a particular faith will accept that their holy book is violated, burnt or dishonoured; This is irrespective of whether they follow its teachings. The act of dishonouring any holy book could easily ignite communities against each other. The people involved in the survey were asked how they felt about the burning of the Qur'an which was publicly organised by the USA Pastor Dr Terry Jones and that of the American soldiers in Afghanistan. They responded by condemning and denouncing such acts which they viewed as blasphemous and offensive. They clearly found it as a barrier to a cohesive society. The following section is an account of the reactions made by the survey participants.[858]

Bhavin Tailor, an RE teacher, William Ellis School, a secondary school in North West London notes how the burning of the Qur'an is an affront to religious values. He feels that some people have got the wrong idea about Islam. He dubs it as a dreadful crime:

The burning of any religious text will be a negative thing because there are a small group of people who have misinterpreted Islam and is a way of showing their dislike. They are annoyed at the disrespect some Muslims show society, but then they are showing disrespect in the burning of the Qur'an. It's a heinous crime, it's disgusting, and one we shouldn't allow whether it's the Qur'an, Bible or anything.[859]

Similarly, Reverend Thomas O'Brien of Our Lady of the Assumption Church, Tower Hamlets, said:

I think it's completely sacrilegious and blasphemous.[860]

Father Allen Green, Chairman, Tower Hamlets Interfaith Forum, also found the burning of the Qur'an an offensive gesture:

I believe it is right to respect faith communities and to respect the sensitivities of these communities. It is simply offensive to trample on what people feel is holy.[861]

Stephen Shashoua, Director, Three Faiths Foundation, Camden, terms it as distasteful and offensive to others:

> *This is abhorrent to me. To insult others in such a way.*[862]

The defilement of the Qur'an is such a heinous crime that, according to UN Secretary General Ban Ki-Moon, no faith can support such an act. He said: *"Such actions cannot be condoned by any religion."*[863]

Aside from causing deep offence to Muslims who revere the Qur'an, burning this book, which is the Holy Scripture of over a billion people worldwide would push back attempts at peacemaking. Ban Ki-Moon adds:

> *The recent burning of a copy of the Qur'an in the United States and similar actions anywhere else contradict the efforts of the United Nations to promote tolerance, intercultural understanding and mutual respect between cultures and religions.* [864]

Lord Norman Lamont sees the burning of the Qur'an as a sacrilegious act:

> *I think it's deeply offensive and I strongly deplore blasphemy in all its forms.*[865]

President Barack Obama condemned the burning of the Qur'an by some American troops in Afghanistan. He apologised to the Afghan people for the act, and in a letter to the Afghan President H Karzai, expressed a general sense of sorrow and regret for what had occurred.[866]

The US government wasted no time apologising for the Qur'an burning incident: Press secretary Jay Carney said it was a 'deeply unfortunate incident'.[867]

The plan to burn the Qur'an was definitely a publicity stunt to promote the views and agenda of far-right extremist. The then US Secretary of State Hilary Clinton expressed her concern over burning the Qur'an. She called it a 'distrustful and disgraceful' action.[868]

The burning of the Qur'an was, in the view of many participants in this research, a shameful act of bigotry, intolerance and insensitivity to the beliefs of others. Many were moved to the point of actively engaging with persons of influence to find ways of preventing the American pastor at the centre of the controversy from being admitted to the UK, on the grounds that his proposed action was so insulting and offensive to ordinary Muslims that his presence on British soil would be catastrophic for social cohesion. Responses also stated the importance of a calm and measured response by the Muslim community to such a senseless and provocative gesture. Mehri Niknam MBE, Executive Director, the Joseph Interfaith Foundation, Camden, London said:

> *I absolutely find it unacceptable, disgraceful and disgusting. In my opinion, people's religious beliefs should be respected and people's religious books should be respected. As Jews, we have suffered because our holy books were burnt so many times in history, so we understand how it hurts to witness such destruction. Therefore, certainly, as a Jew, it is incumbent upon me to object to this, but also because of my professional work, I think this is absolutely and totally unacceptable. The Joseph Interfaith Foundation's Council of Imams and Rabbis wrote a letter to this effect to the Home Secretary, when that Pastor from America wanted to come to England to burn the Qur'an. We wrote an official letter to the Home Secretary both as Jews and Muslims if this man is allowed into the country it will be detrimental to community cohesion and good Interfaith relations in this country. We were very pleased when he was banned from entering the country. I also would like to add this, that although I find the burning of the Qur'an abhorrent, I also disagree strongly with those Muslims who become violent and kill people as revenge. Two wrongs don't make a right.*[869]

Cause of Tension

Reverend John Pritchard, Assistant priest, All Saints Church, West London, views the burning of the Qur'an as a provocative act which presents a barrier to mutual relations in society. In the view of Pritchard:

> *I don't think any text should be burned. I cannot believe that the burning of a holy book can promote social cohesion.*[870]

Canon Paschal Ryan of the Archbishop's House, London, feels that the burning of the Qur'an is destructive for social cohesion efforts; it cannot bring any good, rather, it will only compound the antagonism and distrust among faith communities:

> *I think it's a very harmful thing and no good can come of it. It only creates tension.*[871]

The burning of the Qur'an for almost all participants in this research represented a very divisive and provocative act which only holds back social cohesion efforts and pits communities against each other. A teacher from a Church of England School, North London (who requested anonymity) stated:

> *I completely disagree with that as I would disagree with anybody defacing any religious book. I think it's disrespectful. My difficulty is, everybody has a right to religion and what they believe. Everybody has a right to express their own views. I understand that people want to express that they don't follow Islam and they don't agree with it and they don't see the Qur'an as a holy book. But then I think it's very antagonistic to go and burn it because instead of showing respect to this person and say: 'I understand you believe it and you're fine to believe that', they are causing conflict.*[872]

The Vatican also expressed concern over the action, saying that burning the Qur'an would be an "outrageous and grave gesture." Vatican spokesman Federico Lombardi said burning the holy book will jeopardise the peace plans of religious communities:

> *This act would only call for new hate and violence. It goes directly in the opposite direction to the building of peace to which we all, as faithful in god and as people of peace, are called.* [873]

In order to prevent acts like burning the Qur'an from recurring, it would be a good idea for a legal provision to be introduced in states which ban such actions. However, no amount of education can make up for depraved education and ignorance, which ultimately is the cause behind such antagonistic actions. The teacher goes on saying:

> *Firstly, it should be part of our race relations act, the idea that actually it's part of the law. The problem is, it's a very grey area. You can't say that was racism, because the act itself wasn't racist. However, the act itself was very disrespectful. The majority of these needs are to be dealt with in education.*[874]

The burning of the Qur'an was a senseless act in the view of almost all and it was intended to provoke and cause division among communities. However, it does not help the situation when the Muslims urge violent reprisals. Reverend John Cowie says:

> *I would deplore that. I think it's an insult to somebody else's beliefs to do that. It's disproportionate on the part of Muslims to call for dramatic sanctions and people to be so distressed. I think God can protect himself; he doesn't need us to riot and kill on his behalf.*[875]

The burning of the Qur'an points to a deeper cultural failure for us to appreciate and respect the differences of one another, without letting these differences spill into violence, as Jeremy Corbyn notes:

> *I think burning anyone's book is completely wrong. I think it is appalling and it just simply should not happen and it creates tension. The behaviour of some people in the USA and some people in Afghanistan in the treatment of the Qur'an indicates something very deeper, which is a fear, or suspicion or lack of knowledge or*

lack of respect.[876]

There is unanimity on the view that the burning of the Qur'an was detrimental to social cohesion efforts and represented a deep affront to the religious sensibilities of Muslims worldwide. The cohabitation with plurality and mutual acceptance of different cultures, beliefs and religions is at the heart of fostering good relations and understanding between different groups in society and this is jeopardised when lone groups or individuals do not have a secure sense of identity or belonging. This sense of isolation, coupled with an unfounded hostility towards Islam perhaps explains actions or the calls to censor and burn the Qur'an. According to Right Honourable Stephen Timms MP says:

> *I don't think burning the Qur'an is a helpful thing to do, not an action I would support at all. I think it's quite a damaging thing to do in fact, because it causes very deep offence on the part of quite a large group of people. If you look at our society which has a lot of different faith groups represented in it, people quite often believe that because it's got different faiths in it, it must be a fragmented society. But actually I think it's a misunderstanding... The fact that this particular community where we are today, a lot of people belong to mosques, that's positive for cohesion and not negative.*[877]

As in all groups of people, there are always fringes who depart from the norm and unfortunately adopt a radical stance towards the members of other beliefs. What makes this even worse is when the radicals emanate from religious communities themselves. Michael Meacher commented:

> *Unfortunately, there are in very large populations – 300 million people in America... There will always be a tiny number of people who have all sorts of thoughts which are utterly extremist, fundamentalist, intolerant, sometimes brutal. What is awful is that this man was a Baptist pastor. He purported to be a priest of God and the intolerance is utterly dreadful. You cannot suppress a faith.*[878]

CHAPTER EIGHT

Prophet Muhammad's Teachings on Interfaith Understanding

It has been almost common for many to believe that Islam does not accept the presence of other religions in the world. This chapter discusses the teachings of Prophet Muhammad (ﷺ) regarding how to deal with non-Muslims and live in a cohesive society. Islam offers rights to the non-Muslims amidst them. These rights include freedom of religion, the right to work, housing, freedom of movement, education and security in times of war and hostility. Prophet Muhammad(ﷺ)'s teachings on the behaviour which Muslims should show towards members of other faiths can be neatly encapsulated by the Qur'anic verse: "To you is your religion, to me mine."

The society in which Prophet Muhammad (ﷺ) lived comprised a diverse religious base. Jews, Christians, polytheists and others who did not subscribe to any form of organised religion lived in close proximity. Prophet Muhammad(ﷺ)'s conduct during this time reflected his tolerant nature towards non-Muslims. A good starting point for us to properly understand the level of tolerance displayed by Prophet Muhammad (ﷺ) and Muslims is the period when Islamic laws were implemented on a state level in Madinah. This is not to say that Prophet Muhammad (ﷺ) was not of a tolerant nature in Makkah. Indeed he was, but the principle of religious tolerance was really set in stone once the constitution of Madinah was drafted.

The 'constitution of Madinah' is the clearest example of Prophet Muhammad(ﷺ)'s commitment to religious tolerance. Following his migration to Madinah, Prophet Muhammad (ﷺ) was no longer just a spiritual leader in the eyes of the people. Rather, he was vested with political power and assumed the executive authority of government. He was now tasked with ruling according to Islamic law and bringing understanding to a fragmented society. For Prophet Muhammad (ﷺ), laying down a constitution was of paramount importance, as all religious groups needed to be reminded of their civil obligations towards one another and not to transgress the limits set by the legal framework, which could amount to treason.

The constitution stipulated that the residents of Madinah, Muslims and non-Muslims, and anyone who had entered into a treaty with the state, were "one nation to the exclusion of all others." Irrespective of race, creed or lineage, they were all part and parcel of Madinan society. The life, wealth and property of non-Muslims were to be protected according to the article in the constitution which read: "To the Jews who live there will be help and equity. They shall not be harmed nor their enemies be aided." In the past, alliances between tribes were formed from inside and outside the Madinan territories but Prophet Muhammad (ﷺ) sought to unite these tribes under one government which assimilated the alliances which already existed between tribes. If any tribe or faith group was attacked, the state would consider it an attack on itself. The life of non-Muslims who had a treaty with the Muslims was considered to have the utmost sanctity and was afforded protection. Prophet Muhammad (ﷺ) said:

> *"Whoever kills a person who has a truce with the Muslims will never smell the fragrance of Paradise."* (Sahih Muslim).

As Muslims were in a position of authority, Prophet Muhammad (ﷺ) warned his followers not to abuse this authority and privilege. He said:

> *"Beware! Whoever is cruel and hard on a non-Muslim minority, or curtails their rights, or burdens them with more than they can bear, or takes anything from them against their free will; I (Prophet Muhammad (ﷺ)) will complain against the person on the Day of Judgment."* (Abu Dawud)

In another article, the Madinan constitution states: "The Jews have their religion and the Muslims have theirs." This is one of the clearest indications of tolerance towards non-Muslims, and that their faiths could not be offended. Non-Muslims could go about their religion and way of life without any interference from the state and harassment by authorities. Prophet Muhammad (ﷺ) insisted that the disputes which occurred between the people of Madinah must be referred back to the law, which at that time was Islamic. This was fundamental requirement of being part of Madinan society and enjoying the protection of the state. The Qur'an states: "If any dispute or controversy likely to cause trouble should arise, it must be referred to God and His Messenger." Prophet Muhammad (ﷺ) did not want justice to be dispensed arbitrarily by individual leaders. Although non-Muslims had the freedom of referring their religious specific disputes to their own scholars, the option was always available for them to ask for arbitration from Prophet Muhammad (ﷺ) and Islamic law if they wanted to. God says in the Qur'an:

> *"If they do come to you, either judge between them or decline to interfere..."* (the Qur'an 5:42)

This was a clear demonstration that Prophet Muhammad (ﷺ) was an advocate of religious freedom, providing the main tenets of the state constitution were not violated.

This chapter is divided in two parts: *Diversity in Islam* and *Social Cohesion.*

Part One:

Diversity in Islam

Constitutional Rights for Non-Muslims

Bernard Lewis claims that the Constitution was not a treaty in the modern sense, but a unilateral proclamation by Prophet Muhammad (ﷺ). One of the constitution's more interesting aspects was the inclusion of Jewish tribes in the Ummah because, although the Jewish tribes were one community with the believers, they also have their religion and the Muslims have theirs.

Tolerance in Islam

As far as tolerance is concerned, this is clearly enshrined in Islam and the character of Prophet Muhammad (ﷺ). The Qur'an highlights this principle. The overwhelming number of Islamic traditions which support the principle of tolerance should suffice to prove that compulsion has never been endorsed in Islam. According to Dr N.K. Singh:

> *The Islamic Philosophy of tolerance is derived from the Qur'an and the practice of the Prophet. The Qur'an teaches that "Religion is only for Allah': Ya kunuddinu lillahi. The basis of Islamic toleration is firmly laid in the teaching of the Qur'an, 'toleration' means 'the recognition of free thought and practice in religious matters' (Oxford Dictionary). Toleration is a law, not of Coercion but of Love, not one of violence but of peace.*[879]

Tolerance is a great virtue which is reflected in the practices of Prophet Muhammad (ﷺ) and the caliphs after him. Dr Singh explains how tolerance was discernible in the behaviour of the Arabs. In his words:

> *The Islamic doctrine of tolerance found the fullest expression in the practice of the Prophet and the pious Caliphs. The Ummayad and*

Abbasid Caliphs also practised tolerance in the vast regions which gradually became a part of the Islamic Commonwealth. The term 'practice' should, however, be taken to mean 'usual behaviour' rather than 'invariable behaviour'. The Prophet had brought about the political unification of the Arab tribes shortly before his death. This great achievement represented the combined victory of Arab nationalism over centrifugal tribalism, as also of Islam as the revised version of ancient Judaism and Christianity. The hitherto camel-drivers, petty traders and free-booters of the desert, emerged from the back-waters of history, on the world-stage of history. The almost unbroken chain of military victories against the then superpowers inevitably fostered a new self-image of the Arab emerging elite.[880]

Nelson Mandela acknowledged the debt that ought to be paid to African Muslims and their remarkable struggles in taking up noble causes. Muslims were working there very closely with other communities.

Islam has become part of Africa in a process as complex as the history of the continent itself... In the face of European colonialism, Islamic communities took their place along the whole spectrum of resistance politics, including the struggle against apartheid.[881]

The lives of many African Muslims were taken during the apartheid era, which should remind us how important the Muslims are in Africa's recent political and cultural narrative. According to Mandela:

If I may, I would like to take this opportunity to pay tribute to those South African Muslims who died while in detention because of their resistance to apartheid; Babla Saloojee; Imam Haroun; Ahmed Timol; and Dr Hussein Haffejjee. They represent the involvement of the Muslim community in the struggle for justice and freedom, as does the presence of Muslims as Cabinet Ministers and in the highest office of our judiciary, in the new democratic political dispensation of our country.[882]

Karen Armstrong insists that the Muslims did not have any problems living in harmony with people from other faiths. The Christians and the Jews lived within the Islamic domain for many years but the West felt uncomfortable accepting Muslims within their territories.[883]

The original message of Islam, contained in the Qur'an and carried by Prophet Muhammad (ﷺ), stressed the importance of equality and justice in all spheres of life. Although these principles may have been largely ignored, it is by no means a reflection of what Islam requires of Muslims.[884]

The former Indian Prime Minister Manmohan Singh said that Prophet Muhammad(ﷺ)'s teachings will direct us towards the path of understanding, peace and co-existence. He said:

> *The Prophet's life and work is an inspiration to lead a life of compassion and brotherhood. May the festival (EiD) spread peace, love and tolerance among all.*[885]

Prophet Muhammad's emphasis on interfaith dialogue and enjoining compassionate relations is clear. There are incidents in his life which indicate that he had a high level of respect for non-Muslims. Danny Richmond maintains:

> *Yes. I know there is a famous story – and you'll have to help me out on it – I believe one of his Jewish neighbours who had a funeral and the Prophet attended his funeral. (the coffin was going in front of him and he stood up to respect and told the others). Yes, that's it. The sign of respect when many others wouldn't have thought to respect or were condemning other groups, I think the Prophet multiple times showed that respect above all is an essential trait of an Islamic person. I know that teaching of respect to others came heavily in a lot of his life.*[886]

Dr Henry Stubbe noted that Prophet Muhammad (ﷺ) never forced anybody to embrace Islam and non-Muslims were well protected during his time. According to Dr Stubbe:

I do not find that Mahomet proceeded any further in Arabia the desert then to exterminate Idolatry, but not to force men to the profession to Islamism. He himself gave Letters of security and protection to the Jews and Christians in Arabia, and never used any Violence to them upon the Account of religion.[887]

Jon Dal Din has studied Prophet Muhammad (ﷺ) and says that the Prophet(ﷺ) instructed Muslims to show friendliness and warmth to those belonging to other religions:

The prophet taught his people to be respectful to people from other faiths...what I understand is that the prophet has taught Muslims to have respect for other people. I am not aware of anything that the prophet is saying that you should not have respect for the community.[888]

An objective assessment of Prophet Muhammad(ﷺ)'s life would reveal that he was not aggressively seeking converts to Islam and promoted peaceful living with those belonging to different faiths. According to Reverend Jennifer Potter, Minister, Wesley Chapel, London:

I think Muhammad preached that we should live peacefully with others and in particular with those who acknowledged one God – monotheism, as fellow people and not as outcasts and enemies to aggressively evangelise, but to live with them in peace and harmony.[889]

Prophet Muhammad(ﷺ)'s teachings on neighbourliness encompass the toleration of non-Islamic religions, and he did not show an adversarial attitude to the adherents of other faiths but rather exhibited tolerance at all times. This characteristic of Prophet Muhammad's teachings is often suppressed and not properly practised by Muslims. According to Jeremy Corbyn:

As I understand the teachings, he has a set of values and views, e.g. the food you eat, the way you treat people, the times you pray, the

> *way you lead your life. His values were also respect for other faiths and other religions. There are a lot of disputes about his attitudes to Judaism; I prefer to take the view that he was developing a set of beliefs as a messenger from God, but he was not hostile to people who believed other things. It's that tolerance and respect which I think is a strong feature of the Muslim community in Britain and Europe and it is something which is often misunderstood, deliberately in some cases. Like any other faith, Islam has followers who claim to be followers of Islam who don't fully understand the faith and use their own version.*[890]

According to Mike Stagal, Prophet Muhammad(ﷺ)'s neighbourliness could be seen in the way he respected the differences of others:

> *When dealing with neighbours, he was always very respectful, observing that they were different but respecting those differences. As long as they were not attacking Islam in the way they behaved then there was always to be a respectful relationship between each other. That's my understanding of what Muhammad had to say about neighbours.*[891]

There are aphorisms of Prophet Muhammad (ﷺ) which point to the Muslims' duty to treat neighbours with care and cordiality. There is sometimes a misunderstanding that the Muslim obligation to his fellow man included only co-religionists. However, Prophet Muhammad(ﷺ)'s instruction for neighbourliness and peaceful coexistence and relations with the local community encompassed everybody, including non-Muslims. There was no element of discrimination in his advice for Muslims to be dutiful to their peers and neighbours. Niknam Mehri notes:

> *One of the sayings of the prophet according to hadith is that he said 'be kind to your neighbours, up to 40 households on one side and 40 households on the other side'. When we question this, we try to analyse what the Prophet meant. He was a wise man. If he had said, be kind to your Muslim neighbours up to 40 houses on this*

side and up to 40 houses on that side that would have meant discard anybody who is not a Muslim, he is not your neighbour. But his statement is inclusive, he meant whoever lives within your vicinity, regardless of race, religion or background, they are your neighbours, be kind to them. Also, I have explained this further by saying, in those days if you said be kind to your neighbours ten houses further, or be kind to your neighbours two houses further, it would have a numerical value in people's mind. The number 40 always has the connotation of infinite. If you have 40 of something, it means you have a great number of something. So I always teach why did he say 40, why did he not say 30, or 20 or 10? Does it mean that the streets in Madinah were so long that they had 40 neighbours on one side and 40 neighbours on the other side? No, rather, what he meant was extend your kindness to your neighbours throughout the world. It is infinite. It is not just your next door neighbour but all the world is one neighbourhood. It seems to me that this is the message that should be communicated more than anything else about this teaching of the Prophet.[892]

Prophet Muhammad(ﷺ)'s teachings are conducive to fostering close relations between our peers and the wider society. This is achieved by applying the Islamic dictates of equitable wealth distribution, which is reflected in one of the major pillars of the Islamic faith: Zakat. Mehri comments:

The Qur'an commands the believers to look after the orphans, the needy, the poor, to share your wealth with your fellow citizens and so on. Zakat is a very important aspect of Islam, one of its five pillars. If every Muslim in the world, genuinely and truly gave two and a half per cent of his profit per annum as Zakat for the poor, for the needy, for the widow, for the uneducated, if they build with this money schools, hospitals, universities, welfare houses, social institutions, there would not be a single poor Muslim in the world.[893]

Many are of the view that Prophet Muhammad (ﷺ) and Jesus shared similar visions on how neighbours and those who are different should be treated. There was a common denominator in their religious persuasions.

According to Reverend John Cowie, the English Reformed Church, Amsterdam:

> *I think the teaching of Islam and the prophet is similar to the way Christians would preach dealing with your neighbour. Because they come from the same roots and there was a concern for people amongst whom you lived.*[894]

Both Prophet Muhammad (ﷺ) and Jesus emphasised the importance of maintaining a dutiful regard towards neighbours. They did not restrict the definition of neighbours to mean an exclusive group of people but rather taught that it was a general principle to be courteous with anyone. Reverend Cowie adds:

> *My understanding of the Prophet's teachings or Islam is that we have a responsibility beyond just ourselves but also to the poor and Jesus taught that we have that responsibility to our neighbour. And our neighbour can be anybody – not just people we know but strangers in our midst; that we have a responsibility to them.*[895]

Intolerance in Islam is Denounced

According to British Conservative politician David Amess, social cohesion is fully realisable when considering the wisdom and experience which Prophet Muhammad (ﷺ) imparted to others:

> *The idea that Muslims are trying to undermine other religions is ridiculous and is not the teachings of Muhammad. There are no barriers to Muhammad's teachings to achieve social cohesion. Rather, Muhammad's teachings are conducive to social cohesion.*[896]

Racial Equality and Unity

Magsie Hamilton Little says that one of the final speeches delivered by Prophet Muhammad (ﷺ) showed how important he considered racial equality and unity. We must remember that the attitudes prevailing during his time were no short of being awful and the levels of intolerance, racism and general prejudice were very high. Prophet Muhammad(ﷺ)'s message challenged these social ills and stereotypes, and laid a special emphasis on understanding among all.[897]

A review of the Prophet(ﷺ)'s life shows that he celebrated the ethnic pluralism which God had created, and emphasized the importance of equality among human beings. There is not only a religious but also a historical precedent which reflects the principle of religious freedom in Muslim societies, as examples of interfaith harmony under Muslim statesmanship. The establishment of peace and goodwill between members of different faiths was a special accomplishment under Muslim rule and has not gone unnoticed by many religious scholars. Jon Dal Din, Director, Westminster Interfaith Group, London, points to the mutual expressions of social harmony and cohesion, emphasised by the Islamic and Christian traditions:

> *[S]o far as the teachings of the Qur'an, from the suras I have read talk very much almost in the same way that our own book talking about God creating man and women of different nationality, different background, with a view that they should live together in a harmony. These are the fundamental teachings in the Qur'an to all people – we are all made equal. There is an idea of living in peace and harmony...in Spain and in Africa – there was total freedom of religions – Christian, Muslims and Jews worked very well together – there was no problem at all under Islamic rule. The teachings of Prophet Muhammad (ﷺ) coincided with the practice basically. There was peace. There were times when there was not peace – the time of the crusades – that was a different situation. So my understanding of Islam itself, 'Muslim' means peace; people of peace.*[898]

Part Two:

Social Cohesion

Social cohesion is a complex issue. Many people define it in different ways. However, the participants in this research have defined it as shared social responsibility, securing trust and sustainable social bonds that bring people together, irrespective of religion, colour, creed, ability and social situation, etc. The people interviewed were positive that the Muslims are able to build social cohesion based on the teachings of Prophet Muhammad ( ).

Zakat

The institution of Zakat was introduced by Prophet Muhammad (ﷺ). Zakat is a kind of tax in which Muslims pay 2.5% of their annual income to the poor if their income exceeds a certain threshold. The participants in this research thought this custom was very helpful in increasing the solidarity of the community as well as alleviating poverty. The teachings of Zakat promote unity between the well-to-do and the have-nots within communities. Zakat could be provided to non-Muslims as well, as long as they not fighting against the Muslims.

Zakat Establishes Social Unity

Prophet Muhammad(ﷺ)'s teachings of Zakat are mutually reinforcing healthy neighbourhood ties, according to the RE teacher Bhavin Tailor:

> *I understand Muhammad was very welcoming to others. He is said to have wanted to take care of the most vulnerable and the poorest. So the zakat is a very good example, that 2.5% of a person's wealth goes to the poorest and vulnerable people in society. For me, this practice says that we are taking care of the vulnerable.*[899]

Tailor mentions the benefits which the payment of Zakat can bring, suggesting it could help efforts for social cohesion:

> *I think it's a really good idea. If Muslims are taught to be*

charitable, then why shouldn't we distribute. Religion promoting this can only be a good thing. But regarding this threshold, it shouldn't always be if they have money. Some people might not have enough money to start off with. So we should start with a threshold so people don't think like it's a burden on them.[900]

Prophet Muhammad(ﷺ)'s endorsement and promotion of Zakat benefited the destitute in society and he obliged the wealthy to come to the aid of the less well off by putting aside a portion of their income for them. Regarding Zakat, Jeremy Corbyn likened it to the forms of taxation and benefit systems prevailing in the West:

It's an early form of progressive taxation. Muhammad did not have a concept of a nation state such as one which we recognise now, but he did say that the rich have a responsibility to everyone else and therefore on a grading basis should pay a percentage of their income…Yes absolutely, because the basis of the modern welfare state and taxation system is that everyone should pay on the basis of their ability to pay into a common pot, in order to provide those resources and needs for people.[901]

Reverend John Cowie says that Prophet Muhammad (ﷺ)'s promotion of zakat can be deployed to equalise inequitable distribution of wealth.[902]

Magsie Hamilton Little thinks that Zakat is one of the hallmarks of Islamic faith and a mark of a Muslim's level of piety and God-consciousness. A Muslim owes everything to God and is not the ultimate owner of the things he possesses, whether property or wealth. Therefore, Zakat is analogous to a debt to God. Zakat is essential if Muslims are to establish a fair and equitable society.[903]

Muslims are required to pay a part of their earnings as alms to the poor if their earning has reached the minimum threshold. The alms known as 'Zakat' would be 2.5% of their total earnings. The alms are for those who are less privileged and needy and go a long way to contributing towards an equitable society. Dr Leitner illustrates:

Their alms, which are rightly called only a pecuniary prayer, consist in giving up a portion, not less than a fortieth part, or two and a half percent, of their goods, to the poor. These alms go into the public treasury, and are applied, among other things, to the redemption of slaves; another subject regarding which Christians ignorantly accuse Muhammadans of a state of things which Muhammad did his best successfully to mitigate by a practical legislation towards its eventual abolition. But, reverting to alms, in order that these be acceptable to God, the givers must show that they are in lawful possession of the gift (which, it is needless to add, can be increased beyond the legal minimum). It would not do "to rob a till in order to build a chapel", but those who voluntarily give more than the fortieth part will be rewarded by God.[904]

Unlike other holy sages, Prophet Muhammad (ﷺ) did not spurn the material riches of this earth and condemn his followers to a lifetime of drudgery. There was nothing in his teachings which even remotely suggested that Muslims should avoid earning wealth. However, they were cautioned not to be excessive with whatever God gave to them and told to extend a helping hand to the less privileged. In this regard, the compulsory requirement of Zakat (almsgiving) helped limit the widespread economic differences. As far as economic ethics goes, Prophet Muhammad (ﷺ) instructed his followers to earn without hoarding, avoid the type of competition which leads to rancour and not devour the wealth of orphans, which was common among the Quraish during his time.[905]

The command for Zakat is primarily out of humanitarian considerations and is incumbent on Muslims who are capable of paying it. Instead of viewing the practice of giving Zakat, meaning a portion of one's substance given in order to purify the rest, as the mere giving of money to another soul who is less fortunate, rather it is to be aimed to achieve through this a much deeper, spiritual attainment. Tailor says:

Like a lot of schools, we focus on the 5 pillars of Islam and one that I focus on is Zakat. The idea that charity is so fundamental and not just the giving of money. So charity in year 9 we spent a whole unit looking at what is charity and immediately my students say, it is the

> *giving of money. Then we stop them and say actually, charity is more then that, it's helping someone. It's looking out for your neighbour. Although Zakat is 2.5% of an annual disposable income, I often say to my students that some Muslims cannot even give that because they're in a state where they cannot fend for themselves. But Islam would not then say, they're bad or wrong. So Prophet Muhammad's teachings on Zakat are based on the principles that you help mankind.*[906]

Zakat, which Prophet Muhammad (ﷺ) endorsed as a religious obligation, was a very admirable introduction in a society where poverty was rife. It has the potential to strengthen cohesion in society and help consolidate the principle of equality. A teacher from a Church of England School, North London (who requested anonymity), says:

> *I think it's a wonderful thing to do. I personally am a Christian and I believe I should give 10% of my earnings tithe – I think it's good to expect people to help others and a framework in which to do it is very helpful.*[907]

According to Dr Geoffrey Rowell, the point where Islam and Christianity, and likewise many other faiths, converge is in the teachings on neighbourliness. Both Islam and Christianity place great emphasis on treating neighbours with respect and dignity, and ensuring that their basic needs are met. The mutual teachings on this aspect can certainly help foster a greater sense of belonging and community among both faiths.

Social Brotherhood

HRH Prince Charles states that it is strange that the West and Islam have clashed on many fronts, especially when we consider the similar visions and ideals which both share. The Qur'an affords a special status to the members of the other Abrahamic faiths, and both Islam and Christianity possess a similar belief in the existence of the hereafter, judgement for sins and other social beliefs such as providing relief to those in poverty, the preservation of the family unit, etc. All of these teachings are enshrined in the Qur'an and they seem to correspond with the teachings in other Scriptures as well. It could be that the violent episodes throughout history between Muslims and non-Muslims have contributed to a skewed understanding of each other's beliefs, and therefore historical interpretations could equally be responsible for shaping and distorting our judgment. Prince Charles says:

> *It is odd, in many ways that misunderstandings between Islam and the West should persist. For that which binds our two worlds together is so much more powerful than that which divides us. Muslims, Christians — and Jews— are all 'peoples of the Book'. Islam and Christianity share a common monotheistic vision: a belief in one divine God, in the transience of our earthly life, in our accountability for our actions, and in the assurance of life to come. We share many key values in common: respect for knowledge, for justice, compassion towards the poor and underprivileged, the importance of family life, respect for parents. 'Honour thy father and mother' is a Qur'anic precept too. Our history has been closely bound up together. There, however, is one root of the problem. For much of that history has been one of conflict; fourteen centuries too often marked by mutual hostility. That has given rise to an enduring tradition of fear and distrust, because our two worlds have so often seen that past in contradictory ways.*[908]

In a telegram published on the Kremlin's website, President Vladimir Putin stated that Islam has become integral to Russia's religious, cultural and social fabric. Millions of Muslims are practising and living in the country.

> *Traditions of Islam are based on eternal values of kindness, mercifulness and justice. Millions of people in our country practice this ancient religion.*[909]

President Putin was also full of praise for the Muslim community for being active participants in Russian public life, by launching charities and strengthening family values. He said:

> *I want to stress that the state's estimation of fruitful activities of Muslim organizations is very high and the state guarantees its citizens the opportunity to follow the norms of their religion including the pilgrimage to the holy places of Islam.*[910].

Prophet Muhammad(ﷺ)'s teachings on helping the poor, needy and generally being concerned for the welfare of others helps us to reflect on the grim reality of the contemporary world. Reverend Dr Harriet Harris (May, 2012), the Chaplain and honorary Fellow at the school of divinity, Edinburgh University and former Chaplain and tutor at Oxford University and lecturer of theology at Sussex University says:

> *I think these are wonderful teachings. And I know the number 40 is often used to mean 'many'. What I like about these teachings is that they help you to see yourself in your specific situation and, in a very literal way, to think about those who are around you. So these teachings are very practical. The particular teaching about sharing extra food with others is good – it is like going the extra mile.*[911]

The warmth and friendliness which Prophet Muhammad (ﷺ) encouraged Muslims to show their neighbours is a very effective way of highlighting the principle of equal treatment. It can help those who are new to Muslim circles feel at home and in some sense special, without feeling any discomfort. The Reverend Stephen Williams, Senior Anglican Chaplain, University Chaplaincy, University of London states:

> *I think it's a noble, high ideal and I think it's a way of incorporating and promising someone who comes into your home, so that they are not from a different tribe and are being equitable, but that you are actually giving them an honoured place. It's actually elevating them to being an honoured guest. These teachings have a value.*[912]

Many argue that Prophet Muhammad(ﷺ)'s teachings on neighbourliness can be deployed today as a good way of establishing social cohesion. In particular, his teaching relating to being welcoming and cordial with others, irrespective of religion and race speaks volumes for current experiments with multiculturalism and social cohesion. The Reverend Williams says:

> *Well I think it's a good model of how human beings can interact. We're looking at a model from the 7th century; from a pre-industrial society when the groupings were small.it was the family, the tribe, clan and so on. By extrapolation, I think we can say that the very human model of being hospitable and gracious and respectful to your immediate people who you come across, we can say this is a good way of living in the more complicated societies we have today.*[913]

Mako Nagasawa (May, 2012), is area director, advisor to the Harvard-Radcliffe Christian Fellowship (HRCF), and a staff member with InterVarsity Christian Fellowship, University of Harvard, USA. He thinks that a critical reading of Islamic history would suggest that Muslims are more than capable of being good hosts to civilisation and demonstrate the qualities that are essential for living side by side with those belonging to other faiths.[914]

Prophet Muhammad(ﷺ)'s teachings for behaving in a neighbourly fashion are similar to Christian principles which enshrine the same responsibility. Looking after your neighbours in this sense is a core tenet reflected in Islamic and Christian teachings and was exemplified by Prophet Muhammad (ﷺ). Mako Nagasawa adds:

> *I think there are certainly a lot of positive things. He stood in the Biblical tradition of ethical monotheism. I really appreciated that. I do know for instance that, there was more social equality among the Arab people because of his teaching. What I would like to understand more is how are we to take earlier versus later statements from him in the Qur'an and the Hadith on relations between Muslims and non-Muslims.*[915]

Prophet Muhammad(ﷺ)'s honest nature and teachings on the importance of neighbourliness brings him close to Christian traditions of respecting and loving neighbours. This part of Prophet Muhammad( )'s message reflects the objective behind his prophethood and reveals that the divine revelation has an all- encompassing message and is intended to bring benefit to humanity at large. Professor John Eade observes:

> *I think it's similar to Christian traditions in the sense where they share common ground of being just and fair and honest to another person as a human being. Someone created by God is part of a divine person. It's not just about this world and the short time we have here. It's the notion that we are part of a much wider scheme where we must maintain some kind of relationship with the divine so therefore our religious practice is not just doing things for the sake of doing things but has a purpose behind them in terms of how our lives are linked to the lives of our predecessors and those who come after us.*[916]

Prophet Muhammad(ﷺ)'s teachings on maintaining neighbourly relations were achieved through many ways and had a visible impact on the ways in which the Muslims of 7th-century Arabia interacted with those from multi-faith communities. Some of the core tenets of the Islamic faith also reinforce the importance of being considerate towards others and showing concern for their general welfare. According to Reverend Stephen Coles, St Thomas Church, North London:

> *I know what he said about treatment of the people of the book, where the Christians and Jews have to be treated with respect and not attacked. I know that historically, this has worked out in a variety of different ways. I know that one of the pillars of Islam is almsgiving and that suggests that a faithful Muslim is supposed to look after the needy and the vulnerable and that would come under the Christian definition of a neighbour.*[917]

One of the remarkable feats of the Scripture and religious individuals is the inherent ability to transcend the narrow confines of its beginnings and thereby resist any temptation to be insular. Reverend Coles adds:

> *Well I think it encourages people of a particular faith to look out beyond themselves which are important. I think the danger of separate religious communities is that they become inward looking.*[918]

An understanding of different belief systems is a very good way of becoming more tolerant and less prejudiced about others. Since many are of the view that one single interpretation of Islam is not the be all and end all, different strategies need to be employed in order to exploit the plurality of understandings. Danny Richmond, Faith Act Manager, Tony Blair Faith Foundation says:

> *We should all learn more about faith traditions. If you look at social cohesion on a global level, we have 1.3 billion Muslims today, so when a sixth of the world is Muslim, it's essential, both living in our communities but also at a global level that we understand the influences in each others life. I also know there is an incredible amount of diversity within Islamic thought and various communities, particularly on how they viewed the life and teachings of the Prophet (ﷺ) and so it would be helpful to explore that as well.*[919]

Magsie Hamilton Little said that with Prophet Muhammad(ﷺ)'s religious responsibilities came political ones, and the need to foster healthy relations between Muslims and non-Muslims. In effect, he was laying down the constitutional principles of religious freedom, tolerance and citizenship. This was a remarkable feat of Prophet Muhammad (ﷺ) that he achieved a common and mutual respect among members belonging to all faiths and gave them something which Arabia always craved: unity. Any extreme Muslim thinking of imposing a monoculture which does not respect others betrays Prophet Muhammad(ﷺ)'s example.[920]

Although the early Muslims ventured on expansionist campaigns, this is not to be misconstrued in the way the term is currently used. The spread of Islam did not signal the death knell for other minorities and their beliefs. According to Father Alban McCoy, Cambridge University Catholic Chaplaincy:

> *Historically, Islam has been a military and conquering faith and when it had conquered territories, it was reasonably tolerant of the existence of other faiths.*[921]

The doctrinal and ritual similarities between Muslims and Christians can be taken as a means to promoting social welfare and mutual cooperation between different faiths. In this regard, the Jon Dal Din added that:

> *Our common things are: We believe in one God, We have scriptures from God, we pray and fast, all these things are common, are the parts and parcel of our way of life. It is right and proper that we come together and pray to one God for the good of the society of the world. But we need to work together and need to cooperate each other as an act of solidarity, shared projects, we all have charitable organisations. We worked together during Pakistan and Haiti disaster, there the example of solidarity, we are in the same boat, we need help each other.*[922]

Working upon the elements which are common and familiar to all religious groups can help mitigate any differences and potential conflicts. Pandit Lalit Kumar Sharma makes the point that Muslims and Hindus are capable of living in relative peace:

> *He said that, live together in peace, you are one and not different, never one is different than the other. The holy books did not guide in a bad path, all taught a good way; now it depends on us if we should take the good path or the other one. They have shown us the good paths. They never had said anything wrong. Hindu Muslim is one community.*[923]

The principle of peaceful coexistence was enshrined in the Prophet(ﷺ)'s behaviour. It is sometimes, due to unfounded ideas that this principle becomes clouded or misapplied. There is nothing in Islam or the Prophet(ﷺ)'s teachings which prevents inter-religious coexistence. Pandit Sharma echoes this idea, as he goes on to say that:

> *He has given very good advice in that respect- don't hit the mind of anyone-serve each other-you live and allow the other to live-he has taught the whole world. But we tend to forget it time to time having been influenced by external wrong idea. That is wrong. People from all religions can live together.*[924]

Respecting the religious adherents of non-Islamic faiths is a trait that could be identified in the Prophet(ﷺ)'s character. The Pandit believes that in the teachings of Prophet Muhammad (ﷺ) there is no obstacle for the Muslims to live together with people from different religions:

> *There is nothing working as a barrier towards establishing good social cohesion among the Muslims and Hindus or people of other faiths.*[925]

Another aspect of the Prophetic teachings that can be discerned is its non-coercive nature. British MP Frank Dobson notes:

> *Well my understanding is that generally speaking, he wishes to live in amity not enmity with neighbours, providing they don't provoke him and he will not provoke them, all neighbours. Clear acceptance of the fact that while he would have preferred everyone to be a Muslim, people were I suppose you have to say within limits, entitled to their own views but he didn't want them to force their views on Muslims.*[926]

The concept of *ummah*, according to Father Allen Green, was engendered by Prophet Muhammad (ﷺ) as a way of instilling neighbourliness between Muslims and others:

> *I do understand about the notion of ummah and brotherhood that exists within the people of God. In other words, you cannot be a*

devout Muslim without taking the concerns of your neighbours upon you. My impression is that the Prophet was clear that there is a shared understanding sufficiently between the peoples of the book-other monotheistic religions that share such common heritage. His message was that we should attempt to find that common ground.[927]

Prophet Muhammad(ﷺ)'s neighbourliness and enforcement of just punitive measures is also acknowledged by Right Honourable Lord Kinnock, who says:

From what I know, he said we should treat them with generosity and trust. I'm certain that he advocated in all circumstances co-existence, so far as it could be sustained, and resistance to those who broke the code of that coexistence by being aggressive.[928]

Prophet Muhammad (ﷺ) preached that it was obligatory to assist the poor and less fortunate and this obligation was to be collectively shared by the entire society. Even a part of our wealth, generated through earnings is to be allocated to the poor and religious institutes and places of worship are also entrusted with this responsibility. The Right Honourable Corbyn points out:

He took the view that society as a whole has responsibility for everybody and that responsibility stems to giving a portion of your income to charity and the poor and the function of the mosque is to provide and open house and support for people through charitable needs, housing and so on.[929]

Prophet Muhammad(ﷺ)'s neighbourly inclinations and exhortations to be dutiful to others, irrespective of race or religion speak volumes for his community vision. The generosity which Islam obliges its followers to exhibit to others is one of its distinctive traits and is a clear reflection of Prophet Muhammad(ﷺ)'s true nature. Father Alban McCoy notes:

I think this is integral to a healthy society and it's there in Christianity as well. It's still I think more explicit and more vivid in Islam and well known. I think a society in which hospitality is not a premium value is not a society.[930]

Lord Norman Lamont highlights Prophet Muhammad(ﷺ)'s affability with neighbours:

> *I would have thought that his teachings would be to look after our neighbours and be friendly with them.*[931]

Prophet Muhammad (ﷺ) actively militated against the tendency to be selfish. He always enjoined compassion and care when dealing with the less fortunate in society. This is a trait reflected throughout the course of Prophet Muhammad(ﷺ)'s life. Whether it was through the Prophetic traditions or the Qur'an itself, Prophet Muhammad (ﷺ) was a staunch advocate of sharing space and living with everyone, irrespective of race and creed. Danny Richmond, Faith Act Manager, Tony Blair Faith Foundation says:

> *I know one of his teachings was you're only your best person when you're serving others and your worthiness comes from serving others – I'm paraphrasing something that he said, but it would be pretty easy to look through his teachings and find references to the vulnerable, the poor, the orphan, the woman, and I think that the underpinning for my work in Interfaith engagement is very much inspired by a surah which was conveyed by him which is "O Mankind! We made you into many tribes and nations so that you may come to know one another." and I think that is the essential teaching in terms of social cohesion that its essential that we live side by side with one another and that we can come to know each other and our inspirations and our teachings.*[932]

Care for Neighbours

According to the Buddhist monk, Dhama Caro, Wimbledon Temple, London, the prophetic teachings emphasise concern for the welfare of fellow humans and community members:

> *Muhammad taught about caring for your friend, loving your friend*

> *and looking out for the interest of your friend... He taught people to live in peace, in friendship, loving your neighbour....*[933]

British politician David Amess believes that the Prophet Muhammad (ﷺ) has been grossly misrepresented. His being portrayed as being bent on taking over the world through violence is not consistent with what he preached and practised about neighbourliness and living in peace with others:

> *Well as I understand it, I think Muhammad has been misrepresented. The idea that just because you're non-Muslim you can't have anything to do with them – I don't think it was like that at all. He has been misrepresented as if Muslims are trying to take over the world by violence and to me this is totally against his teachings and he is peace loving. The teaching is to help your neighbour.*[934]

Prophet Muhammad(ﷺ)'s brotherly relations and peaceful co-existence with neighbours is recognised by Former British Home Secretary David Blunkett, who says:

> *He believed my neighbour is my brother, we help each other when in need. He said we should behave with non-Muslims as you would behave with your brother.*[935]

Venkata Ratnam pays glowing tribute to the Prophet of Islam, saying that Islam is a very liberal religion. However, many people resort to publishing fictions rather than the truth about this religion. Prophet Muhammad (ﷺ) taught that there is no God but Him. He is the Creator of everything that is in the universe which He alone rules with mercy and affection. Mankind can seek forgiveness directly without an intermediary. The Prophet advised his followers to take care of the poor on a regular basis by feeding them and giving charity and forbade alcoholic drinks in line with the revelations of the Qur'an.[936]

Lord Kinnock is alive to the fact that the turmoil for which Islam is so often accused is often the product of its erroneous reading and application:

> *Problems with religion derive from the interpretation and manipulation and the distortion.* [937]

Prophet Muhammad(ﷺ)'s promotion of the concept of 'People of the Book' is conducive for multi-faith relations, as Stephen Shashoua mentions:

> *As I understand, his teachings emphasise a respect for neighbours and a relationship to be had with neighbouring groups of other beliefs. The idea of the 'People of the book' enforces a family of faiths and beliefs that came from Abraham and therefore we should live together peacefully.* [938]

Muslims are required to go out of their way to ensure their neighbours' emotional and financial needs are satisfied. Shashoua continues:

> *There is quite a huge responsibility in most of the teachings. It's not just about supporting your neighbours emotionally or talking to them, or financially; if they're in need, you have to make sure that they are ok, especially when you're in a position where you're quite wealthy and able yourself. Your neighbour was not just the person next to you but it was everyone.* [939]

Prophet Muhammad (ﷺ) introduced specific teachings to help relieve the distress of the poor and the less fortunate in society. Some of what he instructed was unprecedented in the sense that it had not been proposed until Prophet Muhammad (ﷺ) advanced it as a workable idea to help those in disadvantaged positions. A principle of living which Prophet Muhammad (ﷺ) routinely emphasised was the concern that should overcome a believer if he knows that those close to him are in difficulties. Danny Richmond says:

> *I think essential to institutionalising his vision and creating very practical implementations of creating a more just world that takes*

into consideration others and the most vulnerable in our society was the teachings of Zakat and sadaqa, and tithing part of your earnings to the most vulnerable, not simply because it's something nice and kind to do but because it's part of our responsibility of living in a society with each other and taking care of the other. I think that was both revolutionary for the time and also showed the very practical nature in which he saw that vision coming into play in society. I think there's also a beautiful saying that he used to say which is, you cannot sleep if someone amongst you is hungry. I think that sense of responsibility to another, in a time from what I know of that time in human history when the poor were both relegated and not seen as each other's responsibility, I think that is an essential teaching. In today's society, you look around the world and you see half the world's population living on less than two dollars a day, that's something that has very real implications for our time. Or even just in the UK, there's poverty here and so the notion of how we're responsible to each other is something that's very important.[940]

Prophet Muhammad(ﷺ)'s teachings on neighbourliness are crucial for developing peace and harmony in the world. Regarding Prophet Muhammad's comments on the one who sleeps while his neighbour is hungry, a teacher from a Church of England School, North London (who requested anonymity) says:

I would say that is something crucial for children to understand and people to understand that if we start seeing everything in the world as our own, then we don't really understand what it means to have a relationship and we don't understand what it means to gain from sharing with others.[941]

Living with Interfaith Communities

According to Reverend Rupert Hoare, the concept of 'ummah' – articulated by Prophet Muhammad (ﷺ) – goes a long way in cementing ties and fraternal links between disparate people. Prophet Muhammad (ﷺ) inhabited a society characterised by a multiplicity of faiths and ethnicities and his inclusive notion of living was very amenable to healthy social relations and can be taken as a precedent for living harmoniously in today's world with members of different faiths and races. Reverend Hoae says:

> *Yes. In his society, one of the great things was the creation of this ummah – fellowship or community which transcended tribal boundaries. So in relation to the time that Muhammad lived, it was a case more of finding a community of human beings who would be one people but our present situation where different religions are living in parallel with one another was true in his day to a more limited extent with the people of the book. So you have the people of the ummah and very closely associated with that are the Christians and the Jews.*[942]

Prophet Muhammad (ﷺ) was a staunch advocate of social cohesion, who according to the British politician David Blunkett instructed harmonious co-existence between people and acknowledged the instrumental role which faith has to play in fomenting good relations. In his words:

> *I think we need a fundamental faith in the family; we need to reach out to our neighbours and hold in common the desire to live together in peace – I think Muhammad enjoined others to go out and live accordingly. I believe faith can be a tremendous foundation for good because it gives people a reason for living their life in a positively good way. The biggest barrier is those who misuse faith for their own purposes, whether it is fundamentalist Christians or Jihadists because they take people away from the true faith and create division and misunderstanding which is then used*

> *by others. I would tell them that we live in common and others who preach evil should not be heard.*[943]

According to the Father Allen Green, Prophet Muhammad (ﷺ) was a man who was ahead of his time and this attribute necessitated practising social cohesion:

> *Muhammad transcended his own society and because of this, it required Muslims to seek unity and cohesion with neighbours. It is quite clear from the Qur'an that Muslims should respect the community and nation where they are living, as long as they can identify principles that accord with Islam.*[944]

Stephen Shashoua, Director, Three Faiths Foundation, Camden, London speaks about the Prophet(ﷺ)'s teachings about building a cohesive society. He says:

> *'Co-exist' just means existing side by side. Tolerance is how much you can tolerate before you get sick. Social cohesion or adhesion is probably the best term you can use to refer to communities and individuals coming together to build society together, to understand similarities and differences. My Muslim friends say the Prophet's teaching was about respect for the diversity that exists in this world and his actions and words said that being together is the paradise we seek.*[945]

A teacher from a Church of England School, North London (who requested anonymity) pays tributes to Prophet Muhammad (ﷺ) for his teachings about the responsibilities towards neighbours and living in a peaceful community. She says:

> *I would see social cohesion as a situation in which everybody in society, whatever religion or race they are, is able to show respect to one another, is able to tolerate each other, is able to let each other have freedoms and rights to the extent where they don't impinge the*

> *rights of others and where people are taken care of.*[946]

She thinks that the teachings of Prophet Muhammad (ﷺ) in the 7th century in relation to social responsibility can still apply in the 21st century if implemented and followed accurately. There are many people who are unemployed, many children who are orphans and require support and sympathy of others. So, people at large would benefit from such teachings. She claims:

> *If there is an expectation to help the poor and needy, then we will not have a situation where people are fighting over taxes, a situation where people are unemployed...we have a huge number of children in the UK living below the poverty line and that should never be the case, we wouldn't have that situation if everybody was willing to support each other.*[947]

Jeremy Corbyn thinks that interfaith understanding is encouraged by the teachings of Prophet Muhammad (ﷺ):

> *Muhammad's teachings that we all have a responsibility for everybody else and society as a whole are the same basic humanitarian principles that everyone should live by.*[948]

Corbyn continues:

> *[The teachings encourage] The ability to live in a community with differences of language, ethnicity, faith, to respect the views of others and afford everyone the space for their own identity and a common set of beliefs and respect for each other and living with each other peacefully.*[949]

Mike Stygal says that it is in Prophet Muhammad(ﷺ)'s promotion of neighbourliness in which social cohesion can be identified, and he does not see any impediment in Prophet Muhammad(ﷺ)'s teaching to achieving a socially cohesive society:

> *Muhammad's teachings said to respect the difference in your*

> *neighbour. If you love your neighbour as yourself, then that gives you the opportunity to form a cohesive bond with your neighbour. The teachings of Muhammad are a very positive example of how social cohesion could work. There's certainly nothing in the teachings of Muhammad that would go against social cohesion, only that would work in a very positive way for social cohesion.*[950]

The longing to belong to a community as part of one's identity lies at the heart of social cohesion for some participants. This communal identity helps to give the individual a sense of the self which can then be used to develop healthy relationships with others. The Reverend Pritchard notes:

> *I think social cohesion should be about the ambition of the individual to not be alone. In what is becoming an ever more lonely planet and for us to be socially cohesive means we find in everyone the possibility of a good relationship and that transcends gender, sexuality, race, culture creed, that sort of stuff. Social cohesion is the possibility of the hope of God revealed.*[951]

When asked to define social cohesion, all participants featured in their definition the principle of mutual understanding of each other's differences. Reverend Dr Harriet Harris defines social cohesion thus:

> *A situation in which people from whatever background, culturally, religiously, socially, have a sense of one another as neighbours, so that in amongst their differences, which can be enjoyed, there is something that binds them together in their place, so that they are able to live and work together companionably.*[952]

Professor John Eade defines social cohesion as:

> *[T]he willingness to tolerate difference. I don't think social cohesion is about homogeneity, that everyone believing in the same thing, doing the same thing. I think what social cohesion is about is an awareness of other people's difference and an ability to cope with*

> *that difference.*[953]

The celebration of difference and social diversity is an essential component of social cohesion according to many participants. The attempts to enforce a monochrome culture often eat away at our efforts in building better relations and understanding with each other. Social cohesion is very much to do with appreciating the unique contributions and efforts which a wide range of people from different backgrounds make to their societies and communities. According to Reverend Stephen Coles, St Thomas Church, North London:

> *My perception of social cohesion is people allowing each other to be different while at the same time understanding that underneath all our differences we have a common humanity. It's not about everybody being the same. It's not about in order for you to live in the U.K. you having to become British in everything you do. It's about saying we all have gifts which we bring to this place. We have to be totally committed that we're in this place and we're here together.*[954]

Recognition of Equality and Humanity

Adopting the interests of others and seeing something familiar in their motivations and aspirations is a key ingredient for social cohesion. According to Reverend Jennifer Potter:

> *The people in a neighbourhood being able to link to each other, to recognise each other as residents and neighbours in that area, to cooperate together, they identify an interest which they can come together on… that Muhammad wanted his followers to live peacefully together and to recognise the equal humanity of everybody else.*[955]

The human need to be a part of a community and not be isolated has featured in the definitions of social cohesion by many. Among them,

Father Alban McCoy says:

> *Social cohesion is the result of our innate need of human beings for society, community and friendship and only though these can human beings flourish. Therefore, social cohesion is an indispensable aspect of human life. I agree with Aristotle that we are social animals.*[956]

Neil Kinnock is of the view that while Prophet Muhammad (ﷺ) had a very compelling and civilising message to preach to the world, the onus is on the Muslims worldwide to dispel any misconceptions surrounding him:

> *I think Muslims have got a mission that must be fulfilled. Is there confidence that the truth about Muhammad was that he was enlightened, non aggressive, non colonialist, not a threat to any neighbour, whether next door or next continent?*[957]

The co-existence of Muslims with the wider non-Muslim society was encouraged by Prophet Muhammad (ﷺ) and the effects of such practice can be seen in the Muslims in the UK, and their conduct with the wider population. Kinnock added:

> *I think there is clear evidence that within this country, most Muslims living in good relations with their non-Muslim neighbours, friends, workmates, fellow pupils, and fellow students. I think most Muslims are well capable of showing respect and living in peace with others.*[958]

Prophet Muhammad (ﷺ) was compassionate to all, regardless of religion. This was central to preaching equality for all. Pandit Thillai K. Rangarathan says:

> *Prophet Muhammad was a good preacher He taught people to like neighbours, share food with them and be helpful and kind to all… Don't harm anyone... try to rectify, love everybody whether believer or non believer… He was a firm believer in social cohesion among*

people.[959]

Prophet Muhammad (ﷺ) had taught his followers not to harm themselves, nor to reciprocate harm and social cohesion features instrumentally in his propagation. In this regard, a spokesman in a Sikh Temple in East London observes:

> *Muhammad taught people to respect the neighbor, which is Allah's teaching. Allah does not hate anybody. Everybody is thesame in the eyes of Allah... the prophet said not to do any harm to anybody; if you do, then you are harming yourself. The Prophets' teaching is about helping each other, to live in a friendly manner in a community with each other. There might be poor people, but the poverty does have a religion.*[960]

Stephen Shashuoa states that Prophet Muhammad (ﷺ) had taught people to respect those from other religions and live with them amicably:

> *[H]e shows there are no divisions between people and we have to develop respect. Even his comments regarding the people of the book, he speaks about respecting all. These things illustrate that he respects 'otherness', which involves acceptance of other types of people, with whom we can live cohesively...*[961]

Prophet Muhammad (ﷺ) taught people to live with each other peacefully irrespective of their colour, religion etc. This is echoed by Gordon Birtwistle, a British Member of Parliament says:

> *I am told that in the Qur'an it says he believes in honesty, peace, families, working together and that we are all equal no matter what colour, creed etc. His teachings are that we should live in peace and harmony.*[962]

Prophet Muhammad (ﷺ) was clear in preaching harmonious coexistence and to be sympathetic to others' concerns. In particular, he taught that a life lived only for selfish concerns at the expense of consideration for others was a disservice to God. Reverend Jennifer

Potter says:

> *Muhammad promoted that we should live in peace and cooperation with people, to not live your life for just your own satisfaction but to think about the community where you live.*[963]

According to Reverend Rupert Hoare, Prophet Muhammad (ﷺ) exemplified a tremendous degree of compassion and hospitality as far as his teachings relating to neighbours was concerned. He berated the practice of infanticide and generally advocated taking care of the less fortunate and those who tended to be left on the margins of society. Reverend Hoare observes:

> *He taught that you live with your neighbours in honesty and in care for them. Particularly for the poor, the orphans, for the destitute. I've been looking up some of the passages. And care for women and a sense of outrage for female babies being put to death. So his teaching is certainly a teaching of care for both the neighbours within the community and strangers.*[964]

Brotherhood in Islam is intended for everyone. There is no class distinction and Muslims are commanded to treat others as their own brothers. Dr R.L. Mellima, a Dutch anthropologist, writer and scholar says:

> *The doctrine of brotherhood of Islam extends to all human beings, no matter what color, race or creed. Islam is the only religion which has been able to realize this doctrine in practice. Muslims wherever on the world they are will recognize each other as brothers.*[965]

A common understanding of each other's faiths and an appreciation for its core tenets is integral for multi-faith communities to live cohesively with each other. There are common denominators between faiths and their followers and this could be the basis upon which mutual acceptance and tolerance can be effectively practised.

Providing Interfaith Values

As far as neighbourliness is concerned, Father Tom Quinn acknowledges Prophet Muhammad(ﷺ)'s endeavours to adopt the interest of the masses and not restrict his activities so that they are in the service of a specific religious group:

> *To work for the common good of everybody, not just the members of a particular faith.*[966]

By observing the conduct of Muslims in his neighbourhood, Father Quinn sees in this proof of Prophet Muhammad's commitment to good relations:

> *From witnessing the good behaviour of Muslim families in the area, I will see in them a reflection of Muhammad's religious values and Interfaith values.*[967]

Muslims are Social

The overwhelming majority of Muslims are peaceful, law-abiding citizens who are eager to coexist on an equal and peaceful basis with the wider community. The importance in engaging with each other, so that Muslims may play their part in the community is pointed out by Jon Dal Din, Director, Westminster Interfaith Group, London:

> *I know maybe 99% of Muslim love to stay peacefully in a community; however, we should know each other, we are brothers and sisters, we have responsibilities towards our society.*[968]

According to Jon Dal Din, Prophet Muhammad (ﷺ) wanted people to interact with their neighbours so that they could live harmoniously in society:

> *My understanding is that he was encouraging different faiths to live*

> *together, but of course that changed fairly quickly within 100 years after his death... changed to a very much more aggressive stance...I think he encouraged interactions with the neighbours and understand people.*[969]

The fact that there was peaceful coexistence between Muslims and those from other faiths throughout history would suggest that this was a reflection of the teachings which Prophet Muhammad (ﷺ) imparted to his followers. Rev. John Pritchard says:

> *I'm very well aware that Muslims and Christians have lived peacefully and very well together and have been able to in the holy land.*[970]

Muslims across the world have embraced a culture of respect and sharing with their non-Muslim neighbours. This is a mandatory requirement of their faith and is reflected in the practices of millions of Muslims across the globe. An example of this kind of cooperation is given by Amit Pal:

> *During Ramadan, I remember Muslim neighbors bringing generous amounts of food to our house in the city of Lucknow, a city heavily imbued with Muslim culture. My maternal grandfather's Muslim friends used to drop by his house. The Muslim residents of our village came to visit us in our ancestral home. I recall the gentle, protective man ferrying my cousins and me to our elementary schools.*[971]

Unity and Brotherhood in Islam

Indian Prime Minister Indira Gandhi admired the teachings of Prophet Muhammad (ﷺ) including those on democracy, equality, brotherhood and peace.

> *The teachings of the prophet Muhammad had an instant and revolutionary appeal because of its democratic feelings and its message of equality and brotherhood of self-help and peace.*[972]

Anita Rai applauds the Prophet Muhammad (ﷺ) in numerous ways for allowing people from different faiths to live in his state. She says there is no evidence to prove that Prophet Muhammad (ﷺ) had ever destroyed any place of worship of the people of other faiths. This means the teachings of Prophet Muhammad (ﷺ) encourage Muslims to live with others cohesively in a society.[973]

Edmund Burke, an Irish statesman, author, orator, political theorist and philosopher who, after moving to England, served for many years in the House of Commons of Great Britain as a member of parliament. He recognises that the Islamic laws and principles are the best on earth to unite the rich and poor:

> *The Muhammadan Law which is binding on all – from the crowned head to the meanest subject is a law interwoven with a system of the wisest, the most learned and the most enlightened jurisprudence that ever existed in the world."*[974]

M.K. Gandhi acknowledged that Islam showed light in the darkness in many parts of the world and created brotherhood in the world:

> *Someone has said that Europeans in South Africa dread the advent of Islam – Islam that civilised Spain, Islam that took the torchlight to Morocco and preached to the world the Gospel of brotherhood. The Europeans of South Africa dread the advent of Islam, for they are afraid of the fact that if the native races embrace Islam they may claim equality with the white races. They may well dread it. If brotherhood is a sin, if it is equality of the coloured races that they dread, then that dread is well founded. For I have seen that any Zulu embracing Christianity does not ipso facto come on a level with the Christians; whilst immediately he embraces Islam, he drinks from the same cup and eats from the same dish as a Mussalman. That is what they dread.*[975]

Magsie Hamilton Little further said that Prophet Muhammad (ﷺ) had given unity to a disunited people and this was unprecedented in Arabia. Even when he had to resort to arms, he did his best to ensure that the unity of the Arabs remained intact and that discord and rancour never set in.[976]

One is not required to completely overlook their differences with the other to foster unity. Rather, unity can be achieved even after acknowledging that some people share different beliefs and values. Despite Prophet Muhammad(ﷺ)'s efforts to establish a fair and equal society, it is unfortunate that the behaviour of some Muslims today contradicts this practice. The sayings of Prophet Muhammad (ﷺ) and Muslim thinkers of the past lay emphasis on establishing relationships based on what humans have in common, and not on those aspects which could possibly deter us from getting along.

Prophet Muhammad (ﷺ) is known to have bred a unique system of brotherhood, which is well documented in the history of Islam. Such was his emphasis on brotherhood that it set a precedent for other nations on how to integrate their minorities, ethnic or otherwise. Dutch scholar Snouck Hurgronje states:

> *The League of Nations founded by the prophet of Islam put the principle of international unity and human brotherhood on such universal foundations as to show candle [sic] to other nations. ... the fact is that no nation of the world can show a parallel to what Islam has done towards the realization of the idea of the League of Nations.*[977]

Reverend Dr Murray Thurston Titus, an American missionary in India especially known for encouraging understanding between Christians and Muslims, felt that Islam is a religion which encourages unity amongst all; it is not only a religion but a social, spiritual and legal system in the society which unites all irrespective of colour, race, status, walks, nationality etc.[978]

The Muslim contribution to British society did not go unrecognised by Prime Minister David Cameron. He recognised the values and overall message of the Eid festival when he said:

> *As families and friends come together in celebration, I want to recognise the immense contribution that British Muslims make to*

our country…Peace and unity are the spirit of Eid and I am proud of the way Britain has demonstrated these values to the world during the Olympics…So to Muslims around the world on this very important day of celebration, I wish you all a very happy and peaceful Eid.[979]

There is an underlying unity among Muslims, and this was true historically as it is today. This unity owes a lot to the fact that in Islam, religion and politics are considered to be one harmonious whole, as a result, religion features prominently in the everyday affairs of Muslims. With social practices rooted in faith, Islam is a current which permeates right through the heart of Muslim society, which helps foster a sense of unity based on religion. According to Dr N.K. Singh:

This reflects the social solidarity of the Muslim community. This solidarity is expressed in the historical fact that in Islam, State and Church are one and the same; the political power goes together with the religious sanctions. It introduces between the social structure and the value system of the Islamic society a remarkable degree of concomitancy and synchronism. Nevertheless, the personal nature of the Islamic faith is the primary factor of which the social solidarity is a derivative.[980]

The Reverend A. Peacock praised Prophet Muhammad (ﷺ) for his dedicated and very effective services to polytheists or infidels as the Prophet (ﷺ) guided them towards monotheism and united them under one brotherhood:

What is there with his life and example that the Christians appreciate? The first thing to appreciate seems to me his deep insight and courage. Muhammad found himself in a world wherein religion was prevalent. Men were either worshipping many gods or no God. Standards were low.… Against this irreligion and this irresponsibility in living, Muhammad spoke vigorously… He (Muhammad) dedicated himself to the building up of the brotherhood of Islam. Muhammad realised that if there was one

God and one God only, there could be but one humanity. His vision was of a world brotherhood uniting all men of goodwill in the one God and one humanity. Further, Muhammad had the insight to stress that while religious disciplines and ceremonies may have a place in the religious life, it was fatal if such disciplines and ceremonies were seen but as ends in themselves. He presented to his people a concept of faith and belief that was simple in its expression, though profound in its basic concepts. He stressed the value of both individual and corporate prayer.[981]

The author mentions that in a famous reported tradition, Prophet Muhammad (ﷺ) articulated the very nature of brotherhood and closeness which humans should feel for one another. The main principle underlying this bond is equality for all, irrespective of race. Islamic rituals such as prayer reflect this spirit of fraternity, as Muslims from all backgrounds are required to stand side by side, feet to feet and shoulder to shoulder in an act of unwavering unity and solidarity before God. Another aspect of Islamic faith which enshrines brotherhood and equality is that there is no clergy or priesthood in the religion. All, regardless of rank, are accountable and equal before Allah. In addition to this, it is a Qur'anic commandment to unite the ranks of Muslims for the sake of God. The factionalism which cut across Arabia was condemned and eradicated by Prophet Muhammad (ﷺ).[982]

By contrast with the West with its rampant secularism, Muslim societies, historically speaking, upheld the union between the religious and the temporal realms, and this helped to cement the ties of brotherhood among Muslims. W.C. Smith writes:

It is well-known that Muslim society has remarkable solidarity, that the loyalty and cohesion of its members are intense. Many have recognised that the community is not only a social group but a religious body; that Church and state are one, to use the inappropriate language of the West. Yet, to stress these facts, to insist upon the centrality of society is not to deny but to interpret our initial emphasis on religion as personal.[983]

Prophet Muhammad (ﷺ) was a very strong advocate of unity and solidarity. This principle is reflected in the Qur'an, which states that man is by nature inclined to peace and tranquillity with others and disposed against violence. Prophet Muhammad (ﷺ) was very vocal in condemning war and unjustified violence. According to Major Arthur Leonard:

And above all things, this Statesman Prophet was the essence and personification of centralization and concord. For unity alone rendered Islam feasible. Thus in the second Surah he insists that mankind was of one faith from the beginning. Thus too as a just, faithful and consistent man, he is opposed to violence and taking the offensive, even in the name and under the cloak of religion; he constantly advocates and authorizes (that is, has God's authority for) the defensive. He even recommends, at the same time that he excuses, war and retaliation on the unbeliever and infidel. On the whole, however, I am bound to admit that Mohammed disapproves of and discountenances violence in religion.[984]

Dr Julius Germanus, an Hungarian Professor of Oriental studies and Islamologist, stated that Prophet Muhammad (ﷺ) had established links with numerous people from diverse social backgrounds and preached the religion of Islam:

Islam in its glorious march has connected millions of people who lived in quite different regions and quite different social and economical environments than the Arabs among whom the Prophet first preached the Qur'an. Islam has proved the most perceptive religion, as in its onward march retaining and strictly clinging to the ethic fundamentals of the revelation has amalgamated in itself all the requirements of the times in order to serve the spiritual needs of its adherents. We may boldly say that God has not created mankind for Islam, but He revealed Islam to serve the moral and spiritual needs of its believers.[985]

Historian H.A.R Gibb noticed that, although there are divisions in Islamic school of thoughts, its followers take a uniform path and a strong brotherhood is found amongst Muslims.[986]

The celebrated author Barnaby Rogerson highlights that Prophet Muhammad (ﷺ) had always taken non-Muslims as friends and encouraged everybody to live cohesively in a society where people from other faiths also lived.[987]

British politician Norman Lamont discerns in Islam a potential to remind others how central religion is as an organisational principle for life's affairs:

> *I personally think Islam enriches Britain. In a society where we have lost sight of God, it is good to be reminded that millions of people in the world still live their lives by religion.*[988]

Tolstoy was very impressed by the Prophet Muhammad (ﷺ), because he was selected by One God to preach His last message as the last Prophet with the acknowledgment of other former Prophets. The main aim of the mission was to build a global society, including the entire humanity:

> *I am one of those who are very much impressed by the Prophet Muhammad who was chosen by the One God to have His last message revealed through his soul, heart and mind. He chose him to be the last prophet; hence, no other prophets would come after him. His acknowledgement of the prophets, who had been sent by God before him to produce the global social building for which Muhammad had been sent to complete, is indubitable evidence that he came with Islam to conclude the social building for the entire humanity everywhere.*[989]

Global Vision

Leo Tolstoy, the Russian author, essayist, novelist and philosopher acknowledges that Prophet Muhammad(ﷺ)'s prophetic responsibilities entailed looking after the community's wellbeing:

> *His acknowledgement of the prophets, who had been sent by God before him to produce the global social building for which Muhammad had been sent to complete, is indubitable evidence that he came with Islam to conclude the social building for the entire humanity everywhere.*[990]

It can be gleaned from the Prophet's teachings that he advocated the values of self-sacrifice and a giving spirit to mankind at large, which manifested itself in brotherhood. The Indian Prime Minister, Dr Manmohan Singh, when greeting the nation on the occasion of the Prophet's birthday in 2011 remarked:

> *The birth and life of the Prophet symbolizes a message of selflessness, brotherhood and amity among people.*[991]

Similarly, the prime minister noted in 2012 on the birthday of the Prophet (ﷺ) that the Prophet's teachings are universal and will always motivate us to support the poor:

> *Prophet Mohammed's teachings are timeless. They will always inspire us to strive for the uplift of the poor and the downtrodden.*[992]

Prime Minister Singh added:

> *May the festival of compassion spread peace, tolerance and brotherhood amongst all.*[993]

The twelfth President of India, Srimati Prativa Patil, also greeted the nation on the occasion of the birthday of the Prophet Muhammad (ﷺ). She wished that the teachings of the Prophet (ﷺ) would lead all to be united together. She said:

> *May the message of service to humanity as taught by the Holy Prophet lead all of us to unity and fellowship.*[994]

The Prime Minister of Fiji, Commodore Josaia Voreqe Bainimarama urged the people of his country in a speech on the birthday of the Prophet Muhammad (ﷺ) to be united with the Muslims in celebrating the Prophet's teachings of love, cooperation, social justice and equality amongst all mankind. The Prime Minister said:

> *But as a people and a nation of many faiths, we Fijians understand that the teachings of our many religions are interconnected; that they cherish and uphold many of the same values and virtues. In this way, we see religion as a bridge, not a barrier. So today, I ask each of us to join with our Muslim brothers and sisters in celebrating the Prophet Muhammad's teachings of love, understanding, social justice and equality amongst all people.*[995]

The Prime Minister also pointed to the prophetic teachings on social unity, responsibilities for neighbours, etc:

> *The celebration of his birth therefore is not only a wonderful opportunity to reflect on the universality of these principles, but it is also a time to consider the special role that faith plays in each of our lives and in the lives of our neighbours. Above all, it is an opportunity for us to appreciate the responsibility we hold to each other. We are reminded to reflect on the values and principles that we all share and on our common goal of advancing peace and prosperity for all Fijians.*[996]

Annemarie Schimmel pays high tribute to Prophet Muhammad (ﷺ) for his teachings on peace among all. One of the Prophet's followers asked him what the best thing in Islam was. He answered that the best thing in Islam is to feed the hungry and to extend peace to everybody.[997]

HRH Prince Charles says that in order to maintain the climate of tolerance for Muslims, the onus is on the majority non-Muslim population to maintain a respectful attitude towards Muslims and not to engage in any provocation. Of course, this works both ways. Muslims are expected to treat non-Muslims with the highest level of compassion and understanding, as well as gratitude for the host community's hospitality:

> *For those of us who are not Muslim, that may mean respect for the daily practice of the Islamic faith and a decent care to avoid actions which are likely to cause deep offence. For the Muslims in our society, there is the need to respect the history, culture, and way of life of our country, and to balance their vital liberty to be themselves with an appreciation of the importance of integration in our society. Where there are failings of understanding and tolerance, we have a need, on our own doorstep, for greater reconciliation among our own citizens. I hope we shall all learn to demonstrate this as understanding between these communities grows.*[998]

The Prince adds that promoting greater understanding between Muslims and non-Muslims requires efforts on the part of both Islamic and non-Islamic countries to cooperate across many fronts, such as trade, education, etc. This requires a determination to do away with any hostility which countries and civilisations may have had throughout history. Once again, tolerance is the key principle here and it requires both sides to pull their weight and make a genuine effort for a harmonious society. According to him:

> *One excellent example of our two cultures working together in a common cause is the way in which the Kingdom of Saudi Arabia is working with Oxford University to set up a research centre into schizophrenia for an organization called SANE, of which I am Patron. Nor can we afford to revive the territorial and political confrontations of the past. We have to share experiences, to explain ourselves to each other, to understand and tolerate - and I know how difficult these things are - and build on those positive principles which our two cultures have in common. That trade has to be two-*

way. Each of us needs to understand the importance of conciliation, of reflection - tadabbur is the word, I believe - to open our minds and unlock our hearts to each other. I am utterly convinced that the Islamic and the Western worlds have much to learn from each other. Just as the oil engineer in the Gulf may be European, so the heart transplant surgeon in Britain may be Egyptian.[999]

The Prince further says that one of Islam's unique characteristics is to view man and nature as an integrated whole, and the idea that our actions and lifestyle are guided by a higher spirit may be a welcome addition to the current thought patterns and practices in the Western world, which is clearly suffering from a spiritual void. Many Christians who can identify with this philosophy will see it in their interests to cooperate with Muslims for the greater good:

At the heart of Islam is its preservation of an integral view of the Universe. Islam - like Buddhism and Hinduism - refuses to separate man and nature, religion and science, mind and matter, and has preserved a metaphysical and unified view of ourselves and the world around us. At the core of Christianity there still lies an integral view of the sanctity of the world, and a clear sense of the trusteeship and responsibility given to us for our natural surroundings. In the words of that marvellous seventeenth-century poet and hymn writer, George Herbert:

A man that looks on glass,
On it may stay his eye;
Or if he pleaseth, through it pass,
And then the heaven espy.[1000]

George Bernard Shaw argued that the present world needs leaders like Prophet Muhammad (ﷺ) for genuine peace and unity. It is Prophet Muhammad (ﷺ) who can solve the present crises of the world and bring happiness in the world. Shaw claimed:

I believe that if a man like him were to assume the dictatorship of the modern world he would succeed in solving its problems in a way that would bring it the much needed peace and happiness: I have prophesied about the faith of Muhammad that it would be acceptable to the Europe of tomorrow as it is beginning to be acceptable to the Europe of today [1001]

Global Peace

We have noted that the world politicians, religious leaders, academics, professors, teachers, historians, sociologists, scientists, biographers, writers, authors, poets, Christian priests, Hindu pandits, Sikh Gurus, Buddhist monks, Jewish Rabbis, etc., have proclaimed in one voice that the teachings and the guidance of Prophet Muhammad (ﷺ), the Holy Book 'the Qur'an' and the religion 'Islam' do encourage living peacefully like brothers of a family, irrespective of the differences due to faiths, nationalities, cultures, colours or any others factors. Every individual belongs to one class which is 'humankind'. Whoever lives in a neighbourhood, Prophet Muhammad (ﷺ) has asked his followers to take care of forty families to his right and forty to his left. By following the prophetic teaching, 'every Muslim family care' for the neighbours can ultimately build the entire neighbourhood.

SELECT BIBLIOGRAPHY

A needful Caveat", appended to the translation of the Alcoran of Mahomet, by Ross, 16

Ahmad, Fazl. Muhammad, The Holy Prophet, Lahore: Ashraf, 1960. Ahmed, Akbar. Discovering Islam: Making Sense of Muslim History and Society Routledge, an imprint of Taylor & Francis Books Lt. 1989

Ahmed, Akbar. Islam Under Siege: Living Dangerously in a Post-honor World (Themes for the 21st Century S.), Polity Press, 2003

Ahmed, Akbar. Postmodernism and Islam: Predicament and Promise, Routledge, an imprint of Taylor & Francis Books Lt, 2004

Ahmed, Akbar. Islam Today: A Short Introduction to the Muslim World, I.B. Tauris, 1998

Akram, Ayesha "What's behind Muslim cartoon outrage". San Francisco Chronicle. http://sfgate.com/cgi-bin/article.cgi?file=/c/a/2006/02/11/MNGRCH6UQK1.DTL.

(2006-02-11). Ali, Muhammad. The Living Thoughts of the Prophet Muhammad London: Cassell, 1947.

Ali, Syed Ameer. A Critical of the Life and Teachings of Mohammed. Amin, Muhammad (ed.). The Sayings of Prophet Muhanamad. Lahore: Lion Press, 1960.

Andrae, Tor. Mohammed: The Man and His Faith, translated by Theophil Menzel. Books, 1971.

Armstrong, Karen. Muhammad: A Western Attempt to Understand Islam. London: Victor Gollancz ltd. 1991

Berkey, Jonathan, The Formation of Islam: Religion and Society in the Near East, 600-1800, Cambridge University Press, p. 64.

Brewer's Dictionary of Phrase and Fable, "Termagant"

Bryman, Alan. Social Research Methods. Oxford University Press, 2012

Cesari, Jocelyne. Muslims and the Republic: Youth, Islam and France, 1998

Cesari, Jocelyne, co-authored with Bernard Botiveau. Gopolitique des islams (Geopolitics of Islam), 1997

Cesari, Jocelyne. When Islam and Democracy Meet: Muslims in Europe and in the United States Palgrave Macmillan, 2004

Chopra, Deepak: Muhammad: The Story of the Last Prophet. New York: Harper Collins, 2010.

Daniel, Norman. Islam and the West: The Making of an Image. Oneworld Publications, 2009

Denison, John Hopkins. Emotion as the Basis of Civilization. New York; London: Charles Scribner's Sons, 1928.

Draycott, Gladys M. Mohomet Founder of Islam. New York: Dodd, Mead and Co. 1916.

Draz, Muhammad 'Abd Allah. "Muhammad" in Islam: The Straight Path, ed. by T. H. Weir. Edinburgh: J. Grant, 1923.

Emil Dermenghem, The Life of Mahomet, translated by Arabella, Yorke, New York: The Dial Press, 1930

Encyclopaedia Britannica Online. Sinnite. Encyclopaedia Britannica, INC. Retrieved 2007-04-11

Ernst, Carl. Following Muhammad: Rethinking Islam in the Contemporary World. University of North Carolina Press, 2004

Ernst, Carl. Following Muhammad, Rethinking Islam in the Contemporary World, Universityof North Carolina Press, 2003

Esposito, John. Political Islam: Revolution, Radicalism or Reform, Lynne Rienner Publishers, 1997

Esposito, John. Islam, The Straight Path. , Oxford University Press; 3rd edition. 1997

Esposito, John. Islam: The Straight Path. Oxford University Press, 1998.

Esposito, John. The Islamic Threat: Myth Or Reality?. Oxford University Press, 1999

Esposito, John. What Everyone Needs to Know About Islam, Oxford University Press, 2002

Esposito, John. Unholy War: Terror in the Name of Islam, Oxford University Press, USA, 2003

Firestone,Reuven Jihad: the origin of holy war in Islam ,1999

Foster, H. Frank. "An Autobiography of Mohammed," The Moslem World, XXVI (1936), 130-152.

Gibbon, Edward. 'The Decline and Fall of the Roman Empire'. London: John Murray, 1838-1839

Gulick, Robert. Muhammad, the Educator. Lahore: Institute of Islamic Culture, 1953.

Hilliard, Frederick Hadaway. The Buddha, the Prophet, and the Christ. London and Hippler,

Jochen and Lueg, Andrea. The Next Threat, Western Perceptions of Islam, Pluto Press Ltd,1995

Jeffery, Arthur. Islam: Muhammad and His Religion. New York: Liberal Arts Press, 1958

Johnstone, P. De Lacy. Muhammad and His Power. New York: Charles Scribner's Sons, 1901.

Justo Perez de Urbe, A Saint under Moslem rule: [a narrative of Moslem rule in the days of St. Eulogius of Cordova] / Trans. by a Benedictine of Stanbrook Abbey, Worcester, England; Adapted by the editor, [J. Husslein]., Milwaukee : Bruce Pub. Co., 1937

Kennedy, Pringle. At the Time? Mohammad'. Calcutta, India, 1966

Kenneth Meyer Setton. "Western Hostility to Islam and Prophecies of Turkish Doom". DIANE Publishing. July 1992

Khan, Muhammad Mojlum. The Muslim 100. UK. Kube Publishing

Ltd. 2010

Lacy, Norris J. Lancelot-Grail: The Old French Arthurian Vulgate and Post-Vulgate in Translation, Volume 1 of 5. New York: 1992

Lewis, Bernard, The Arabs in History.

Lewis, Bernard. The Crisis of Islam: Holy War and Unholy Terror. Random House, 2004

Lundequistska Bokhandeln, 1955. ?

Madison: University of Wisconsin Press, 1970. ?

Mahomet and His Successors, edited by Henry A. Pochmann and E. N. Feltskog.

Margoliouth, D. S. Mohammed and the Rise of Islam. London: G. P. Putnam's Sons, 1905.

Maundeville, John. The voyages and travels of Sir John Maundeville: Cassell and Co, 1909.

Merrick, J. L. (tr.). Life and Religion of Mohammed as Contained in the Sira.

Muhammad the Prophet. Lahore: Ahmadiyya Anjuman-i-Isha'at-iIslam, 1933.

"Muhammad", Encyclopedia of Islam Online

Muir, Sir William. The Life of Mohammad from Original Sources.

Nahim, Hassan A. The Division After Muhammad. Published in USA 2012 Neuman, W Lawrence. Social Research Methods: Qualitative and Quantitative Approaches.Pearson, 2010 New York: Barnes and Noble, 1957. ? New York: G. Allen and Unwin and Macmillan, 1956. ?

Pike, Edgar Royston. Mohammed, Prophet of the Religion of Islam. 2nd ed.; London: Weidenfeld, 1968.

Polo, Marco. The Travels Of Marco Polo. Translated by William Marsden London, 1828.

Poole, Elizabeth. Reporting Islam: Media Representations of British

Muslims, I.B. Tauris, 2002.

Promoting Christian Knowledge; and New York: Pott, Young, and Co., 1877. ?

Reeves, Minou. Muhammad in Europe: A Thousand Years of Western Myth-Making. NYU Press 2003.

Richardson, Robin. Islamophobia - issues, challenges and action, Trentham Books, 2004.

Rodinson, Maxime. Mohammed, translated by Anne Carter. New York: Pantheon

Roger of Wendover's Flowers of history / translated from the Latin by J. A. Giles. Vol.2. Part 2, 1215-1235.

Sahas, Daniel J. John of Damascus on Islam: The 'Heresy of the Ishmaelites.' Leiden: Brill, 1972.

Said, Edward W. Orientalism. Penguin. 2003.

Said, Edward. Covering Islam: How the Media and the Experts Determine. How We See the Rest of the World, Vintage, 1996

Schimmel, Annemarie. Islam: An Introduction. SUNY Press, 1992
Schimmel, Annemarie. Mystische Dimensionen des Islam. Insel, Frankfurt.

Serjeant,R. B. "Sunnah Jami'ah, pacts with the Yathrib Jews, and the Tahrim of Yathrib: analysis and translation of the documents comprised in the so-called 'Constitution of Medina'", Bulletin of the School of Oriental and African Studies (1978), 41: 1-42.

Shaheen, Jack., Arab and Muslim Stereotyping in American Popular Culture, Georgetown University Center for Muslim,1997

Smith, Reginald Bosworth. Mohammed and Mohammedanism, lectures delivered at

Sprenger, Aloys. Life of Mohammad from Original Sources. Allahabad, 1851.

Stobart, James William Hampson. Islam and Its Founder. London: Society for Promoting Christian Knowledge; New York : E. & J.B. Young, 1895)

Stubbe, Henry (Dr). An Account of the Rise and Progress of Mahometanism. London: Luzuc & Co. 1911.

The Spirit of Islam, A History of the Evolution and Ideals of Islam with a Life of The Travels of Sir John Mandeville.

The Poems of William Dunbar (Assoc. For Scottish Lit. Studies: Glasgow, 1998).

Theophanes the Confessor (trans. Cyril Mango and Roger Scott). The Chronicle of Theophanes Confessor: Byzantine and Near Eastern History AD 284-813. Oxford: Clarendon Press, 1997

Traditions of the Hyat-ul-Kuloob. Boston: Phillips, 1850.

Turner, William. "Raymond Lully." The Catholic Encyclopaedia. New York: Robert Appleton, 1914

Walter Emil Kaegi, Jr., "Initial Byzantine Reactions to the Arab Conquest", Church History, Vol. 38, No. 2 (June, 1969), p. 139-149, p.139-142, quoted from Doctrina Jacobi nuper baptizati p 86-87

Watt, W. Montgomery Muhammad: Prophet and Statesman. Oxford University Press, 1974.

Watt, William Montgomery. Muhammad at Makkah. Oxford: Clarendon Press, 1960.

Widengren, George. Muhammad, the Apostle of God, and His Ascension.

Uppsala: Willan, Philip "Al-Qaida plot to blow up Bologna church fresco". The Guardian

http://arts.guardian.co.uk/news/story/0,11711,742914,00.html. 2002-06-24).

Wisdom of Muhammad. Lahore: Lion Press, 1960. Wolfe, Michael. Taking Back Islam, Rodale Press, 2003

Zimmerman, Seth. The Inferno of Dante Alighieri. Universe. 2003

REFERENCES

[1]http://www.brainyquote.com/quotes/authors/w/william_makepeace_thacker.h tml

[2] Denison, John Hopkins. *Emotion as the Basis of Civilization*. New York; London: Charles Scribner's Sons, 1928.p 269

[3] Edward Gibbon (1737 - 1794) was an English historian and Member of Parliament. His mostimportant work, *The History of the Decline and Fall of the Roman Empire*, was published in six volumes between 1776 and 1788

[4] Rogerson, Barnaby. *The Prophet Muhammad: A Biography*. London: Little Brown Book Group. 2011

[5] Rai, Anita. *Muhammad: Uncovering the true story*. London: Starsighter ltd. 2006

[6] Glubb, Sir John. *The life and Times of Muhammad*. England: Madison Books, 1998

[7] Karen Armstrong. *Muhammad: Prophet for our time*. London: Harper Perennial, 2007

[8] Watt, W Montgomery. *Muhammad: Prophet and Statesman*. Oxford: Oxford University press, 1961

[9] Rogerson, Barnaby. *The Prophet Muhammad: A Biography*. London: Little Brown Book Group, 2011

[10] Glubb, Sir John. *The life and Times of Muhammad*. England: Madison Books, 1998

[11] Irving, Washinton. *The Life of Muhammad* Bernh. Tauchnitz Jun, 1850

[12] Rodinson, Maxime. *Muhammad, New York*: Alfred a Knopf, 1980

[13] Hart, Michael H: *The 100: A ranking of the Most Influential Persons in History*. New York. Carol Publishing Group, 1989, P33

[14] Ibid, p39

[15] Ibid

[16] Ibid, p40

[17] Liu Chai-Lien. *The Arabian Prophet: A Life of Mohammed from Chinese and Arabic Sources*. Published in 1921, p4

[18] Ibid

[19] Brown, K and Palmer, M. *The Essential Teachings of Islam*. London, Arrow Books Limited, 1987

[20] Renan, Ernest wrote in 1851, as in Robert Spencer, *The Truth About Muhammad.* US, Regnery Publishing, 1962, p20

[21] Bainimarama, Commodore Josaia Voreqe, Prime Minister, Fiji. *Prophet Muhammad's message for Prophet Prophet Muhammad birthday.* Fiji Sun, January 28, 2013. http://www.fijisun.com.fj/?p=139324,

[22] Mason, Isaac. *The Mohammedans Of China*, 1922, p3

[23] Wu, Hong (the Emperor of China, 1368 - 1398). *http://en.wikipedia.org/wiki/The_Hundred-word_Eulogy*

[24] Thomas Carlyle. *On Heros, Hero-Worship and the Heroic in History.* USA: Press, 184, p43-44

[25] Ibid, p 45

[26] Glubb, Sir John. *The life and Times of Muhammad.* England: Madison Books, 1998

[27] Rai, Anita. *Muhammad: Uncovering the true story.* London: Starsighter Ltd. 2006

[28] Pal, Amit. '*Islam Means Peace'.* USA, Praeger Publishers Inc, 2011, p5

[29] Leonard, Major Arthur Glyn. *Islam: Her Moral and Spiritual Values.* London: Luzac & Co. 1909, p37. Online book: file:///C:/Users/M%20A%20Lais/Desktop/Major%20AG%20Leonard.htm

[30] Ibid, p27

[31] Sell, Edward. *The Life of Muhammad.* Forgotten Books, 1913, p. 94

[32] Chopra, Deepak, *Muhammad: A Story of The Last Prophet.* New York, HarperOne, 2010

[33] Rogerson, Barnaby. *The Prophet Muhammad: A Biography.* England. Little Brown, 2003

[34] Draper, John William, *A History of the Intellectual Development of Europe,* London 1875, Vol.1, pp.329-330

[35] Ibid, p 52-53

[36] Andrae, Tor. *Mohammed: The man and his faith.* New York: Harper and Row, 1936

[37] Ibid

[38] Armstrong, Karen. *Muhammad: A Western Attempt to Understand Islam.* London: Victor Gollancz,1991, p52

[39] Wollaston, Arthur Naylor, *The Sword of Islam.* New York. E T Dutton & Company, 1905, p 1

[40] Ibid

[41] Ibid

[42] Stubbe, Henry (Dr). *An Account of the Rise and Progress of Mahometanism.* London: Luzuc & Co. 911. P211

[43] Das, Rana Bhagwan, as in KHJ Ahmad, Pakistan: Ferozesons, 1983

[44] Ibid 29

[45] Ibid, p50

[46] Sharma, Diwan Chand, *The Prophets of the East,* Calcutta 1935, p. l 22.

[47] Gibbon, Edward and Ockley, Simon. *The Saracens: Their History and the Rise and Fall of their Empire.* Published by Alex, Murray & sons, 1869, p 54

[48] Austin, John, *Muhammad. The Prophet of Allah in T.P.'s and Cassel's Weekly* for 24th September 1927

[49] Ibid

[50] Ibid

[51] Christiaan Snouck Hurgronje, as quoted in *Encyclopaedic Survey of Islamic Culture* (1997) by Mohamed Taher, p. 260

[52] Watt, W Montgomery. *Mohammad At Makkah,* Oxford, 1953

[53] Ibid, p237

[54] Lane-Poole, Stanley. *The story of the Moor Spain.* Republished by Cossimo Classics in 2010.P 2-3

[55] Ibid

[56] Ibid, *The Table Talk of Muhammad,* Online book, page 49

[57] Ibid, p 37

[58] Ibid, Lane Poole, quoted in Introduction to Higgins' *Apology for Mohammad* pp ixxi) (this has already been quoted and analysed in pg 16

[59] Eade, John, Professor, Roehampton University, UK. Interview: February, 2012

[60] Parrinder, Geoffrey - *Mysticism in the World's Religions,* New York: Oxford University Press, 1976.p 121

[61] Ibid. p 93

[62] Ibid, *Mehomet and his successors* New York : G. P. Putnam's Sons, 1881. p192- 93, 199

[63] Michener, James A "Islam: The Misunderstood Religion," *Reader's Digest* (American), May 1955, pp. 68-70

[64] Forlong, J.G.R (Major General) *Short Studies in the Science of Comparative Religions.* London: Bernard Quaritch, 1897, p 488

[65] Montet, Edward, as in Arnold, T.W. *The Preaching of Islam:* A History of the Propagation of the Muslim Faith. London: Constable and Company ltd. 1913. Online Book. P307

[66] Johnson, G Lindsay. *The Two Worlds*, Manchester 1940, 9th August.

[67] Dr Emanuel Deutsch. *The Quarterly Review*, London: 954, p315

[68]Le Bon, Gustave. *The Religion and Life* p67

[69] Le Bon, Gustave. "*Civilization of the Arabs*" p. 115

[70] Davenport, John. *An Apology for Muhammad and The Koran*. London: Dreyden Press, 1882, p1

[71] Carlyle, Thomas, *Muhammad*: *The Hero as Prophet*, England in 1841, p 29-30

[72] Bell, Richard. Introduction to the Qur'an Edited by M Watt. (Edinburgh, 1970), 67 as in Malise Ruthven (2012)

[73] Besant, Annie , *The Life and Teachings of Muhammad* (1932), p. 4

[74] Ibid

[75] Tolstoy, Leo. http://www.islamgate.org/?p=238&upm_export=pdf.This page was exported from - IslamGate. Export date: Sat Jan 26 21:15:45 2013 / +0000 GMT

[76] Ibid

[77] Arnold, Edwin. *Pearls of the Faith* (Preface). Boston. Roberts Brothers, 1883

[78] *Irving,* Washington, *"Mahomet and His Successors".* New York: G.P Putnams and sons, 1868, p 332.

[79] Durant, Will. Translated from Persian. *Islam Faith* Newspaper, p 76

[80] Durant, Will: Excerpts from Will Durant's *The Age of Faith* Pages 162-186 Pub. 1950

[81]Shaw, George Bernard (Sir), in 'The Genuine Islam,' Vol. 1, No. 8, 1936. (The Society of Authors, on behalf of the Bernard Shaw Estate)

[82] Smith, Bosworth, *Mohammed and Mohammedinism* page 75

[83]*Lings, Martin. Muhammad: His life based on the earliest sources.* Cambridge: Islamic Texts Society, 1991, p30

[84] Marston, Elsa. *Muhammed of Makkah: Prophet of Islam.* USA, Franklin Watts, 2001

[85] Ibid

[86] Ibid, p36

[87] Reverend Stephens, as in the Last Law Giver by Mahmood Vanderman, Printed at Premier Press, Secundabad, 1935, p116

[88] Carlyle, Thomas, *On Herons, Hero-Worship and the Heroic in History*. USA: Press, 184, p74

[89] Ibid

[90] Alphonse de Lamartine in *'Historie de la Turquie,'* Paris, 1854. Vol. 11, pp. 276-77. [Translated from *Histoire De La Turquie*, Paris, 1854, vol. II, pp. 276-277]

[91] Ibid

[92] Alphonse de Lamartine in 'Historie de la Turquie,' Paris, 1854. Vol. 11, pp. 276-77. [Translated from *Histoire De La Turquie*, Paris, 1854, vol. II, pp. 276-277

[93] Bodley, R.V.C. *The Messenger*. Double Day and Company Inc, New York 1946. Page 339

[94] Ibid, p9

[95] Sale, George, *The Koran: Commonly called the Al-Koran of Mohammed.* New York: Frederick Warne and co. 1909, p33

[96] Wells, H.G, The Outline of History, Published in 1920, p 269

[97] Vaswani, Sadhu T. L. as in the *Last Law Giver* by Mahmood Vanderman, Printed at Premier Press, Secundabad, 1935,p72-73

[98]Leonard, Arthur Glyn in *Islam, Her Moral and Spiritual Values*, London. Luzac and Co. 1909

[99] Gibbon, Edward. *History of the Decline of and Fall of the Roman Empire*: Vol. 5-50. Chapter L: Description Of Arabia And Its Inhabitants.-Part VI. H. H. Milman, 1845, Online Books: http://www.gutenberg.org/files/25717/25717- h/files/735/735-h/gib5-50.htm#note-1

[100] *Islam, its Moral and Spiritual* Values, p. 9; 1909, London

[101] Rai, Lala Lajpat as in the *Last Law Giver* by Mahmood Vanderman, Printed at Premier Press, Secundabad, 1935,,p74

[102] Davenport, John, *An Apology for Muhammad and The Qur'an*. London: J. Davy & Sons, 1882, p92

[103] Andrae, Tor. *Mohammed: The man and his faith. New York*: Harper and Row, 1936

[104] Sale, George as in Tor Andrae, *Mohammed: the Man and Faith*, 1936

[105] Sale, George, *The Koran: Commonly called the Al-Koran of Mohammed.* New York: Frederick Warne and co. 1909, p32

[106] Rao, K. S. Ramakrishna in *'Mohammed: The Prophet of Islam,'* 1989

[107] Ibid

[108] Ibid

[109] A British Politician (requested to be anonymous), Interviewed in June 13, 2011

[110] Rodwell, John Medows (1808-1900)

[111] Pershad, Maharaja Peshkar Sir Kishen as in *The Last Law Giver* by Vanderman, p69

[112] Reverend Stephens, as in as in *the Last Law Giver* by Mahmood Vanderman, Printed at Premier Press, Secundabad, 1935, p116

[113] Sharma, Sunder Lal, *Glory of Muhammad*. 1941

[114] Royden, Dr Mawde *The Problem of Palestine*, Hutchinson & Co., 1939

[115] Archer, John Clark, *Our Debt to The Muslim Arab, The Muslim World*, Volume 29, Issue 3, pages 248-264, July 1939

[116] Sadhu T. L. Vaswani

[117] Zwemer, Samuel Marinus. *A Canadian Orientalist's speech in Princeton University*, 1929

[118] Nanak, Guru. By S. Piaras Singh as in The Last Law Giver by Mahmood Vanderman, Printed at Premier Press, Secundabad, 1935, p72

[119] Editor, Sat Updaish, Lahore, 7 July 1915; see *Barguzida Rasul Ghairon Main Maqbul*, 12, 13.

[120] Gavin, James, Speeches of a U.S. Army General, h ttp://www.paklink.biz/articles/islam5.html

[121] Forlong, J.G.R (Major General) "*Short Studies in the Science of Comparative Religions*. London: Bernard Quaritch, 1897, p 482

[122] Gandhi, M.K., Preface to *The Sayings of Muhammad* by Abd Allah al-Ma'mun Suhrawardi, 1992

[123] Dr Gokalchand as in *The Last Law* Giver, by Mahmood Vanderman, Printed at Premier Press, Secundabad, 1935, p113

[124] Alphonse de LaMartaine in *'Historie de la Turquie,'* Paris, 1854. Vol. 11, pp. 276-77. [Translated from *Histoire De La Turquie*, Paris, 1854, vol. II, pp. 276-277]

[125] Martin, Alfred. *The Great religious Teachers of the East*, The Macmillan Company, 1911, *p227*

[126] Hardayal, Lala, as *the Glory of Islam* By Mian Abid Ahmad: Lahore, Pakistan: Time Publishers, 1993, p38

[127] Nicholson, Reynold. *A Literary History of the Arabs*, Published in 1907

[128] Muir, William, *Life of Mahomet, 1887*, p 613

[129] Ibid

[130] Johnson, Samuel (Dr), *Glory of Islam* By Mian Abid Ahmad: Lahore, Pakistan: Time Publishers, 1993, p56

[131] Glubb, Sir John. *The life and Times of Muhammad*. England: Madison Books, 1998

[132] Bonaparte, Napoleon, as in KHJ Ahmad. Freedon Act, 1976: Pakistan, Feroze and sons, 1983

[133] Masserman, Jules in "Who Were Histories Great Leaders?" *TIME Magazine*. Monday, July 15, 1974

[134] Peterson, Daniel C (Dr). *Muhammad: Prophet of God.* Wm. B. Eerdmans Publishing Company, USA, 2007

[135] Hitti, P.K. *Makers of ArabHistory.* New York, St. Martins Press, 1968.

[136] Stobart, J.W.H. *Islam and Its Founder.* Published in 1878, p228

[137] Ibid

[138] Johnstone, Pierce De Lacy, *Muhammad and His Power.* UK. T & T Edinburgh, 1901, p225

[139] Adair, John. *The Leadership of Muhammad.* USA & UK, Kohan Page, 2010 p88

[140] Masserman, Jules in "Who Were Histories Great Leaders?" *TIME Magazine*. Monday, July 15, 1974

[141] Lewis, Bernard. *The Crisis of Islam.* Holy war and Unholy Terror. London. Weildenfeld & Nicolson.

[142] Watt, W Montgomery. *Muhammad: Prophet and statesman.* London, Oxford University Press, 1961

[143] Ibid

[144] Marston, Elsa. *Muhammed of Makkah: Prophet of Islam.* USA, Franklin Watts, 2001, p 60.

[145] Ibid

[146] Marston, Elsa. *Muhammed of Makkah: Prophet of Islam.* USA, Franklin Watts, 200, p 114

[147] Kinnock, Neil (Right Honourable) Lord, the former leader of Labour Party, UK. Interview: January, 2012.

[148] Rivorie, George, Visages de L' Islam.

[149] http://islamgreatreligion.wordpress.com/2012/09/25/prophet- muhammad-pbuh-listed-as-greatest-law-giver-of-the-world-in-us-supreme- court/

[150] Boulainvilliers, Henri de as in Tor Andrae, *Mohammed: the Man and Faith,* 1936

[151] Singh, N.K. (Dr), *Islam: A Religion of Peace.* India: Global Vision Publishing House, 2002, p 46

[152] John Alden Williams, *Islam*, Forgotten Books, 1962, p69

[153] Sell, Edward. *The Life of Muhammad.* Forgotten Books, 1913, p94

[154] Forlong, J.G.R (Major General) *Short Studies in the Science of Comparative Religions.* London: Bernard Quaritch, 1897, p 482

[155] Martin, Alfred. *The Great religious Teachers of the East*, The Macmillan Company, 1911, p306

[156] Krishna, Pandit Gopal, as in KHJ Ahmad, Pakistan: Ferozesons, 1983

[157] Muller, Max (Professor) as in Forlong, J.G.R (Major General) *Short Studies in the Science of Comparative Religions*. London: Bernard Quaritch, 1897, p 491

[158] Muir, William. *The life of Muhammad*. 1887

[159] Bodley, R.V.C. *The Messenger*. Double Day and Company Inc, New York 1946

[160] Ibid

[161] Ibid

[162] Ibid

[163] Glubb, Sir John. *The Life and Times of Muhammad*. USA, Madison Books, 1988

[164] Marston, Elsa. *Muhammed of Makkah: Prophet of Islam*. USA, Franklin Watts, 2001

[165] Peterson, Daniel C (Dr). *Muhammad: Prophet of God*. Wm. B. Eerdmans Publishing Company, USA, 2007

[166] Dr Rowell, Geoffrey, Right Reverend. European Diocese, Bishop of Gibraltar in Europe, Interview: London, May, 2011

[167] Haaren, John Henry was an American Educator and Historian. He wrote in his *Famous Men of the Middle Ages* (1904) p.51

[168] Haaren, John Henry was an American Educator and Historian. He wrote in his *Famous Men of the Middle Ages* (1904) p.51

[169] Johnstone, Pierce De Lacy. *Muhammad and His Power*. Forgotten Books, 1901, *P57*

[170] Smith, RB. *Mohammed And Mohammadanism*; Lectures Delivered at the Royal Institution of Great Delivered at the Royal Institution, 1874

[171] Irving, Washington. *The Life of Muhammad*. Bernh. Tauchnitz Jun, 1850. *P 197- 8*

[172] Scott, Samuel Parsons, a lawyer and writer from Hillsboro Ohio, History of the Moorish Empire in Europe (Vol I), attributing all the success of Europe to the prophet Muhammad.

[173] Bodley, R.V.C. *The Messenger*. Double Day and Company Inc, New York 1946

[174] Carlyle, Thomas, *On Herons, Heroes-Worship and the Heroic in History*. USA: Press, 184, p74

[175] Park, Mung, as " in the *Last Law Giver* by Mahmood Vanderman, Printed at Premier Press, Secundabad, 1935, p124

[176] Tolstoy, Leo. http://www.islamgate.org/?p=238&upm_export=pdf.This page was exported from - IslamGate. Export date: Sat Jan 26 21:15:45 2013 / +0000 GMT

[177] Denison, J. H. *Emotion as the Basis of Civilization*. Harvard University, 1928, p266-9

[178] H.A.R. Gibb. *Muhammedanism.* USA, Oxford University Press, 1953

[179] Rai, Anita. *Muhammad: Uncovering the True Story.* London, Starsighter Ltd, 2006

[180] Sell, Edward. *The Life of Muhammad.* Forgotten Books, 1913, p229-230

[181] Vaswani, Professor T.L.. *The Spirit and Struggle s Islam.* Published by Ganesh & sons, Madras, 1921, p13

[182] Sarton, George. *The Civilization of the Renaissance* (Chicago, 1929); *Six Wings: Men of Science in the Renaissance* (Bloomington, 1957); and *The Appreciation of AncienSt and Medieval Science during the Renaissance,* 1450-1600 (Philadelphia, 1955)

[183] Hughes, Thomas Patrick. *Notes on Muhammadanism.* Forgotten Books, 2012. P4-5

[184] Sale, George, *The Koran: Commonly called the Al-Koran of Mohammed.* New York: Frederick Warne and co. 1909, p42

[185] Dods, Marcus, Dr., *Muhammad, Buddah, and Christ,* p 17

[186] Bodley, R.V.C. *The Messenger.* Double Day and Company Inc, New York 1946. Page 339

[187] Savary, Claude- Etienne, as in Tor Andrae, *Mohammed: the Man and Faith,* 1936

[188] Russell, Bertrand *in Reflection on re-awakening East,* Published in Pakistan Quarterly, Vol 4, No.3, 1954, p4-7

[189] Watt, W Montgomery. *Muhammad: Prophet and Statesman.* London, Oxford University Press, 1961

[190] Geothe, JWV.Noten und *Abhandlungen zum Weststlichen Dvan,* WA I, 7, 32

[191] Ibid

[192] Hart, Michael H: *The 100: A ranking of the Most Influential Persons in History.* New York. Carol Publishing Group, 1989

[193] Cook, Michael. *Muhammad.* London, Oxford University Press, 1983

[194] Gilman, Arthur. *The story of the Saracens, from the earliest times to the fall of Bagdad,* London, T. Fisher Unwin, p *75*

[195] Ibid, p184

[196] Leitner, GW (Dr), *Muhammadanism as in the Quarterly Message,* March, 2002, p7

[197] Andrae, Tor. *Mohammed The Man And His Faith.* New York, Harper and Row, 1960

[198] Walid. A Saleh. The *Cambridge Companion to Muhammad. Edited by Jonathan E. Brockopp.* UK, Cambridge University Press, 2010.

[199] Zwemer, Samuel Marinus. *Islam, A Challenge to Faith; Studies on Mohammadan Religion And.* Forgotten Books, 2012, p52

[200] David Kerr, *Prophet Muhammad in Christian Theological Perspectives: Islam in a world of diverse faiths*. Edited by Dan Cohn-Sherbok, London, MacMillan, 1991

[201] Ibid

[202] Singh, Sarder Diwan, as in KHJ Ahmad, Pakistan: Ferozesons, 1983

[203] Marston, Elsa. *Muhammed of Makkah: Prophet of Islam.* USA, Franklin Watts, 2001, p37

[204] Alfred Martin (1911), *Great Religious Teachers of the East.* New York. The MacMillan Company, P246-248

[205] Smith, Bosworth, *Mohammed and Mohammedinism* page 81

[206] Kaltner, John. *Islam: "What Non-Muslims should Know".* USA, Fortress Press, 2003

[207] Irving, Washington. *The Life of Muhammad.* Bernh. Tauchnitz Jun, 1850. *P 199*

[208] Armstrong, HC, *Lord of Arabia, A Biography of Abdul Aziz bin Saud*, GB, 1939

[209] Karl Marx, http://www.radioislam.org.za/a/index.php?option=com_content&task=view&id=16316&Itemid=143

[210] Weber, as in Peterson, Daniel C (Dr). *Muhammad: Prophet of God.* Wm. B. Eerdmans Publishing Company, USA, 2007

[211] Freedman as in Peterson, Daniel C (Dr). *Muhammad: Prophet of God.* Wm. B. Eerdmans Publishing Company, USA, 2007

[212] Roy, MN. An essay on Islamic Culture: *The Historical Role of Islam*, Published in 1939, pp. 4-5

[213] Ratnam, Vankata, *An Essay on Islam*, with illustrations, by M. Venkata Ratnam. Madras. 1922 pp. 208

[214] Carlyle, Thomas, *Muhammad: The Hero as Prophet,* England in 1841, p 29-30

[215] Martin, Alfred. *The Great Religious Teachers of the East,* The Macmillan Company, 1911*p 265*

[216] Richmond, Danny, Faith Act Manager, Tony Blair Faith Foundation. Interview: February 2012

[217] Gandhi, MK, *Young India* (periodical), 1928, Volume X

[218] Alfred Martin , *Great Religious Teachers of the East.* New York. The MacMillan Company, 1911, p 232-233

[219] Ibid *p238-239*

[220] Ibid 264-265

[221] Davenport, John. *An Apology for Muhammad and the Qur'an*, 1882, p52

[222] Rao, Professor Ramakrishna, "*Islam and Modern Age*"

[223] *Irving,* Washington, *"Mahomet and His Successors*". New York: G.P Putnams and sons, 1868, p 332. Online book

[224] *Irving,* Washington, "*Mahomet and His Successors*". New York: G.P Putnams and sons, 1868, p 332. Online book

[225] Johnstone, Pierce De Lacy. *Muhammad and His Power.* Forgotten Books, 1901, *P149-150*

[226] Johnson, Dr Samnal as in the *Glory of Prophet Muhammad* **(ﷺ)** by Mian Abid Ahmad

[227] Shaw G.B., THE GENUINE ISLAM, Singapore Vol. 1, No. 8, 1936(The Society of Authors, on behalf of the Bernard Shaw Estate)

[228] Leronge, Raymond. *Life de Mehomet.* Publisher Fasquelle, 1939

[229] Hogarth, David George *(1862-1927)? Oxford* Arabia, Oxford, 1922, p. 52

[230] Schimmel, Annemarie. *And Muhammad is His Messenger: The Veneration of the Prophet in Islamic Piety.* USA, University of North Carolina, 1985.

[231] Ibid

[232] Ibid

[233] bid

[234] Adair, John. *The Leadership of Muhammad.* USA & UK, Kohan Page, 2010, p88

[235] Ibid, p89

[236] Satillan, De David. *The Legacy of Islam.*

[237] Leitner, GW (Dr), *Muhammadanism as in the Quarterly Message,* March, 2002, p5

[238] Sir William Muir - *Life of Mohammad.,* Cornwell University, 1878

[239] Chazali, !hya 'ulum a! Din 2:300-44, tr. Leo Zolondek (Leiden: Brill, 1963), cited by Schimmel, 31 as in Malise Ruthven, Islam: A very short Introduction, (2012)

[240] Singh, N.K (Dr), *Islam: A Religion of Peace.* India: Global Vision Publishing House, 2002, p 4

[241] Ibid, p148

[242] Singh, N.K (Dr), *Islam: A Religion of Peace.* India: Global Vision Publishing House, 2002, p 4

[243] Smith. R. Bosworth. *Lecture on Muhammad and Muhammadism* at Royal Institution of Great Britain. 1874. Online book, page 94-95

[244] Ibid, p235

[245] Muir, Willam (Sir) as in Forlong, J.G.R (Major General) "*Short Studies in the Science of Comparative Religions.* London: Bernard Quaritch, 1897, p 473

[246] *And Muhammad Is His Messenger* (Chapel Hill: University of North Carolina Press, 1985), 34 as in Malise Ruthven (2012)

[247] *Irving,* Washington, *"Mahomet and His Successors".* New York: G.P Putnams and sons, 1868, p 332. Online book

[248] Bodley, RVC, *The Messenger*. New York. Double Day INC. 1946, p8

[249] Bodley, RVC, *The Messenger*. New York. Double Day INC. 1946, p338

[250] Smith. R. Bosworth. *Lecture on Muhammad and Muhammadism at Royal Institution of Great* Britain. 1874. Online book, page 94-95

[251] Gibbon, Edward and Ockley, Simon. *The Saracens: Their History and the Rise and Fall of their Empire.* Published by Alex, Murray & sons, 1869, p 44

[252] Irving, Washington. Life of *Muhammad.* Online Book,1850; http://books.google.co.uk/books/about/The_life_of_Mahomet.html?id=Brg9AAAAYAAJ&redir_esc=y

[253] Schimmel, Annemarie. *And Muhammad is His Messenger: The Veneration of the Prophet in Islamic Piety.* USA, University of North Carolina, 1985

[254] John Alden Williams, Islam, *Forgotten Books,* 1962, p73

[255] Dr E.B. Hocking, *The Universal Faith*

[256] Cranston, Ruth. *World Faith.* Ayer Publication and Co. 1949

[257] Gibbon, Edward. *History of the Decline of and Fall of the Roman Empire*: Vol. 5-50. Chapter L: Description Of Arabia And Its Inhabitants.-Part I. H. H. Milman, 1845, Online Books: http://www.gutenberg.org/files/25717/25717-h/files/735/735-h/gib5-50.htm#note-1

[258] Davenport, John. *An Apology for Muhammad and the Qur'an,* Published in 1982.

[259] Marston, Elsa. *Muhammad of Makkah: Prophet of Islam.* USA, Franklin Watts, 200, p90

[260] Irving, Washington. *The Life of Muhammad.* Bernh. Tauchnitz Jun, 1850. *P 197*

[261] Magsie Hamilton Little, *The thing about Islam: Exposing the myths, facts and controversies.* London. Max press. 2012.

[262] Gibbon, Edward and Ockley, Simon. *The Saracens: Their History and the Rise and Fall of their Empire.* Published by Alex, Murray & sons, 1869, p17

[263] Ibid p17

[264] Peterson, Daniel C (Dr). *Muhammad: Prophet of God.* Wm. B. Eerdmans Publishing Company, USA, 2007

[265] Watt, W Montgomery. *Muhammad: Prophet and statesman.* London, Oxford University Press, 1961

[266] Davenport, John. *An Apology for Muhammad and the Qur'an,* 1882.

[267] Gibbon, Edward as in Davenport. *An Apology for Muhammad and the Qur'an,* 1882, p1-12

[268] Lord Headley, Rowland George Allanson - Winn. *A Western Awakening to Islam.* Forgotten Books.*2013, p32*

[269] Bodley, R.V.C. *The Messenger.* Double Day and Company Inc, New York 1946.

[270] Muir, William, Sir; *The Life of Mahomet,* Volume IV, Smith, Elder, & Co., London, 1861

[271] Magsie Hamilton Little, *The thing about Islam: Exposing the myths, facts and controversies.* London. Max press. 2012.

[272] Johnstone, Pierce De Lacy Henry. *Muhammad and His Power.* Forgotten Books, 1901, P148

[273] Singh, N.K(Dr), *Islam: A Religion of Peace.* India: Global Vision Publishing House, 2002, p 5

[274] Ibid p 6

[275] Dods, Marcus, Dr., *Muhammad, Buddah, and Christ*

[276] Harayal, Lala, as in , *'Muhammad: In non-Muslims Eyes'*, 1983,

[277] Harayal, Lala as in KJ Ahmad, 1983, 82

[278] Carlyle, Thomas, *Muhammad: The Hero as Prophet,* England in 1841, p 29-30

[279] Ibid p 123

[280] Nehru, Jawaharlal. *Glimpses of World History.* Delhi: Oxford University Press, 1989, Centennial Edition

[281] Hyndman, M.H. *The Awakening of Asia* 1919 p9

[282] Forlong, J.G.R (Major General) *Short Studies in the Science of Comparative Religions.* London: Bernard Quaritch, 1897, p 482

[283] Andrews, C.F, in the 'The *Third Companion* of *the* Prophet, as in KHJ Ahmad. Pakistan: Ferozesons, 1983

[284] Carlyle, Thomas, as in Tor Andrae, *Mohammed: the Man and Faith*, 1936

[285] Kennedy, Pringle. *At the Time Mohammad'.* Calcutta, India, 1966

[286] Ibid

[287] Sale, George, *The Koran: Commonly called the Al-Koran of Mohammed.* New York: Frederick Warne and co. 1909, pvii

[288] Sir William Muir - *Life of Mohammad.*, Cornwell University, 1878, p326

[289] Phesrisai, Sangthong (Dhamacaro) Buddhist Monk, Buddhist Temple, South London, October, 2011 Interview.

[290] Hoare, Rupert, Reverend. Former Dean of Liverpool Cathedral and Chair of the Council of Faiths, Liverpool, UK. Interview: April, 2012

[291] Bodley, R.V.C. *The Messenger.* Double Day and Company Inc, New York 1946.

[292] Timms, Stephen, Right Honourable, British MP; Interview: London, March, 2012.

[293] Spokesman, Sikh Temple, East London, Interview, November, 2011

[294] Mehta, Piyuskumar, Pandit, Jalaram Hindu Mandir, Greenford, London. Interview: December 2011

[295] Kinnock, Neil (Right Honourable) Lord, the former leader of Labour Party, UK. Interview: January, 2012.

[296] Tailor, Bhavin, RE teacher, William Ellis School, North West London. Interview: March, 2012

[297] Niknam, Mehri, MBE, Executive Director, the Joseph Interfaith Foundation, Camden, London, Interview: February 2012

[298] O'Brien, Thomas (Rev), Our Lady of the Assumption Church, Tower hamlets, London Feb, 2012.

[299] Amess, David (Right Honourable), British MP, UK. Interview: January 2012

[300] Corbyn, Jeremy, Right Honourable British MP. Interview: London March 2012

[301] Ibid

[302] Stygal, Mike. Chairman, Camden Interfaith Foundation, London. Interview: January 2012

[303] Ibid

[304] Haaren, John Henry was an American Educator and Historian. He wrote in his *Famous Men of the Middle Ages* (1904) p.5

[305] Watt, William Montgomery, *Mohammad At Makkah*, Oxford, 1953

[306] *Encyclopaedia Britannica*, Volume 12

[307] Margoliuth, D.S. *Mohammed and Rise of Islam*, London: Putnam and Sons, 1905.

[308] Mills, Charles Stuart. *History of Mohammadanism*, 1818.

[309] Scott, Samuel Parsons. *History of the Moorish Empire in Europe*, J B Lippincot Company, 1904. p. 124-127.

[310] Taylor, W. C. *The History of Mohammedanism and its sects*, John W. Parker, London, 1834.

[311] Weil, Dr Gustav. *History of the Islamic Peoples*, University of Calcutta, 1914

[312] Williams, Stephen, Rev. Senior Anglican Chaplain, University Chaplaincy, University of London. Interview: May, 2012.

[313] Meacher, Michael. Interview: March, 2012.

[314] Ibid

[315] Cranston, Ruth (1949) *'World Faith'*. Pp 138-139. Harper and Row Publishers

, Re printed in 1968

[316] Warren, Ruth, *Muhammad: Prophet of Islam,*: Published by F. W 1965

[317] Warren, Ruth, *Muhammad: Prophet of Islam,*: Published by F. W 1965

[318] Geoffrey, Dr Rowell, , Right Reverend. European Diocese, Bishop of Gibraltar in Europe, Interview: London, May, 2011

[319] Din, Jon Dal, Director, Westminster Interfaith Group, London, Interview: October, 2011

[320] Gill, Shiv Charan Singh, Spokeman, Sikh Temple, Southall,. Interview: London, December 2011

[321] Blunkett, David, Right Honourable, MP (Former Home Secretary), UK. Interview: Jan, 2012

[322] Green, Allen (Father). Tower Hamlets Interfaith Forum, London. Interview: January 2012

[323] Shashoua, Stephen. Director, Three Faiths Foundation, Camden, London. Interview: January 2012

[324] Lamont, Norman, Rt. Hon. Lord, British politician and former Conservative MP and Chancellor of the Exchequer, Interview: January,2012

[325] Charles, HRH Prince. *Lecture Delivered at the Oxford Centre of Islamic Studies, Oxford, Uniskill Ltd., 1993, p15*

[326] A Teacher from a Church of England School, North London (requested anonymity), London. Interview: March, 2012

[327]A Teacher from a Church of England School, North London Interview, March, 2012

[328] Ibid

[329] Quinn, Tom, Father, Shadwell Catholic Church, East London, Interview:January 2012

[330] Irving, Washington. *The Life of Muhammad.* Bernh. Tauchnitz Jun, 1850. *P 199*

[331] Dobson, Frank, Rt. Hon. MP, London. Interview: September 2010

[332] Vaglieri, LV, *'An Interpretation. of Islam'* p 78

[333] Martin, Alfred. *The Great religious Teachers of the East,* The Macmillan Company, 1911, *p263*

[334] Blunkett, David, Right Honourable, MP (Former Home Secretary), UK. Interview: Jan, 2012

[335] Green, Allen (Father). Tower Hamlets Interfaith Forum, London. Interview: January 2012

[336] Kinnock, Neil (Right Honourable) Lord, the former leader of Labour Party, UK. Interview: January, 2012

[337] A Teacher from a Church of England School, North London (requested anonymity), March, 2012

[338] Mehri Niknam MBE, Executive Director, the Joseph Interfaith Foundation, Camden, London, February 2012

[339] Dobson, Frank, Rt. Hon. MP, London. Interview: September 2010

[340] Ibid

[341] Niknam, Mehri, MBE, Executive Director, the Joseph Interfaith Foundation, Camden, London, Interview: February 2012

[342] O'Brein, Reverend Thomas. Bishop of Our Lady of the Assumption Church, East London. Interview February, 2012.

[343] Muller, Max, as Forlong, J.G.R (Major General) *Short Studies in the Science of Comparative Religions*. London: Bernard Quaritch, 1897, p 480

[344] Vaglieri, LV, *'An Interpretation of Islam'* p 72

[345] Gill, Shiv Charan Singh, Spokeman, Sikh Temple, Southall,. Interview: London, December 2011

[346] Marston, Elsa. *Muhammed of Makkah: Prophet of Islam.* USA, Franklin Watts, 2001,

[347] Piyuskumar, Mehta, Pandit Jalaram Hindu Mandir, Greenford, Interview: London: December 2011

[348] Esposito L John, *What everyone needs to know about Islam,* London, University Press, Oxford Esposito 2002, p 14-15

[349] Rai, Anita. *Muhammad: Uncovering the true story.* London: Starsighter Ltd. 2006

[350] Rai, Anita. *Muhammad: Uncovering the true story.* London: Starsighter Ltd. 2006

[351] Farah, Caesar E. *Islam: Beliefs and Observances. P69*

[352] Spokesman from a Sikh Temple in East London, November, 2011 Interview.

[353] Cowie, Reverend John. The English Reformed Church, Amsterdam, Holland. Interview: February, 2012

[354] Blunkett, David. Rt. Hon. British MP and Former Home Secretary. Interview: London, January 2012

[355] Ibid

[356] O'Brein, Reverend Thomas. Bishop of Our Lady of the Assumption Church, East London. Interview February, 2012.

[357] Green Allen,(Father). Chairman, Tower hamlets Interfaith Forum, London. Interview February, 2012

[358] Ibid

[359] Armstrong, Karen. *Muhammad.* London, Victo Gollancz Ltd. 1991

[360] Kinnock, Neil (Right Honourable) Lord, the former leader of Labour Party, UK. Interview: January, 2012.

[361] Ibid

[362] Shashoua, Stephen. Director, Three Faiths Foundation, Camden, London. Interview: January 2012

[363] Vaglieri, LV, '*An Interpretation. of Islam'* p 71

[364] Besant, Annie. *The Life And Teachings Of Muhammad*, Madras, 1932, p. 4

[365] A Teacher from a Church of England School, North London (requested anonymity), March, 2012

[366] Corbyn, Jeremy (Right Honourable), British MP, UK. Interview: March, 2012.

[367] Stygal, Mike. Chairman, Camden Interfaith Foundation, London. Interview: January 2012

[368] Ibid

[369] Harris, Harriet, Reverend (Dr), the Chaplain and honorary Fellow at the school of divinity, Edinburgh University, Interview: May 2012

[370] Nagasawa, Mako. Director and Adviser, Harvard-Radcliffe Christian Fellowship (HRCF), University of Harvard, USA. Interview, April, 2012

[371] Coles, Stephen, Reverend. St. Thomas Church, North London. Interview, February 2012

[372] McCoy, Alban, Father, Cambridge University Catholic Chaplaincy. Interview May 2012

[373] Schimmel, Annemarie. *And Muhammad is His Messenger: The Veneration of the Prophet in Islamic Piety.* USA, University of North Carolina, 1985

[374] Rai, Anita. *Muhammad: Uncovering the true story*. London: Starsighter ltd. 2006

[375] Leitner, GW, *Muhammadanism as in the Quarterly Message*, March, 2002, p8

[376] Singh, N.K(Dr), *Islam: A Religion of Peace.* India: Global Vision Publishing House, 2002, p77

[377] Vaglieri, LV, *An Interpretation of Islam* p 35

[378] Armstrong, Karen: *Muhammed, A Western attempt to understand Islam,* London. Voctor Gollancz ltd, 1991

[379] Cranston, Ruth. *'World Faith'*.. Harper and Row Publishers , Re printed in 1968

[380] Rai, Anita. *Muhammad: Uncovering The Truth.* London, Starsighter Limited, 2006.

[381] Ibid

[382] Mian Abid Ahmad (1993) *The Glory of Prophet Muhammad (SAW).*

[383] Hoare, Rupert, Reverend. Former Dean of Liverpool Cathedral and Chair of the Council of Faiths, Liverpool, UK. Interview: April, 2012

[384] Richmond, Danny. Danny Richmond, Faith Act Manager, Tony Blair Faith Foundation Interview: February 2012

[385] Glubb, Sir John. *The life and Times of Muhammad.* England: Madison Books, 1998

[386] Singh, N.K(Dr), *Islam: A Religion of Peace.* India: Global Vision Publishing House, 2002, p 58

[387] Christian Priest, Church based in East London, Interview: February, 2012.

[388] Williams, Stephen, Reverend. Senior Anglican Chaplain, University Chaplaincy, University of London, Interview: May 2012

[389] Gill, Shiv Charan Singh, Spokesman, Sikh Temple, Southall, Interview: London December 2011

[390] Tailor, Bhavin, RE teacher, William Ellis School, North West London, Interview March, 2012

[391] Amess, David (Right Honourable), British MP, UK. Interview: January 2012

[392] Vaglieri, LV, '*An Interpretation of Islam*' p 79

[393] Forlong, J.G.R (Major General) *Short Studies in the Science of Comparative Religions.* London: Bernard Quaritch, 1897, p 481

[394] Forlong, J.G.R (Major General) *Short Studies in the Science of Comparative Religions.* London: Bernard Quaritch, 1897, p 481

[395] Shashoua, Stephen, Director, Three Faiths Foundation, Camden, Interview: London, January 2012

[396] A Teacher from a Church of England School, North London, Interview March, 2012

[397] Stygal, Mike, Chairman, Camden Interfaith Foundation, London, Interview January 2012

[398] Lane-Poole as in the *Glory of Prophet Muhammad (SAW)* by Mian Abid Ahmad.

[399] Gandhi, M.K. *Young India* (periodical), 1928, Volume X

[400] Thomas, Bertram, *The Arabs: The Life story of a people who have left this Deep Impress on the World*, 1937

[401] Cranston, Ruth (1949) '*World Faith*'. Harper and Row Publishers, Reprinted in 1968

[402] Dobson, Frank, Right Honourable MP, Labour Party, UK, Interview: London, October 2011

[403] O'Brien, Rev Thomas, Our Lady of the Assumption Church, Tower hamlets, London, Interview Feb, 2012

[404] Priest, Catholic Church, North West London, Interview November 2011.

[405] Mehri Niknam MBE, Executive Director, the Joseph Interfaith Foundation, Camden, London, Interview February 2012

[406] Wells, H.G, *The Outline of History*, Published in 1920, p 270

[407] Levy, Reuben (Professor of Persian at the University of Cambridge). "*The Social Structure of Islam*". Cambridge University Press, 1969

[408] Armstrong, Karen. *Muhammad.* London, Victo Gollancz Ltd. 1991

[409] Ibid.

[410] Gibb, H.A.R.: *"Whither Islam"* London, 1932, p.

[411] Forlong, J.G.R (Major General) *Short Studies in the Science of Comparative Religions.* London: Bernard Quaritch, 1897, p 482

[412] Crabites, Pierre, cited in Allama Sir Abdullah Al-Mamun Al-Suhrawardy, *The Wisdom of Muhammad* (New York: Citadel Press, 2001), p. 20

[413] Ibid

[414] Besant, Annie , *The Life and Teachings of Muhammad* (1932), p. 4

[415] *Bodley, RVC. The Messenger*. Double Day and Company Inc, 1946. Page 227

[416] Roy, M.N. *Historical Role of Islam: An Essay on Islamic Culture.* **Published:** 1939

[417] Ruthven, Malise, *Islam. A very short Introduction*, USA. Oxford University Press 2012

[418] Lamont, Norman, Lord (Baron Lamont of Lerwick), British politician and former Conservative MP and Chancellor of the Exchequer. Interview: January, 20012

[419] Ibid

[420] Richmond, Danny. Director, Tony Blair Faith Foundation. London. Interview: February, 2012

[421]Ibid

[422] Lord Headley, Rowland George Allanson - Winn. *A Western Awakening to Islam.* Forgotten Books.*2013, p40*

[423] Singh, N.K. (Dr), *Islam: A Religion of Peace.* India: Global Vision Publishing House, 2002, p VI

[424] Armstrong, Karen. *Muhammad.* London, Victo Gollancz Ltd. 1991

[425] Hamilton, Sir Archibald Watkin, 5 and 3rd Baronet, *Islamic Review*, 1924

[426] Ibid

[427] Smith, W.C. as in Singh, N.K (Dr), *Islam: A Religion of Peace.* India: Global Vision Publishing House, 2002, p140

[428] Leitner, GW (Dr), *Muhammadanism in the Quarterly Message*, March, 2002, p8

[429] Montet, ,Edward *'La Propaganda Chretienne et ses Adversaries Musulmans,'* Paris 1890. (Also in T.W. Arnold in *'The Preaching of Islam,'* London 1913.)

[430] Wu, Hong (the Emperor of China, 1368 - 1398 http://en.wikipedia.org/wiki/The_Hundred-word_Eulogy

[431] Roy, MN, An essay on Islamic Culture: *The Historical Role of Islam*, Published in 1939, p 1-2

[432] Ibid

[433] Ibid p 14

[434] Pal, Amit. *'Islam Means Peace'.* USA, Praeger Publishers Inc, 201, p1

[435] Ibid, p12

[436] Ibid, p5

[437] *http://www.teachislam.com/index.php?option=com_content&task=view&id=907& Itemid=45*

[438] *General Gordon (1884)*; *The Brisbane Courier*, Tuesday, April, 29, Page 3. Source: Trove Digited Newspapers and more.

[439] Shaw, George Bernard (Sir), in *'The Genuine Islam,'* Vol. 1, No. 8, 1936.(The Society of Authors, on behalf of the Bernard Shaw Estate)

[440] Gibbon, Edward. *History of the Decline of and Fall of the Roman Empire*: Vol. 5-50. Chapter L: Description of Arabia And Its Inhabitants.-Part III. H. H. Milman, 1845, Online Books: http://www.gutenberg.org/files/25717/25717- h/files/735/735-h/gib5-50.htm#note-1

[441] Arnold, T.W. *The Preaching of Islam:* A History of the Propagation of the Muslim Faith. London: Constable and Company ltd. 1913. Online Book. P12

[442] Bodley, R.V.C. "*The Messenger: The Life of Mohammed". Doubleday & Company ,1946*

[443] Balbir Singh, Navan Hindustan, 1947, http://www.theuniversalmessenger.co.uk/orators.html

[444] Martin, Alfred, *Great Religious Teachers of the East.* New York. The MacMillan Company P262

[445] Andrae, Tor, Dr *Mohammed: The man and his faith,* Translated by Theophil Menzel, New York 1936

[446] Bevan, Anthony Ashley in Bury *Mahomet and Islam .The Cambridge Medieval History,* etc. vol. 2. 1911

[447] Lewis, Bernard, *The Crisis of Islam.* Holy war and Unholy Terror. London. Weildenfeld & Nicolson

[448] Ibid

[449] Nicolson, Angus Ph. D., *A Guide to Islam,* Stirling, 1951, p. 16.

[450] Watt, W. Montgomery.*"Islam and Christianity Today",* London, 1983

[451] Leonard, Major Arthur Glyn. *Islam: Her and Spiritual Value.* London: Luzac & Co. 1909, p32. Online book: file:///C:/Users/M%20A%20Lais/Desktop/Major%20AG%20Leonard.htm

[452] Hamilton, Frederick Marquis of Dufferin and Ava, *Speeches Delivered in India,* London, 1890, p. 24

[453] Stoddard, Lothrop, Dr *The New World of Islam, (Forgotten Books)*, 1921. P1

[454] Ibid

[455]Eid Speech, Vatican City, 3rd August,2012; http://www.vatican.va/roman_curia/pontifical_councils/interelg/documents/rc_pc_interelg_doc_20120803_ramadan2012_en.html

[456] Muir, Willam, Life of Mahomet, 1887

[457] Baboona, M.S. as " in the *Last Law Giver* by Mahmood Vanderman, Secundabad, 1935, p119

[458] Hearnshaw, F. J. C, *The Book Reference: The Science of History.*

[459] Greenlees, Duncan. *The Gospel of Islam.* Adyar 1948, page 27, *M.A. [Oxon]*).

[460] Bertherand, A, Dr *'Contribution des Arabs au Progress des Science Medicales',* Paris 1883, p. 6

[461] Watson, Charles R. *What is this Moslem World?* London 193, p. 38

[462] Ibid

[463] Smith. R. Bosworth. *Lecture on Muhammad and Muhammadism* at Royal Institution of Great Britain. 1874. Online book, page 185

[464] Ibid p 63

[465] Ibid 69

[466] Smith,Wilfred Cantwell. *Islam In the Modern World*, London 1946, Pages 22-23.

[467] Toynbee, A. J., *Civilisation on Trial*, New York 1948, pp.208-208

[468] Bonaparte et *l'Islam*, France, Page 105-125 - Cherfils.

[469] Leonard, Major Arthur Glyn. *Islam: Her and Spiritual Value.* London: Luzac & Co. 1909,. Online book: file:///C:/Users/M%20A%20Lais/Desktop/Major%20AG%20Leonard.htm

[470] Arnold, T.W. *The Preaching of Islam:* A History of the Propagation of the Muslim Faith. London: Constable and Company ltd. 1913. Online Book. P29

[471] Arnold, T.W. *The Preaching of Islam:* A History of the Propagation of the Muslim Faith. London: Constable and Company ltd. 1913. Online Book. P30

[472] Schimmel, Annemarie. *And Muhammad is His Messenger: The Veneration of the Prophet in Islamic Piety.* USA, University of North Carolina, 1985.

[473]Leonard, Major Arthur Glyn. *Islam: Her and Spiritual Value.* London: Luzac & Co. 1909, Online book: file:///C:/Users/M%20A%20Lais/Desktop/Major%20AG%20Leonard.htm

[474] Ruthven, Malise, *Islam: A Very Short Introduction.* USA. Oxford University Press. 2012

[475] Ibid

[476] Leitner, GW (Dr), *Muhammadanism* as in the *Quarterly Message,* March, 2002, p5

[477] Ibid p6

[478] Ibid p 7

[479] H.A.R. Gibb. *Muhammedanism.* USA, Oxford University Press, 1953

[480] Din, Jon Dal, Director, Westminster Interfaith Group, London, Interview: October, 2011

[481] Dobson, Frank, Rt. Hon. MP, London. Interview: September 2010

[482] Singh, N.K. (Dr), *Islam: A Religion of Peace.* India: Global Vision Publishing House, 2002

[483] Becker, C.H. *The Project Gutenberg EBook of Christianity and Islam,* 1907

[484] Roy, MN, *An essay on Islamic Culture: The Historical Role of Islam,* Published in 1939, p 57

[485] Kaltner, John. *Islam: "What Non-Muslims should Know".* USA, Fortress Press, 2003

[486] Charles, HRH Prince. *Lecture Delivered at the Oxford Centre of Islamic Studies, Oxford, Uniskill Ltd., 1993, p17*

[487] Leitner, GW (Dr), *Muhammadanism* as in the *Quarterly Message,* March, 2002, p8

[488] The Bishop of London, *The Times, 17th April,* 1893 as in Forlong, J.G.R (Major General) "Short Studies in the Science of Comparative Religions. London: Bernard Quaritch, 1897, p 473

[489] Hick, John, *Jesus and Muhammad: Islam in a world of diverse faiths.* Edited by Dan Cohn-sherbok, London, MacMillan, 1991.

[490] Wells, H.G, *The Outline of History*, 1920, p 271

[491] Singh, N.K(Dr), *Islam: A Religion of Peace.* India: Global Vision Publishing House, 2002, 64

[492] Muller, Max (Professor) as in Forlong, J.G.R (Major General) *Short Studies in the Science of Comparative Religions.* London: Bernard Quaritch, 1897, p 473

[493] Cook, Michael. *Muhammad.* Oxford. 1983

[494] Nehru, Jawaharlal. *Glimpses of World History.* Delhi: Oxford University Press, 1989, Centennial Edition

[495] Spronle James A, as " in *the Last Law Giver* by Mahmood Vanderman, Printed at Premier Press, Secundabad, 1935, p120

[496] Taylor, Isaac Canon, Speech, as in Spread of Islam, Page 369

[497] Vaglieri, LV, 'An Interpretation. of Islam' p55

[498] Forlong, J.G.R (Major General) *Short Studies in the Science of Comparative Religions.* London: Bernard Quaritch, 1897, p 468

[499] Pal, Amit. '*Islam Means Peace'.* USA, Praeger Publishers Inc, 2011, p5

[500] Bums, J Patout as in Pal, Amit. '*Islam Means Peace'.* USA, Praeger Publishers Inc, 2011

[501] Arnold, Edward, as " in *the Last Law Giver* by Mahmood Vanderman, Printed at Premier Press, Secundabad, 1935, p118

[502] Vaswani, Sadhu T. L. in *the Last Law Giver* by Mahmood Vanderman, Printed at Premier Press, Secundabad, 1935, p73-74

[503] Germanus, Julius (Dr), lecture delivered in Lahore, December, 1930 in *"Last Law Giver"* by Mahmood Vanderman, Printed at Premier Press, Secundabad, 1935, p108

[504]Clinton, Hilery. Larry B. Stammer, Times Religion Writer, "First Lady Breaks Ground With Muslims," *Los Angeles Times,* Home Edition, Metro Section, Part B, May 31, 1996, p.3.

[505] Leitner, GW (Dr), *Muhammadanism* as in the *Quarterly Message,* March, 2002, p8

[506] Roy, MN, An essay on Islamic Culture: *The Historical Role of Islam*, Published in 1939, p 34

[507] Marchant, Kerena, *Great Religious leaders: Muhammad and Islam.* UK. Whit Thomson Publishing, 2002. p18

[508] Ibid p5

[509] Marchant, Kerena, *Great Religious leaders: Muhammad and Islam.* UK. White Thomson Publishing, 2002. p14

510 Powell, E. Alexander, *The Struggle for Power in Muslim Asia.* New York 1923, p.48.

511 Little, Magsie Hamilton *The thing about Islam: Exposing the myths, facts and controversies.* London. Max press. 2012. p96

512 Ibid

513 Taylor, Isaac Canon, Speech, *in Spread of Islam*, Page 369

514 Charles, HRH Prince. *Lecture Delivered at the Oxford Centre of Islamic Studies, Oxford, Uniskill Ltd., 1993, p22*

515 Charles, HRH Prince. *Lecture Delivered at the Oxford Centre of Islamic Studies, Oxford, Uniskill Ltd., 1993, p18*

516 Charles, HRH Prince. *Lecture Delivered at the Oxford Centre of Islamic Studies, Oxford, Uniskill Ltd., 1993, p18*

517 Armstrong, H.G, as the Glory of Islam By Mian Abid Ahmad: Lahore, Pakistan: Time Publishers, 1993, p59

518 Reverend Stephens, in *the Last Law Giver* by Mahmood Vanderman, Printed at Premier Press, Secundabad, 1935, p117

519 Martin, Alfred. *The Great religious Teachers of the East,* The Macmillan Company, 1911*,p230-231*

520 Martin, Alfred. *The Great religious Teachers of the East,* The Macmillan Company, 1911,p*262*

521 Arnold, T.W. *The Preaching of Islam:* A History of the Propagation of the Muslim Faith. London: Constable and Company ltd. 1913. Online Book. P304

522 Montet, Edward, as in Arnold, T.W. *The Preaching of Islam:* A History of the Propagation of the Muslim Faith. London: Constable and Company ltd. 1913. Online Book. P307

523 Montet, Edward, as in Arnold, T.W. *The Preaching of Islam:* A History of the Propagation of the Muslim Faith. London: Constable and Company ltd. 1913.

524 Vaswani, Sadhu T. L. as in the Last Law Giver by Mahmood Vanderman, Printed at Premier Press, Secundabad, 1935, p73

525 Lawton, Lancelot, *The Sphere*, London, May 12, 1928

526 Cranston, Ruth *'World Faith'.* Harper and Row Publishers , Re printed in 1968

527Cranston, Ruth 'World *Faith'.* Harper and Row Publishers , Re printed in 1968

528 Gandhi, MK as in *The Last Law Giver* by Mahmood Vanderman, p 68

529 Michener, James A *"Islam: The Misunderstood Religion,"* By. Reader's Digest (American), May 1955, pp. 68-70

530 Stoddard, Lothrop, Dr *The New World of Islam,* Forgotten Books, 1921. P5-6

531 Davenport, John, *An Apology for Mohammad and The Qur'an.* London: J. Davy & Sons, 1882, p77

[532] Wells.H.G. *Outline of History.*. Garden City Publishing Co. 1926. 24 pts. in 1 v. cm

[533] Germanus, Julius, Dr *Muslims and Learning* as in http://info.ukimdawahcentre.com/download/some%20Prominent%20Westerners%20Views%20About%20Islam.pdf

[534] Nehru, Jawaharlal. *Glimpses of World History*. Delhi: Oxford University Press, 1989, Centennial Edition, pp. 145-149.

[535] Bonaparte, Napoleon, *Bonaparte et l'Islam*, France, Page 105-125 - Cherfils.

[536] Bonaparte, Napoleon, *Bonaparte et l'Islam*, France, Page 105-125 - Cherfils.

[537] Leonard, A G. *Islam: Her Moral and Spiritual Value*, London 1927

[538] Lewis, Bernard *The Crisis of Islam.* Holy war and Unholy Terror. London. Weildenfeld & Nicolson.

[539] Hitti, PK. *The History of the Arabs*. London, MacMillan, 1962

[540] Vaglieri, LV, *'An Interpretation of Islam'* p 35

[541] Leonard, A G. *Islam: Her Moral and Spiritual Value*, London 1927

[542] Draper, John William, *A History of the Intellectual Development of Europe*, London 1875, Vol.1, pp.329-330

[543] Michener, James A *"Islam: The Misunderstood Religion," Reader's Digest* (American), May1955, pp. 68-70

[544] Cook, Michael. *Muhammad.* London, Oxford University Press, 1983

[545] Wollaston, Arthur Naylor. *The Sword of Islam*. The Forgotten Books, 2012, p254

[546] Savory, R.M. *Introduction to Islamic Civilization.* London, Cambridge University Press, 1976

[547] Vaglieri, LV, *'An Interpretation.* of Islam' p18

[548] Dawson, Christopher, *Religion and the Rise of Western Culture*, Shed and Ward, 1950

[549] Kaltner, John. *Islam: "What Non-Muslims should Know"*. USA, Fortress Press, 2003

[550] Gandhi, Indira (Prime Minister of India). *Selected Thoughts of Indira Gandhi.* By K Dhawan. New Delhi, Mittal Publications, 1985; online book, page 198

[551] Smith. R. Bosworth. *Lecture on Muhammad and Muhammadism* at Royal Institution of Great Britain. 1874. Online book, page 13

[552] Hart, Michael H: *The 100: A ranking of the Most Influential Persons in History.* New York. Carol Publishing Group, 1989

[553] Cranston, Ruth. *World Faith.* Ayer Publication and Co. 1949

[554] Germanus, Julius (Dr), lecture delivered in Lahore, December, 1930 as in *"Last Law Giver"* by Mahmood Vanderman, Printed at Premier Press, Secundabad, 1935, p107

[555] Taylor, Canon, Paper read before the Church Congress at Walverhamton, Oct. 7, 1887, *Quoted by* Arnold *in The Preaching of Islam, pp. 71-72.*

[556] Leeder, S.H, *Veiled Mysteries of Egypt,* London, 1912,pp.332 - 335

[557] Marston, Elsa. *Muhammed of Makkah: Prophet of Islam.* USA, Franklin Watts, 2001,

[558] Naidu, Sarojini, Lecture on "The ideals of Islam" vide *Speeches and Writings of Sarojini Naidu,* Madras, 1918, p.169

[559] Ibid

[560] Toynbee, A.J. *Civilization on Trial,* New York, 1948, p.205.

[561] Ibid

[562] Mellema, R. L. Dr published in *Pakistan Quarterly,* Vol. V. no. 4, 1955.

[563] Naidu, S. IDEALS OF ISLAM, vide Speeches & Writings, Madras, 1918, p. 169

[564] Potter, Jennifer, Reverend. Minister, Wesley's Chapel, London. Interview: February, 2012

[565] Browne, Laurence E. *The Prospects of Islam,* London, 1944, p.12

[566] Leeder, S.H, *Veiled Mysteries of Egypt,* London, 1912,pp.332 - 335 [570] Ibid

[567] Ibid

[568] Gibb, H.A.R. *Whither Islam,* London, 1932,Oxford University press p. 379

[569] Michener, James A *"Islam: The Misunderstood Religion," Reader's Digest* (American), May1955, pp. 68-70

[570] Robinson, Victor, as in Dr Danial Zainal Abidin, *Islam the Misunderstood Religion,* Malaysia.

[571] Pal, Amit. '*Islam Means Peace'.* USA, Praeger Publishers Inc, 2011, p 30

[572] Vaswani, Professor T. L.. *The Spirit and Struggle s Islam.* Published by Ganesh & sons, Madras, 1921, (Preface)

[573] Gibbon, Edward, *History of the Saracen Empires,* London, 1870. p54

[574] Bonaparte, Napolean as Quoted in Christian Cherfils, *'Bonaparte et Islam,'* Pedone Ed., Paris, France, 1914,pp105,125. Original References: *"Correspondence de Napoléon Ier* Tome V piece n° 4287 du 17/07/1799..."

[575] Hunter, Shireen, as in *The Spirit of Islam,* by Syed Ameer Ali, Published in New York, 1891

[576] Leonard, Major Arthur Glyn. *Islam: Her and Spiritual Value.* London: Luzac & Co. 1909, Online book: file:///C:/Users/M%20A%20Lais/Desktop/Major%20AG%20Leonard.htm

[577] Vaglieri, LV, *An Interpretation.* Of Islam' 1957

578 Sarton, George. *The Civilization of the Renaissance* (Chicago, 1929); *Six Wings: Men of Science in the Renaissance* (Bloomington, 1957); and *The Appreciation of Ancient and Medieval Science during the Renaissance, 1450-1600* (Philadelphia, 1955)

579 Lord Headley, Rowland George Allanson - Winn. *A Western Awakening to Islam.* Forgotten Books.*2013, p32*

580 Singh, N.K (Dr), *Islam: A Religion of Peace.* India: Global Vision Publishing House, 2002, p187

581 Singh, N.K (Dr), *Islam: A Religion of Peace.* India: Global Vision Publishing House, 2002, p187

582 Vaglieri, LV, *An Interpretation.* of Islam' p20

583 Johann Wolfgang Von Goethe

584 Stanton, Dr H.U.W. *The Teachings of The Qur'an: With an account of its growth and a Subject Index. Published in 1919, p62*

585 Bachchan, Amitabh. *Amitabh Bachchan Reads the Qur'an.* The News Tribe, December 8th, 2011 by Jitender Singh. http://www.thenewstribe.com/2011/12/08/amitabh-bachchan-reads-the- Qur'an/#comments

586 Ibid

587 Ibid

588 Vaglieri, LV, *'An Interpretation of Islam'* pp 21-22

589 Chopra, Deepak, *Muhammad: A Story of The Last Prophet.* New York, HarperOne, 2010

590 A British Politician (requested to be anonymous), Interviewed in June 13, 2011

591 Ibid

592 Ibid

593 Ibid

594 Armstrong, Karen. Muhammad: *A Western Attempt to understand Islam.* London: Victor Gollancz ltd. 1991

595 Ranganathan, Thillai K. Pandit, Chairman, Britannia Hindu Temple, Highgate, London: Interview-November,2011.

596 Cranston, Ruth. *'World Faith'.* Page 138. Harper and Row Publishers , Re printed in 1968

597 Sikh Temple, East London, Interview: November, 2011

598 Little, Magsie Hamilton, *The thing about Islam :Exposing the myths, facts and controversies.* London. Max press. 2012.

599 Smith, Bosworth, *Mohammed and Mohammedinism*

600 Briffault, Robert, *Making of the Humanity*, Islamic Book Foundation, 1919, p 191-192

[601] Briffault, Robert, *Making of the Humanity*, Islamic Book Foundation, 1919

[602] Margoliouth, G. in his Introduction to J. M. Rodwells - *'The Koran", New York* - 'Everyman's Library, 1977, p VI

[603] Gibbs, Philip said in *the Glory of Muhammad.* https://www.facebook.com/MuhammadSawwInOthersViews?filter=1

[604] Gregory, Richard Arman Sir. Religion In Science And Civilization. Macmillan & Co Ltd, 1940.

[605] Michener, James in 'Islam: *The Misunderstood Religion,' Reader's Digest*, May 1955, pp. 68-70.

[606]Savory, R.M. Law and Traditional Society as in RM Savory. *Introduction to Islamic Civilisation*: Cambridge University press, 2003, p54

[607] Clinton, Bill, Former United States President. Bill Clinton Hosts Eid-al-Fitr at the White House (2000), Encyclopaedia Of Muslim American History, New York, Facts On File Publishing, © 2010, p. 253. Reprinted by permission of the Publisher.

[608] *Encyclopaedia Britannica,* " in the *Last Law Giver* by Mahmood Vanderman, Printed at Premier Press, Secundabad, 1935, p122

[609] The Chambers of Cyclopaedia, Vol, 6 as in the Last Law Giver by Mahmood Vanderman, Printed at Premier Press, Secundabad, 1935, page 118

[610] Dorman, Harry Gaylord. *Toward understanding Islam; contemporary apologetic of Islam and missionary policy.* New York, Bureau of Publications, Teachers College, Columbia University, 1948

[611] Sale, George, *The Koran: Commonly called the Al-Koran of Mohammed.* New York: The Koran: The Preliminary Discourse. London & New York: 1891, 47

[612] Carlyle, Thomas, *Muhammad: The Hero as Prophet.* Published in England in 1841, p 97

[613] Singh, N.K(Dr), *Islam: A Religion of Peace.* India: Global Vision Publishing House, 2002, p 12

[614] Ibid p 12-13

[615] Pal, Amit. '*Islam Means Peace'.* USA, Praeger Publishers Inc, 2011, p 30

[616] Dobson, Frank, Rt. Hon. MP, London. Interview: September 2010

[617] Arberry, Arthur J. *The Koran Interpreted*, London: Oxford University Press, 1964, p. x.

[618] Arberry, Arthur J. *The Koran Interpreted*, London: Oxford University Press, 1964

[619] Draper, John William, *A History of the Intellectual Development of Europe,* London 1875, Vol.1, pp.340

[620] Ibid pp.343-344

[621] Ibid, pp.347

[622] Gibbon, Edward and Ockley, Simon. *The Saracens: Their History and the Rise and Fall of their Empire.* Published by Alex, Murray & sons, 1869, p55

[623] Gibb, H. A. R., *Arabic Literature-An Introduction* (Oxford at Clarendon Press: 1963), 36

[624] Wollaston, Arthur Naylor. *The Sword of Islam*. The Forgotten Books, 2012, p254

[625] Goethe, quoted in T. P. Hughes' *Dictionary of Islam*, 526

[626] Steingass, F, Dr quoted in T.P. Hughes-*Dictionary of Islam*', pp256-257

[627] Ibid

[628] Ibid

[629]Source: http://answeringprophetofdoom.net/Feedback_Non_Muslim_Scientists.ph p

[630] www.al-sunnah.com/call_to_islam/articles/what_they_say_about_islaam.html

[631] A British Politician (requested to be anonymous), Interviewed in June 13, 2011

[632] Ibid

[633]A British Politician (requested to be anonymous), Interviewed in June 13, 2011

[634] Ibid

[635] Naish, John, M. A. (Oxon), D. D., *The Wisdom of the Qur'an* (Oxford: 1937), viii.

[636] *The Popular Encyclopaedia*, (Davison) VII p 3ZG4, as " in *the Last Law Giver* by Mahmood Vanderman, Printed at Premier Press, Secundabad, 1935, p121

[637] Martin, Alfred. *The Great religious Teachers of the East*, The Macmillan Company, 1911, *p253*

[638] Margoliouth, George, *The Koran*, translated by J. M. Rodwell, New York - 'Everyman's Library, 1977, p VI

[639] Smith. R. Bosworth. *Lecture on Muhammad and Muhammadism* at Royal Institution of Great Britain. 1874. Online book, page 124

[640] Watt, W Montgomery. *Muhammad: Prophet and statesman.* London, Oxford University Press, 1961

[641] Bucaille, Dr Maurice - author of "*The Bible, the Qur'an and Science*" 1978, p. 125

[642] Bucaille, Dr.Maurice, THE QUR'AN AND MODERN SCIENCE, 1981, p. 18.

[643] Bucaille, Dr Maurice. *The Bible, The Qur'an, and Science*, Pub. Seghers, Paris

[644] Bucaille, Dr Maurice. *The Bible, The Qur'an, and Science*, Pub. Seghers, Paris

[645] Picktall, M. *Cultural Islam.* Kitab Bhaban. P67

[646] Wilson, J.Christy in *"Introducing Islam"* New York 1950

[647] Charles Francis Potter: *The Faiths Men Live* By, Kingswood, Surrey 1955, p.81

[648] Montet, Edward, as in Arnold, T.W. *The Preaching of Islam:* A History of the Propagation of the Muslim Faith. London: Constable and Company ltd. 1913. Online Book. P307

[649] Montet, Edward, as in Arnold, T.W. *The Preaching of Islam:* A History of the Propagation of the Muslim Faith. London: Constable and Company ltd. 1913. Online Book. P307

[650]Diamond, Jared. Guns, Germs, and Steel - *The Fates of Human Societies*, 1997, p. 253

[651] Professor Dorja Rao .http://answeringprophetofdoom.net/Feedback_Non_Muslim_Scientists.php

[652] Ali Selman Benoist, France, Doctor of Medicine

[653] Stanley, Dean, as " in *the Last Law Giver* by Mahmood Vanderman, Printed at Premier Press, Secundabad, 1935, p121

[654] Armstrong, Karen. *Muhammad: A Western Attempt to understand Islam*. London: Victor Gollancz ltd. 1991

[655] Vaglieri, Laura Veccia. *An Introduction of Islam*.p43-44

[656] Casanova, Paul:Source http://www.miraclesoftheQur'an.com/perfection_02.html: Paul Casanova, *L'Enseignement de I'Arabe au College de France* (The Arab Teaching at the College of France), Lecon d'overture, April 26, 1909.

[657] Irving, Washington. *The Life of Muhammad*. Bernh. Tauchnitz Jun, 1850. *P 197*

[658] Carlyle, Sir Thomas; *Sartor Resartus and On Heroes and Hero Worship*, page 287. Everyman's Library, New York 1965

[659] Bodley,RVC. *The Messenger*. Double Day and Company Inc, 1946. Page 2.

[660] Bose, Basanta Coomer, *Mohammadenism*, Calcutta 1931

[661] Smith. R. Bosworth. *Lecture on Muhammad and Muhammadism* at Royal Institution of Great Britain. 1874. Online book, page 17

[662] Irving, Washington in *'Life of Muhammad,'* New York, 1920

[663] Bodley, RVC. *The Messenger*. Double Day and Company Inc, 1946. Page 236.

[664] Ibid Page 237-8

[665] Little, Magsie Hamilton, *The thing about Islam: Exposing the myths, facts and controversies.* London. Max press. 2012.

[666] Ibid

[667] Ibid

[668] Otto Eduard Leopold, Prince of Bismarck, Duke of Lauenburg *Source: http://www.nur.org/treatise/articles/muslim_christian_alliance.htm*

[669] Gibb, H. A. R., *Islam-A Historical Survey* (Oxford University Press: 1980), 28.

[670] *Noten und Abhandlungen zum Weststlichen* Dvan, WA I, 7, 32

[671] Cranston, Ruth. *World Faith.* Ayer Publication and Co. 1949

672 Marmura, E Michael, *God and His Creation: Two medieval Islamic Views*, as in RM Savory. *Introduction to Islamic Civilisation.*

673 Jenz, Jaims: http://www.radioislam.org.za/a/index.php?option=com_content&task=view&id=16316&Itemid=143

674 Kozan, Yoshido :http://www.imamilyas.com/archives/truthofislam.html

675 Kroner, Alfred: http://www.imamilyas.com/archives/truthofislam.html

676 Chopra, Deepak, *Muhammad: A Story of The Last Prophet.* New York, HarperOne, 2010.

677 Broomhall, Marshall. *Islam In China: A Neglected Problem.* Published in 1910, p305

678 Meacher, Michael, Right Honourable, a British MP. Interview: March, 2012

679 Timms, Stephen, Right Honourable, British MP; Interview: London, March, 2012

680 Din, Jon Dal, the Director of Westminster Interfaith, London. Interview: October, 2011

681 Dev, Ram, *The Prakash*, see *Burguzida Rasul Ghairon Main Maqbul* , 24.

682 Kaltner, John. *Islam: "What Non-Muslims should Know".* USA, Fortress Press, 2003

683 Lord Headley, Rowland George Allanson - Winn. *A Western Awakening to Islam.* Forgotten Books.*2013, p19*

684 Ben, Tony Right Honourable MP, Labour Party, UK, Interview: London, December 2011

685 Spokesman, Sikh Temple, East London, Interview November, 2011

686 Tailor, Bhavin, RE teacher, William Ellis School, North West London, Interview March, 2012

687 Rai, Anita. *Muhammad*: *Uncovering the true story*. London: Starsighter ltd. 2006

688 Amess, David (Right Honourable), British MP, UK. Interview: January 2012

689 Stygal, Mike, Chairman, Camden Interfaith Foundation, London, Interview January 2012

690 A Priest from a Church, East London. Interview: March 2012

691 Corbyn, Jeremy, Right Honourable MP, Finsbury Park, London, Interview March 2012

692 Fulbrook, Julian (Dr), Councilor of London Borough of Camden, February, 2012

693 Ibid

694 Lamont, Norman, Lord (Baron Lamont of Lerwick), British politician and former Conservative MP and Chancellor of the Exchequer. Interview: January, 20012

695 Gandhi, MK as in *The Last Law Giver* by Mahmood Vanderman, p 68

696 Gandhi, MK as in *The Last Law Giver* by Mahmood Vanderman, p 68

697 Gibbon, Edward. *History of The Saracen Empire*, London, 1870

[698] Browne, Laurence E. *in the Prospects of Islam, 1944*

[699] Browne, Laurence E. *in Christianity and Islam'. 1944*

[700] Uri Avnery, September 23, 2006

[701] The Editor, Sat Updesh, Lahore as in the *Last Law Giver* by Mahmood Vanderman, Printed at Premier Press, Secundabad, 1935, page 112

[702] Potter, Jennifer, Minister, Wesley's Chapel, London, Interview February, 2012

[703] Dev, Ram, *The Prakash* , see *Burguzida Rasul Ghairon Main Maqbul* , 24.

[704] Aumie, a senior member of the Jewish community, North West London, Interview February, 2012

[705] Singh, N.K(Dr), *Islam: A Religion of Peace.* India: Global Vision Publishing House, 2002, p 8

[706] Rai, Anita. *Muhammad: Uncovering the true story*. London: Starsighter ltd. 2006

[707] Rev Thomas O'Brien, Our Lady of the Assumption Church, Tower hamlets, Interview London Feb, 2012

[708] L a p i d u s , I r a a s i n Pal, Amit. *'Islam Means Peace'.* USA, Praeger Publishers Inc, 2011

[709] Hoare, Rupert, Reverend. Former Dean of Liverpool Cathedral and Chair of the Council of Faiths, Liverpool, UK. Interview: April, 2012

[710] MN Roy, An essay on Islamic Culture: *The Historical Role of Islam*, Published in 1939. PP 10

[711] Quinn, Father Tom, Shadwell Catholic Church, East London, Interview: January 2012

[712] Hoare, Rupert, Reverend. Former Dean of Liverpool Cathedral and Chair of the Council of Faiths, Liverpool, UK. Interview: April, 2012

[713] De Lacy, O'Leary. Islam at the Crossroads, London, 1923, page 8.

[714] Singh, N.K(Dr), *Islam: A Religion of Peace.* India: Global Vision Publishing House, 2002, p 15

[715] Stubbe, Henry (Dr). An Account of the Rise and Progress of Mahometanism. London: Luzuc & Co. 1911, p 181

[716] Stygal, Mike, Chairman, Camden Interfaith Foundation, Interview London, January 2012

[717] Arnold, T.W. *The Preaching of Islam: A History of the Propagation of the Muslim Faith.* London: Constable and Company ltd. 1913. Online Book. P12-13

[718] Esposito L John, *What everyone needs to know about Islam,* London, University Press, Oxford Esposito 2002, p 119

719 Singh, N.K(Dr), *Islam: A Religion of Peace.* India: Global Vision Publishing House, 2002, 74

720 Blunkett, David, Right Honourable, MP (Former Home Secretary), UK. Interview: Jan, 2012

721 Eade, John. Professor of Sociology and Anthropology Roehampton University, England, Interview February, 2012

722 Sale, George, *The Koran: Commonly called the Al-Koran of Mohammed.* New York: Frederick Warne and co. 1909, p38

723 H.A.R. Gibb. *Muhammedanism.* USA, Oxford University Press, 1953

724 Esposito L John, *What everyone needs to know about Islam,* London, University Press, Oxford Esposito 2002

725 Vaglieri, LV, '*An Interpretation.* of Islam' p10

726 Phesrisai, Sangthong (Dhamacaro) Buddhist Monk, Buddhist Temple, South London, Interview October, 2011

727 Dobson, Frank, Right Honourable MP, Labour Party, UK, Interview: London, Interview October 2011

728 Tolstoy, Leo. http://www.islamgate.org/?p=238&upm_export=pdf.This page was exported from - IslamGate. Export date: Sat Jan 26 21:15:45 2013 / +0000 GMT

729 Cowie, Reverend John. The English Reformed Church, Amsterdam, Holland. Interview: February, 2012

730 A Sikh Journalist, *Nawan Hindustan* , Delhi, 17 November 1947.

731 Pal, Amit. '*Islam Means Peace*'. USA, Praeger Publishers Inc, 2011

732 Potter, Jennifer, Reverend, Minister, Wesley's Chapel, London, Interview February, 2012

733 Mehri Niknam MBE, Executive Director, the Joseph Interfaith Foundation, Camden, London, February 2012

734 Archer, John Clark, Our Debt to The Muslim Arab, The Muslim World, Volume 29, Issue 3, pages 248-264, July 1939

735 Aumie, a senior member of the Jewish Community, North West London, Interview February, 2012

736 Draper, John William, *A History of the Intellectual Development of Europe,* London 1875, Vol.1, p332

737 Green, Allen (Father). Tower Hamlets Interfaith Forum, London. Interview: January 2012

738 Kinnock, Neil (Right Honourable) Lord, the former leader of Labour Party, UK. Interview: January, 2012

[739] Shashoua, Stephen, Director, Three Faiths Foundation, Camden, Interview: London, January 2012

[740] A Teacher from Church of England School, North London, Interview March, 2012

[741] Harris, Harriet, Reverend the Chaplain and honorary Fellow at the school of divinity, Edinburgh University, UK, Interview May 2012

[742] Richmond, Danny. Director, Tony Blair Faith Foundation. London. Interview: February, 2012

[743] Shastri,Pandit Gyanandra Dev Sharma, at a meeting in Gorakhpur (India), 1928

[744] Dobson, Frank, Right Honourable MP, Labour Party, UK, Interview: London, October 2011

[745] Dobson, Frank, Right Honourable MP, Labour Party, UK, Interview: London, October 2011

[746] Roy, MN, An essay on Islamic Culture: *The Historical Role of Islam*, Published in 1939, p 28-27

[747] Sharma, Lalit Kumar, Pandit. Hindu Temple, East London, Interview September, 2011

[748] Tolstoy, Leo. http://www.islamgate.org/?p=238&upm_export=pdf.This page was exported from - IslamGate. Export date: Sat Jan 26 21:15:45 2013 / +0000 GMT

[749] Tolstoy, Leo. http://www.islamgate.org/?p=238&upm_export=pdf.This page was exported from - IslamGate. Export date: Sat Jan 26 21:15:45 2013 / +0000 GMT

[750] O'Brien, Rev Thomas, Our Lady of the Assumption Church, Tower hamlets, London Interview Feb, 2012.

[751] Niknam, Mehri MBE, Executive Director, the Joseph Interfaith Foundation, Camden, London, Interview February 2012

[752] Cowie, Reverend John. The English Reformed Church, Amsterdam, Holland. Interview: February, 2012

[753] Bhavin Tailor, RE teacher, William Ellis School, North West London, Interview March, 2012

[754] Blunkett, David, Right Honourable, MP (Former Home Secretary), UK. Interview: Jan, 2012

[755] Kinnock, Neil (Right Honourable) Lord, the former leader of Labour Party, UK. Interview: January, 2012

[756] Shashoua, Stephen, Director, Three Faiths Foundation, Camden, Interview: London, January 2012

[757] A Teacher from a Church of England School, North London, Interview March, 2012

[758] Shaw, George Bernard, in KJH Ahmad, 1983(The Society of Authors, on behalf of the Bernard Shaw Estate)

[759] Charles, HRH Prince. *Lecture Delivered at the Oxford Centre of Islamic Studies, Oxford, Uniskill Ltd., 1993, p9*

[760] *Ibid p910*

[761] Gyanandra Dev Sharma Shastri; *Dunya ka Hadi Ghairon Ki Nazar Main*, 7th July, pp. 57, 61

[762] Benn, Tony Right Honourable MP, Labour Party, UK, Interview: London, December 2011

[763] Glubb, Sir John. *The Life and Times of Muhammad.* USA, Madison Books, 1988

[764] Ibid

[765] Ibid

[766] Ibid

[767] Hoare, Rupert, Reverend. Former Dean of Liverpool Cathedral and Chair of the Council of Faiths, Liverpool, UK. Interview: April, 2012

[768] Armstrong, Karen. *Muhammad: A Western Attempt to understand Islam.* London: Victor Gollancz ltd. 1991

[769] Meacher, Michael. Interview: March, 2012

[770] Stubbe, Henry (Dr). *An Account of the Rise and Progress of Mahometanism.* London: Luzuc & Co. 1911.

[771] Stubbe, Henry (Dr). *An Account of the Rise and Progress of Mahometanism.* London: Luzuc & Co. 1911

[772] A Teacher from a Church of England School, North London, Interview March, 2012

[773] Corbyn, Jeremy, Right Honourable MP, Finsbury Park, London, Interview March 2012

[774] Ibid

[775] Buaben, J.M.. *Image of the Prophet Muhammad in the West: A study of Muir, Margoliouth and Watt,* 1996

[776] Watt, "What is Islam" pg 1 & 2 as in (Buaben, 1996: *Image of the Prophet Muhammad in the West:* A study of Muir, Margoliouth and Watt

[777] Daniel, N. *I Islam and the West – The Making of an Image*, 1980, reprint, as in Buaben

[778] Spokesman, Sikh Temple, East London, Interview November, 2011

[779] Dr Rowell, Geoffrey, Right Reverend. European Diocese, Bishop of Gibraltar in Europe, Interview: London, May, 2011

[780] Dr Rowell, Geoffrey, Right Reverend. European Diocese, Bishop of Gibraltar in Europe, Interview: London, May, 2011

[781] Tolstoy, Leo. http://www.islamgate.org/?p=238&upm_export=pdf.This page was exported from - IslamGate. Export date: Sat Jan 26 21:15:45 2013 / +0000 GMT

[782] Green, Allen (Father). Tower Hamlets Interfaith Forum, London. Interview: January 2012

[783] Smith, Jane as in *the Qur'an and the sayings of Prophet Muhammad.* Skylight Paths Publishing, 2007

[784] Stubbe, Henry. *An Account of the Rise and Progress of Mahometanism.* London: Luzuc & Co. 911. P238

[785] Cowie, Reverend John. The English Reformed Church, Amsterdam, Holland. Interview: February, 2012

[786] Hoare, Rupert, Reverend. Former Dean of Liverpool Cathedral and Chair of the Council of Faiths, Liverpool, UK. Interview: April, 2012

[787] Kremer, Alfred von. Editor: *History of Prophet Muhammad's Campaign* by Aboo Abdullah Muhammad Omar Al- Waqidy. 1886

[788] Muir, Sir William. *The Life of Muhammad from original sources.* Published by Smith, 1878.

[789] Lyall, C. J (Sir). "Obituary Notices: Sir William Muir," *The Journal of the Royal Asiatic Society of Great Britain and Ireland*, 37 (1905)

[790] Mehri Niknam MBE, Executive Director, the Joseph Interfaith Foundation, Camden, London, February 2012

[791] Armstrong,Karen: Muhammed, *A Western attempt to understand Islam,* London. Voctor Gollancz ltd, 1991

[792] Eade, John. Professor of Sociology and Anthropology Roehampton University, England, Interview February, 2012

[793] Ibid

[794] McCoy, Alban, Father, Cambridge University Catholic Chaplaincy. Interview May 2012

[795] Lamont, Norman, Lord (Baron Lamont of Lerwick), British politician and former Conservative MP and Chancellor of the Exchequer. Interview: January, 20012

[796] Pal, Amit. '*Islam Means Peace*'. USA, Praeger Publishers Inc, 2011, p 49

[797] Griffin, Sir Lepel Henry in discussion of the paper '*Pan-Islamism*' by Sir Ignatius Valentine Chirol, Published by Central Asian Society, London, Nov,1906, p17

[798] Richmond, Danny. Director, Tony Blair Faith Foundation. London. Interview: February, 2012

[799] Richmond, Danny. Director, Tony Blair Faith Foundation. London. Interview: February, 2012

[800] Williams, Stephen, Rev. Senior Anglican Chaplain, University Chaplaincy, University of London. Interview: May, 2012

801 Bhavin Tailor, RE teacher, William Ellis School, North West London, Interview March, 2012

802 Meacher, Michael. Interview: March, 2012

803 A Teacher from a Church of England School, North London, Interview March, 2012

804 Mehri Niknam MBE, Executive Director, the Joseph Interfaith Foundation, Camden, London, Interview February 2012

805 Spokesman, Sikh Temple, East London, Interview November, 2011

806 Sharma, Lalit Kumar, Pandit. Hindu Temple, East London, Interview September, 2011

807 .Carr, E.H. *What is History,* Page 26

808 Martin, Alfred. The Great religious Teachers of the East, The Macmillan Company, 1911, *P327*

809 Armstrong, Karen: *Muhammed, A Wetsren attempt to understand Isla*m, London. Voctor Gollancz ltd, 1991

810 Armstrong, Karen: *Muhammed, A Wetsren attempt to understand Isla*m, London. Voctor Gollancz ltd, 1991

811 Armstrong, Karen: *Muhammed, A Wetsren attempt to understand Isla*m, London. Voctor Gollancz ltd, 1991

812 Armstrong, Karen: *Muhammed, A Wetsren attempt to understand Isla*m, London. Voctor Gollancz ltd, 1991

813 Benn, Tony, Right Honourable MP, London, Interview December, 2011

814 Ibid

815 Ibid

816 Shiv Charan Singh Gill, Spokeman, Sikh Temple, Southall, London, Interview December 2011

817 Tailor, Bhavin, RE teacher, William Ellis School, North West London, Interview March, 2012

818 Amess, David (Right Honourable), British MP, UK. Interview: January 2012

819 Kinnock, Neil (Right Honourable) Lord, the former leader of Labour Party, UK. Interview: January, 2012

820 A Teacher from a Church of England School, North London, Interview March, 2012

821 Corbyn, Jeremy, Right Honourable MP, Finsbury Park, London, Interview March 2012

822 Nagasawa, Mako. Area director, an advisor to the Harvard-Radcliffe Christian Fellowship (HRCF), and a staff member with InterVarsity Christian Fellowship, University of Harvard. Interview: May 2012

823 Ibid

[824] Eade, John. Professor of Sociology and Anthropology Roehampton University, England, Interview February, 2012

[825] Armstrong, Karen: Muhammed, *A Western attempt to understand Islam*, London. Voctor Gollancz ltd, 1991

[826] Armstrong, Karen: Muhammed, *A Western attempt to understand Islam*, London. Voctor Gollancz ltd, 1991

[827] McCoy, Alban, Father, Cambridge University Catholic Chaplaincy. Interview May 2012.

[828] Lamont, Norman, Lord (Baron Lamont of Lerwick), British politician and former Conservative MP and Chancellor of the Exchequer. Interview: January, 20012

[829] Richmond, Danny. Director, Tony Blair Faith Foundation. London. Interview: February, 2012

[830] Fulbrook, Julian (Dr), Councilor of London Borough of Camden, Interview February, 2012

[831] Coles, Stephen, Reverend, St. Thomas Church, Interview February, 2012

[832] Pal, Amit. *'Islam Means Peace'.* USA, Praeger Inc, 2011

[833] Ibid

[834] Charles, HRH Prince. *Lecture Delivered at the Oxford Centre of Islamic Studies, Oxford, Uniskill Ltd., 1993, p14*

[835] Clinton, Hilary, Secretary of State ,USA, in an Article: Hillary Clinton: Koran Burning, by Huff Post, *Online Newspaper*, 9th of August, 2010.

[836] Amess, David (Right Honourable), British MP, UK. Interview: January 2012

[837] Revd John Pritchard, Assistant Priest, All Saints Church, West London, Interview February 2012

[838] Little, Magsie Hamilton, *The thig about Islam: Exposing the myths, facts and controversies.* London. Max press. 2012

[839] Taylor, Isaac Canon, Speech, in *Spread of Islam*, Page 369

[840] Cowie, Reverend John. The English Reformed Church, Amsterdam, Holland. Interview: February, 2012

[841] Cowie, Reverend John. The English Reformed Church, Amsterdam, Holland. Interview: February, 2012

[842] Eade, John. Professor of Sociology and Anthropology Roehampton University, England, Interview February, 2012

[843] Fulbrook, Julian (Dr), Councilor of London Borough of Camden, Interview February, 2012

[844] Lakhan, Jay, Hindu Priest, Hindu Academy, London, Interview December, 2011

845 Niknam, Mehri MBE, Executive Director, the Joseph Interfaith Foundation, Camden, London, Interview February 2012

846 Shashoua, Stephen. Director, Three Faiths Foundation, Camden, London, Interview January 2012

847 O'Brien Thomas. Reverend, Our Lady of the Assumption Church, Tower hamlets, London Interview Feb, 2012.

848 Quinn,Tom. Father Shadwell Catholic Church, East London, Interview January 2012

849 Stygal,Mike. Chairman, Camden Interfaith Foundation, London, Interview January 2012

850 Potter, Jennifer, Reverend. Minister, Wesley's Chapel, London. Interview: February, 2012

851 Smith, Jane as in *the Qur'an and the sayings of Prophet Muhammad.* Skylight Paths Publishing, 2007

852 Buddhist Monk, West London, Interview November, 2011.

853 Bhavin Tailor, RE teacher, William Ellis School, North West London, Interview March, 2012

854 Stygal, Mike, Chairman, Camden Interfaith Foundation, London, January 2012

855 Meacher, Michael. Interview: March, 2012

856 Hoare, Rupert, Reverend. Former Dean of Liverpool Cathedral and Chair of the Council of Faiths, Liverpool, UK. Interview: April, 2012

857 Armstrong, Karen (1991) *Muhammad: A Western Attempt to understand Islam.* London. Victor Gollancz Ltd

858 John L. Esposito, (2002) *What everyone needs to know about Islam,* London, University Press, Oxford

859 Bhavin Tailor, RE teacher, William Ellis School, North West London, Interview March, 2012

860 O'Brien, Rev Thomas, Our Lady of the Assumption Church, Tower hamlets, London, Interview Feb, 2012.

861 Green, Allen (Father). Tower Hamlets Interfaith Forum, London. Interview: January 2012

862 Shashoua, Stephen, Director, Three Faiths Foundation, Camden, Interview: London, January 2012

863 Ban Ki-moon, UN Secretary, Dwan Media Group Online, 6th April, 2011

864 Ibid

[865] Lamont, Norman, Lord (Baron Lamont of Lerwick), British politician and former Conservative MP and Chancellor of the Exchequer. Interview: January, 2012

[866] Obama, Barak, President of USA. BBC, News Asia, 23 February 2012

[867] Carney, Jay. Press Secretary, USA Government, published in the *Daily Mail*, 22 February, 2012

[868] Clinton, Hilary, Secretary of State ,USA, in an Article: Hillary Clinton: Koran Burning, by Huff Post, *Online Newspaper*, 9th of August, 2010

[869] Mehri Niknam MBE, Executive Director, the Joseph Interfaith Foundation, Camden, London, Interview February 2012

[870] Pritchard, John. Reverend, Assistant Priest, All Saints Church, London, Interview February, 2012

[871] Ryan, Canon Paschal, Episcopal Vicar, Archbishop's House, London. Interview: February,2012

[872] A Teacher from a Church of England School, North London (requested anonymity), March, 2012

[873] Lombardi, Federico. Vetican. The Article: Talk of Qur'an burning leads to spreading of sacred word' BY NISA ISLAM *Muhammad* -STAFF WRITER- I LAST UPDATED: SEP 16, 2010

[874] A Teacher from a Church of England School, North London, Interview March, 2012

[875] Cowie, Reverend John. The English Reformed Church, Amsterdam, Holland. Interview: February, 2012

[876] Corbyn, Jeremy, Right Honourable MP, Finsbury Park, London, Interview March 2012

[877] Timms, Stephen, Right Honourable, British MP; Interview: London, March, 2012

[878] Meacher, Michael. Interview: March, 2012

[879] Singh, N.K(Dr), *Islam: A Religion of Peace.* India: Global Vision Publishing House, 2002, 64

[880] Singh, N.K (Dr), *Islam: A Religion of Peace.* India: Global Vision Publishing House, 2002, p77

[881] Mandela, Nelson. President, South Africa. In a lecture at the Oxford Centre for Islamic Studies. *"Renewal and Renaissance - Towards a New World Order"* 11 July 1997, Oxford

[882] Mandela, Nelson. President, South Africa. In a lecture at the Oxford Centre for Islamic Studies. *"Renewal and Renaissance - Towards a New World Order"* 11 July 1997, Oxford

[883] Armstrong, Karen, *Muhammad: A Western Attempt to Understand Islam*, London. Victor Gollancz Ltd. 1991

884 Ibid

885 Singh, Manmohan. Indian Prime Minister. The article, *Manmohan Singh greets Nation on Milad-Un-Nabi.* Thaindian News, by ANI, Feb 15, 2011

886 Richmond, Danny. Director, Tony Blair Faith Foundation. London. Interview: February, 2012

887 Stubbe, Henry (Dr). *An Account of the Rise and Progress of Mahometanism.* London: Luzuc & Co. 1911. P181

888 Din, Jon Dal, Director, Westminster Interfaith Group, London, Interview: October, 2011

889 Potter, Jennifer, Reverend, Minister, Wesley's Chapel, London, Interview February, 2012

890 Corbyn, Jeremy, Right Honourable MP, Finsbury Park, London Interview March 2012

891 Stygal, Mike, Chairman, Camden Interfaith Foundation, London, Interview January 2012

892 Niknam, Mehri MBE, Executive Director, the Joseph Interfaith Foundation, Camden, London, Interview February 2012

893 Niknam, Mehri MBE, Executive Director, the Joseph Interfaith Foundation, Camden, London, Interview February 2012

894 Cowie, John, Reverend, the English Reformed Church, Amsterdam, Holland, Interview February 2012

895 Cowie, John, Reverend, the English Reformed Church, Amsterdam, Holland, Interview February 2012

896 Amess, David (Right Honourable), British MP, UK. Interview: January 2012

897 Little, Magsie Hamilton, *The thig about Islam: Exposing the myths, facts and controversies.* London. Max press. 2012

898 Din, Jon Dal, Director, Westminster Interfaith Group, London, Interview: October, 2011

899 Tailor, Bhavin, RE teacher, William Ellis School, North West London, Interview March, 2012

900 Tailor, Bhavin, RE teacher, William Ellis School, North West London, Interview March, 2012

901 Corbyn, Jeremy, Right Honourable MP, Finsbury Park, London Interview March 2012

902 Cowie, Reverend John. The English Reformed Church, Amsterdam, Holland. Interview: February, 2012

[903] Little, Magsie Hamilton, *The thig about Islam:Exposing the myths, facts and controversies.* London. Max press.

[904] Leitner, GW (Dr), Muhammadanism in the *Quarterly Message*, March, 2002, pp 7-8

[905] Armstrong, Karen: *Muhammed: A Western attempt to understand Islam,* London. Voctor Gollancz ltd, 1991

[906] Tailor, Bhavin, RE teacher, William Ellis School, North West London, Interview March, 2012

[907] Ibid

[908] Charles, HRH Prince. *Lecture Delivered at the Oxford Centre of Islamic Studies, Oxford, Uniskill Ltd., 1993, p12*

[909] Putin, Vladimir, President, Russia. Islam is inseparable part of Russia's society and culture - Putinhttp://rt.com/politics/islam-inseparable-russias-society- 915/, Published on 3^{0th} August, 2012

[910] Ibid

[911] Harris, Harriet, Reverend (Dr). the Chaplain and honorary Fellow at the school of divinity, Edinburgh University, UK, Interview May 2012

[912] Williams, Stephen, Rev. Senior Anglican Chaplain, University Chaplaincy, University of London. Interview: May, 2012

[913] Williams, Stephen, Rev. Senior Anglican Chaplain, University Chaplaincy, University of London. Interview: May, 2012

[914] Nagasawa, Mako. Area director, an advisor to the Harvard-Radcliffe Christian Fellowship (HRCF), and a staff member with InterVarsity Christian Fellowship, University of Harvard. Interview: May 2012

[915] Nagasawa, Mako. Area director, an advisor to the Harvard-Radcliffe Christian Fellowship (HRCF), and a staff member with InterVarsity Christian Fellowship, University of Harvard. Interview: May 2012

[916] Eade, John. Professor of Sociology and Anthropology Roehampton University, England, Interview February, 2012

[917] Coles, Stephen, Reverend, St. Thomas Church, Interview February, 2012

[918] Coles, Stephen, Reverend, St. Thomas Church, Interview February, 2012

[919] Richmond, Danny. Director, Tony Blair Faith Foundation. London. Interview: February, 2012

[920] Little, Magsie Hamilton, *The thig about Islam: Exposing the myths, facts and controversies.* London. Max press. 2012

[921] McCoy, Alban, Father, Cambridge University Catholic Chaplaincy. Interview May 2012

[922] Din, Jon Dal, Director, Westminster Interfaith Group, London, Interview: October, 2011

[923] Sharma, Lalit Kumar, Pandit. Hindu Temple, East London, Interview September, 2011

[924] Ibid

[925] Ibid

[926] Dobson, Frank, Right Honourable MP, Labour Party, UK, Interview: London, October 2011

[927] Green, Allen. Father, Tower Hamlets Interfaith Forum, London Interview January 2012

[928] Kinnock, Neil (Right Honourable) Lord, the former leader of Labour Party, UK. Interview: January, 2012

[929] Corbyn, Jeremy, Right Honourable MP, Finsbury Park, London Interview March 2012

[930] McCoy, Alban, Father, Cambridge University Catholic Chaplaincy. Interview May 2012

[931] Lamont, Norman, Lord (Baron Lamont of Lerwick), British politician and former Conservative MP and Chancellor of the Exchequer. Interview: January, 20012

[932] Richmond, Danny. Director, Tony Blair Faith Foundation. London. Interview: February, 2012

[933] Phesrisai, Sangthong (Dhamacaro) Buddhist Monk, Buddhist Temple, South London, Interview October, 2011

[934] Amess, David (Right Honourable), British MP, UK. Interview: January 2012

[935] Blunkett, David, Right Honourable, MP (Former Home Secretary), UK. Interview: Jan, 2012

[936] Ibid

[937] Kinnock, Neil (Right Honourable) Lord, the former leader of Labour Party, UK. Interview: January, 2012

[938] Shashoua, Stephen, Director, Three Faiths Foundation, Camden, Interview: London, January 2012

[939] Ibid

[940] Richmond, Danny. Director, Tony Blair Faith Foundation. London. Interview: February, 2012

[941] A Teacher from a Church of England School, North London, Interview March, 2012

[942] Hoare, Rupert, Reverend. Former Dean of Liverpool Cathedral and Chair of the Council of Faiths, Liverpool, UK. Interview: April, 2012

[943] Blunkett, David, Right Honourable, MP (Former Home Secretary), UK. Interview: Jan, 2012

[944] Green, Allen. Father, Tower Hamlets Interfaith Forum, London Interview January 2012

[945] Stephen Shashoua, Stephen, Director, Three Faiths Foundation, Camden, Interview: London, January 2012

[946] A Teacher from a Church of England School, North London Interview March, 2012

[947] Ibid

[948] Corbyn, Jeremy, Right Honourable MP, Finsbury Park, London Interview March 2012

[949] Ibid

[950] Stygal, Mike. Chairman, Camden Interfaith Foundation, London, Interview January 2012

[951] Pritchard, John. Reverend, Assistant Priest, All Saints Church, West London, Interview February 2012

[952] Harris, Harriet, Reverend (Dr). the Chaplain and honorary Fellow at the school of divinity, Edinburgh University, UK, Interview May 2012

[953] Eade, John. Professor of Sociology and Anthropology Roehampton University, England, February, 2012

[954] Coles, Stephen, Reverend, St. Thomas Church, Interview February, 2012

[955] Ibid

[956] McCoy, Alban, Father, Cambridge University Catholic Chaplaincy. Interview May 2012.

[957] *Kinnock, Neil (Right Honourable) Lord, the former leader of Labour Party, UK. Interview: January, 2012*

[958] Dobson, Frank, Right Honourable MP, Labour Party, UK, Interview: London, Interview October 2011

[959] Rangarathan, Thillai K, Pandit. Hindu Temple, Highgate, North London, Interview November 2011

[960] Spokesman, Sikh Temple, East London, Interview November, 2011

[961] Shashoua, Stephen, Director, Three Faiths Foundation, Camden, Interview: London, January 2012

[962] Right Honourable Gordon Birtwistle, MP, Burnley, Lib Dem: Interview: London, Feb 2012.

[963] Potter, Jennifer, Reverend, Minister, Wesley's Chapel, London, Interview February, 2012

[964] Hoare, Rupert, Reverend. Former Dean of Liverpool Cathedral and Chair of the Council of Faiths, Liverpool, UK. Interview: April, 2012

[965] Mellema, R. L., Holland, Anthropologist, Writer and Scholar.

[966] O'Brien, Rev Thomas, Our Lady of the Assumption Church, Tower hamlets, London Interview Feb, 2012.

[967] Quinn, Tom, Father, Shadwell Catholic Church, East London, Interview January 2012

[968] Din, Jon Dal, Director, Westminster Interfaith Group, London, Interview: October, 2011

[969] Ibid

[970] Pritchard, John. Reverend, Assistant Priest, All Saints Church, West London, Interview February 2012

[971] Pal, Amit. '*Islam Means Peace'*. USA, Praeger Publishers Inc, 201, p1

[972] Gandhi, Indira (Prime Minister of India). *Selected Thoughts of Indira Gandhi.* By K Dhawan. New Delhi, Mittal Publications, 1985; online book, page 198

[973] Rai, Anita. *Muhammad: Uncovering the true story*. London: Starsighter ltd. 2006

[974] Burke, Edmund, 'The Impeachment of Warren Hastings,' in Kh. Jamil Ahmed, ' *Muhammad in Non-Muslims'* Eyes,' p. 51

[975] Gandhi, MK in *The Last Law Giver* by Mahmood Vanderman, p 68

[976] Little, Magsie Hamilton, *The thig about Islam: Exposing the myths, facts and controversies.* London. Max press. 2012

[977] Hurgronje, Christiaan Snouck, as quoted in *Encyclopaedic Survey of Islamic Culture* (1997) by Mohamed Taher, p. 260

[978] Titus, M. Thurston, *Indian Islam: A Religious History of Islam in India, 1930*

[979] Cameron, David, Prime Minister, UK. Prime Minister's Message for Eid. Prime Minister's Office, 10 Downing Street, Published in 17the August, 2012, https://www.gov.uk/government/news/prime-ministers-message-for-eid

[980] Singh, N.K (Dr), *Islam: A Religion of Peace.* India: Global Vision Publishing House, 2002, p120

[981] Peacock, A. Reverend, *Muhammad through the eyes of a Christian.* The Islamic Review, September Issue, 1958, pp17-19

[982] Little, Magsie Hamilton, *The thig about Islam: Exposing the myths, facts and controversies.* London. Max press. 2012

[983] Smith, W.C. as in Singh, N.K (Dr), *Islam: A Religion of Peace.* India: Global Vision Publishing House, 2002, p120

[984] Leonard, Major Arthur Glyn. *Islam: Her and Spiritual Value*. London: Luzac & Co. 1909, p72

[985] Germanus, Julius (Dr), lecture delivered in Lahore, December, 1930 as in *"Last Law Giver"* by Mahmood Vanderman, Printed at Premier Press, Secundabad, 1935,p106

[986] H.A.R. Gibb. *Muhammedanism.* USA, Oxford University Press, 1953

[987] Rogerson, Barnaby. *The Prophet Muhammad: A Biography.* England. Little Brown, 2003

[988] Lamont, Norman, Lord (Baron Lamont of Lerwick), British politician and former Conservative MP and Chancellor of the Exchequer. Interview: January, 20012

[989] Tolstoy, Leo. http://www.islamgate.org/?p=238&upm_export=pdf.This page was exported from - IslamGate. Export date: Sat Jan 26 21:15:45 2013 / +0000 GMT

[990] Tolstoy, Leo. http://www.islamgate.org/?p=238&upm_export=pdf.This page was exported from - IslamGate. Export date: Sat Jan 26 21:15:45 2013 / +0000 GMT

[991] Singh, Manmohan. Indian Prime Minister. The article, *Manmohan Singhs greets Nation on Milad-Un-Nabi.* Thaindian News, by ANI, Feb 15, 2011

[992] Singh, Manmohan. Prime Minister of India. Thaindian News, The article, *President, PM greet nation on Milad-un-Nabi(Lead)* by Ians, 04 February, 2012

[993] Ibid

[994] Patil, Pratiba. 12th President of India. Thaindian News, The article, *President, PM greet nation on Milad-un-Nabi(Lead)* by Ians, 04 February, 2012

[995] Bainimarama, Commodore Josaia Voreqe, Prime Minister, Fiji. *PM's message for Prophet Muhammad's birthday.* Fiji Sun, January 28, 2013.http://www.fijisun.com.fj/?p=139324,

[996] Ibid

[997] Schimmel, Annemarie. *And Muhammad is His Messenger: The Veneration of the Prophet in Islamic Piety.* USA, University of North Carolina, 1985

[998] Charles, HRH Prince. Lecture Delivered at the Oxford Centre of Islamic Studies, Oxford, Uniskill Ltd., 1993, p. 22.

[999] Ibid p. 21

[1000] Ibid p. 19

[1001] Shaw, George Bernard (Sir), in *'The Genuine Islam,'* Vol. 1, No. 8, 1936. (The Society of Authors, on behalf of the Bernard Shaw Estate)

Printed in Great Britain
by Amazon

27726156R00270